AS & A-Level
Business

Exam Board: Edexcel

OK, so studying Edexcel AS or A-Level Business is a tough job. And the pay isn't great. It'll all be worth it when you're a wildly successful entrepreneur five years from now, but in the meantime, this CGP book is here to keep you motivated...

It explains the whole course, from Ansoff's matrix to zero-based budgets, with realistic exam-style questions to test you on every topic. And of course, we've included plenty of top advice on all the skills you'll need to boss the exams!

There's even a <u>free</u> Online Edition of the whole book to read on your computer or tablet.

How to access your free Online Edition

This book includes a free Online Edition to read on your PC, Mac or tablet.
You'll just need to go to **cgpbooks.co.uk/extras** and enter this code:

2552 3246 3750 2088

By the way, this code only works for one person. If somebody else has used this book before you, they might have already claimed the Online Edition.

A-Level revision? It has to be CGP!

Published by CGP

Editors:
Daniel Fielding, Emily Garrett, Rachael Rogers, Hannah Taylor and Caroline Thomson.

Contributors:
Paul Brockbank, Angela Duffy, Peter Gray, Tony Gray, Alison Hazell, Lynda Turner and Keith Williamson.

ISBN: 978 1 78908 242 5

With thanks to Charlotte Burrows, Katie Burton, Duncan Lindsay, Glenn Rogers and Victoria Skelton for the proofreading.
With thanks to Jan Greenway for the copyright research.

Clipart from Corel®
Printed by Elanders Ltd, Newcastle upon Tyne.

Based on the classic CGP style created by Richard Parsons.

Contents

If you're revising for the **AS exams**, you'll need to revise Themes 1 and 2.
If you're revising for the **A-level exams**, you'll need to revise the whole book.

We deliberately haven't included answers to most of the questions — that's because there are lots of valid ways to give your answers. Instead, we've put in a section on how to write answers and do well (p.187-192). Answers to numerical questions are included though, on pages 193-194.

The Market

Before you delve into the wonders of business, you need to learn some basics about markets...

Businesses can Target Mass and Niche Markets

1) The term **market** generally refers to all of the **buyers** and **sellers** that trade a **particular type of product** in a particular **place**. For example, the UK clothing market includes all of the businesses that **buy** and **sell** clothing to each other, as well as the **consumers** in the UK who buy the clothes to wear.

2) In most markets, there's a **mass market** and several smaller **niche segments** (niche markets):

   • Products in a **mass market** are aimed at a **large group** of buyers. The product has a **wide appeal** and is useful to a variety of people, not just small segments of the population.
   • Products in a **niche market** are aimed at a **specific group** of buyers. The product is **specialised** to meet the **particular requirements** of buyers in the niche market.

3) For example, the confectionary market has a mass market and niche segments. There is a **mass market** for **standard** chocolate — businesses such as Cadbury are part of this market as they sell a **wide range** of standard chocolate to a **large range** of consumers. There are **niche markets** for **special types** of chocolate — for example, Moo Free® is a business in a niche market as one of its **specialities** is in **dairy free** chocolate.

Julian couldn't understand why beard baubles were classed as a niche market product.

4) Businesses in mass markets sell to **more consumers** than those in niche markets, so **sales volume** in mass markets is **higher** than in niche markets. This means that businesses in mass markets are more likely to benefit from **economies of scale** (see p.49), meaning products sold in mass markets can be **cheaper** to produce than those sold in niche markets. However, to meet the large sales volume needed to be successful in a mass market, businesses need a lot of **capital**, so **new** or **small** businesses can find it **hard to succeed** in mass markets.

5) Businesses in niche markets can be **more risky** than businesses in mass markets as they sell to a **smaller number** and **narrower range** of customers — if there's a **change** in the market that affects what customers want to buy, they could quickly **lose sales** and struggle to survive.

6) Usually there's a lot **less competition** in niche markets than in mass markets (see below). This, coupled with the fact that niche markets sell **specialised products**, means that businesses in niche markets can usually charge **higher prices** than those in mass markets.

Market Size is Different to Market Share

1) **Market size** is the **total value of sales** in a market over a certain time period (usually a year). It could also be measured by the **total number of consumers** in that market.

2) The **market share** of a business is the **proportion** of the **total market** that the business holds — it's calculated by dividing **their sales** in a certain time period by the **total sales** in the **total market**. Market share is usually shown as a **percentage**.

3) Mass markets have a **larger market size** than niche markets. There are usually **many more** businesses in a mass market than in a niche market. Each business within a mass market is likely to have a **smaller market share** than each business within a niche market.

Firms in Mass Markets Need to Make Their Brand Distinctive

1) **Branding** creates a clear and obvious **logo**, **name** or **statement** that customers can instantly **recognise**. It helps consumers to **differentiate** a business's product from that of its competitors.

There's loads more on branding on pages 20-21.

2) Branding is important in all markets, as it can encourage consumers to buy products and therefore affect the **market share** that a business has.

3) In mass markets there are more businesses selling **similar products** than in niche markets, so there is **more competition** in mass markets. This means businesses in mass markets might focus **more heavily** on strong **branding** than businesses in niche markets. In niche markets consumers are more likely to be interested in whether the product meets their **particular requirements** rather than being influenced by branding.

The Market

Firms in **Dynamic Markets** Need to **Adapt to Change**

Some markets are more 'static' than dynamic, e.g. markets selling staple products such as bread and fruit.

1) Most markets are **dynamic** — they **change** and **evolve** rapidly. Markets can change in a **variety of ways**, for example:

- **Consumer preferences** can change — e.g. due to changes in **fashion** or **advances** in **technology**.
- **Innovation** means that **new** products or processes emerge — this can lead to the **growth** of some markets and the **decline** of others. For example, the development of **digital cameras** meant that this market grew and the market for older camera types such as **Polaroid** or **disposable cameras** declined.
- The **ways** in which customers **want to shop** can change, like the growth of **online shopping**, see below.
- **Competitors** can enter or leave the market.
- There can be **changes** in **legislation** — these can affect the products sold in a market. For example, in 2018 the UK government introduced a **tax** on sugary drinks — many drinks manufacturers responded to this by **changing their products** so they contained less sugar, so they didn't have to pay the tax.

2) Businesses need to **adapt** to changes in the market in order to be **successful** and **maintain** their **market share**.

3) For example, firms may need to **change existing products**, develop **new products** or change how they **market** their products to keep up with **competition** and changing **consumer preferences**. They may also need to find ways to **cut costs** so they can **lower prices** and maintain demand for their products in a changing market.

Online Retailing has Changed how Markets Operate

There's lots more about online retailing on page 25.

1) **Online retailing** is **selling** products via the **internet**, e.g. through apps or websites.

2) The growth of online retailing and the presence of big online retailers has had a **negative impact** on traditional retailers who have a **shop-front** on the **high street**. Many high street retailers have been forced to **close down** completely, while others have survived by starting to **sell online** themselves.

3) There are **benefits** and **drawbacks** of online retailing for both businesses and customers. For example:

Benefits
- A business's **costs** are lower as it doesn't need to have a **physical shop** or hire as many **staff** — lower costs allow it to sell **lower priced** products or keep prices the same and **make more profit**.
- Customers can order **any time** they want and often from **anywhere** in the world — this is **convenient** for the customer and increases the opportunity for **sales** for the business.
- Customers can easily **compare prices** between different firms and find the **lowest prices**.

Drawbacks
- Businesses face **more competition** as customers can easily **shop around**. Retailers try to combat this by making the shopping experience on their website better than on their competitors' websites, e.g. saving payment and delivery details so it's **easier** for customers to make repeat purchases.
- Some consumers like to **see products** before they buy and some like to speak to **staff**. Ways to tackle this include **free returns** to encourage consumers to purchase and **online chat services**.
- Businesses need to make sure their customers' **personal details** are protected from **cyber criminals** and that they aren't processing **fraudulent transactions**. Maintaining security is **expensive** but the consequences of having an insecure site can cost the firm lots of **money** and damage its **reputation**.

Warm-Up Questions

Q1 What is the difference between a mass and niche market?
Q2 Define the term market share.

PRACTICE QUESTIONS

Exam Question

Q1 A retailer sells a wide range of household electrical appliances in a high-street store. In order to combat falling profits, it is considering either operating in a more niche market or closing its store to become an online retailer. Evaluate these two options and recommend which option the retailer should choose to increase profits. [20 marks]

Online retailing has had a negative impact on my bank balance...

Exam questions will give you information about a business before asking you any questions. You need to know key facts and definitions, but also be able to relate these to the business depending on their product, size, market, etc...

More on The Market

You're not finished yet with the basics of a market — here are another two pages packed with info to get stuck into...

Competition in a Market can be Direct or Indirect

1) In a **competitive market**, products are sold to the **same group** of **customers** by many **competing businesses**.

2) **Direct competition** is when two or more businesses sell **similar products** that **appeal** to the same group of customers. For example, in the grocery market, Sainsbury's, TESCO, ASDA and Waitrose & Partners are all in direct competition as they all sell similar **food** and **household** products.

3) **Indirect competition** is when two or more businesses sell products that are **different**, but they are **competing** for the **same customers**. For example, an **Indian** takeaway restaurant sells completely **different food** to an **Italian** takeaway restaurant, but they are in indirect competition as they are both **competing** for customers who want a takeaway meal.

Competition Affects How Firms Operate

The **level of competition** a firm faces affects many of the **decisions** it makes. For example, competition has a lot of influence on the decisions a firm makes about its **marketing mix**:

- **Product** — A competitive market contains lots of similar products. Competition means that firms need to make sure that the product they are providing is of a good quality — if it's not, then customers can easily choose to buy from a competitor. Firms also need to make sure that their products are distinctive from competitor products — this can mean that there is lots of innovation in competitive markets in order to create products that have a unique appeal over competitor products.

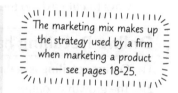
The marketing mix makes up the strategy used by a firm when marketing a product — see pages 18-25.

- **Promotion** — Competition means that firms have to try really hard to get their products noticed and encourage customers to buy them over competitor products. This means that there's often a lot of promotional campaigns and advertising in competitive markets, which inform customers about the business's products. Businesses in competitive markets may also focus heavily on branding and use methods such as celebrity endorsement to try to entice customers to buy their product.

Competition in this market had gotten slightly out of hand.

- **Pricing** — Firms in a competitive market often use a competitive pricing strategy, which means prices are based on competitor prices — if a similar competitor product is of a similar quality but is cheaper, then customers are more likely to buy the cheaper product. Sometimes firms with new products on the market try to tempt customers away from competitors by using a penetration pricing strategy, which is where they set low prices for their products initially. Overall, prices are often cheaper for customers in a competitive market than in less competitive markets.

There's more about different pricing strategies on pages 22-23.

- **Place** — In a competitive market, businesses need to make sure it's as easy (or easier) for customers to access their product as it is to access competitor products. This can mean that in a competitive market lots of businesses sell online — for many this includes apps so customers can buy more easily on the go.

Firms have to be **aware** of what competitors in the market are doing and be ready to **take action** if the market becomes **more competitive**.

> **Example:** If a **large and popular** high street **clothes retailer** were to open up a store near to an **independent** clothes shop, the independent clothes shop might need to **respond** to this **new competition**.
> The independent clothes shop could focus on **advertising** its clothes as **unique** and **higher quality** than those from the high street retailer. It could also **promote** its clothes using promotional offers such as **buy one get one free**.
> The independent clothes shop might need to **research** the **prices** of clothes in the high street retailer's store, and think about **reducing** its clothing prices if necessary.

More on The Market

Competition Affects the Nature of Ownership

1) Many **competitive** mass markets are dominated by a few **national** or **global** businesses — for example, the UK **breakfast cereal market** is dominated by firms such as Kellogg's®, Nestlé® and The Weetabix Food Company.

2) **New** and **smaller** firms often struggle to survive in these competitive markets as they haven't got the **budgets** needed to make themselves stand out from the bigger firms and win **market share**. These businesses might need to get **investors** to help raise more **funds** in order to compete successfully — this means there's more incentive for firms in a competitive market to be **limited companies** rather than operate as **sole traders** or **partnerships**.

3) Even **big** and **established** companies might need to change the nature of their ownership in order to gain **more market share** in a competitive market — e.g. a **private** limited company might transition into a **public** limited company.

4) A new firm can find it easier to succeed in a competitive market by operating as a **franchise**. A franchise is an **agreement** that allows a **business** to use the **idea**, **name** and **reputation** of an established business (see p.52).

> *Limited companies, sole traders, partnerships and franchises are all different forms of business — there's more about them on pages 50-52.*

> **Example:** An entrepreneur wants to open a **restaurant** in his home town but there are already **a lot** of eating establishments in the area. He decides to open an Italian restaurant but opts to be a **franchisee** for **Bella Italia** rather than setting up his own independent business. Customers will already be familiar with the Bella Italia **brand name** and he will get **support** from Bella Italia to help make the business a success in a **competitive market**.

All Businesses in a Market Face Risks and Uncertainties

1) All business activity comes with an element of **risk** — there's always a chance that something could go **wrong**.

2) When taking a risk, the **probabilities** of different **outcomes** are often known. Before making a **decision**, businesses can consider the **probability** of a **negative outcome** and think about how they can **minimise** the chance of this happening. They can make a **conscious decision** about whether or not to take the risk — this means that risks are **controllable**.

3) **Uncertainties** are **unexpected** events — they're often things that firms know **could** happen, but it's very difficult for them to predict **if** or **when** they'll actually happen, or what their **outcome** will be. Uncertainties are usually **external things** that businesses can't control, like unexpected bad weather. They're things that often affect the **market** as a **whole** rather than just **individual businesses**.

> **Example:** A **car manufacturer** brought out a **new model** of diesel car. There was a **risk** that the car wouldn't be as **popular** as expected but the firm tried to control the risk, e.g. it did **market research** to **predict** demand and had **strategies** in place ready to **promote** the car differently if demand was low. However, shortly after the release of the car there were a lot of media stories about the **damaging environmental effects** of diesel engines, and the UK government increased the **tax** on diesel cars. This caused the **demand** for the new model to be much **lower** than expected. The change in **consumer preferences** and change in **legislation** that led to the low demand were **uncertainties** — the firm couldn't accurately predict that they were going to happen and couldn't control them.

Warm-Up Questions

Q1 Describe the difference between direct and indirect competition.
Q2 Describe the difference between risk and uncertainty for a business.

Exam Questions

Q1 Explain how the nature of ownership of a clothing retailer operating in a competitive mass market may differ compared to a clothing retailer operating in a less competitive niche market. [4 marks]

Q2 A franchise of a large, national driving school has started operating in a town. Assess how this event may affect the marketing decisions made by an independent driving instructor working in the same town. [10 marks]

There's usually a large risk of me writing a bad joke here...

Competition is a good thing for consumers but can be a right pain for firms — it affects many of the decisions they make. And if you haven't got the message, risk is NOT the same as uncertainty — make sure you know the difference.

Market Research

Market research is important for a business, especially before launching a new product — it helps prevent terrible errors.

Businesses Can Have a **Product** or **Market Orientation**

1) If a business is **product orientated** then when making production and marketing decisions it focuses most heavily on the **design**, **quality** or **performance** of its products, rather than what consumers actually **want**.

2) Product orientated businesses might use advances in technology to develop **new products** and **functions** that they **think** customers will like. They often create **new** and **innovative** products and then put them on the market and hope that they can persuade consumers to **buy them**.

3) For example, Apple® continuously develops the design and quality of its iPhones® and focuses on **innovative** new functions to capture its market — it can be classed as a product orientated business.

4) **Market orientation** is when a business focuses most heavily on selling products that match **customer preferences**. It **invests** lots in **market research** to find out what consumers **want** and will be **willing to buy**.

5) A market orientated business is considered to be a more **modern** and **successful** approach than a product orientated one. It provides products tailored to what consumers want, so it can often charge **higher prices**.

6) Market orientation could be viewed as a more **low-risk strategy** compared to product orientation — it's based on **consumer feedback** so firms can predict more accurately how much **demand** there'll be for the product.

Businesses Need **Effective Market Research**

Market research is the **collection** and **analysis** of **market information**. It can include looking at the **market** as a **whole**, the **competitors** in the market and **their products**, and the **consumers** in the market. **Effective market research** is important to a business for many reasons, for example:

1) Market research finds out what customers **need** and **want**. **Needs** are **essential** things such as food and water, whereas **wants** are things that customers can **choose** whether they buy, like jewellery and holidays. As well as identifying the **current** needs and wants of customers, market research tries to **anticipate** what the needs and wants will be in the **future** so that the business can get **one step ahead** of the market.

2) Market research allows a business to **predict** how much **demand** there will be for its products. Researching the level of demand can help a business to know how much of the product it will need to **supply**. If research shows that demand for an existing product is likely to **fall** it can take action, e.g. it can **promote** the product to increase demand.

3) Market research allows a business to learn more about how consumers **behave** in relation to a product. E.g. it could learn how consumers **buy** the **product** (e.g. in store or online) and how they **use** the product. This could help the business to understand how best to **market** its product.

4) Businesses use market research to work out how much consumers would be **prepared to pay** for a product — they usually want to charge enough to make a **profit**, but not so much that customers **won't buy it**.

5) Identifying **competitors** is a big part of market research — businesses need to research what their competitors may be doing **better** than them, to see where they can **improve** their own business.

6) As part of market research, a business may gain insight into aspects of the **business environment** that could affect the market — these are called **SLEPT** (social, legal, economic, political and technological) **factors**.

Overall, market research helps businesses to make **informed decisions** about business operations, which helps to **reduce** the **risks** involved in such decisions.

Market Research can be **Quantitative** or **Qualitative**

1) **Quantitative** research produces **numerical statistics** — facts and figures. It often uses multiple-choice **questionnaires** that ask questions like: "When did you last buy this product? **A:** within the last day, **B:** within the last week, **C:** within the last month, **D:** within the last year, **E:** longer ago, **F:** never." These are called **closed questions** because they have **fixed**, **predetermined** answers.

2) **Qualitative** research is based on the **opinions** of consumers, and doesn't produce numerical or quantitative results. It often involves questions like: "How does this product make you **feel**?" These are called **open questions**. The answer isn't restricted to multiple-choice options.

3) Quantitative research and closed questions give data that can be **statistically analysed**, which makes analysis **quicker** and **easier**. However, qualitative research may be more **informative** as the responses can be more **flexible**. The most effective type of market research **combines** both qualitative and quantitative research.

Market Research

Market Research can be Primary or Secondary

Primary market research is where a business **gathers new data** (or employs someone to do it on their behalf). **Secondary market research** involves **using data** that's already available.

Primary

1) Primary data can be collected in a number of ways. Methods include: **questionnaires** or **surveys** (these ask **lots of questions** and can be done via post, phone, internet or in person), **observations** (where consumers are **watched** in a normal shopping environment to get an insight into their **behaviours**), **interviews** (usually done **one-on-one** with a researcher) and **focus groups** (where a **group** of around 8 people discuss their opinions, e.g. about a product).

2) Businesses do **test marketing** — e.g. they launch a product in one **region** and measure **sales** and **customer response** before launching it across the country.

3) **Sampling** might be used to make predictions about the **whole market** based on a sample (see below).

4) Primary data is needed to find out what consumers think of a **new product** or **advert**. You can't use secondary data because, erm, there won't be any secondary data on a brand new product.

5) Primary data is **specific** to the purpose it's needed for. This is great for **niche markets** (see p.2) — secondary data might be too broad or too mainstream to tell you anything useful.

6) Primary data is **exclusive** to the business who researched it, so **competitors can't benefit** from it.

7) However, primary research is **labour-intensive**, **expensive** and **slow**.

Secondary

1) Secondary data includes information from **Government publications**, reliable **internet sources** such as Statista (a website that gives access to statistics), **trade magazines** and **market reports** such as those by MINTEL.

2) Secondary data is much **easier**, **faster** and **cheaper** to get hold of than primary data.

3) Secondary data collected for a different reason may be **unsuitable**. It may have **errors** or be **out of date**.

4) Secondary data is often used to get an **initial understanding** of a market. A firm may then do more specific primary research to investigate any **issues** or problems that are shown by the secondary data.

Market Researchers need a Representative Sample

1) When primary market research is done, **samples** of people are used rather than the **whole market** — this is valuable as it keeps **costs down** and saves a lot of **time** and **resources**.

2) The sample needs to **represent** the market. It must have **similar proportions** of people in terms of things like age, income, gender, etc. A **more representative** sample will be more likely to give **accurate** results.

3) A **big sample** has a better **chance** of being representative than a **small sample** — but even a big sample won't necessarily be 100% representative. There's always a **margin of error**.

4) The **size** of the **sample** may depend on how many people a firm can **afford** to ask. If the **money** available for research is **limited**, the **risk** of the information being **inaccurate** increases. Whether a firm **prioritises cost** or **accuracy** often depends on the **type** of **market**, the **size** of the business and the business **context** — e.g.:

- A new business launching a product in a niche market is risky. It will benefit from accurate research to find out what consumers really want, so it may prioritise accuracy over cost.
- A business launching a product in a competitive market which is similar to products already on the market is likely to prioritise cost over accuracy — it might not need to spend much on market research because it is already clear that the product is in demand.

Market Research needs to Avoid Bias

1) To **increase the accuracy** of market research, researchers have to be careful to avoid any possible **bias**.

2) Questionnaires, surveys and interviews should avoid **biased questions** — e.g. questions that are phrased in a way that **leads** the respondent to give a particular answer, e.g. "You do like chocolate, don't you?"

3) Both interviewers and respondents can cause bias. **Interviewer bias** can be caused by the **personality** of the interviewer — their **opinions** can **influence** the interviewee. **Respondents** can give biased answers — this is when the **response** isn't the **true answer**, often because they don't think their true answers are **socially acceptable** (like saying they eat 3 chocolate bars in a week, when really it's 23).

Market Research

Technology Can be Used to Support Market Research

1) Many firms now use **ICT** (information and communication technology) to help them with market research.
2) Using technology makes market research **easier**, **cheaper** and **quicker**. It can be used to get a lot **more** information than traditional research methods and it's easier to reach a **wider sample** of consumers.
3) **Websites**, **social networking** and **databases** are examples of ICT that firms can use:

Businesses Can Use a Range of Different Websites

1) A business can use its **own** website for market research. This could be done by using the website as a platform to conduct short **surveys** or by **analysing** the **activities** of people using the site. For example, they could analyse information about:

- What times of day/year the website is used the most.
- What visitors are clicking on when they use the website.
- How likely it is that visitors will buy products via the site and how much they're likely to spend, etc.

There are **limitations** to the data that can be gathered from a business's website, e.g. a business might discover that many people visiting its site **don't** end up buying products, but it still won't know **why**.

2) A business can look at **competitor websites** to gather information about their **new products**, **prices**, etc.
3) A business can read **reviews** about their products that have been written on other websites. For example, they could read customer reviews on an **online retailer's** website, such as Amazon®. They could also look on specific **review websites**, such as TripAdvisor®. However, consumers are **more likely** to leave a review if they have had a **bad experience** with a product, so reviews might not be **representative** of what **all consumers** think.

Social Networking Can be Used for Market Research

1) **Social networking** is the use of **internet-based** platforms to make connections with people. Firms can **connect** with their customers through well-known social networking sites, such as **Facebook®** or **Twitter**. They could also use less well-known, niche social networking sites to connect with users that have **certain interests**, e.g. **Ravelry** is a social networking site for people that like crafts, such as knitting and crochet.
2) Firms can **post content** on social networking sites and monitor the **responses** they get. This may allow them to find out what **people** are **saying** about their **products** and their competitor's products, which is a **quick** and **cheap** way to carry out market research.
3) Many social networking sites have tools that can be used for **market research**. For example, firms can pay social networking sites to post **survey** questions about products on consumers' news feeds. **Facebook®** also has tools that **analyse** the demographics of its followers, as well as which other pages a firm's **followers** are **interested** in — so a firm can easily and cheaply build a **profile** of its **followers**.

4) Social networking sites can be used to **track current trends**, for example businesses can search for **hashtags** on Twitter to see what products and trends are **popular**.
5) A **limitation** of using social networking for market research is that not all **consumers** use the same social networks — for example, fewer **older people** use Twitter than Facebook®. So market research could produce very **different results**, depending on the social networking site that's used.

Marshall was pleased to discover that all of his followers also had an interest in blindfolds.

Business Databases Contain lots of Useful Data

1) Businesses can collect their **own data** to form a **database** about their **products** and **consumers**. For example, lots of **supermarkets** offer **loyalty cards** which give customers money back according to how much they spend — these allow supermarkets to form a **database** of customer names and addresses, and also their **preferences** based on what they **buy**. E.g. they could target an offer on pet insurance at people who bought pet food. This would make the campaign **cheaper** and **more effective**.
2) Firms can also use **other databases** as a source of secondary research. These are usually accessed **online** for a **fee** and can provide information about the **trends**, **businesses** and **consumers** in a particular market. These databases are a **quick** and **cheap** source of information but the data is mostly **quantitative** — it doesn't give much information about **consumer opinions** and how they actually feel about a product.

Market Research

Market Research Allows Businesses to Segment Their Market

1) **Segmentation** means **dividing** a market into **groups** of buyers — consumers in **each segment** share one or more **characteristic**, e.g. age, income, hobbies, etc. (see below).

2) **Market research** helps a firm to segment a market by revealing more about the **types** of **consumers** in the market.

3) Each segment of consumers has different **wants** and **needs**, and so requires a **different marketing mix** (see p.18). Segmenting a market allows businesses to **target** their **marketing** towards **specific groups** of buyers.

4) Segmentation can also help to identify segments of a market whose needs and wants **aren't being met**, which could lead to **new products** being developed.

There are Different Ways to Segment a Market

Here are some of the ways in which a market can be segmented:

As the only 18-year-old, Tyler wasn't sure that he was really welcome on his Saga Holiday.

Demographic segments:

- **Age**, e.g. Saga Holidays are aimed specifically at the over-50s.
- **Gender**, e.g. yoghurts are mainly marketed towards women.
- **Socio-economic class**, e.g. businesses can segment their market based on the kind of jobs people have — e.g. modern one bedroom flats might be marketed at young professionals.

Geographic segments:

- The market can be divided according to neighbourhood, city, county, country, or world region, e.g. Asia. It's a method mostly used by multinational companies as their customers have a range of cultures, lifestyles and climates and are likely to need different marketing mixes.

Income segments:

- E.g. CHANEL makeup is aimed at customers with high incomes and Superdrug's own-brand makeup is aimed at lower-income customers. Luxury products are usually aimed at high income groups.

Behavioural segments:

- **Amount of use**, e.g. mobile phone suppliers market differently to heavy users and light users.
- **Lifestyle**, e.g. busy young workers might tend to buy lots of microwaveable ready-meals, so a business making ready-meals might target this market segment.
- **Hobbies and interests**, e.g. snack foods with a high protein content might be mainly marketed towards people who like playing sports and going to the gym, and people who are interested in health.

Warm-Up Questions

Q1 Explain three reasons why effective market research is important for a business.

Q2 Describe the difference between primary and secondary market research.

Q3 Give eight ways that a market could be segmented.

PRACTICE QUESTIONS

Exam Questions

Q1 What is meant by product orientation? [2 marks]

Q2 A manufacturer is launching a new brand of luxury gym clothing.
Assess two ways in which the firm could use ICT to support its market research. [8 marks]

Surveys show that most people lie in surveys...

Market research needs to be done properly — if the data's not accurate it'll be as much use as a chocolate teapot.

Market Positioning

A brand or product's 'market position' is how consumers perceive it compared to competitor brands or products.
You can see a brand or product's market position by looking at a neat little thing called a market map...

Market Mapping Compares Two Features of Products or Brands

1) A **market map** shows **extremes** for **two measures** that are important to customers, e.g. low price vs. high price, low quality vs. high quality, basic vs. luxurious, young customer appeal vs. mature customer appeal, mass market vs. niche market (p.2).

2) It's laid out as a **matrix**, and the products or brands are **positioned** on it according to where they are judged to lie between each pair of extremes.

3) This market map shows how customers ranked 8 **supermarkets**, labelled A to H, in terms of **price** and **quality**.

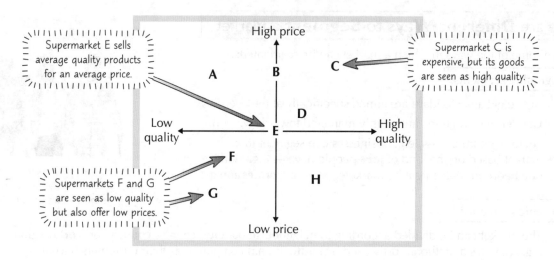

Supermarket E sells average quality products for an average price.

Supermarket C is expensive, but its goods are seen as high quality.

Supermarkets F and G are seen as low quality but also offer low prices.

Businesses can get Lots of Information from Analysing Market Maps

1) Market maps can reveal **gaps in the market**. These gaps can be **spotted** and **filled** by people starting up **new businesses** or by **existing businesses**. Businesses can fill the gaps with new products or brands, knowing that there won't be any close competitors. Other **market research** will be needed to find out if there is actually **demand** for a product in that gap though. E.g. is there a market for high-quality shirts for children?

As soon as Saskia found a gap in the market, she sat down and refused to move.

2) Market maps can show a business who its **closest competitors** are. It can then plan the best **marketing strategy** to persuade customers away from them.

3) If the sales of a product are **declining**, the business might use a **market map** to find out how customers view their product and then try to **reposition** it on the map. Market maps can show the features provided by the most popular brands, which can indicate the **benefits** considered most desirable by the target market.

4) Market maps can show how much customers expect to **pay**, e.g. for cameras of varying quality. This can help a business with its **pricing strategy**.

5) However, market mapping can **simplify** things too much. E.g. in the map above, supermarket A manages to successfully sell **lower quality** goods for **high prices** — this could be due to its **location**, e.g. if it is **conveniently** located within walking distance it means you don't have to drive or use public transport.

6) The positions of products and brands on a market map are usually a **matter of opinion**, and may be **biased**. For example, different people might have **different views** on whether a product is high or low quality.

Market Positioning

A **Competitive Advantage** Helps a Business Increase **Sales** and **Profits**

A **competitive advantage** is a condition which allows a firm to generate **more sales** or be **more profitable** than its rivals. To achieve a competitive advantage, a firm needs to be doing something **different** to its competitors. E.g.:

1) Lower costs — producing a similar product to a competitor's product but at a lower cost means a business can charge a lower price for its product, which should generate more sales. The business may decide to still charge a similar price to its rivals, but the lower costs will mean that it makes more profit on each item sold. Either way, the lower cost gives it a competitive advantage.

2) Product innovation — a business can aim to be the first in the market to introduce new functions for an existing good or create a new, unique product altogether. By producing new and unique products that consumers want to buy, sales will increase — this gives the business a competitive advantage.

3) Advertising and marketing — the more a firm advertises its product and markets it to make it attractive to buyers, the more likely it is to generate sales. The firm could also focus on creating a strong brand image to attract consumers to a product — for example, big global brands use distinctive logos and celebrity product endorsements to help make their products memorable and encourage people to buy them.

4) Product differentiation — this is where businesses distinguish their products from competitors' products. They can do this by creating a unique selling point (USP) — this is an aspect of the product that makes it different from any other on the market. A firm can emphasise the product's USP in its marketing or branding so that the product really stands out from competitors' products.

   There's more about USPs and branding on page 21.

5) Reliability and quality — some consumers are prepared to pay more for a product that is seen to be more reliable and better quality than a competitor product. Maintaining a good reputation for these things helps a business to gain a competitive advantage as it enables higher prices to be charged for its products and generates more sales.

6) Good customer service — good customer service is really important before, during and after the time of purchase. Polite, efficient and knowledgeable staff can make a customer more likely to make a purchase and more likely to make repeat purchases in the future. Customers may also be prepared to pay more for a product if they feel they are receiving good customer service and know that they will be offered after sales service. For example, Apple® Stores attract customers by having a good reputation for helpful after sales service and offer workshops on how to get the most out of their products.

7) Convenience — generally, anything a firm can do to make the buying experience quicker and easier will attract customers, e.g. next day delivery can attract customers to buy from websites.

Firms Often Gain a **Competitive Advantage** by **Adding Value**

Adding value means increasing the **difference** between the **cost** of making the product and the **price** that the customer pays. This usually increases **profits**.

> ### ADDED VALUE = PRICE PRODUCT IS SOLD FOR – COST OF MAKING PRODUCT

Added value can be achieved by either **increasing** the **selling price** of the product or by **reducing** the **costs** of making the product. Lots of the strategies businesses use to gain a competitive advantage (e.g. strong branding, good customer service) encourage customers to pay a **higher price** and so **add value** to a product.

Warm-Up Questions

Q1 Describe what is shown on a market map.

Q2 What is meant by a competitive advantage?

Exam Question

Q1 Assess the ways in which a large firm operating in the games console market could gain a competitive advantage over its rivals.

[12 marks]

Say it three times... Market mapping makes marketing meetings more meaningful...

Every business strives to be better than its competitors in some ways. Market maps can help a business understand how it's viewed by consumers and can highlight ways in which it could alter its activities to gain a competitive advantage.

Supply and Demand

These pages are all about supply and demand — businesses want demand to be high, and supply needs to be able to keep up with demand. If that doesn't tickle your taste buds, there are some fun diagrams coming up too.

You Need to be able to Draw **Supply** and **Demand Diagrams**

1) **Effective demand** (sometimes this is just referred to as '**demand**') is the **quantity** of a **product** that **consumers want** and are **able to buy** at a **given price**, at a **particular time**.

2) Supply is the **quantity** of a **product** that **suppliers** are **willing** and **able to supply** to a market at a **given price**, at a **particular time**.

3) A supply and demand diagram, like the diagram on the right, plots the **quantity** (Q) of a product in **supply** or **demand**, against a range of **different prices** (P) of the product. It's made up of **two curves** — one for demand and one for supply.

4) The **demand curve** (D) usually slopes downwards. It shows that as the **price** of a product increases, the **demand** decreases. This is because, at a **higher price**, fewer buyers will be **able** or **willing** to buy the product so **demand is lower**.

5) The **supply curve** (S) shows the **relationship** between **price** and **quantity supplied**.

6) Supply curves usually **slope upwards**. This means that the **higher** the **price** charged for a product, the **higher** the **quantity supplied**.

7) **Producers** and **sellers** aim to **maximise** their **profits**. Other things being equal, the **higher** the **price** for a product, the **higher** the **profit**. **Higher profit** provides an **incentive** to **expand production** and **increase supply**, which explains why the **quantity** of a product supplied **increases** as **price increases**.

8) However, increasing **supply** increases **costs**. Firms will only **produce more** if the **price increases** by **more** than the costs.

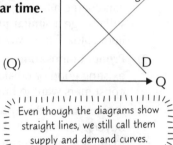

Even though the diagrams show straight lines, we still call them supply and demand curves.

Everyone agreed that Maximus Profitus was a bit weird and no fun at parties.

Equilibrium Price is when the Amount Demanded **Matches** The Amount Supplied

1) When the quantity that buyers demand is **the same** as the quantity the sellers wish to supply, an **equilibrium** price and quantity is achieved. This is sometimes referred to as the **market clearing price**.

2) The equilibrium price (P_e) and equilibrium quantity (Q_e) is where the **two curves meet**.

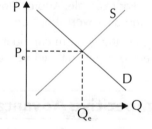

A **Surplus** Occurs when the Price **Increases**

1) If the **price** of a product was **increased**, this would cause a movement to the **right** along its supply curve, and a movement to the **left** along its demand curve.

2) This would mean the quantity demanded (Q_d) would be **less** than the quantity supplied (Q_s), and so there would be **excess supply** and therefore a **surplus** in the market.

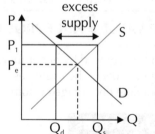

In this diagram, the price needs to decrease from P_1 to P_e to reach equilibrium.

A **Shortage** Occurs when the Price **Decreases**

1) If the **price** of a product was **decreased**, this would result in a movement to the **left** along its supply curve, and a movement to the **right** along its demand curve.

2) This would mean there would be **more** demand than supply, and so there would be **excess demand** and therefore a **shortage** in the market.

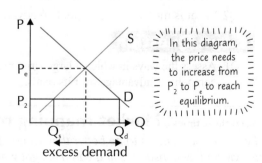

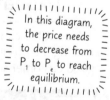

In this diagram, the price needs to increase from P_2 to P_e to reach equilibrium.

Supply and Demand

Demand is Influenced by Lots of Factors

You saw on the previous page that a **change** in the **price of a product** will give a **movement along** the demand curve — if the product price **increases**, the demand for the product will **fall**. Similarly, if the price of the product **falls**, demand will **rise**. But it's not just price that can affect demand — there are **loads** of factors. These other factors cause a **shift** in the **demand curve** rather than a movement **along** the curve (see the next page), for example:

1) **Substitutes** — the demand for a particular brand or product type can be affected by a price change of a substitute. For example, if the cost of margarine increased by a huge amount, then demand for butter would rise.

   Substitutes are products that can be used to replace another — customers see them as very similar products.

2) **Complementary products** — these are products which are used together, e.g. printers and ink cartridges. So if the price of printers were to increase, the demand for printers might fall, and so the demand for ink cartridges could fall too.

3) **Consumer income** — a higher income can lead to an increase in demand for more expensive products, whereas a fall in income can increase the demand for cheaper goods and services (see p.16).

4) **Fashion, consumer tastes and consumer preferences** — demand for a product relies on what consumers want. For example, warnings about the dangers of eating too much sugar could lead to a change in consumer diets — this could lead to a fall in demand for sugary drinks and an increase in demand for healthier drinks.

5) **Advertising and branding** — this aims to increase demand for a product, or encourage existing consumers to be loyal to the product brand and repeatedly buy the product, even when faced with a good substitute, to stop demand falling.

6) **Demographics** — changes in population can lead to changes in demand. For example, advances in healthcare mean that, on average, people are living longer. This has led to an increase in demand for goods and services for the older generation.

   Demographics looks at the number of people with different characteristics in a population, such as the number of people in different age groups.

7) **Seasonal changes** — demand for goods and services can change throughout the year. For example, a long, cold winter often leads to an increase in demand for gas used in central heating. A hot summer is likely to lead to an increase in demand for fans and air conditioning units.

8) **External shocks** — these include the threat of war, diseases and extreme weather. For example, a risk of flooding may lead to an increase in demand for sandbags as people try to protect their homes.

Supply can be Affected by Various Factors

The quantity of the product that a business is **willing** to **supply** is determined by the **price** at which it can sell the product (see the previous page). A change in the **price** of the product will cause a **movement along** the supply curve — e.g. if the product price **increases**, the supply for the product will **rise**. There are lots of other **factors** that can **affect supply**. These other factors cause a **shift** in the **supply curve** (see the next page). For example:

1) **Costs of production** — if the **cost of production** for a product **increases** then the **profit** made from selling the product at a given price **decreases**, so there'll be a **fall** in supply.

2) **Indirect taxes** — these are taxes on a **good** or **service**, like VAT. The **government** can influence supply by **changing taxation**. If tax on a good or service **increases**, then this effectively increases the **costs** for the producer and they are likely to **reduce** their supply.

3) **Subsidies** — a subsidy is **money** given to a **business** by the **government** to help it with **costs** and **encourage** it to produce **more** of a particular product. For example, the EU began a scheme in 1962 to provide **farmers** with subsidies to help them with any large costs and to secure the **supply of food**.

4) **New technology** — this can lead to more **efficient production techniques** and therefore **cost savings**. Lower costs would mean that a firm would be willing and able to **increase the supply** of its good or service.

5) **Weather conditions** — a severe **change in weather** can affect the supply of goods and services, especially in **agriculture** where the weather affects harvests. Bad weather such as too little rain can cause crops to **die early** and therefore supply will be lower. However, good weather like a warm spring and summer can lead to good growth and an **abundance** of certain fruit and vegetables, so **supply** is **increased**.

6) **External shocks** — this includes shocks such as **war**, which can affect supply. If a nation finds itself at war then the supply of certain products from the country can decrease, as the country **focuses** its efforts and factories on **producing supplies** for its **armed forces** instead.

Supply and Demand

Demand Curves and Supply Curves can Shift

1) Changes in the **market** can cause demand or supply to change, as you saw on the previous page.
2) These **changes** in supply or demand cause supply curves or demand curves to **shift** — the curve moves to the **left** or to the **right**.
3) A shift in either curve will change the **equilibrium** price and quantity.

> Remember — a price change will cause a movement along the curves, but changes in supply or demand will shift a curve.

A **Rise in Demand** Shifts the Demand Curve to the **Right**

1) An **increase** in customer **demand** shifts the demand curve to the **right** from D_1 to D_2.
2) However, at a price of P_1 there is a **shortage** in the market. The **price** needs to **rise** to clear the market of **excess demand**.
3) A new **equilibrium quantity** (Q_2) is reached at a **higher price** than before (P_2).

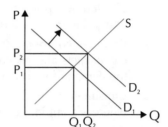

A **Fall in Demand** Shifts the Demand Curve to the **Left**

1) A **fall** in customer **demand** shifts the demand curve to the **left** from D_1 to D_2.
2) However, at a price of P_1 there's a **surplus** in the market. The **price** needs to **fall** to clear the market of **excess supply**.
3) A new **equilibrium quantity** (Q_2) is reached at a **lower price** than before (P_2).

A **Rise in Supply** Shifts the Supply Curve to the **Right**

1) An **increase** in **supply** shifts the supply curve to the **right** from S_1 to S_2.
2) At a price of P_1 there's a **surplus** in the market. The price needs to fall to clear the market of excess supply.
3) A new **equilibrium quantity** (Q_2) is reached at a **lower price** than before (P_2).

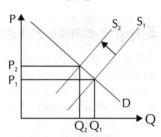

A **Fall in Supply** Shifts the Supply Curve to the **Left**

1) A **decrease** in **supply** shifts the supply curve to the **left** from S_1 to S_2.
2) At a price of P_1 there is a **shortage** in the market — the price needs to **rise** to clear the **excess demand**.
3) A new **equilibrium quantity** (Q_2) is reached at a **higher price** than before (P_2).

Warm-Up Questions

Q1 Is a surplus in the market caused by the price of a product being too high or too low?
Q2 State five factors that could lead to an increase in demand for a good or service.

PRACTICE QUESTIONS

Exam Questions

Q1 What is meant by equilibrium price? [2 marks]

Q2 Caitlin's Cake Creations makes handmade, bespoke cakes for special occasions.
Assess two factors that may influence the number of cakes it is able to supply to the market. [8 marks]

Q3 Roger's Railways makes toy trains for children. Assess how an increase in the population of children aged 3-7 years may affect the equilibrium price and quantity of Roger's Railways' products.
Include a supply and demand diagram in your answer. [10 marks]

I demand that you supply me with cake — immediately...

Boy that's a lot of diagrams... Make sure you know how to draw a supply and demand diagram to show what happens when the supply or demand changes. And don't forget to clearly label all the curves and axes on your diagram.

Interpreting Elasticity of Demand

Calculators at the ready — time for some maths. I know, I know, it's thrilling stuff, but try to contain your excitement.

Price Elasticity of Demand Shows how Demand Changes with Price

1) The **price elasticity of demand** (PED) of a product is how much the price change **affects** the demand. It's found using this **formula:**

$$\text{Price elasticity of demand} = \frac{\%\ \text{change in quantity demanded}}{\%\ \text{change in price}}$$

2) Price elasticity of demand is **always negative** (a positive change in price causes a negative change in demand, and a negative change in price causes a positive change in demand) so you can just **ignore** the **minus sign**.

3) If the price elasticity of demand is **greater than 1** (ignoring the minus sign), the product is **price elastic**. If the price elasticity of demand is **less than 1**, it's **price inelastic**. So, –1.5 is price elastic and –0.5 is price inelastic.

> **Example:** A price **rise** of **20%** results in a **30% reduction** in demand.
>
> *As price goes up, demand falls — and vice versa.*
>
> **Price elasticity of demand** = $\frac{-30\%}{+20\%}$ = **–1.5** so this product is **price elastic**.
>
> **Example:** A price **reduction** of **20%** results in a **5% increase** in demand.
>
> **Price elasticity of demand** = $\frac{+5\%}{-20\%}$ = **–0.25** so this product is **price inelastic**.

4) For **price elastic** products, the **% change in demand** is **greater than** the **% change in price**.

5) For **price inelastic** products, the **% change in demand** is **less than** the **% change in price**.

Price Elasticity of Demand Depends on Lots of Factors

1) **Necessity** (or **necessary**) **products** like milk are **price inelastic**. Changing the prices doesn't affect demand much. If customers can **switch** to **similar** or **competitor** products (**substitutes**), demand will be **price elastic**. E.g. if Princes tuna increases in price, people might buy John West tuna instead.

2) Businesses try to **differentiate** their products to create **brand loyalty**. **Loyal** customers won't switch even if the price goes up, so this makes the product **less** price elastic.

iPhones® are price inelastic due to the strength of the Apple® brand.

3) Price elasticity of demand increases over time as customers have the chance to find alternative products. The **internet** makes it easy to find alternatives and so **increases price elasticity**.

4) **Product types** tend to be **price inelastic**, but individual **brands** tend to be **price elastic**.

Petrol sales are inelastic but sales of an individual business's petrol are elastic.

5) Items costing a **greater proportion** of customers' incomes will be more **price elastic**. Customers won't be too concerned about a 20% rise in the cost of a newspaper, but a 20% increase in the price of a car might cause them to look for **alternatives**.

6) How **often** a customer buys a product affects price elasticity of demand. A product that customers buy **regularly** is likely to be **price inelastic**. This is because a product that is bought **more frequently** is more **likely** to be a **necessity** to the customer.

7) The price elasticity of demand of a product could **change**, for example:
   - If a **competitor** were to **enter the market**, then it would be **easier** for customers to **switch** to a **different product**. This means that the product could become **more price elastic**.
   - An increase in **brand awareness** (see p.20 for more on branding) can lead to more **customer loyalty**, which could make the product **less price elastic**.
   - If the product became more of a **necessity**, this would make the product **less price elastic**. For example, mobile phones were once thought of as a **luxury** item, but are now seen to be a **necessity**.

Demand Curves Show Price Elasticity and Inelasticity

A product that is price **elastic** has a **shallow** demand curve. This shows that the demand for the product is very **dependent** on the **price** — a small change in price leads to a **large** change in **demand**.

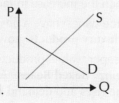

A product that is price **inelastic** has a **steep** demand curve. The product **isn't** very **dependent** on price — a large change in price **won't** lead to a large change in demand.

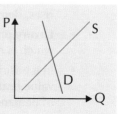

Interpreting Elasticity of Demand

Price Elasticity of Demand Affects Sales Revenue

Sales revenue and total revenue are the same thing if a business doesn't get revenue from elsewhere (like selling assets).

1) **Sales revenue = selling price × sales volume** (see p.63). Price elasticity shows how price affects sales revenue (and therefore total revenue).

2) If a product is **price elastic**, a **price increase** will make **sales revenue go down**. The money lost from the **% decrease in sales** will be **more than** the money gained from the **% increase in price**.

> **Example:** **100 scarves a year** are sold for **£10 each** giving a revenue of **£1000**.
> Price elasticity of demand = **−2.5**.
> If the business **increases** the price by **10%** to **£11**, demand will **change** by:
> % change in quantity demanded = % change in price × price elasticity of demand
> = 10% × −2.5 = −25%
>
> So 75 scarves will be sold at the new price, which **decreases sales revenue** to:
> sales revenue = selling price × sales volume = £11 × 75 = **£825**

This is just the equation from the previous page, but it's been rearranged.

3) For **price elastic products**, a firm can **increase sales revenue** by reducing price — a small **decrease** in **price** will cause a large **increase** in **demand**.

4) If a product is price **inelastic**, a rise in **price** will make **sales revenue go up**. The money lost from the **% decrease in sales** will be **less than** the money gained from the **% increase in price**.

> **Example:** If the scarves' PED is **−0.5** and price **increases** by **10%**, demand will **change** by:
> % change in quantity demanded = % change in price × price elasticity of demand
> = 10% × −0.5 = −5%
>
> So 95 scarves will be sold at the new price, which **increases sales revenue** to:
> sales revenue = selling price × sales volume = £11 × 95 = **£1045**

5) For **price inelastic products**, **decreasing** the **price** will make **sales increase** slightly, but sales **revenue goes down** because the price has fallen and only a few more units have been sold.

Income Elasticity of Demand Shows how Demand Changes with Income

1) A person's income can **change**, for example because of **changing jobs**, getting a **promotion**, getting a **pay rise** or being **dismissed**. The **average** income of a nation will **increase** during economic growth and **decrease** during economic decline (a recession).

2) **Income elasticity of demand** (YED) shows how the demand for a product changes as incomes change. Income elasticity of demand is calculated with this equation:

$$\text{Income elasticity of demand} = \frac{\%\text{ change in quantity demanded}}{\%\text{ change in income}}$$

> **Example:** A rise in income of **20%** results in a **5% increase** in demand.
> $$\text{Income elasticity of demand} = \frac{+5\%}{+20\%} = +0.25$$
>
> **Example:** A fall in income of **15%** results in a **10% increase** in demand.
> $$\text{Income elasticity of demand} = \frac{+10\%}{-15\%} = -0.67$$

3) The income elasticity of demand of a product depends on whether the product is a **normal product** (a **necessity** or a **luxury product**) or an **inferior** product. **Normal products** have a **positive** income elasticity of demand and **inferior products** have a **negative** income elasticity of demand.

- **Necessity products** (e.g. fruit and vegetables) have a **positive income elasticity of demand** that's **less than 1**. This means that as **income rises, demand rises** — but at a **slower rate** than the increase in income.

  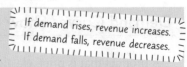
  If demand rises, revenue increases. If demand falls, revenue decreases.

- **Luxury products** (e.g. designer clothes and fine wines) have a **positive income elasticity of demand** which is **more than 1**, meaning **demand for luxury products** grows **faster** than the increase in income.

- In a business sense, **inferior products** are cheaper 'value' products — e.g. a **cheaper supermarket value brand** of baked beans compared to **Heinz® Baked Beans**. A **negative income elasticity of demand** means **demand falls** when **income rises** and **demand rises** when **income falls**.

Interpreting Elasticity of Demand

Elasticity Helps a Business Make Choices

1) **Price elasticity** helps a business **decide** whether to **raise** or **lower** the price of a product. They can see what might happen to the **sales**, and ultimately what will happen to **sales revenue**.

2) If a product is price elastic, then businesses are more likely to set **low** and **competitive prices** (p.23) to increase **revenue**, whereas for a price inelastic product it's likely that businesses will use **high prices** and **price skimming** (p.22) to increase revenue.

3) **Income elasticity** helps a business see what will happen to sales if the **economy** grows or shrinks.

4) Here are examples of the **marketing decisions** that might be made about two products:

> Tin of value tomato soup — price elasticity of demand = –3.0, income elasticity of demand = –0.5

- Reduce the price to increase demand and sales revenue, but only if the profit margin is big enough.
- In times of economic growth, sales will fall so the brand image of the product may need to be changed to appeal to better-off customers. In times of recession, demand for the product will increase.

> New designer kitchen — price elasticity of demand = –0.4
> income elasticity of demand = +1.5

- Increase the price — demand will fall slightly, but revenue will still increase.
- In times of economic growth, sales will grow so the aspirational brand image should be maintained. In times of recession, demand for the product will fall, so incentives such as discounts and interest-free repayments over a number of years could be introduced to encourage sales.

Although the bows helped to make them more price inelastic, neither Nigel nor Vince was convinced it was worth it.

5) Businesses that sell a **range** of products may decide to **promote** different products if incomes **increase** or **decrease**. For example, **supermarkets** such as Sainsbury's sell a range of **luxury**, **necessity** and **inferior products**. Sainsbury's might focus on promoting products with a **negative income elasticity of demand** during times of **low income**, such as **Sainsbury's basics** products, but focus on promoting items with a **positive income elasticity of demand** during times of higher income, such as **Sainsbury's Taste the Difference** products.

Warm-Up Questions

Q1 If a product has a price elasticity of demand of –0.9, is it price elastic or inelastic?

Q2 Give three factors that affect price elasticity.

Q3 Does a shallow demand curve show a price elastic product or price inelastic product?

Q4 The income elasticity of demand for a brand of champagne is 2.8. Calculate the percentage change in quantity demanded if incomes were to decrease by 1.2%.

Q5 What kind of products become less popular when there's an increase in income — necessity, luxury or inferior?

Answers on p.193.

Exam Questions

Q1 A company sells 200 horses a year for £1500 each. If the price elasticity of demand is –0.7, calculate the new sales revenue per year if there was a 15% increase in prices. You are advised to show your working. [4 marks]

Q2 The price elasticity of demand for a pack of sausages is estimated to be –0.2. Assess the effect changes in price will have on total revenue for the sausages. [10 marks]

Rubber prices are usually the most elastic...

The clues are in the names — price elasticity of demand shows how much the price of a product influences demand, and income elasticity of demand shows how much income affects demand. You could be asked to calculate the price or income elasticity of demand in the exam, and as the wise old saying goes — practice makes perfect...

Design Mix

This section's all about marketing strategies — that's right, all twelve pages of it. Get ready for some exciting stuff...

The **Marketing Mix** is Made Up of the **4Ps**

The **marketing strategy** is the **plan** a business uses to reach its **marketing objectives** (p.48-49). The **marketing mix** makes up this **strategy**. There are **four** key components of the **marketing mix**, known as the **4Ps**:

1) The design of the **product** (see below).
2) The **promotion** and branding techniques (p.19-21).
3) The **pricing** strategy used for the product (p.22-23).
4) The type of distribution or **place** in which the product is sold (p.24-25).

A business will need to **consider** the 4Ps when deciding on a marketing strategy. The best strategy for the business will depend on the **types of market** it operates in.

Cindy thought the 4Ps were Party, Party, Party and Party.

The Design Mix Includes **Function, Aesthetics** and **Cost**

1) When designing a product, a business needs to make sure that the product is **fit for purpose** (functional) and has a **good look** (aesthetics), but that it isn't **too costly** to produce. This is called the **design mix**.

2) The product must meet the **needs of the consumer** and be able to fulfil its **intended function**. For example, a chair that has a beautiful design but is uncomfortable to sit on is not meeting its intended function.

3) The design of the product must also be **aesthetically pleasing**. For example, a good value, functional car may be difficult to market if its shape and interior are seen as cheap and clunky. But the design **shouldn't** be so **complicated** or use such **expensive materials** that it's **too costly** to produce.

4) A business might **focus** on different **parts** of the **design mix**. For example, a **jewellery** business may be more concerned with **aesthetics** than cost, but a **paperclip** business may be more concerned with **cost** than aesthetics.

Changing **Social Trends** Can Influence The **Design Mix**

1) Businesses may need to alter the **aesthetics** or **function** of their products in response to changing **social trends**.

2) Many consumers are concerned about the **overuse of resources** and want businesses to **minimise** the amount of **waste** they produce by making products more **reusable** and **recyclable**.

> In 2013, Starbucks began selling **reusable coffee cups**. It also offered customers a **discount** on hot drinks if they brought in their reusable cup.

> In 2008, Dell™ switched from **plastic** to **bamboo** packaging for some of its devices. Bamboo is quick to grow (compared to other plants) and is **biodegradable**.

Firms can also reduce waste by making their production processes more efficient (p.82-83).

3) Consumers are also increasingly **demanding** that **raw materials** should be **ethically sourced**. Materials that are ethically sourced help to **preserve** the **environment** and **protect local communities**.

> **Palm oil** is used in many **food products** and **cosmetics**, but there's concern that rainforests are being destroyed to make way for palm oil plantations. This may mean that businesses **alter** their products so that they only contain **ethically sourced** palm oil or that they use an **alternative ingredient** instead.

4) Consumers may **choose** one producer over another if its **products** are **recyclable** or **reusable**, or if its ingredients came from an **ethical source**. These products could command **higher prices**, but not all consumers may be **willing** to pay this. So businesses need to **carefully consider** whether it's worth making any changes.

Warm-Up Questions

Q1 What are the four components of the marketing mix?
Q2 What are the three components of the design mix?

PRACTICE QUESTIONS

Exam Question

Q1 Marlton's want to launch individually wrapped, single portion, processed cheeses aimed at the lunchbox market. Assess how changing social trends may influence the design mix for this product. [10 marks]

That's one **P** down, only three more to go...

...sounds like my mum trying to get me to eat my petit pois. Bleurgh. A jícama though — now there's a vegetable.

Promotion and Branding

Without promotion, businesses won't get very far. I mean, have you tried that new teleporting machine? No, I didn't think so. That's because they won't promote it. Something about destroying the space-time continuum.

Promotion is Part of the Marketing Mix

1) Promotion is designed to **inform** consumers about a product, or **persuade** them to buy it.
2) **Promotional objectives** include increasing **sales** and **profits**, and increasing **awareness** of the product.
3) All promotion has to get the customer's **attention** so they can be informed or persuaded about the product.

Many Businesses Choose to Advertise Through the Media

1) Adverts are used to **promote goods** and **services** — and also to promote a firm's **public image**. Advertising uses various **media** including print, film, TV, radio, billboards (also called hoardings) and the Internet.
2) The choice of media depends on who the **target customers** are and how many of them **see** or **hear** the ad. TV adverts at prime times are very expensive. Ads shown when fewer people are watching are cheaper, but don't reach as many people. The cost must be **worth it** in terms of the **extra sales** or **awareness** created.
3) **Digital communications**, like online adverts and social media, are used by many businesses. For example:

   - Online adverts can be **targeted** at customers who've shown an **interest** in a product by browsing for it.
   - Advertising on **mobile phones** is becoming increasingly important, e.g. banners in apps — sometimes the advertiser is only charged when their advert is **clicked on**, so no money is wasted on unseen ads.
   - **Viral marketing** is when businesses get users to **pass on adverts** to their friends through, for example, social networking platforms or email (p.21). The adverts have to be considered **interesting enough** for people to pass along, e.g. a hilarious video, or something that offers something for **free**.

4) **Digital communications** are often **cheaper** than traditional forms of advertising.
5) However, many customers are exposed to a **large number** of digital ads so they may **ignore** digital advertising, e.g. by closing pop-ups as soon as they appear or by installing ad-blocker software.
6) The **impact** of an ad is very important. An advert that covers a two-page spread in a magazine has much more impact than a single page, or a small ad stuck in the classified section at the back.
7) **Specialist media** are used to advertise specialist products to **niche markets**. For example, a manufacturer of fish hooks would do better to advertise in a monthly fishing magazine than in the Daily Telegraph newspaper.
8) Businesses need to follow **legal constraints** on advertising some products. E.g. cigarette advertising is banned.

Not All Promotion Involves Advertising

1) Businesses often offer **sales promotions**. These are things like competitions, free gifts and **special offers**, e.g. "buy one get one free" (**BOGOF**). Sales promotions can aim to **raise awareness** or **increase sales**. Manufacturers also aim sales promotions at **retailers** to encourage them to **stock** more of their products. However, customers could become aware of this technique and **wait** to purchase non-essential items until they enter a promotional offer. This may **increase sales** but it would also **reduce** the **profits** made on each sale.
2) **Direct marketing** can include **mailshots**, which are promotional materials sent in the **post** to customers. The customer usually hasn't **asked** to receive them. Businesses that keep information about their customers on a database can **target** their marketing to particular consumer groups through post. Direct marketing that is untargeted ("**junk mail**") can sometimes be a **waste of money**, because it often just gets thrown away.
3) **Personal selling** or **direct selling** is personal communication between a **salesperson** and a customer. Personal selling can involve sales assistants in shops as well as travelling salespeople and phone salespeople. However, the **salary** and **travel costs** of the salesperson can be **expensive**, and personal selling has a much more **limited reach** compared to other promotional methods, like a TV ad.
4) **Event sponsorship** makes consumers **aware** of a firm and its products. But sponsoring **large events** could be **expensive**, which increases **costs** for the business.
5) **Public relations** (PR) involves **liaising** with the **media**, setting up **TV interviews** and organising **product launches**, **conferences** and other **special events**. This is done to help **raise awareness**, and to try to create a **good public image** of a business. But it can be **difficult** for a business to control exactly what the media **reports** about it. For example, a **comment** in an interview could be **misinterpreted** and result in a **negative story** being spread. This would create a **negative public image** of the business.

Promotion and Branding

Promotion Relies on **Clear Branding** of a Product

Branding creates a clear and obvious **logo**, **name** or **statement**. This means that customers will instantly **recognise promotional material** from a particular **business** or for a particular **product**.

Manufacturer or Corporate Branding

1) **Corporate branding** is how a business **presents** itself.
2) **Within** the corporate brand there may be **separate product brands** aimed at different groups of consumers.
3) For example, the **corporate brand** Kellogg's® has a **recognisable** red font used for its name, and **several product brands** within in. Consumers **trust** that products with this logo will be of **good quality**.

Product Branding

1) Product branding relates to specific **individual products** that a corporate brand makes.
2) The individual product will have its own **logo** and **slogan** but it will also often have the corporate brand **included** in its packaging to show that it's associated with a **business** that **consumers** may **trust**.
3) For example, Kellogg's® produces many **breakfast cereal** products each with its own **distinctive brand**. Its **Rice Krispies®** cereal is associated with the slogan "**Snap, Crackle & Pop®**". The product **Frosties®** is associated with **Tony the Tiger®** and his phrase "They're Gr-r-reat!®". Each is **instantly recognisable** by its unique product branding but **also** by the **Kellogg's®** logo in the **top corner** of the cereal box.
4) Branded products usually have **expensive marketing** so they usually have a **higher retail price**. Many consumers are **willing** to pay more if they're buying a **trusted product**, because it appeals to their **sense of wellbeing** and gives them a **feel-good factor**. However, **some consumers** may **not** be happy paying **higher prices**.

Own Branding

1) Own branding refers largely to brands that are **in-house** to a supermarket or retailer.
2) It's **unlikely** that **large budgets** have been spent on the **branding** of these products. Usually they don't have a **distinctive slogan** or **attractive logo** used to promote them, therefore these are **cheaper** to produce. However, the producer may **not** be able to charge a **high price** for an own brand product.
3) The advantage to the consumer of buying own brand products is that they usually get a product at a **cheaper price** than if they bought branded. But consumer's often consider own branded products to be of a **lower quality** so they don't get the same sense of wellbeing as they do from a branded product.

Sometimes a **Business** or **Product** Needs **Rebranding**

1) Rebranding is a **marketing strategy** that can involve a **change** to the **design**, **promotion**, **pricing** or **distribution** of an **existing brand**. A business might want to reposition a product and **aim** it at a different **target market** or try to **overcome competition** from another business.
2) Rebranding can also be used to create a **new identity** when a brand name is **no longer suitable**. For example, a charity formerly known as the Royal National Institute of the Deaf **changed its name** in 2011 to Action on Hearing Loss. The **aim** of this rebranding was to **incorporate all** people who are suffering from a hearing impairment and not only those who are deaf.

Strong Branding has Several **Benefits** to a Business

1) One of the main reasons for a business to **build** a strong brand is to **add value** to its product. Strong branding makes the price elasticity of demand for a product **less price elastic** (p.15).
2) The consumer perceives the product to be of a **higher quality** or more **desirable** than any substitutes and is prepared to pay a premium price — they'll be **loyal** to the brand and make **repeated purchases**. For example, Apple® can charge a lot for the iPhone® because the brand is so strong.
3) Strong branding can create a **barrier** so that it's **harder** for **newcomers** to **enter** the market.

There are certain brands which have become brandnomers, which is where the product becomes known by a brand name rather than its general name. For example, Post-It® Notes is a brand but it's now common to refer to any sticky note as a post-it. This is an example of successful and strong branding.

Promotion and Branding

There Are **Several Ways** to **Build** a Brand

1) One way to create a brand is to base it around the product's **unique selling point** (USP). A **clear** USP will help consumers with **product differentiation** (see p.11), which may convince them to buy one brand over another. For example, the USP of **Harris Tweed** is that it's **handwoven** in the Outer Hebrides of Scotland.

2) Sometimes the USP might not be an **obvious** or **unique feature**, but it might be more about the **image** associated with the brand. If consumers **perceive** it to be a **superior brand** then this is its USP. For example, a restaurant that's been in a town for many years may be **perceived** to be better than a new restaurant simply because it's been there for such **a long time** — even if the food and the customer service is of a similar quality.

3) **Advertising** (p.19) is used to promote and maintain **consumer awareness** of a brand. Businesses use it to persuade consumers that their brand is **unique**. In **competitive markets**, lots of money is spent on advertising.

4) **Sponsorship** is widely used in certain competitive markets. Corporate brands might **sponsor large outdoor events** such as music festivals and sports events. For example, Emirates began sponsoring the FA Cup in 2015. Sponsorship advertises the brand to anyone **watching** or **attending** these events.

Social Media Channels are Increasingly Used to **Communicate** with Consumers

1) Many businesses have **changed** their **methods** of **promotion** and building a **brand** to include the use of **social media**, as social media has become more **popular**.

2) **Viral marketing** involves platforms such as YouTube, Instagram, Facebook® and Snapchat. These can be used by businesses to share **news** and **updates** that consumers can then **share**. This helps to **spread awareness** of a brand and **advertise** it. These messages can spread at a **rapid rate** and the audience is **potentially huge**.

3) This can be a very **low cost** technique if successful as there are **no huge advertising budgets** required, such as those needed for **traditional advertising** (e.g. TV adverts, billboards, etc.).

4) However, the business can experience a **loss of control** as **negative images** or **messages** about a brand can be spread and damage the business's **reputation**. This may take a **long time** and **great expense** to recover.

Luiza misunderstood when her friends suggested she try Facebook®.

Emotional Branding Helps **Engage** Consumers

1) Sometimes, in order to engage a consumer, the branding of a product is matched to the **lifestyle**, **values** or **aspirations** of consumers to trigger an **emotional response**, so that they **buy** the product. This is known as **emotional branding**.

2) An example of emotional branding is for MALTESERS® chocolate which has an **emphasis** on **sharing**, **enjoying time** with **friends** and not taking life too seriously. This attracts consumers who **share** these **ideals** about life.

3) To be successful at emotional branding, businesses need to **understand** the values and purchasing behaviour of consumers and how they **change over time**. This means businesses may need to do **market research** (p.6-9).

Warm-Up Questions

Q1 Describe what corporate branding, product branding and own branding are.
Q2 Give one disadvantage of viral marketing.

Exam Questions

Q1 SportsLog produce a sports watch that can record pulse rate and physical activity. Assess a benefit and a drawback to SportsLog of using social media to help build a strong brand. [8 marks]

Q2 Assess how, in addition to advertising, a manufacturer of breakfast cereal could promote its product. [10 marks]

We want them to buy our product — that's why we tell them to BOGOF...

Promotion and branding go together like tea and cake — branding, such as a logo or slogan, should be added to any promotional material. It's no good if consumers can't recognise which business the promotional material is for.

Pricing Strategies

It can be annoying when your favourite bottle of shampoo goes up in price (mine's ylang ylang flower with coconut and honey — smells wonderful) but businesses put a lot of thought and effort into their pricing strategies.

Several Factors Affect Pricing Decisions

1) The **price** of a product is affected by all of the other Ps in the **marketing mix** — e.g. during heavy **promotion** of a product, its **price** may be **reduced**.

2) The price is often set to **cover the cost** of making the product (or buying it from a wholesaler) and to **make a profit**.

3) The price must be **acceptable to customers** — it depends how **price sensitive** the target market is. Affluent consumers are less price sensitive than those at the other end of the scale.

4) The **price elasticity of demand** (see page 15) influences the pricing of a product. This depends on the **availability of substitutes**, the **type** of product, whether it's an **expensive purchase**, and the **strength** of the brand.

5) The **stage** of the **life cycle** that the product's in (see page 26) will also affect pricing decisions — for example, if sales are declining then the price may be **reduced**.

6) The price has to be in line with the business's **objectives**. E.g. it might be aiming to increase its **market share**, make the **maximum profit**, or keep its **brand image** up-market.

7) The **level of competition** in the market influences pricing decisions. If the price is set **above** that of competitor products without it being **differentiated** in some way by having a **USP** (p.11) then no one will buy it and it may bring the business **bad publicity**. However, if the price is too far **below** that of others, particularly the major players', then customers will question its **quality**.

8) A product with a **strong USP** would be able to **command** a **higher price** because it is **highly differentiated** from any competitor products.

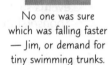

No one was sure which was falling faster — Jim, or demand for tiny swimming trunks.

Businesses Use Promotional Pricing Strategies for New Products

Price Skimming

1) **Price skimming** is when **new and innovative products** are sold at **high prices** when they first reach the market. Consumers will pay more because the product has **scarcity value**, and the high price boosts the **product's image** and increases its appeal. **Technological products**, e.g. computers, tend to be priced using this method.

2) Prices are usually then **dropped considerably** when the product has been on the market for a year or so — by this point everyone prepared to pay extra for being one of the first to own the product has got one. Also, competitors might have entered the market with **imitative products** at **lower prices** — although a business can prevent this using **patents** or **trademarks**.

3) Some businesses use price skimming as a **long term strategy** to keep their brands **more exclusive**, e.g. Apple® and Ray-Ban® sunglasses.

4) However, **potential customers** can be put off by the initial high price and customers who bought the product at its initial price may be **annoyed** and **frustrated** when it suddenly drops in price after launch.

Penetration Pricing

1) **Penetration pricing** is the opposite of skimming. It means launching a product at a **low price** in order to **attract customers** and gain **market share**. It is especially effective in markets which are **price-sensitive**, e.g. a new washing powder or food product.

2) Penetration pricing works best for businesses that can benefit from **lower costs** when manufacturing **large quantities** of a product.

3) A **problem** with penetration pricing is that customers may expect the low price to **continue**, so it's difficult to raise it without losing customers. It can also damage how the **brand image** is perceived.

4) Price penetration isn't just for new products — it can be used as an **extension strategy** to prolong a product's life (see page 27).

5) Penetration can also be used to target a more **budget-conscious** market segment. E.g. an airline might set up a **no-frills, low-cost service** in addition to its **regular service**. That way they can appeal to a **new segment of the market**, whilst also keeping their **existing customer base** who are prepared to pay more, and maintaining their premium brand image.

Pricing Strategies

There Are Lots of Other **Pricing Strategies**

1) One type of **cost-plus pricing** is when a firm adds a percentage **mark-up** to the costs of making or buying a single product (the unit cost).

$$price = unit\ cost + \left(\frac{unit\ cost}{100} \times mark\text{-}up\right)$$

2) For example, if a product's unit cost is **£30** and the business wants a mark-up of **25%**, it'll price it at **£37.50**.

3) **Predatory pricing** is when a business **deliberately lowers prices** to force another business **out of the market** — e.g. a large nationwide business might target a successful but small local competitor by lowering their prices in that specific area until the small competitor **goes out of business**. Once the competitor has gone it will **raise** its prices again. Predatory pricing is illegal under EU and US laws.

4) **Competitive pricing** is when businesses **monitor** their **competitors' prices** to make sure that their own prices are set at an equal or lower level. **Supermarkets** and **department stores** often use this method. Some stores will **refund the difference** in price if the product is cheaper somewhere else.

5) **Psychological pricing** bases the price on customers' **expectations**. For example, a **high price** may make people think the product is really **high quality**. An **insignificant** price change can have a big **psychological impact** on the customer, e.g. £99.99 seems a lot better than £100 even though it's only 1p difference.

Changes in **Social Trends** Can Affect Pricing Strategies

The internet has led to the rise of online retailers and price comparison sites. This is useful for customers as it allows them to **shop around** to find the **best deals** more easily.

Customers Are Increasingly Using **Online Retailers**

1) **Online retailers** need to be more **price competitive**, as it's very easy for customers to **compare prices** for identical products. If there are many **substitutes** of a similar quality available, the cheapest online retailer will usually **achieve the sale**.

2) Online retailers may choose instead to compete with **other aspects** of final pricing, such as offering **free delivery** or **free returns**, which affect the final price for the customer. These **extra benefits** may make the customer more willing to pay a higher price for the product itself.

The Use of **Price Comparison Sites** is Increasing

1) **Price comparison** sites make it **even easier** for customers to compare the prices for a **product** between **many different** retailers or suppliers. They're very popular for comparing the price of services such as **car insurance**, **flight prices** and retail prices of **popular goods**.

2) These sites are popular as they save customers **time** and **effort** in their search for the lowest price.

3) The consequence for retailers is that they need **effective information** systems so that they're aware of prices charged by their **competitors**, so they can be **price competitive**.

Warm-Up Questions

Q1 Explain how the level of competition can affect the pricing decision of a business.

Q2 Give one disadvantage of a penetration pricing strategy.

Q3 Give one benefit to customers of using price comparison sites.

Exam Questions

Q1 What is meant by predatory pricing? [2 marks]

Q2 Repas is an expensive gourmet food shop that is currently operating as a chain of physical shops but wants to begin retailing online.
   a) Explain a pricing strategy that Repas could use when it makes this move. [4 marks]
   b) Assess the factors that will affect the pricing decision of Repas. [12 marks]

My gecko's tail fell off — so I compared the prices of some retailers...

The internet has made it easier for competing businesses to keep an eye on each others' prices — but it's also meant that customers are able to be more choosy about which businesses they buy from. Personally, I'd buy everything online if I could — I'd never need to change out of my PJs and I could avoid bumping into Linda at the butchers again.

Distribution

It's no good for a business to make a fantastic product and successfully promote it to a whole bunch of people if it can't actually get the product to the consumer. That's where distribution channels come in.

It's **Vital** to Get the **Product** to the **Consumer**

A **channel** of **distribution** is the route a product takes from the manufacturer or producer to the consumer. A product usually passes through **intermediaries** on the way from producer to consumer — e.g. **retailers**, **wholesalers** and **agents**.

The research team had almost finished their work on the new distribution method.

1) **Retailers** are **shops** who sell to consumers. They're usually the **final stage** in the distribution channel. TESCO, Argos and Amazon® are **retailers**. Retailers can be physical shops or online "e-tailers".

2) **Wholesalers** make life **easier** for retailers and manufacturers:

- Wholesalers **buy** goods from manufacturers in bulk and **sell** them in **smaller quantities** to **retailers**. This is called **"breaking bulk"** — a wholesaler takes the goods off the manufacturer's hands and **pays** for the whole lot. Manufacturers don't have to **wait** for customers to buy the goods before they see any cash.
- Wholesalers make distribution **simpler**. Without a wholesaler, the manufacturer would have to make **separate deliveries** to lots of retailers, and send each and every retailer an **invoice**. Selling to one wholesaler cuts down the paperwork and the number of journeys.
- Wholesalers can **store more goods** than a retailer can — they act as the retailer's storage cupboard.

3) **Agents**, such as travel agents, **sell** products to customers **on behalf** of businesses. They're often **paid commission** for the products that they sell.

There are **Different Channels** of **Distribution**

A business will look at the product, the market and the size of the business when deciding which distribution channel to use.

Direct Selling (Two stage channel): Manufacturer ⇒ Consumer

The **Internet** has made it **easier** for producers to sell **directly** to the consumer. Buying and selling on the Internet is called **e-commerce**. This allows access to a **worldwide market**. For small firms, a low-cost option is to sell goods using **electronic marketplaces** (e.g. eBay®).

Direct selling can also be done through door-to-door sales, TV shopping channels, telephone sales and websites. Accountants, electricians and hairdressers sell their **services** direct to the consumer.

Indirect Selling (Three stage channel): Manufacturer ⇒ Retailer ⇒ Consumer

This is a **common** distribution channel for **recreational items** such as clothes, shoes and homeware. **Retailers** are usually in places that are **convenient** for the consumer, such as a **shop** on the **high street**.

Indirect Selling (Four stage channel): Manufacturer ⇒ Wholesaler ⇒ Retailer ⇒ Consumer

This is a **traditional** distribution channel used for **groceries**, e.g. by supermarkets. However, because those at **each stage** of the distribution channel want to make a **profit**, it can increase the **cost** to the consumer.

Retailers Often use **Multi-Channel Distribution**

Multi-channel distribution is when businesses sell through more than one method, e.g. online and in-store. It gives **flexibility** for customers and a **wide market coverage** for manufacturers.

1) Supermarkets and fashion retailers which have **high street stores** as well as an **internet store** are using a **multi-channel strategy**. This may lead to added costs, but it allows them to target a wider market.

2) Stores which **only** sell **online** may have **cheaper costs**, because they use a **single** channel of distribution. However, they can have **problems** establishing **brand loyalty**. Also, customers often like to see and feel goods before they buy them, which is a **limitation of e-commerce**.

> **Example:** Apple® uses multi-channel distribution. You can buy an iPad® **directly** from an **Apple® Store**, either **online** or in a **physical shop**. Alternatively, you can buy it from an **online retailer** such as Amazon®, or from a retailer such as ASDA or PC World, either **online** or from a **retail outlet**.

Distribution

Online Distribution Means Firms can Provide Services Instead of Products

1) **Online distribution** is the **streaming** or **downloading** of **media content** (like games, films, music and books) via the internet.

2) The consumer is purchasing the **right to download** the media content as opposed to buying a good — they're purchasing a **service** instead of a **physical product**.

3) Delivery via online distribution is **direct** and almost **immediate** once an item has been purchased. In **certain markets**, the **traditional** distribution channels are being replaced by online distribution.

4) There are **cost savings** for the business because there is no need to **spend money** on producing **boxed products**, whereas there is for traditional distribution.

5) The **price** of downloads for the consumer can be **cheaper** than actually buying a physical film or book, due to these **reduced costs** for the business.

6) Online distribution is more **environmentally friendly** than the production of physical goods such as DVDs which contain non-biodegradable plastics. Using online distribution also reduces the **pollution** from **transporting physical goods** across countries.

7) Setting up online distribution can be **relatively easy** and can be **run from anywhere** with an internet connection. The **set-up costs** are also **low**, which means that there are **opportunities** for **fast growth** and **return**.

8) However, this requires a **different** set of **skills** to traditional distribution, so staff may need **further training** in **IT skills**.

9) Businesses can respond to changing customer needs more **quickly** as goods do not need to be packaged and distributed but can instead be **updated online** ready for download.

10) These businesses will also have more **working capital** as it's not tied up in stock, which also needs to be **stored** in distribution centres. This money that was previously invested in production and distribution can be **invested** elsewhere in the business.

Online Distribution Is Becoming More Popular

1) Because buying through online distribution is **easy** and **cheap**, more and more consumers are **buying online**. To stay **competitive**, more businesses are **moving** to **online distribution**.

2) This has also led to changes in **social trends**. For example, many people now watch **shows** on **streaming services**, such as NETFLIX, instead of on **TV**.

3) There has also been a rise in the popularity of **reading devices** such as Amazon Kindle®, which has resulted in **fewer people** buying **physical books** but instead choosing to **download books**.

4) So now, instead of needing to store **books, CDs** and **DVDs** in houses, all of the downloaded media content is stored on **computers**, **mobile devices** or **virtual hard drives**.

5) This means there's been a **growth** in **third party service providers**, such as Spotify® and Amazon®'s prime video®, who provide downloadable or streaming services.

Warm-Up Questions

Q1 What is a wholesaler?

Q2 What are the stages of a four stage distribution channel?

Q3 What is online distribution?

Q4 Give two advantages to the consumer of online distribution.

Exam Question

Q1 Legend Ltd make educational films. Traditionally all its films were available as DVDs and were distributed through a traditional three stage distribution channel. It's now considering only having its films available to stream through online distribution from its own website. Assess two benefits to Legend Ltd of this decision. [8 marks]

Shopping channels — my favourite channels of distribution for trashy tv...

I know, it's not exactly rocket science* that a business needs to actually get its products to consumers, but there's a bit more to it than that — make sure you understand the different ways that a business can distribute its products.

*Keep your eyes peeled for our Rocket Science Revision Guide. Coming early 3019.   Theme 1: Section 3 — Marketing Mix and Strategy

Marketing Strategy

Cash cows give you cash. But brown cows don't give you chocolate milk — that would be udderly ridiculous.

Products Have a Life Cycle

1) The **product life cycle** shows the **sales** of a product over **time**.
2) It's **valuable** for planning **marketing strategies** and has implications for **cash flow**.
3) **Marketing decisions** will be based on where a product is in its **life cycle**.

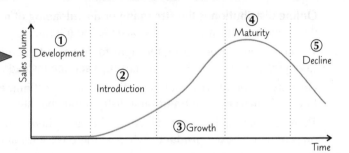

1) Development

1) The **research and development** (R&D) department **develop** the product.
2) The **marketing** department does **market research**.
3) The **costs** are **high**, and there aren't any sales yet to cover the costs.
4) Development has a **high failure rate**. This is because there's often **not enough demand**, or because the business can't make the product **cheaply** enough to make a profit.

2) Introduction

1) The product is **launched**, either in one market or in several markets. It's sometimes launched with **complementary** products — e.g. the PlayStation® was launched with games.
2) The business often **promotes** the product heavily to build sales — but businesses need to make sure they've got enough **resources** and **capacity** to **meet the demand** that promotions create.
3) The **initial price** of the product may be **high** to cover **promotional costs**. This is price **skimming**.
4) Alternatively, the price can start off **low** to encourage sales. This is **penetration pricing**.
5) Sales go up, but the sales revenue has to pay for the high **fixed cost** of development **before** the product can make a **profit**. The business usually ditches products with disappointing sales after this stage.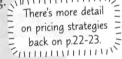
6) There may not be many **outlets** for the new product — businesses will have to work hard to persuade retailers to sell it.
7) Competition may be **limited** (if it's an **innovative** product).

3) Growth

1) Sales grow fast. There are **new customers** and **repeat** customers.
2) **Competitors** may be attracted to the market. Promotion shows **differences** from competitors' products.
3) The product is often **improved** or **developed**, and it may be targeted at a different market segment.
4) Rising sales encourage **more outlets** to stock the product.

4) Maturity

1) **Sales** reach a **peak** and profitability increases because **fixed costs** of **development** have been **paid for**.
2) At **saturation** (when the market is full and has reached maximum growth) sales may begin to drop, depending on the product. Sales are more likely to drop for long-lasting products that customers do not need to replace regularly. The price is often reduced to stimulate **demand**, which reduces profits.
3) There aren't many new customers. **Competition** within the industry becomes fierce so sales might **fall**.

5) Decline

1) The product doesn't **appeal** to customers any more. **Sales fall** rapidly and profits decrease.
2) On the other hand, the product may stay profitable if **promotional costs** are **reduced** enough.
3) If sales carry on falling, the product is **withdrawn** or **sold** to another business (**divestment**). Sometimes, sales might pick up again if competitors leave the market first.
4) **Decline isn't inevitable.** It's usually caused by products becoming obsolete, changing consumer tastes or poor marketing. Quality products with great design (e.g. Cadbury Dairy Milk) can sell for **decades**.

Marketing Strategy

Extension Strategies Keep a Product Going Strong for Longer

1) **Extension strategies**, like **product development** and **promotion**, are used to improve the **sales** of products that are starting to **decline**.

2) **Product development** involves businesses **improving**, reformulating or **redesigning** a product. They can change the design of **packaging** to make it look more up to date, or make **special editions** of the product. This can also give a **new focus** to existing **marketing** campaigns.

3) A business can change the way it **promotes** the product — for example, by running a new **ad campaign**, or by using **special offers** or **competitions**.

Businesses Need a Variety of Products — a Mixed Product Portfolio

1) A **product line** consists of related products (including different sizes of the same product) with similar **characteristics**, **uses** or **target customers**.

2) The **product portfolio** is the **combination** of all the **product lines** that a business produces.

3) For example, the Nestlé® **KitKat®** product line includes **2 Finger** KitKat®, **4 Finger** KitKat®, KitKat® **Chunky**, etc. Nestlé's® **product portfolio** includes all the product lines they make — **KitKat®**, **Nescafé®**, **Maggi®**, **Shredded Wheat®**, etc.

The product portfolio is also called the product mix.

4) Businesses aim to have a **product portfolio** that contains a variety of different products, all at different stages of the **product life cycle** (see previous page). That way if one product fails, the business should still be able to depend on the others.

The Boston Matrix is a Model of Product Portfolio Analysis

The Boston Matrix is also known as the Boston Box.

1) The Boston Matrix compares **market growth** with **market share**. Each **circle** in the matrix represents **one product**. The **size** of each circle represents the **sales revenue** of the product.

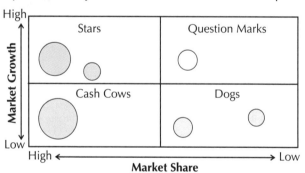

All **new products** are **question marks** (sometimes called **problem children**) and they have small market share and high market growth. These aren't profitable yet and could succeed or fail. They need **heavy marketing** to give them a chance. A business can do various things with question marks — **brand building**, **harvesting** (maximising sales or profit in the short term) or **divestment** (selling off the product).

Cash cows have high market share but low market growth. They're in their **maturity** phase. They've already been promoted and they're produced in high volumes, so costs are low. Cash cows bring in plenty of **money**.

Stars have high market growth and high market share. They're in their profitable **growth** phase and have the **most potential**. They're future **cash cows**. BUT... competitors are likely to try to take advantage of this **growth market** too, so a firm will need to **spend** a lot on **promoting** their product to keep their **market share**. Also, money might need to be spent to **increase capacity** (see page 84) to keep up with **demand**.

Dogs have low market share and low market growth. They're usually pretty much a lost cause. If they're still profitable, e.g. a chocolate bar that is still popular, but no longer growing, the business will **harvest profit** in the **short term**. If the product is no longer making a profit it can be **sold off**.

2) The **Boston Matrix** is a **valuable** way of showing where a business's products are **positioned** in the market.

3) A business's marketing **decisions** will depend on the products' **positions** in the matrix. For example, a business can use money from its **cash cows** to **invest** in its **question marks** so they can become **stars**.

4) But the Boston Matrix **can't predict exactly** what will happen to a product. A product's **profit** may be **different** from what the matrix suggests (e.g. a dog can have a strong cash flow and be profitable despite falling sales).

Marketing Strategy

A **Mass Marketing Strategy** is Intended to **Appeal** to a **Wide Audience**

1) A **mass marketing strategy** needs to **appeal** to the **whole market** instead of individual market segments.

2) The product needs to have **mass appeal**, which may mean that it's not very different from competitor's alternatives. In this case it is very important that any advertising **clearly** shows any **USPs** the product does have.

3) Mass markets tend to be **dominated** by a few competing products so businesses in **mass markets** may need to **promote** their **products** in certain ways to stay **competitive**:

- **Expensive advertising campaigns** can maintain brand awareness.

- **Sponsorship** and **product endorsement deals**, such as the 2016 TV ad for Pantene Pro-V shampoo, featuring singer Ellie Goulding.

- **Promotional activities** at the point of sale such as **percentage discounts** and BOGOF offers (see page 19).

- Being price competitive is important as it's often pricing that customers use to decide between competitors. This can lead to **price wars** between businesses.

- **Customer loyalty cards** and **saver schemes** (see next page) can get customers to make **repeat purchases**.

A **Niche Marketing Strategy** Focuses on a **Specific** Market Segment

1) In a **niche market** there is more emphasis on creating a product that is **differentiated** or **unique** compared to what is available in the mass market. The development of the USP of a product is **key** in a niche market.

2) Niche marketing is more **specialised** and requires the business to have done **effective market research** into understanding the customer's **needs**, **values** and **aspirations**.

3) Businesses operating in niche markets will need to find more **cost-effective** means of raising awareness as they don't tend to have **big budgets** to spend on expensive advertising campaigns.

Buster's favourite niche.

4) Given that their market size is smaller, they will be concentrating more on **building a reputation** and establishing **customer loyalty**. They may concentrate on adding value through **strong customer service** and introducing **loyalty schemes** (see next page).

5) The pricing strategy used in niche marketing will **depend on the products** — if it's recently developed and a highly specialised product it may be appropriate to use **price skimming**. This is because there are unlikely to be **substitutes** and consumers will be **prepared to pay** the price.

Check out pages 22-23 for a reminder on pricing strategies.

Different **Marketing Strategies** Are Used for **B2B** and **B2C** Marketing

1) **Business to business** (B2B) marketing is the sale of one business's product to **another business** or organisation. For example, the marketing of surgical gloves to a local hospital trust.

2) **Business to consumer** (B2C) marketing is the sale of a business's product to a **consumer**. For example, the marketing of ready meals to shoppers in a supermarket.

3) B2B marketing doesn't need to focus on an emotional component. It will instead focus on being more **informative** than B2C marketing.

4) B2B marketing rarely uses traditional advertising media, like TV and radio, as these are costly and most of the viewers or listeners will not be the target audience. **Trade journals** and **trade shows** are more likely to be used to advertise the products.

5) B2B customers will be interested in the quality of the product, but they'll be more **concerned** with any **cost savings** or **potential revenue**, as they don't have an emotional interest in the product.

6) There will be a much stronger emphasis on building a **long-term relationship** between the two businesses and having a **highly effective customer service**, compared to B2C marketing.

7) It's important in B2B marketing to understand the client's **particular needs**, so it's **more specialised** than B2C marketing. The **volume** (number of units purchased) for sales orders may be **very large**, therefore the **stakes are high** as each contract successfully negotiated could be very **profitable**.

Marketing Strategy

Customer Loyalty is Important for Repeated Purchases

1) A strong customer service both **before** and **after** sales is a key aspect to building a **strong brand** and **customer loyalty**. It creates **good relationships** with customers and may lead to **repeated purchases**.

2) **Salespeople** try to make customers feel **happy** so they're **more likely** to make a **sale**. The emphasis on customer service is important if the item purchased represents a **large proportion of total income**, like a car or a house. In these cases customers need **information** on the **performance** and **functionality** of the good before buying it.

3) **After sales service** is also important to customers, so they can get help with any problems with their product after buying it. This makes the customer **feel valued** and they're more likely to **return** to the business again in the future. This is more important for **more expensive items**.

4) The **more expensive** the brand, the more a business will invest in a strong customer service. This could include a luxury waiting room whilst waiting to speak to a customer service advisor, or the offer of complementary water and hot drinks. It's all about ensuring that the experience for the customer is **good** and that they **feel valued**. These expenditures can be seen as **investments in the customer** themselves, as it's more likely that the customer will **spend a large sum of money** if they feel valued.

Loyalty Cards and Saver Schemes Can Promote Customer Loyalty

1) Loyalty cards help **tie** a customer in to a **particular service provider** or **retailer**. This is useful in markets where there are **many substitutes** or where the product is **regularly** purchased, i.e. daily or monthly.

2) For example, many coffee shops give out **loyalty cards** where the customer gets a **stamp** each time they buy a drink. Once the customer has collected a certain number of stamps they receive a **free drink**. This encourages the customer to **regularly return** to that business.

3) **Saver schemes**, where customers **collect points** based on the amount that they spend, have been very successful, especially in **UK supermarkets**.

4) One example is TESCO'S CLUBCARD, where the points earned give customers **vouchers** for money off their next shop. TESCO have also **teamed up** with other organisations to offer **discounts** on **leisure activities** such as holidays in **exchange** for these **points**.

Jonny only needed to buy one more stamp to have enough stamps to get a free stamp.

Warm-Up Questions

Q1 Explain what happens to the sales and profits of a product when it enters the maturity stage of its life cycle.

Q2 Explain why a business may choose to sell off a dog product.

Q3 Explain why a business operating in a niche market may not advertise through national TV.

Q4 Describe two differences in strategy between B2B marketing and B2C marketing.

Q5 State three techniques for building customer loyalty.

Exam Questions

Q1 What is meant by a cash cow? [2 marks]

Q2 Franco's is a local business looking to set up a new Italian restaurant in town. It's decided to focus on a niche marketing strategy and will specialise in only preparing gluten free pasta and pizza dishes.
Assess the advantages and disadvantages to Franco's of operating such a niche marketing strategy. [10 marks]

Q3 Gecko Sodas (GS) produces sodas that it sells successfully nationwide through supermarkets. Its lemon and thyme soda with added vitamins recently became a star product. GS needs to decide whether it is going to use a niche marketing strategy or a mass marketing strategy to turn this product into a cash cow. Evaluate these two marketing strategies and recommend which is most suitable for GS to use for this product. [20 marks]

The Boston Matrix for my telescope business shows only star products...

Remember, the marketing strategy and pricing strategy can change depending on where the product is in its life cycle and the type of market it's in. In your exam, read any information you're given carefully before answering. You don't want to write about a cash cow in a mass market if the product you're asked about is a dog in a niche market.

Employees

Most businesses need employees (or 'human resources' if you're being posh). Unless you become a business owner or a lottery winner, chances are you'll end up as someone's employee. Time to see what joys await you in the future...

Employees are an Asset to a Business

1) **Staff** are an **asset** to a business, which means that they are something a business has that is **valuable**.

2) The **skills** and **abilities** of staff mean that they are able to **add value** to a product (see p.11). They can do this in a number of ways — for example, their skills in the **manufacturing process** may ensure that **high quality** products are produced as **efficiently** as possible, or their ability to provide **excellent customer service** could mean that customers are willing to pay a higher price for the business's products.

3) Businesses should treat their staff as a **valued asset** and **invest** in them (e.g. by training them and looking after their welfare) — this will help to **motivate** staff and increase their **productivity**.

> An employee's productivity is the output they generate in a given time period (see p.81). There's more about the relationship between motivation and productivity on page 38.

Employees are Also a Cost to a Business

1) Employees get **remuneration** (payment) for the work they do, so they are a **cost** to a business.

2) Remuneration is usually in the form of **wages** or a **salary**.

3) A **wage** is paid to a worker based on the **amount of work** they have done, e.g. the number of hours worked. Wages are often used for **lower-skilled** or **manual workers**, such as those that do shop work or cleaning.

4) To protect workers from being **underpaid**, the UK government sets **National Minimum Wage** (NMW) rates — this is the legal minimum that businesses must **pay** their employees per **hour**. NMW rates vary depending on the **age of the worker** and whether or not the worker is an **apprentice**. E.g. in April 2018, NMW rates were:

> The rate for workers aged 25 or over is called the National Living Wage.

Employee	Minimum hourly wage rate (£)
Aged 25 plus	7.83
Aged 21-24	7.38
Aged 18-20	5.90
Aged under 18	4.20
Apprentice	3.70

NMW rates can lead to better **motivated** staff, which could increase **productivity**. However, it can also lead to **increasing costs** for businesses as the rates usually increase each year.

5) A **salary** is a **fixed amount** that is usually paid **monthly**. It's the amount earned for doing a particular job — the worker doesn't usually get paid any **extra** for **working harder** or doing **extra hours**. Salaries are usually paid to workers who are **highly skilled** or **not directly** involved in making a product, such as engineers or office staff.

6) As well as remuneration, employees **cost** a business money in other ways. For example, there are costs involved in **recruitment** and **training** of staff (see p.34), staff **welfare** (e.g. making sure that staff have safe and comfortable working conditions) and **severance** (when they leave the firm, see below).

There is a Difference Between Dismissal and Redundancy

1) Every employee has a **contract of employment**. This is a **legally-binding** agreement between the employer and the employee about what the **duties** and **rights** of the employee and the employer are, including **hours**, **salary**, etc.

2) An employee could be **dismissed** if they have **breached** their **contract** of employment. Their contract is **ended** — this is the **choice** of the **employer** and **not** the **employee**.

> Dismissal can also be referred to as being 'fired' or 'sacked'.

3) **Redundancy** occurs when the employee's job role is **no longer required**. For example, this could be because the business is **reducing** the **number of staff** it employs, is **closing down** or because changes in **technology** result in a job role no longer being needed.

4) Redundancies **cost a business money** as the business needs to pay a minimum **redundancy payment** to employees that have been with the firm for at least **two years**. When possible, a business will often ask if any employees want to take **voluntary redundancy** before it chooses who will lose their job.

Employees

A **Modern Workplace** has a **Flexible Workforce**

It's **beneficial** to a firm if its workforce is **flexible**, as it means it's easier to match the **work done by employees** to the **needs of the business**. Flexibility in a workforce can refer to the variety of **different ways** in which employees work and the **different contracts** that they can be offered, or it can refer to employees being **multi-skilled** so that they can perform a **variety of tasks**.

Flexible Working can Affect the **Ways Staff Work** and the **Contracts They Have**

- **Full or part-time contracts** — Employees that work full-time usually work at least **35 hours a week**. Part-time workers work **fewer hours** than **full-time** workers. Employing **more part-time workers** (and therefore having fewer full-time workers) can be beneficial for firms as it means they've got **more staff** who could come in to **cover** any **absent workers**.

- **Zero hours contracts** — A firm **employs** a worker but does not offer them **guaranteed hours**. This means staff only work **as and when** they're needed, so employers don't waste money paying for labour when it isn't needed. But staff are under **no obligation** to accept work, so it could be difficult for employers to find **enough staff** in **busy times**. Employees might prefer zero hours contracts because it means they can **work around** other commitments. However, zero hours contracts provide **little financial security**.

- **Permanent or temporary (fixed term) contracts** — A permanent contract has **no end date**, whereas a temporary contract does (e.g. the contract might be for one year). Temporary contracts are beneficial for businesses as they can be issued to cover a **temporary increase** in need for a particular job, or if a **current employee** will be **off work** for a **long period** of time (e.g. due to **sickness** or **maternity leave**). Permanent contracts might be more **motivating** for employees as they provide **more financial security**.

- **Shift work** — This is used when a job role needs filling for **more hours** in a day than can be completed by a **single worker**. The working day is **divided** into **shifts** (e.g. day shifts and night shifts) and staff work different shifts to make sure that there's **always** somebody doing the job. Shift work is **necessary** for a business that needs **24 hour cover**, such as factories in which production **never stops**, or **services** such as hospitals. Shift workers can often **choose** the shifts that they prefer, which gives some **flexibility**. However, working **irregular shifts** or **night shifts** can be **hard** for employees.

- **Home working** — Employees can work from home **some** or **all** days of the week. The employee can save on **travel costs** and can work around **outside commitments**. However, workers might find working from home **harder** or **more distracting**. Employers may gain from **freeing up desk** and **office space** for other workers. However, it can be difficult to **monitor** the **performance** of staff who are working from home.

- **Flexible hours (flexitime)** — Workers complete a **set number** of **daily/weekly/monthly hours** at times that **suit them** — e.g. they may prefer to **start work earlier** in order to **leave earlier** at the end of the day. There are usually **core hours** in the middle of the day when that **all** workers need to be present for. This helps workers to achieve a work-life balance and can improve **employee motivation**. However, it can be harder for a firm to set up **meetings** if it doesn't know **exactly** when all of its staff will be in work.

- **Outsourcing** — Businesses can **outsource** some tasks to **external businesses** — for example, they could get other businesses to assemble a product for them or produce marketing materials. This is advantageous to employers as they don't have to **invest money** in **training staff** for tasks that may only need doing **now and again**.

If you're taking the full A-level course, there's more on outsourcing on p.165.

A **Flexible Workforce** can be **Multi-Skilled**

1) Having a **multi-skilled workforce** means that a business can employ **fewer workers**, as it doesn't need to hire and train a different worker for every single **different job** aspect. This can lower a firm's **recruitment costs**.

2) Having a multi-skilled workforce also means that workers can be **moved** between jobs **when necessary** — e.g. if production of a certain item has to **stop** for some reason, workers can be moved on to **another task** rather than standing around with nothing to do. It also means that any **absent staff** can easily be covered by other workers, which helps to **maintain output levels**.

3) Being multi-skilled can **increase motivation** as employees have more **variety** in their job — this can lead to **increased productivity**.

4) However, a firm may face **additional training costs** in order to make its workforce multi-skilled, and the **cost of labour** may **increase** as multi-skilled workers may expect to be **paid more**.

Kinga was loving her firm's new flexible working policy.

Employees

Employer-Employee Relationships are Very Important

1) Employers and employees need each other. Employers need **hard-working** staff to contribute to the **production** of products that can be **sold** for a **profit**. Employees need a **secure income** to support themselves and their families.

2) A successful **employer-employee relationship** maximises the **cooperation** and minimises the potential for **conflict** between these two groups. It is built on a culture of **trust** between the two groups.

3) Having a good employer-employee relationship **benefits** both the employer and the employee. For example, it can increase employee **motivation** and **productivity**, which can increase **profits** for the business.

Each Employee has an Individual Relationship With Their Employer

1) All employees are treated as **individuals** for some purposes, such as employee appraisals. When **individual employees** negotiate with their employer about their own **pay** and **working conditions**, it's known as **individual bargaining** (or an 'individual approach').

2) **Individual bargaining** for **pay** means that employers can decide to pay an employee what they think he or she is **worth** to the firm. It might be **more** or **less** than other employees in the same role. This provides a financial **incentive** to the employee to work productively.

3) **Individual bargaining** is also used for things like **flexible working arrangements** — they're often based on the employee's **personal circumstances**, e.g. if an employee cares for young children or an elderly parent, the employer might allow that employee to work from home or work flexible hours.

Employees can Also Have a Collective Relationship With Their Employer

1) **Collective bargaining** is when a **group of employees** is represented by **workforce representatives** — these negotiate with the employers on issues such as **pay** and **working conditions**.

2) A common example of workforce representatives is **trade unions**. For example, **UNISON** is a large trade union that typically serves workers in the public sector. By joining with others and belonging to a union, an employee **strengthens** their **bargaining power** in a way that wouldn't be possible if they tried to bargain as an **individual**.

> Collective bargaining can also be done through a works council. A works council is a group of employers and employees that meet to discuss work-related issues.

- Trade unions can **take action** in the **workplace** to protect or improve conditions — for example, they can **negotiate** pay and productivity bonuses, reasonable **hours of work**, **paid holiday** entitlement, safe and civilized **working conditions**, and protect against **mistreatment**, **discrimination** and **unfair dismissal**.

- Trade unions can also **take action** at a **national level**. They can put **pressure** on the **government** to bring in **legislation** that will serve the interests of the trade union members. For example, things like the **minimum wage**, **redundancy payments** and the **Pension Protection Fund** were all introduced as a result of efforts from trade unions.

Warm-Up Questions

Q1 State three ways in which employees are a cost to a business.

Q2 What is the difference between dismissal and redundancy?

Q3 Give two advantages to a business of having a multi-skilled workforce.

Exam Questions

Q1 What is meant by collective bargaining? [2 marks]

Q2 Wheels Meals provides a takeaway delivery service from local restaurants. Assess two ways that flexible working for staff could benefit Wheels Meals. [8 marks]

Increase the flexibility of your workforce through daily yoga sessions...

What do you mean it's not that kind of flexibility? Anyway, make sure you've properly understood everything on the last three pages about employees, then have a go at those questions above to test your knowledge.

Recruitment and Training

Businesses need to find the right person for a job and then the new person needs to be trained. If this isn't done effectively it can be a right pain for employers — they might end up with rubbish employees who can't do their jobs very well, or employees might leave and the business will have to start the whole process all over again. Grrrr...

Recruitment is Finding the Best Person for a Job

1) Recruitment is the process of **finding** and **hiring** someone for a **job role** that needs filling. It has lots of **stages**:

Identify vacancy. → Write job description and job specification. → Advertise job. → Process applications. → Shortlist most suitable candidates. → Assess most suitable candidates. → Appoint most suitable candidate.

2) Once the business has identified what new staff are needed, a **job description** is drawn up — this document includes the **job title**, the main **roles** and **responsibilities** of the job, the **salary**, etc. A **job specification** is also drawn up — this document includes the **qualities** and **qualifications** required for the job.

> **Example:** A restaurant is advertising for a new **head chef**.
>
> **Job Description:** **Head Chef. Restaurant Delizioso**, Central London.
> **Salary:** £36 500.
> **Working hours:** Full-time, 40 hours weekly.
> **Duties and responsibilities:** Controlling food preparation, constructing menus, approving dishes before they reach the customer.
>
> **Job Specification:** We are recruiting an **experienced chef** with at least **3 years experience**. You must be an inspirational **leader** and be able to **work under pressure**. You will need strong **people management** and **communication** skills.

3) The business then decides whether it wants to recruit **internally** or **externally** (see next page) before **advertising** the job.

4) Candidates then **apply** for the job. The **way** in which candidates apply will be stated in the **job advert** — common methods include completing an **application form**, writing a **cover letter** and giving the business a copy of their **CV** (a summary of their work and education history).

5) The business can then begin the **selection process**.

The Selection Process Involves Assessing Candidates

There are a variety of ways that a business can **assess** potential candidates:

Interviews

- **Interviews** are the most common way of choosing candidates.
- Candidates can be interviewed **one-to-one** or by a **panel** of interviewers. Phone interviews are thought to be less effective than **face-to-face** interviews.

So Mr Johnson, tell us a bit about yourself.

I'd rather not, I really need this job.

Assessment days

- Some organisations use assessment days to help them test candidates. Assessment days include a range of activities to test the candidates.
- Tests include psychometric testing which assesses personality, aptitude tests which find out how good the candidate is at job tasks, and group exercises which show how candidates interact with other people in various situations. Assessment days can also include in-tray exercises (see below).

In-tray exercises

- In an in-tray exercise, a candidate will be given a scenario in which they play a member of staff, and be given a list of tasks that need completing. These tasks could include telephone calls, e-mails, meetings, etc.
- The candidate has to put the tasks in order of importance and say what action should be taken for each task.

Recruitment and Training

Businesses Can **Recruit** for a **Positive Attitude** or **Skills**

1) When businesses are **recruiting** for new employees, they can focus on hiring people with the **right attitude** or the **right skills** for the job — or a mix of both.

2) Hiring employees with a **positive attitude** means that employees are more **driven** and may be motivated to learn **new skills** at a **faster rate**. They are also likely to work better in **teams** and be motivating for **co-workers**.

3) If a business employs people that are already **highly trained** in the **skills** needed for the job, then this could **reduce training costs**. However, if the potential employee doesn't have a positive attitude or lacks team working skills then they might **not** be **enjoyable** or **easy** to work with, and could **demotivate** other employees.

4) Overall, it's easier to **learn new skills** than to **learn** how to have a **good work attitude**. So, if a business can't find a candidate with a good **mix** of **both**, they will often hire for a positive attitude and train for skills.

There are **Pros** and **Cons** of **Internal** and **External Recruitment**

Internal recruitment is when a business recruits someone who **already** works for them, and **external recruitment** is when it hires someone from **outside** the business. There are **pros** and **cons** of each approach:

	Internal recruitment	External recruitment
Pros	• Candidates already **know** the business, and the business knows the candidates. • **Short** and **cheap** process. • **Motivates** workers to go for a promotion.	• Brings in fresh **new ideas**. • Brings in **experience** from other organisations. • **Larger** number of applicants.
Cons	• Leaves a **vacancy** in another department. • Can cause **resentment** among colleagues who aren't selected.	• **Long** and **expensive** process. • Candidates will need a **longer** induction process. • Will have only seen a candidate at recruitment — might **not** be **representative** of what they're like at work.

Recruitment and **Training** Have **Costs** for a Business

1) Recruitment has significant **costs** to a business — for example:

- The cost of **advertising** the **vacant post** — adverts may be placed in **specialist magazines** or **newspapers** to attract the **right staff**, which can be expensive. Sometimes professional **social media** sites such as LinkedIn will be used — this allows businesses to reach a **large** number of people with very **specific skills**, but it can be **expensive**.

- A business might pay for a **specialist recruitment agency** in order to help recruit professional staff. This is often used if the job is **unique** or if it is a more **senior** position. A recruitment agency **advertises** and **shortlists** candidates, and in some cases will **interview** and make the **final choice**.

- **Shortlisting** and **assessing** candidates might be done by **existing staff**. This costs money as they can't do their **usual job** whilst taking part in the shortlist and assessment processes. The **more senior** the staff involved in these selection processes, the **more expensive** it is, as their labour hours are more expensive than **junior staff**.

- There may be other **expenses** involved in recruitment such as sending existing staff to **recruitment fairs** to talk to **potential applicants**, or paying **travel expenses** for interview candidates.

2) Once a person is appointed to a position, they need **training** — this costs money as the business needs to **pay** for people to **deliver** their training. There may be a **handover period** in which the new employee **shadows** the role of a person who is leaving the firm. During this period the firm has to pay **two sets of wages** for the same job role.

There's more on training on the next page.

3) It is important that the recruitment and training process is **effective** due to the high costs involved.

4) If the person appointed is **not suitable** or **not trained effectively** they may **leave the job**.

5) The more people that **leave** a job, the higher a business's **labour turnover** — labour turnover is the **percentage** of employees who leave a business over a **period of time** (usually a year).

6) Having a high labour turnover is **costly** for a business as it means it has to **spend more** on **recruiting** and **training new employees**.

If you're doing the full A-level, there's more on labour turnover on p.143.

Recruitment and Training

Induction Training is Important for New Recruits

1) Once the **right person** has been chosen and is employed by the business, they will start a **period** of **induction training** to **introduce** them to their workplace and their new role.

2) Induction training usually starts with an **introduction** to the **business**. This could include its **history** and **background**, and familiarisation with all the **key policies** and **procedures** used in the business. Induction training also includes **health and safety** and information on **line management**.

3) During induction training an employee will also be given more information about their **job role** — this can involve some **training** on how to do their job. The **amount** and **depth** of job-specific training given during an induction period depends on the **business** and the **nature of the job**.

4) Induction training needs to be **effective** — if it's **not effective** or **not long enough**, the new employee could **make mistakes** that could cost the business money.

5) If the employee if not **fully supported** at the beginning in their new role, they may become **overwhelmed**, **demotivated** and unable to work **effectively**. This could lead to lower **productivity** or poor **quality** work, or even cause them to **leave** the business.

> Full induction training often isn't needed if the firm has recruited internally — the employee will already know all about the firm and its policies.

Tom misread the memo — he thought he was attending seduction training.

Training Can be Done Inside or Outside of Work

1) New recruits need **training** to become fully **competent** and **confident** in their new role. This training can be done **off-the-job** (e.g. studying part-time at a local **college**) or **on-the-job** (e.g. where the new worker is trained by an experienced worker in the workplace). Training can also be given to **existing employees** to **develop** their **skills**.

2) **On-the-job training** is most suitable where **practical skills** are being taught, providing it's **safe** to do so in the **work environment**, e.g. picking stock in a warehouse.

3) **Off-the-job training** is appropriate when the employee needs to know **general information** about the business or its procedures. It's also useful for when employees are **learning a new skill** that would be difficult to learn while in a **real work environment**, e.g. learning how to manage people or drive a fork-lift truck.

	On-the-job training	Off-the-job training
Pros	• Easy to organise. • Lower cost of training. • Training is job specific.	• Trainers are specialists. • New ideas are brought to the business. • No job distractions during training.
Cons	• Trainers are not fully productive during training. • Bad practices are passed on. • No new ideas are brought to the business.	• Can be expensive. • No benefit to the business while training. • Training might not be specific to their day-to-day job.

Warm-Up Questions

Q1 What is an in-tray exercise?

Q2 Give two costs of recruitment for a business.

Q3 What is induction training?

Q4 Give two advantages of on-the-job training and two advantages of off-the-job training.

PRACTICE QUESTIONS

Exam Question

Q1 Jazz-it-up Pens makes multi-coloured permanent markers. It is looking to recruit a team leader for its innovation department. Assess the likely benefits to Jazz-it-up Pens of recruiting internally for the role. [10 marks]

Entrée exercises — the most delicious way of assessing candidates...

It's important that you understand why effective recruitment and training are essential for a business. If either of these are done wrong, a business could have a high labour turnover — this increases recruitment and training costs.

Organisational Structure

Hurray, two pages on organisational structure. It must be your lucky day.

Organisations Usually Have a **Hierarchical Structure**

1) The traditional business structure is a series of levels, where each level has responsibility for, and **authority** over, the levels below. This is called a **hierarchy**, and can be shown on an organisational chart.

2) An **organisational chart** sets out who has **authority** and **responsibility** to make decisions.

3) It shows who individual employees are **accountable** to (who is directly **above** them in the hierarchy) and who employees are **responsible** for (who is directly **below** them in the hierarchy).

4) An organisational chart shows the **chain of command**. This is the path of **communication** and **authority** up and down the hierarchy.

5) The chart also shows how the organisation is divided up, e.g. by **department**, by **product** or by **location**.

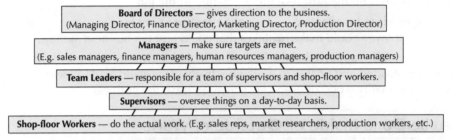

Board of Directors — gives direction to the business.
(Managing Director, Finance Director, Marketing Director, Production Director)

Managers — make sure targets are met.
(E.g. sales managers, finance managers, human resources managers, production managers)

Team Leaders — responsible for a team of supervisors and shop-floor workers.

Supervisors — oversee things on a day-to-day basis.

Shop-floor Workers — do the actual work. (E.g. sales reps, market researchers, production workers, etc.)

Structures Can be **Tall** or **Flat** and Have Wide or Narrow **Spans** of **Control**

1) Organisations with **lots of levels** in their hierarchy are called "**tall**". Tall structures have long **chains of command**.

2) Tall structures can negatively impact **communication** and **efficiency**. **Vertical communication** (getting messages between the **different levels**) can take a **long time**, especially for messages going from the very **top** to the very **bottom** of the structure. **Decisions** take a long time to make and there's a lot of **paperwork** to deal with.

3) In tall structures, there are lots of layers of management so there are more opportunities for **promotion** — this can be **motivating** for employees.

4) "**Flat**" organisations only have a few levels in their hierarchy. People are given more **responsibility** and **freedom**, which can be motivating for employees.

5) **Horizontal communication** (getting messages throughout one level) can be **slow** in a flat structure due to the relatively **large number** of people at each level.

6) The **span of control** is the **number of people** who report directly to a manager. Managers in **flat** structures have **wide** spans of control. This means they have a lot of workers answering to them.

7) If the span of control is **too wide**, managers find it hard to manage **effectively** and can become demotivated.

8) Managers in tall structures have **narrow** spans of control — they aren't responsible for many people. This allows them to **monitor** the people below them **more closely**.

9) If the span of control is **too narrow**, workers can become **demotivated** — they may feel that they're being **micromanaged** by interfering bosses.

10) It can be hard for a manager to keep a close eye on workers if the span of control is bigger than about 6 people. But if the workers are all doing the **same routine task**, they don't need as much supervision — so a span of control of 10-12 people (or more) is fine.

Director
|
Manager

Team Leader   Team Leader

Supervisor   Supervisor   Supervisor   Supervisor

Workers   Workers   Workers   Workers

Here, the manager has a span of control of two people.
Each supervisor has a span of control of five people.

Organisational structure can be improved through delayering

- **Delayering** means **removing** parts of the hierarchy — it creates a **flatter** structure with **wider** spans of control.

- Delayering can help to **lower costs**. Cutting management jobs can save a lot of money in salaries. It gives junior employees more responsibility and can improve **efficiency** and **communication**.

- It can **cost businesses money** in the short term as the remaining staff need to be **retrained** in their new roles. The business might also have to give **redundancy pay** to people it has made redundant.

- If there's **too much** delayering, managers can end up **stressed** and overworked with **huge** spans of control.

Organisational Structure

Organisations can be Centralised or Decentralised

In **centralised** organisations all decisions are made by **senior managers** at the **top** of the business, whereas in **decentralised** structures authority is shared out to more **junior** employees (e.g. to branch managers).

	Advantages	Disadvantages
Centralisation	• Business leaders have lots of experience of making business decisions. • Managers get an overview of the whole business, so decisions are consistent throughout the business. • Senior managers aren't biased towards one department so they can make the best decisions for the business as a whole. • Senior managers can make big decisions quickly because they don't have to consult anybody else.	• Not many people are expert enough to make decisions about all aspects of the business. • Excluding employees from decision-making can be demotivating. • The organisation reacts slowly to change, allowing its competitors to get ahead. This is because the senior managers who make the decisions don't spend time on the shop floor, so they're slow to notice consumer trends.
Decentralisation	• Involvement in decision-making motivates employees. • Employees can use expert knowledge of their sector. • Day-to-day decisions can be made quickly without having to ask senior managers.	• Junior employees may not have enough experience to make decisions. • Inconsistencies may develop between divisions in a business. • Junior employees may not be able to see the overall situation and needs of an organisation.

The **size**, **nature**, **objectives** and **culture** of a business will all affect whether a centralised or decentralised approach is used — this will then have an impact on the **structure** of the business.

- Businesses might **centralise** in order to save money in a more competitive market. A **centralised** approach can result in a **flat** and **wide** structure as levels of middle management are no longer needed.
- Businesses might **decentralise** as they are **expanding** and operating from a number of **different locations**. A **decentralised** approach will create **more levels of authority** and increase the amount of **delegation**.

Organisations can Have a Matrix Structure

1) **Matrix structures** organise staff by **two different criteria**. Businesses might use matrix structures if their operations tend to be **project-based**.

2) The diagram opposite shows a business organised by **project** and **function**. Each project team has workers from different functions. The red circle shows a **salesperson** working in **Project B** — they **report** to a sales manager and the manager of Project B.

3) The matrix structure ensures that staff are pursuing **clearly defined objectives**, and it **encourages** departments to build **relationships** with one another — this can lead to increased employee motivation and efficiency.

4) However, this structure could lead to **conflict** — e.g. project managers and department managers might have different ideas about how a strategy should be implemented.

Warm-Up Question

Q1 Explain whether managers in a tall or flat structure are likely to have a greater span of control.

Exam Question

Q1 Moors Ltd is a large accountancy firm with a centralised structure. It has recently expanded and now has three offices, all in the north of England. The firm is deciding whether to keep its centralised structure or become decentralised. Evaluate these two options and recommend which one is most suitable for Moors Ltd. [20 marks]

It was 27 °C today, but apparently it's not OK to delayer in the office...
It's a shame you can't delegate the learning of your Business course, but then you'd have missed out on this nice page.

Employee Motivation

For the past 150 years, industrial psychologists and sociologists have tried to figure out what motivates workers...

Motivated Employees get More Done than Non-Motivated Employees

1) The value of motivation should not be **underestimated** — a motivated workforce is likely to be more **productive** (and therefore the firm's productivity is higher) as they are **happy** in their jobs and are willing to **work hard** for the firm to do well. They're also more likely to be **reliable** and more aligned with **business objectives**.

2) Motivated workers are more **loyal**, which will decrease both **labour turnover** and **absences**, which reduces costs.

3) **Customer satisfaction** usually increases when a workforce feels **engaged** with what they are doing.

When Paul stopped working his bosses motivational thumbs went down but the staring continued. He'd never been more ~~scared~~ productive in a job before.

4) A business that **motivates** and **engages** its employees is a more attractive prospect for **future employees**. Businesses with a **good reputation** will attract the **best employees** and gain a **competitive advantage**.

5) There are several different **motivational theories** — they each suggest different ways to motivate employees.

1) Taylor's Scientific Management — Concentrate on Efficiency

1) In the early 20th century, F.W. Taylor thought that workers were motivated by **money**. He believed workers would do the **minimum** amount of work if left to their own devices.

2) Taylor's goal was to figure out the **most efficient** way to do a job, and then make sure every single worker did it that way. Also, making sure that each task was being done by the **right worker**. This approach is called **scientific management**.

3) He favoured **division of labour** — breaking work down into a lot of **small repetitive tasks**, with managers taking **responsibility** for the workforce.

4) Taylor believed in paying workers according to the **quantity** they produced — the most **productive** workers got a **better rate**. He believed that financial incentives would **motivate** workers and raise **productivity**.

5) Increased productivity meant that **fewer workers** were needed — workers worried about losing their jobs.

6) There were other disadvantages, too — increased productivity could lead to a reduction in **quality**. **Supervisors** were needed to monitor efficiency and for quality control purposes.

Taylor's approach wouldn't work for modern businesses — it would be seen as **exploitation**. It also ignores the **demotivating** effect of doing very repetitive boring work. However, aspects of Taylor's theory have survived — **piecework** (see p.40) is based on his ideas, and the **supervisor role** still exists.

2) Maslow's Hierarchy of Needs — People Need the Basics

Maslow and Herzberg (see next page) both believed that workers had needs which were specific to them as individuals.

Maslow said that people start by meeting the needs at the **bottom** of the pyramid. Once they've sorted out those needs, they can move on to the needs on the **next level** up.

Businesses meet these needs by giving the opportunity to develop new skills and take responsibility.
→ **Self-actualisation** meeting potential

Businesses give employees recognition (e.g. by giving awards) and offer promotion.
→ **Self-esteem** — achievement

Team working and social outings are designed to meet these.
→ **Social Needs** — friendship, teamwork

Health and safety policies and secure employment contracts meet these needs.
→ **Safety** — safe work environment with job security

Businesses meet these needs by paying workers enough and providing a warm, dry work environment.
→ **Basic Physical Needs** — food, water, shelter, clothes

Maslow's theory is **appealing** as each of the five different needs have some **importance** to workers. However, it isn't always **obvious** which level an **individual** is at. Different workers may put their needs in a **different order**, e.g. some may value friendship and team work over achievement and meeting potential.

Theme 1: Section 4 — Managing People

Employee Motivation

3) Herzberg's Two Factor Theory

In the 1950s and '60s, Frederick Herzberg interviewed accountants and engineers to find out what **motivated** and **satisfied** them at work. He identified **two groups of factors** which influenced the motivation of workers:

1) **Hygiene factors** are things like good **company policy**, **supervision**, **working conditions**, **pay**, and **relations** with fellow employees. They don't motivate as such, but if they **aren't good**, workers get **dissatisfied**.

2) **Motivating factors** are things like **interesting work**, personal **achievement**, **recognition** of achievement, and scope for more **responsibility** and personal **development**. These factors **do** positively motivate workers.

Herzberg's theory recognises that motivation comes from the **individuals' needs** and has influenced **motivational techniques** today — it provides clear solutions for businesses. However, it is often criticised for being based on a **small sample** of people and it doesn't consider that people have **different** hygiene and motivation needs.

4) Mayo's Human Relations Theory of Motivation

1) In the 1920s and '30s, Elton Mayo was involved in the Hawthorne Experiments — these investigated whether **certain factors** affected workers' **productivity**.

   - As part of the experiments, one group of employees worked in their usual working conditions for the duration of the experiment, whilst one group had their working conditions changed. E.g. employees had changes in the length and number of rest breaks and changes in the brightness of the workplace.

   - The experiments found that the group that had been exposed to changes showed an increase in productivity, even if the changes made their working conditions worse. Mayo concluded that it was the attention given to the workers by management during the experiment that improved productivity, and not any specific change in working conditions.

   - The experiments also showed that productivity increased if employees worked together in teams rather than by themselves (as long as they were still getting attention from management). Mayo concluded that workers benefit from informal social interaction and working in groups.

2) Mayo's **human relations** theory suggested that managers need to **improve communication** with workers and **value** their **opinions**.

3) Managers must meet the workers' **social needs** in order to improve motivation. This was a change from **Taylor's scientific management theory** that suggested that workers were only motivated by **pay**.

4) **Modern** methods used to improve motivation at work might include staff **social clubs** where workers can meet informally, **team working** and setting up opportunities for regular **feedback** meetings between workers and management.

Warm-Up Questions

Q1 Give three benefits of a motivated workforce.
Q2 Briefly describe Maslow's hierarchy of needs.
Q3 Give five factors that Herzberg would describe as 'hygiene factors'.
Q4 Give two modern methods for improving motivation at work that have been influenced by Mayo's theory.

PRACTICE QUESTIONS

Exam Question

Q1 Connor's Cars make high performance sports cars. Explain how Connor's Cars could use the principles of Taylor's scientific management approach to motivate its employees. [4 marks]

Motivational theory 5 — more tea and biscuits = higher productivity levels...
Make sure you know the four theories of motivation on these pages — the ideas might well come in handy in the exams if you're asked to give examples of how managers today can increase the motivation of their workers.

More on Employee Motivation

Businesses can offer financial and non-financial incentives to motivate their employees and improve employee performance. Personally I'm motivated by the thought of cheese and biscuits at the end of the day.

Non-Financial Motivation — Jobs are **Designed** to be More **Satisfying**

1) Lots of businesses today **design jobs** to be **motivating**. There are **different ways** to do this:

- **Job enlargement** gives the employee a greater range of work to do at the same level.
- **Job enrichment** gives workers more challenging work, and the training they need to do it. It gives employees more responsibility for organising their work and solving problems.
- **Job rotation** is where workers are occasionally moved from one task to another. It's often used where a job involves very repetitive tasks, such as on a production line. Job rotation means that workers become multi-skilled in a range of different tasks and have some variety in their job.
- **Empowerment** gives people control over their work and a greater role in decision-making — quality circles let groups of workers from various departments meet to suggest improvements to productivity and quality.

  See p.89 for more on quality circles.

- **Consultation** between managers and employees shows employees that their opinions are important and valued. In addition, employees may have direct contact with customers or first-hand experience of production processes, so may be able to suggest improvements that the managers wouldn't have thought of.
- **Delegation** gives employees more responsibility for decision-making. The manager needs to trust the people they are delegating responsibility to and the person being delegated to needs to trust that their manager isn't just passing on the work they don't like doing themselves.
- **Team working** puts workers into small teams and lets them organise their own work — this can lead to job enrichment and empowerment as workers get a greater role in a variety of tasks.
- **Flexible working** (see p.31) can allow employees to work whilst still having time for personal roles, such as being a student or as a carer to children or sick relatives.

2) You should be able to **link** these methods of motivation to the **motivational theories** covered on pages 38-39.

3) For example, Kellogg's® has weekly informal **team meetings** called huddles, which covers the **social needs** of employees according to **Maslow's hierarchy of needs** and is in line with **Mayo's theory** that workers benefit from feeling part of a **team**. Kellogg's® also provide employees with challenging opportunities such as **leading projects** — this fits on the **top level** of **Maslow's hierarchy of needs** (self actualisation) and could be classed as one of **Herzberg's motivating factors** as it leads to **more responsibility** and **personal development**.

Financial Motivation — **Money** is Used as an Incentive

As well as paying a **salary** or **wages** (see p.30) there are several different methods of **financial motivation** that businesses use:

Just like for the non-financial methods, you need to be able to link the financial methods of motivation to the motivational theories covered on pages 38-39.

Piecework is Often Used for **Assembly Line** Workers

Piecework (or 'piece rate') is when workers are paid per **unit produced** — they **don't** get a fixed salary. Piecework is used when the **quantity** produced can be measured easily — it can motivate workers to produce a **high quantity** of products. However, **quality** can **suffer** and the manager will need to make sure some **quality control** measures are put in place.

Commission Can be Used in Many **Sales Roles**

Commission is money paid to workers for completing tasks (e.g. making sales), which is often a bonus on top of their salary. This is often used in sales roles in firms such as estate agencies and car dealerships — workers are rewarded for selling certain products. The commission is often a percentage of the value of the sales they make — for example, if a TV business offered its sales employees 5% commission on any items sold, they would be paid an extra £50 on top of their normal salary for each £1000 TV they sold. Earning commission can increase motivation and performance of sales staff. However, it can also lead to overselling, and customers can feel like they are overwhelmed by staff whenever they enter the store. The business also doesn't know how much its labour costs will be each month.

More on Employee Motivation

Performance-Related Pay can be Used to Reward the Best Workers

With **performance-related pay**, workers are paid based on **their performance** or on the **performance of the business**. The amount is determined by both the **individual** and the **business** meeting **targets** — this is often done in annual **appraisals**. Workers are motivated to meet their own **targets** and ensure the business meets its **objectives** — however, it can lead to **demoralisation** of staff if only certain people are getting increased pay when the **whole business** is doing well.

Bonus Schemes Motivate Workers to Reach Targets

Bonus schemes mean that workers are paid extra on top of their salary once an agreed target has been met — this target could be in sales, profit, productivity, customer services, etc. Targets can be set for individual workers, teams and departments, or the firm as a whole. The bonus could be a fixed payment to all workers, or it might be based on a percentage of the worker's salary. Targets are negotiated with managers and should be set at a level that is achievable for the employees, but high enough to benefit the firm.

Profit Sharing Shares out a Business's Annual Profit

A firm using **profit sharing** will often **set profit targets** and share a **proportion of its profit** if these targets are met — the amount of money that a worker receives usually depends on their salary. If the business makes a **small profit** one year, then the employees **might not** get a share of the profit. **Profit sharing schemes** usually include **all employees** and so are used to help **motivate all employees** to meet the business's **main goals**. This encourages employees to work hard for the overall good of the organisation throughout the year.

The Motivational Techniques Used Depend on the Type of Business and the Job

1) **Non-financial** incentives are a **long-term** type of motivation — a business and its management invest a lot of **time**, **money** and **effort** into getting it right. Therefore, non-financial methods are more likely to be effective for **permanent staff**, whereas **temporary staff** are more likely to be motivated by **financial methods** of motivation — they may not be with the firm **long enough** to really benefit from non-financial incentives.

2) **Organisational structure** (see p.36-37) can affect the methods of motivation a business chooses. For example, a business with a **flat structure** might not want to introduce **team working**, because team leaders introduce an extra **level** of hierarchy. They might try to motivate people through **job enlargement** or **enrichment** instead. Businesses with a flat structure may also be more likely to use **empowerment** and **consultation** as motivational techniques, as **vertical communication** is easier than in a tall structure.

3) The **financial methods** of motivation that a firm chooses are also influenced by **organisational structure**. E.g. a business with a **tall structure** might be more inclined to use **piecework** or **performance-related pay** because there are lots of **levels** of authority to monitor the **productivity** and progress of the people below them.

4) It's **easier** for **employees** to **compare** the **financial rewards** that different firms offer than it is to compare the different **non-financial methods** of motivation firms use. Therefore, to attract and retain staff when there's a shortage of labour, a firm may need to concentrate on providing better **financial rewards** than competing firms.

Warm-Up Questions

Q1 Give five non-financial motivation techniques that businesses use.

Q2 Define the term 'piecework'.

Exam Question

Q1 Fall 2 is a small, start-up clothes retailer. The firm is planning to motivate its employees by focusing on financial incentives. Assess two ways in which financial incentives could be used to motivate Fall 2's employees. [8 marks]

Sadly I don't get paid on commission for all these gags...

Believe it or not, people aren't just in it for the money. Shocking, I know. Businesses also need to offer their workers some sort of non-financial motivation. Getting the balance right is what businesses usually strive to achieve...

Leadership

There's no denying that employees are important in a business — they do all the work after all. But to keep all those employees happily beavering away and striving towards a common goal requires good leadership...

There Are **Differences** Between What **Leaders** And **Managers** Do

1) Businesses often have lots of **managers**, but **not all** managers are **leaders**.

2) **Leaders** have a **vision** which they **share** with others, while **pushing** them in the right direction. Leaders often think in the **long-term** and are always thinking of ways to **improve** and to **innovate**. The power held by a leader can be **temporary** and is held only as long as the leader **continues** to **inspire** and **motivate** those that are following them.

3) **Managers** make **decisions** that affect the **day-to-day** running of a business. They **set objectives** for their department, and for the people under them. They decide what **work** needs to be done to **meet** the objectives, and what **resources** and **staff** they need. Managers tend to focus more on **meeting targets** and **maintaining** the **status quo** than on **innovation**.

4) However, **good managers** should also show **leadership skills**. That way employees won't just follow instructions because they're **obliged** to do so, but because they feel **motivated** and **inspired** by the manager.

Leadership Styles Can Vary

1) **Autocratic** style — the leader **makes decisions** on their **own**. They identify the objectives of the business or department and say **exactly** how they're going to be achieved. It's useful when dealing with lots of **unskilled** workers and in **crisis management**. This method requires lots of **supervision** — workers can't make their own decisions. This style can **demotivate** able and intelligent workers.

2) **Paternalistic** (fatherly) style is a softer form of the autocratic style and is used in **similar situations**. However, this style **focuses** on **employee wellbeing** and **motivation** more than the autocratic style. The leader **consults** the workers before making decisions, then **explains** the decisions to them to **persuade** them that the decisions are in their interest. Paternalistic leaders think that getting **involved** and caring about human relations is a **positive motivator**.

3) **Democratic** style — the leader encourages workers to **participate** in the decision-making process. They **discuss** issues with workers, **delegate responsibility** and **listen** to advice. This style shows leaders have a lot of confidence in the workforce — which leads to increased employee **motivation**. It also takes some of the **weight** of decision-making off the leader. However, this style can be **difficult** to implement in firms with **many employees** — if too many people are involved then it can take a **long time** to make decisions.

4) **Laissez-faire** style is a very **hands-off** form of leadership. **Leaders** might offer employees coaching and support, but they **rarely interfere** in the running of the business. This style of leadership is appropriate for a small, **highly motivated** team of **able** workers.

5) **Transformational leadership** is used when a business needs to **drastically change**. The leader has highly **innovative** ideas about how to **improve** the business and will need to **inspire** the employees to make these changes. This style of leadership requires an **existing business structure** that needs **fixing**. It's best used in businesses that need **modernising** or to help **small** businesses achieve their **big ambitions**.

Leaders don't usually **stick rigidly** to one style of leadership — they **adapt** their style to **suit the situation**. For example, when developing a new product, a **laissez-faire** leadership style may be best in the **early stages** when highly skilled staff are designing the product, but then a **more direct** (autocratic or paternalistic) style could be used during production to ensure that any **targets** are met.

Warm-Up Questions

Q1 Describe two qualities a leader should have that a manager might not have.

Q2 Describe how a paternalistic style of leadership differs from a democratic style of leadership.

Exam Question

Q1 Halina is the manager of a large production team in a textile factory that frequently has many orders to fill. Explain how having an autocratic leadership style might benefit Halina. [4 marks]

Fun fact: "laissez-faire" is French for "let-do" — the more you know...
Of course, knowing French terms won't help much with your Business exam. Better get back to revising then. Eurgh.

Entrepreneurs

Entrepreneurs make me feel like I'm on a train. Entrepreneurs... Entrepreneurs... Entrepreneurs... Toot-tooooot!

Entrepreneurs Are Important for Setting Up New Businesses

1) An **entrepreneur** is a **person** who **sets up** a **business**. They take on the **risks** of **new business activity** with the aim of **gaining a reward** (usually **profit**).

2) Entrepreneurs are **really important** as without them there'd be **no new businesses**. They have **several key roles**: **creating** and **setting up** a business, **running** and **developing** a business, **bringing innovation** to the business world, **overcoming barriers** to entrepreneurship, and **anticipating risk** and **uncertainties**.

3) Here's **more** on what **each** of these roles **involves**:

Creating and Setting Up a Business

Setting up an underwater café wasn't a great business idea.

1) Before starting a business, an entrepreneur needs to identify a **gap in the market** and a **need** for a product. They may do this through **market research** (see p.6-9).

2) Once they're confident they've got a **good business idea**, they'll usually write a **business plan** (a document that describes the main aims and objectives of the business and says how they'll be achieved). They'll have to **research** their business idea **thoroughly** and make sure they've considered everything, like the **marketing mix** (page 18), where the business will be **located** and what its **finance requirements** will be. They'll also need to decide on the form of **legal ownership** they want the business to have — entrepreneurs of **small start-up** businesses often set up as **sole traders** (see p.50).

3) The entrepreneur will then have to **raise the money** needed to start the business and **acquire** all the **other resources** they need to get the business up and running (e.g. a premises, equipment, staff, materials, etc.).

Running and Developing a Business

1) Once they've set the business up and started trading, an entrepreneur needs to keep the business **running** by keeping **up-to-date** with things like the **law**, the business's **sales** and **marketing** techniques and **accounting**.

2) They'll usually continue doing **market research** to check for **changes** that could affect their business — e.g. customer needs might change or there may be new competitors in the market.

3) They'll also need to continue to **set aims** and **objectives** for the business as it **grows**. They can use these to **monitor performance** and make **decisions** to ensure that the business is on the **right track**. They'll need to come up with **strategies** to grow and develop the business based on their successes and failures.

4) As the business grows, it'll become **harder** for the entrepreneur to **manage** all the business **functions** that they did when the business was first set up. They might need to **hire** some (or more) **employees** to help **manage different areas** of the business.

Bringing Innovation to the Business World

1) Entrepreneurs need to be **innovative** — they need to think of **new products** or ways of doing things and be prepared to take on the **risks** of making these **new ideas** a **reality**.

2) Once a business is up and running, the original entrepreneur may not think of new ideas **personally** — if they **employ staff**, they can **encourage** their **workers** to be **innovative**. For example, entrepreneurs can allow their employees to **take risks** and **experiment** with lots of different ideas until they find the **most productive** and **effective** way to complete a task — their solution can then be implemented across the **whole department** or **business**.

3) When an employee shows **entrepreneurial skills within a business** (e.g. having ideas for new products or processes and developing plans to put them into action), the employee is showing **intrapreneurship**.

Examples:
- Intrapreneurship can lead to **innovation** of the **technology** used by the business. E.g. in a publishing firm, an intrapreneur might investigate different **software** in order to find the most efficient type for making a book — this software could then be implemented across the whole editing department.
- Intrapreneurs can also come up with **innovative goods and services** during their experiments and research. E.g. Google™ allows its workers time to be **creative** and work on **personal projects** — one of the biggest successes to come out of this is Gmail™.

44

Entrepreneurs

Overcoming Barriers to Entrepreneurship

1) Some great business ideas never actually become a business due to a **lack of money**. This often occurs when a business idea has very high **start-up costs**, such as a business which requires an **initial investment** in **large machinery** or **technology**. An entrepreneur has to **overcome** this barrier by **raising capital**. They could try to raise large amounts of capital by getting a loan from a **bank**, but they may be rejected if the bank thinks the new business idea is **too risky**. The entrepreneur could also try to raise the money needed from **other sources**, such as business angels, peer-to-peer lenders or crowd funding (see p.55).

2) Another barrier occurs when the entrepreneur **lacks confidence**. The **fear of failure** and the **risk** of losing their **investment** or the security of a **regular wage** is **not worth** the gamble for some people. A successful entrepreneur needs to overcome this by developing a **strong belief** that their business **will succeed** and **communicating** this **confidence** to other people — **investors**, potential **employees**, **customers**, etc. are **unlikely** to **support** a business if it's clear the entrepreneur doesn't really believe in the idea.

3) Even if an entrepreneur has a **great business idea** and the **money** and **confidence** to get a business going, they may not have had the **training** or **know enough** about **running a business** to make it succeed. To overcome this barrier, entrepreneurs should make sure they **learn** as much as they can about running a business before they begin. For example, they could **get a job** working for a **similar business** before they start up, they could do an approved **entrepreneurship course** or they could get **specific training** related to the product they'll be selling (e.g. someone who wants to own a plumbing business will probably benefit from training as a plumber first).

Oliver wouldn't rest until he'd found a way through this barrier.

4) A firm might lack **entrepreneurial capacity** — this is a business's **ability** to identify **growth** and **development opportunities** and use its **resources creatively** to pursue these. To **overcome** this barrier, an entrepreneur will need to find ways to **develop** their business's **entrepreneurial capacity** — e.g. by **encouraging employees** to put **ideas** forward and investing **more time and money** into **developing** new ideas.

Anticipating Risk and Uncertainty

1) All business decisions carry an **element of risk**. For any decision, an entrepreneur can consider the **probability** that what they decide will have a **negative effect** on the business. They can weigh this up against what they would **gain** if things **went well**, and then make a **conscious decision** about **whether or not to take the risk**.

2) It's often considered that the **riskier** a **project** the **greater** the potential **financial gain**. For example, setting up a business in a **niche market** where there are **no current competitors** would be **high risk** — the market **hasn't been tested** and there could be **very little demand** for the products offered. However, if the business was successful, being the **only one** in the market could mean the business could charge **higher prices** and generate **larger sales volumes** than if they had competitors. The entrepreneur would need to try to **minimise** the **risks involved** before starting the business, e.g. by doing thorough market research into consumer trends and only producing small volumes initially.

3) **Uncertainties** differ from risks as they're usually **unpredictable** and **beyond** the entrepreneur's **control**. They tend to be associated with **external factors** that affect the business. For example:

- Health scares — e.g. in 2001, a severe outbreak of foot-and-mouth disease affected UK livestock. Many animals had to be killed, which affected the profits of farmers and firms selling meat and other animal-derived products.

Commodities are basic goods from primary industries, such as agriculture or mining — they're often used as raw materials in production.

- Political factors — e.g. if a new political party is elected, it may make changes to taxation, funding, regulations, etc. that affect a firm. The period leading up to an election can be a time of major uncertainty for firms.

- Commodity price shocks (sudden or drastic changes in the prices of commodities) — e.g. in 2014, the price of oil fell (due to a fall in demand), which reduced profit margins for businesses selling oil.

- Changes in exchange rates — e.g. if the pound's value falls, imported goods will cost UK firms more.

- Changes in legislation — e.g. in 2018, the European General Data Protection Regulation (GDPR) came into force — this legislation sets out how businesses need to handle people's personal data. Changing their existing procedures to be in-line with the new rules was very costly for most firms.

4) Although entrepreneurs **can't accurately predict** uncertainties, there are still steps they can take to **anticipate** and **prepare** for them. E.g. they can **keep up to date** with **predicted economic changes** and come up with **strategies** for a **worst-case scenario** to try to minimise any potential losses.

8

Entrepreneurs

Entrepreneurs Often **Share** Common **Characteristics**

Not everyone is **cut out** for **running their own business** — a **successful** entrepreneur is usually:

1) **Someone with initiative** — An entrepreneur needs to be able to **analyse** a situation and decide what's the **best course of action**, **without** being directed to do so by **someone else**.

2) **Hard-working** — Running a business is not a job with **fixed hours**. An entrepreneur may need to tend to a **problem** at any time of the **day or night** and during the **weekends**. If there's a problem that needs fixing, there may be no one for the entrepreneur to **delegate to** — they must **sort it out** themselves.

3) **Creative** — When developing a business idea, an entrepreneur needs to think up **new ideas** and look for **business opportunities** to exploit. This is still relevant when the business is up and running as the entrepreneur needs to think of creative ways to **improve** and **develop** the business.

4) **Self-confident** — An entrepreneur needs to **believe** in their **abilities**, **judgement** and their **business idea**.

5) **A risk-taker** — An entrepreneur needs to be **willing to try** things that don't have a certain outcome and could potentially have a **negative outcome** — this helps them to come up with **innovative products**.

6) **Resilient** — An entrepreneur needs to have the ability to **keep going** and **remain optimistic** even when things aren't going well, e.g. when **sales** aren't as **high** as expected or customer **feedback isn't good**.

Entrepreneurs Need **Specific Skills** to be Successful

1) As the owner of a business, an entrepreneur will have to **communicate** with **many** different **people** (e.g. customers, staff, investors, suppliers, etc.). It's important the entrepreneur has good **communication skills** so they can get across the **messages** they want to in a **confident**, **concise** and **polite** manner.

> A person's characteristics tend to be natural traits that they have, whereas skills are things that a person can learn to do better the more they practice.

2) An entrepreneur is unlikely to work completely alone in their business, so they need good **team-working skills** — these involve being able to **share responsibilities**, consider the **opinions of others** and be **reliable**.

3) The entrepreneur is likely to be responsible for **solving problems** that arise in the business — good **problem-solving skills** involve being able to **clearly identify** a problem, **assess different solutions** and **put a plan into action** to sort the issue.

4) There are lots of **numbers and figures** involved in running a business, so **numeracy skills** are really important. For example, a numerate entrepreneur will be better able to **work out costs** and **revenues** and therefore make accurate **sales** and **profit forecasts** (see p.62 for more on sales forecasts). Without **accurate analysis**, decision making can't be **effective**, which could prove **damaging** to the business.

5) An entrepreneur needs to have good **organisation skills**. They need to have **reliable systems** in place to keep on top of the **day-to-day running** of the business as well as **monitoring** the business's **overall performance**, **planning strategies** for the **future**, **solving problems** that arise, etc.

6) It's important the entrepreneur has good **IT skills**. Particularly when the business is **new** and the entrepreneur has **very few** (if any) **staff**, the entrepreneur may need to use IT a lot, e.g. to conduct **market research**, **communicate** with people (via email, social media, etc.) or to **promote** the business (e.g. by building a website).

Warm-Up Questions

Q1 What is an entrepreneur?
Q2 Describe what an entrepreneur's role of 'running and developing a business' involves.
Q3 Give four common characteristics of an entrepreneur.
Q4 Give four important skills needed by an entrepreneur.

Exam Question

Q1 Paula wants to set up a small business as a personal trainer.
Give two potential barriers to entrepreneurship that she may face as a business start-up. [2 marks]

Not revising every section in this book might be high risk...

... but the exam hall getting attacked by laser cannon wielding sharks is unpredictable and out of your control.
Not out of my control, though — I always carry my shark repellent spray with me wherever I go. Now, that's smart.

More on Entrepreneurs

More on entrepreneurs? Yes. Sorry. Now it's on to their motives — what gives them the get up and go, go, go they need to run their own business. Get through these next two pages, then you can go, go, go to make yourself a cuppa...

There Are **Financial Motives** For Setting up a Business...

1) The main **financial motive** for many entrepreneurs is to **earn enough** money to support themselves, although many are **also motivated** by knowing they could **earn more** than they could do in **employment**.

2) To be able to **make money** from a business, the business will need to be **generating profit** — this means that the business is making **more money** than it **costs to run**, so the entrepreneur can use the **surplus money** (the **profits**) to pay themselves lots of lovely cash.

3) **How much profit** the entrepreneur wants to generate depends on whether they decide to follow a **profit maximisation** or a **profit satisficing** approach:

Profit Maximisation

1) **Profit maximisation** means making as **much profit as possible**.

2) This can be achieved by **reducing costs** to their minimum and **increasing sales revenue** to its maximum.

> There's more on how a business can maximise profits on pages 48-49.

3) Generally, the more money a business makes, the more money the entrepreneur will be able to take as a **salary**. If the business is set up as a **limited company**, then maximising profits will mean that **shareholders** get higher **annual dividend** payments (see page 51).

Profit Satisficing

1) **Profit satisficing** means **making enough profit**, but **not pushing to maximise** it.

2) If the business **doesn't** have shareholders, the entrepreneur may be happy to make enough profit so that they can have an **enjoyable lifestyle** and no more — they may **not be motivated** to keep **increasing profits** year after year. This type of business is called a **lifestyle business** (see page 52).

3) If there are **shareholders** in the business, profit satisficing means the entrepreneur only wants to make enough profit to keep the shareholders **satisfied**, but no more.

...as Well as **Non-Financial** Motives

1) Many entrepreneurs crave the **independence** that running their own business brings — not having to **report to a boss** and having the freedom to pursue their **own ideas** can be very motivating. It can help the entrepreneur to achieve the **work-life balance** that they want.

2) Some entrepreneurs are motivated by the **flexibility** that being their own boss can bring. For example, they may be able to **choose** which **hours of the day** they work and be able to **take time off** without needing to ask for **permission**.

3) Some are motivated by having the opportunity to **work from home** — not having a **long, daily commute** or not having to work away from home for **long spells** can make life much more enjoyable.

Being an entrepreneur meant that Emma could wear whatever she liked at work.

4) Many people enjoy the **challenge** of building a business. They may find it more **rewarding** to start up a business and see it become successful, than if they succeeded as an employee. Others may do it because they simply enjoy the **thrill** of taking a **risk**.

5) Some entrepreneurs might be motivated by their desire to make a difference to a **social problem**. An entrepreneur like this is known as a **social entrepreneur** and the firm they set up is called a **social enterprise** (see page 52). Their business might be designed to improve the **quality of life** of a particular group of people or for society in general. For example, a social entrepreneur might set up a **youth group** to improve the quality of life for **young people** in a **deprived area**.

6) Entrepreneurs may also be motivated by **ethical issues**. For example, an entrepreneur that sets up a **café** in which customers are encouraged to bring in their own **re-usable coffee cups** has a clear **ethical stance**.

More on Entrepreneurs

Over Time An Entrepreneur May Need to Develop Into a Leader

1) Most businesses are **very small** to start with — maybe **just the entrepreneur** or just the entrepreneur and a **handful of staff**.

2) If the business idea is a **success** and the business is able to **grow**, **more staff** will need to be employed to **help run** the business.

3) With more staff in the business, the entrepreneur has to **develop into a leader**.

4) This **transition** can be **difficult** for many entrepreneurs. They have to be prepared to do the **following things**:

A leader is someone who has a vision that they share with others, while motivating them — see page 42.

Delegate Responsibility

The entrepreneur will have to **delegate responsibility** to other members of staff to **manage** specific functions of the business. They will need to **develop trust** that these individuals will carry out tasks **as well as** they would do themselves. In the early days this may mean the entrepreneur spends a lot of time **consulting** with the employees and **verifying** the **decisions** they make. The entrepreneur may find it easier to build trust and delegate responsibility if they hire people with similar **beliefs**, **principles** and **visions** for the business as themselves.

Develop Emotional Intelligence

Emotional intelligence is the ability to **identify** and **manage** your **own** emotions, as well as to **recognise** the emotions of **others** and be able to **respond** to them **appropriately**. It's important in fostering a sense of **wellbeing** in staff and keeping them **motivated**. The entrepreneur needs to learn to **listen to others** and to have an **open mind**. Others might have **ideas** on ways to do things and may have opinions about what is good or bad about the business. Getting a **new perspective** on things could help the business to **grow** and it will be **motivating** for staff to be listened to. The entrepreneur needs to **understand** and **accept** that other individuals in the business will be **better at dealing** with certain **issues** or have **more experience** in certain areas than themselves.

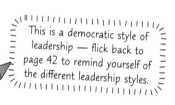

The new staff member was really testing Doug's leadership skills.

Become Less Reactive

When the business was only managed by the entrepreneur they could be very **reactive** — they could **make decisions quickly** and **instinctively**. However, with more staff, the entrepreneur is **responsible** for a **greater number of people** and needs to consider what **consequences** their decisions could have on these people. They may even need to **consult** their staff to help them make decisions about the business.

This is a democratic style of leadership — flick back to page 42 to remind yourself of the different leadership styles.

Warm-Up Questions

Q1 Give one financial motive of an entrepreneur.

Q2 What does profit satisficing mean?

Q3 Explain why an entrepreneur may need to develop emotional intelligence in order to expand their business.

PRACTICE QUESTIONS

Exam Question

Q1 Rory currently works as a mechanic in a garage. He wants to set up his own business of restoring vintage campervans. Assess two non-financial motives Rory might have for becoming an entrepreneur. [8 marks]

Single, creative entrepreneur seeking business for profit maximisation...

Make sure you know what tends to motivate people to start their own businesses — remember it's not all about wanting to be filthy rich. Make sure you know why entrepreneurs might find it hard developing into leaders too.

Business Objectives

Objectives set out what the business hopes to achieve — your revision objective should be to learn these two pages...

A Business Needs to Set Out Its **Aims** and **Objectives**

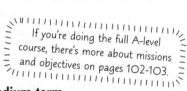

If you're doing the full A-level course, there's more about missions and objectives on pages 102-103.

1) An **aim** is a broad **target** or goal set by the business for the **long-term**. For example, an **aim** could be to become the **number one seller** of books. A business's main aims are also known as its **mission**.

2) An **objective** is a specific **target** or goal set by the business in the **short-** to **medium-term** to help achieve an aim. Businesses usually have **more than one** objective they're working towards at any one time, although they may consider some to be **more important** than others.

3) **Profit maximisation** is a very common **aim** for businesses — the more profit a firm makes, the more capital it has available in order to **grow** and **expand**.

4) Profit maximisation also helps a firm to **survive**, as the more money a firm has, the better able it is to deal with any large **expenses** it may face that are needed to **keep it operating**, such as replacing old machinery.

5) In order to **maximise profits**, firms need to try to **reduce costs** to a **minimum** and/or **increase sales revenue** to its **maximum**. A firm's **objectives** will often help them to achieve one of these two things.

Survival is the Most Important **Short-Term** Business **Objective**

1) Before a business can concentrate on maximising profits, its **main objective** may simply be **survival**. A survey in 2014 showed that **less than half** of small UK businesses will still be trading five years after they start up.

2) **Poor cash flow management** is one of the main reasons why new businesses **struggle to survive**. This can happen if the business **expands too quickly**, resulting in higher costs before they've seen any increase in sales.

3) If a business is able to **break even** (enough **sales revenue** is being made to **cover** all of its **costs** — see p.64), then the business can start concentrating more heavily on objectives other than survival.

4) It's not just start-ups that have survival as an objective though — **established businesses** can also have a survival objective. This may be necessary when factors arise that make the **future** of the business **uncertain**, e.g. if the **market becomes** very **competitive** or if **economic changes** cause the firm's **costs to increase**.

Objectives can be **Directly Focussed** on **Maximising Profit**

1) Although **profit maximisation** is **often** a **long-term aim**, a business may still set **profit objectives** to act as **short-** to **medium-term** goals. For example, a business could set an objective to **achieve** a **certain amount** of **profit** each **month**, or to **increase** profits by a **certain percentage** over a **year**.

2) Profit objectives will help the business to **monitor** how well it's achieving its overall profit aim.

Sales Maximisation Objectives can Help to **Boost Revenue**

1) **Sales maximisation** is where the business focuses on **increasing sales**.

2) This might be measured by the **value** of total **sales** and so may help increase **profits**.

3) Alternatively, it might be measured by the **volume** of sales, so the business may try to increase the **number of items sold** with less concern for making a large profit from these sales.

4) Increasing the number of items sold helps **increase market share**, which can increase profits (see below).

Increasing **Market Share** can Also **Increase Revenue**

1) **Increasing market share** may be an important objective for a **new business** when they're trying to gain a **foothold** and become **more established** in a market. As they gain more market share the firm is likely to become **more well-known** — this may help to **increase sales further** as **retailers** will be encouraged to **stock** the firm's products, and **more customers** will be tempted to **buy** them.

2) To increase market share, a firm may need to **heavily promote** their products or put their **prices really low** in order to tempt customers **away from competitors**.

3) For an established business, having an objective to increase market share may mean that they're trying to **dominate** the market and **reduce** the number of **competitors** in the **market**.

Business Objectives

Improving **Cost Efficiency** is a Common Objective

1) Improving cost efficiency focuses on **saving money** for the business by **reducing unit costs**.
2) If **unit costs** are **reduced** then the business will generate **more profit** on each unit sold, assuming the business doesn't reduce its prices.
3) Alternatively, with lower unit costs, the business may be able to **reduce prices** — this may **generate more sales** and therefore lead to **increased profits**.
4) **Cost efficiency** can be **increased** by **scaling up** and taking advantage of **economies of scale**. Economies of scale occur when **unit costs fall** as **a result** of producing on a **larger scale**. They can happen for several reasons, e.g. because firms that **produce more** need **more materials**, which often means they can **buy in bulk** and pay a **lower unit price**.
5) Cost efficiency can also be improved by looking for **cheaper suppliers**, using more **efficient production** methods, **reducing waste**, etc. (There's more about how a firm can improve efficiency on pages 82-83.)

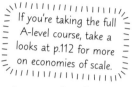
If you're taking the full A-level course, take a looks at p.112 for more on economies of scale.

Improving **Employee Welfare** can Lead to **Lower Costs** and **More Sales**

1) Improving **employee welfare** relates to anything that will **improve** the **happiness** or **wellbeing** of staff. Improving employee welfare will help **staff** to stay **motivated**.
2) A more **motivated workforce** is likely to be more **productive** — this leads to a **fall in costs** as each worker produces **more output** in a given time. Motivated staff may also produce **better quality work**, which may reduce **wastage costs** and lead to **more sales** as customers are more likely to buy good quality products. More motivated staff will also be more likely to **stay** with a firm, reducing the amount a firm needs to **spend** on **recruitment** and **training**.

Increasing **Customer Satisfaction** can be an Important Objective

1) A **satisfied customer** may become a **loyal customer**, and a loyal customer is more likely to make **repeated purchases**. In addition, a satisfied customer is more likely to **recommend** a business to others.
2) So having a **high level** of **customer satisfaction** may lead to **increased revenue** and may allow a firm to **charge more** for its products.

A Business May Pursue **Social Objectives**

1) A firm may focus on **social objectives** as a way of maximising profits, as customers may be **more likely** to **buy** from a firm that they know is **socially responsible**.
2) For example, in 2005 Starbucks purchased Ethos® Water, a company that sells bottled water and uses some of its **profits** to support water projects in water-stressed countries. This has benefitted more than **500 000 people** globally. Some people may be **persuaded to buy** from Starbucks knowing that they made this move.
3) Alternatively, some firms are set up with their **overall aim** being to **improve a social problem** — these firms are known as **social enterprises** (see p.52). Social enterprises are likely to have **ongoing** social objectives they want to meet.

Warm-Up Questions

Q1 What are the two main ways that a business can achieve an objective of profit maximisation?
Q2 Give five business objectives other than profit maximisation.

Exam Question

Q1 WaxyDays makes handmade candles in a niche market. The firm has been operating for three months and employs ten people. The firm's aim is one of profit maximisation. To achieve this, the owners are considering setting new objectives based on either improving employee welfare or increasing market share. Evaluate these two options and recommend which is more likely to help WaxyDays achieve its aim of profit maximisation. [20 marks]

What makes a good objective is subjective...

A business can set itself whatever objectives it wants, but the eight on these two pages are common ones. Have a go at covering up the pages and seeing if you can list all eight with a brief description of each. Boring but effective.

Forms of Business

Businesses can take several different forms, depending on how many owners there are and how much risk they want to take on. There's quite a lot to learn on these three pages. The first two are about different forms of legal ownership businesses can have and the last page is about the different types of business an entrepreneur can own.

Sole Trader Businesses Are Run by an Individual

1) A sole trader is an **individual** trading in their own name, or under a suitable trading name. Sole traders are **self-employed**, for example as shopkeepers, plumbers, electricians, hairdressers or consultants. They don't necessarily **work alone** — they can also **employ staff**.

2) The main feature of this type of business is that the sole trader has **full responsibility** for the **financial control** of their own business and for meeting **running costs** and paying **taxes**. Having full responsibility for all the **debts** of the business is called **unlimited liability**. This can be **risky**, as if the business goes bust with huge debts, the owner is responsible for paying **all** of the money back, even if this means they have to sell their **personal assets**, such as their house.

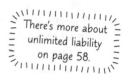
There's more about unlimited liability on page 58.

3) There are **minimal legal formalities** when setting up as a sole trader — the individual simply has to start trading.

4) Being a sole trader has **advantages** and **disadvantages**:

   Advantages

   - **Freedom** — the sole trader is his or her **own boss** and has complete **control** over decisions.
   - **Profit** — the sole trader is entitled to **all the profit** made by the business.
   - **Simplicity** — there's **less form-filling** than for a limited company. Bookkeeping is less complex.
   - **Savings on fees** — there aren't any legal costs for drawing up an ownership agreement.

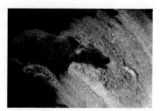
Bears — just another hiccup in Sally's plan to become a sole trader.

   Disadvantages

   - **Risk** — there's **no one to share the overall responsibility** of running the business with.
   - **Time** — sole traders often need to **work long hours** to meet tight deadlines.
   - **Expertise** — the sole trader may have **limited skills** in areas such as finance.
   - **Vulnerability** — there might be no one to **cover** if the trader **gets ill** and can't work.
   - **Unlimited liability** — the sole trader is **responsible** for all the debts of the business.

5) A **small business** that isn't **very profitable** is most likely to be a sole trader enterprise.

6) However, over time a sole trader enterprise may **grow** and **expand** and take on a **different form of legal ownership**. The form of business it expands into depends on a number of different factors, such as the **owner** (e.g. what size of business they want to run), the **product** (e.g. whether there's enough demand for the business to become very big), the **nature** and the **size of market** (e.g. in a very competitive market the business might need lots of investors if they want to have a significant market share) and how **profitable** the business is (e.g. the business might not generate enough profit to support more than a few owners).

A Business Can Be a Partnership

1) A business can **start off** as a **partnership**, or **develop** from a sole trader into a partnership as the business **grows**.

2) The **minimum number** of owners needed to set up a **partnership** is **two people** (there's usually between two and twenty people).

3) Partnerships have **unlimited liability**, so the owners have **shared responsibility** for the business's **debts**.

4) There are **advantages** of partnerships over sole trader businesses. For example, the owners have **shared responsibility** in **decision making**, and they **share** the **costs** and **risks** of setting up and running the business. Also, having **more owners** in the business will **extend the variety** of **skills** and **ideas** that can be used.

5) Having **more owners** also means that **more capital** could be **put into the business**, so it could **grow faster**.

6) However, there are also **disadvantages** to being a partnership rather than a sole trader. For example, the partners **all** have to **agree** on **big business decisions**, which can lead to **stress** and **conflict**. Also, any **profits** will need to be **shared** between all of the owners.

Forms of Business

A Business Can Become a **Limited Company**

1) There are **two** kinds of limited company — **private limited (Ltd)** and **public limited (PLC)**.

2) Both types of limited company are **owned** by **shareholders**. The main **difference** is **who** owns the shares. In a **private** limited company, the owners (the **other shareholders**) have to **agree** before **anyone buys or sells** shares (the sale of shares is done **privately** within the business). Often, the shareholders **run** the business.

3) In a **public** limited company, **anyone** can **buy shares** in the business — the **shares are sold publicly** on the **stock market**. This means that the **general public** can buy shares in the business. Most shareholders have **very little power** when it comes to decision making in the business (unless they **hold lots of shares**).

4) **All shareholders** (whether in a private or public limited company) are **paid a dividend** in return for their **investment**. Dividends are a **proportion** of the **profits** earned by the company which are split and paid out to the shareholders. Dividends are paid as a **fixed amount per share** — the **more shares**, the **larger** the **dividend**.

5) Both private and public limited companies have **limited liability**. The **business** and the **owners** have **separate** legal **identities**, so the **money** that owners **risk** losing if the company goes bankrupt is **limited** to the amount that they have invested — their **personal assets** are **not at risk**.

Sole Traders and **Partnerships** may Become **Private Limited Companies**

1) An entrepreneur can **set up** their business as a **private limited company**, but many private limited companies arise as sole traders or partnerships **grow** and **develop** into this form of business.

2) Becoming a Ltd company lets the business **sell shares**, which provides it with **more money** to use for **growth**.

3) A Ltd company has **limited liability**, which means the owners have **more financial protection** if the **company goes bust**. This means they may take **more financial risks** with the business than a sole trader or partnership.

4) Ltd companies can be perceived as having more **credibility** than sole traders or partnerships as they have their own **identity** and appear more **professional**, so many customers have more **confidence** buying from them.

5) However, a Ltd company requires **lots of paperwork** — e.g. unlike sole traders or partnerships, Ltd companies are legally obliged to **publish their accounts** each year.

6) Also, it can be **harder** for a Ltd company to **borrow** money from banks as the owners aren't **risking** their **personal assets**. This may mean that the banks are **less able** to get their money back if the company **fails**.

7) There are **more owners** in a Ltd company, so there is **less profit** available **for each owner**. Also, having more owners can mean **decision making** is **slower** or **harder** (the original entrepreneur or owners have **less control**).

Private Limited Companies May **Grow** Into **Public Limited Companies**

1) A **Ltd company** that has the **potential for growth** may opt for **stock market flotation** and **transition** into a **PLC**. Stock market flotation is when a business **publicly sells shares** on the stock market for the first time.

2) This means the business can **raise lots of capital** by **selling shares** — it can have **thousands** of shareholders. This **shares the financial risks** between a much larger number of people than in a Ltd company. It also **extends decision making** because shareholders can vote on certain decisions — e.g. a **change** in the **company name** or the **appointment** of a **director** can't be **approved** unless the decision is backed by **more than 50%** of shareholder votes. Voting usually takes place at **annual general meetings**, which all PLCs have to have.

3) There is a **higher prestige** for a business if it can put PLC after its name.

4) However, having **more shareholders** means that the business has to **share** the **profits** with more people. The business will need to **generate a huge profit** in order to be able to **pay decent dividends** to each shareholder.

5) **Share prices** on the stock market are influenced by the **national** and **global economy**. This means that the owners have **less control** over the **share price** than in a Ltd company, which can make the business **vulnerable**.

6) **Supply** and **demand** affect share value — if a business is doing **well**, then **demand** for shares will **increase**, which will cause the **value** of the shares to **increase**. If a business is doing **poorly** then more people will choose to **sell off** their shares and there will be **less demand** for them, so the **value** of the shares will **drop**. So, the financial value of the business is **unstable**, which can make it difficult to plan for the future.

To transition from a Ltd company to a PLC, the business needs over £50 000 of share capital, and if they're listed on the stock market, at least 25% of this must be publicly available. So it's usually only big, global or national companies that are PLCs — the vast majority of limited companies are Ltd companies.

7) If a person (or another business) buys **more than 50%** of shares in the company, they become very **powerful** — they often have **control** over the **outcome** of any shareholder **votes** and could even **take over** the firm.

Forms of Business

There Are **Different Types** of Business

This page isn't about the **legal ownership** of the business (like we've been talking about for the last two pages) — this page is about some of the different **types** of business an entrepreneur might set up.

Franchising Allows a New Business to Be **Set Up Quickly**

1) A **franchise** is an **agreement** (contract) which allows an entrepreneur to use the **business idea**, **name**, **model** and **reputation** of an **established business**. In return, the entrepreneur usually has to pay the established business an **initial fee**, plus **ongoing royalty payments** — these are usually a **percentage** of their **revenue** or **profit**.

2) The **franchisor** is the established business which is willing to **sell**, or **license**, its idea, name, model and reputation. The **franchisee** is the entrepreneur that **buys** into the franchise.

3) Franchising allows the franchisor to **grow quickly** as most of the **costs** and **risks** are taken on by the franchisee.

4) Franchising can be an easy way for an **entrepreneur** to **start up** a business, as they're using an **existing business model**. It's often **cheaper** than starting from scratch, they may get **support** and **advice** from the franchisor, and **customers** may **already know** the brand.

In need of a business model? Never fear, Jimmy's here!

Online Businesses Have Become More Popular

1) **Online businesses** are businesses that trade through the **internet**. They're **relatively cheap** and **easy** to set up, because the **overheads** and other **fixed costs** are **low** — they just require an internet connection.

2) An online business may be an attractive option for an entrepreneur wanting a good **work-life balance** — they can generally be **run from anywhere** and often don't require **regular working hours**.

3) However, entrepreneurs may **not** have the **IT skills** they need to **set up** and **safely run** an online business. **Technical issues** such as **fraud**, **spam** and **viruses** can cause lots of **problems**, especially for someone with poor IT skills.

Lifestyle Businesses Focus on **Lifestyle** And Not Profit

1) A lifestyle business focuses on **profit satisficing** (see p.46) to obtain and maintain a **desired lifestyle**. The entrepreneur is motivated by having **flexibility** in what they do and achieving a good **work-life balance**.

2) These businesses tend to have **lower start-up costs** and more **limited growth** compared to traditional businesses, as **investing** lots of money and time in a business **goes against** the **goals** of a **lifestyle business**.

3) For example, many people making videos for YouTube are running a **lifestyle business**. They can produce video content **whenever** it suits them, **wherever** they are and about **whatever they want**. Many **aren't concerned** with making **huge profits**, only that they have a **high enough income** to support themselves.

Social Enterprises are Set Up to **Benefit Society**

1) A **social enterprise** is a business that's set up with a **core aim** to use its **profits** to **benefit society** in some way.

2) They can often get **government grants** and their social benefits can **encourage customers** to buy from them.

3) An example of a social enterprise is **THE BIG ISSUE FOUNDATION** — this was set up to help **homeless people** try to **earn an income** for themselves to help them get off the streets and living in their own home.

Warm-Up Questions

Q1 Describe two advantages and two disadvantages of:
a) a partnership becoming a Ltd company, b) a Ltd company becoming a PLC.

Q2 What is: a) a franchise, b) an online business, c) a social enterprise?

Exam Question

Q1 Peter owns a coffee van and operates as a sole trader. Over the last three years he has been making a loss. If this continues, the business may face bankruptcy. Peter is attempting to turn the business around. Explain how being a sole trader could be a disadvantage to Peter in this situation. [4 marks]

Sole traders — they're not just shoemakers...

They can also be plumbers, greengrocers... You get it. Make sure you know the four different forms of legal ownership that a business can have and understand the reasons why business owners might choose one form over another.

Business Choices

To revise? Or to watch your favourite TV programme? The choice might not be as simple as it first seems...

Firms Need to Consider the **Trade-Off** and **Opportunity Cost** of Decisions

1) Businesses **don't** have an **infinite supply of resources** (e.g. money), so they have to think very carefully about how **best** to use their resources.

2) Any business **decision** will involve **weighing up alternatives** in order to make a **choice**.

3) Often, deciding how to use resources means that **one thing** has to be **reduced** or **given up** in order to **increase** or **gain another**. This is called a **trade-off**.

4) For example, in 1997 Apple® **reduced** its **range of products** dramatically so that it could **focus** on creating **fewer, higher quality** products. The **trade-off** worked though, as Apple® went on to be extremely **successful**.

5) Businesses have to consider the **opportunity cost** of the choices they make — this is the **benefit** that's **given up** in order to do something else.

6) Using the above example about Apple®, the **opportunity cost** was the **lost sales** from the scrapped products.

7) Another example would be if a sandwich shop had **£5000 to invest**, they may consider spending the money on **advertising** their business **or** on **extending** their shop. If they chose to **extend their shop**, then the **opportunity cost** would be the **advertising campaign** and the **potential sales** it would have generated.

8) In more formal terms, opportunity cost is the **value** of the **next best alternative** that's been **given up**.

Lots of **Choices** Need to Be Made in **Business**

It's important that you're able to discuss the **potential trade-offs** of different **business decisions**.
Here are some **examples** of situations in which businesses might need to make trade-offs:

- Design Mix: If a decision was made to try to minimise the cost of making a product, the trade-off might be that it doesn't look as good as a competitor's product. However, a low quality, cheap product may sell better than a more expensive, better quality product.

- Market Research: A business might decide that thorough market research is too costly. They might be confident that their product has a strong USP and instead choose to invest in developing the product. So the trade-off is that they'll get less information than they could do from market research, but gain a more well-developed, unique product.

- Business Ownership: A sole trader may choose to change the ownership of their business to a partnership to help spread the risk (see page 50). However, the trade-off is that the entrepreneur now has to share the profits with all the partners.

- Promotion: A firm may try to promote its brand so it appeals more to buyers from a younger generation. The trade-off is that in doing so, it may lose some of its customers from older generations.

- Pricing Strategy: Launching a product with a penetration pricing strategy (see page 22) may help to boost sales initially, but the trade-off is that it reduces the profit per sale.

Warm-Up Questions

Q1 What is a trade-off?
Q2 What is an opportunity cost?

Exam Question

Q1 Kylie has a dog-grooming business, which she runs from home. She has lots of loyal customers and a waiting list of people wanting to use her services. She is planning to expand her business by renting a small shop in a nearby town and hiring two members of staff. She plans to temporarily close her business for a month while she sets up the shop and trains her staff.
Assess the effect that trade-offs could have on the success of Kylie's expansion plans. [10 marks]

Would you rather have fingers for toes or toes for fingers? A tough choice...

Decisions, decisions... they're never easy. But you should make the right decision now and get this page well and truly learnt. The trade-off is probably less time on your phone for more chance of exam success. Although the opportunity cost is that you might not find out the latest gossip until after (yes, after) your friends. Oooh, I know, life sure is tough.

Sources and Methods of Finance

It's no great surprise that businesses need money to be able to operate. The next few pages are all about the different places that they can get the money from and different ways that they can get it...

All Businesses Need a Source of Finance

1) Businesses need **finance** to buy **fixed assets**, like factories and machinery. Finance is also needed to pay **day-to-day costs**, like wages, so that the business can **survive**.

2) A **source** of finance is a **provider** of finance. The **way** in which a provider **gives** finance is a **method** of finance. E.g. a sole trader has an overdraft on her bank account — the **bank** is the **source** of finance and the **overdraft** is the **method**.

3) **Sources** of finance can be **internal** (see below) or **external** (see next page).

4) A business may require **short-term** finance to pay its suppliers or cover temporary shortages of cash. Short-term finance is usually repaid **within 1 year**. **Long-term** finance is needed for long-term investments. It can take a while for a business to benefit financially from investments like new machinery, so repayments of long-term finance are due over a longer period, usually **3 years or more.**

5) When **choosing** a **source** of finance, a business must consider various things, including:
   - **Amount of money required** — the larger the amount, the less likely it is that internal sources can be used.
   - **Level of risk involved** — a risky business is less likely to find a source willing to lend it money.
   - **Cost of the finance** — some sources charge interest on the finance they offer (e.g. interest is paid on a bank loan). Other sources of finance may want a share of the business and its profits.

It's important you know the distinction between sources and methods of finance. Methods of finance are coming up on pages 56-57.

Internal Sources of Finance Come From Within the Business

Internal finance can be raised by using the **owner's money**, **selling assets** or putting **profits** back into the business:

Owner's capital

1) **Owner's capital** is **money** the **owner** (or owners) **invest** in the business, often from their **personal savings**.
2) **Sole traders** or **partnerships** are likely to use this as a source of finance when they're starting up or expanding — they're often relatively **small businesses** that **don't** need **huge sums** of money. Also they might **not** be able to access **other sources** of finance.
3) The **advantages** of using owner's capital are that it's **easy to access** and **doesn't** need **paying back**.
4) However, the amount of finance that can be raised is **limited** — it depends on the **personal wealth** of the owner(s).

Selling assets

1) Businesses can **sell** some of their **assets** (e.g. factories, machinery, etc.) to generate capital.
2) This source of finance is only appropriate for businesses with **spare assets**, so it's **not** suitable for **very new** businesses or **very efficient** businesses (as they're unlikely to have assets they don't use).
3) Businesses **don't** need to pay **interest** on money they raise by selling their assets, which makes it a **cheap** source of finance.
4) However, selling assets means that the business **no longer owns** the asset. Also, it can take a **long time** to sell the asset and **get the cash.**

Retained profit

1) **Profit** can be **retained** and built up over the years for **later investment**. This can work in the **short-** and **long-term**.
2) **Not all businesses** can use this as a source of finance — some (especially recent starters) won't be making **enough profit** to be able to retain much.
3) The main **benefit** of using retained profit is that the business doesn't have to pay **interest** on it.
4) However, **shareholders** may object to using this source of finance as they may wish to receive the profit as **dividends**. Also, retaining profit may cause the business to **miss out** on investment opportunities.
5) In many businesses, retained profit **isn't** used **on its own** to fund **expansion** — its level often isn't built **high enough**.

Sources and Methods of Finance

External Sources of Finance Come From Outside the Business

There are **loads of places** a business can get **external finance** from:

Family and Friends

1) Owners of small or new businesses may ask family and friends to help them out financially.

2) An advantage is that family and friends may offer the money as a gift or be willing to agree to a flexible repayment with little or no interest.

3) However, the amount of money available may only be small, and borrowing money from family and friends could place a strain on the relationship if they need the money back quickly.

Banks

1) **Banks** are a common source of finance for all different types of businesses. They can **offer** methods of finance such as **loans**, **overdrafts** and **mortgages**.

2) Advantages of using banks as a source of finance are that they are **recognised financial institutions**, and the **terms** and **conditions** of their financial products are **clear**. They can also **advise** a business and provide other services, such as **completing financial documents**.

3) However, banks often have **strict lending criteria** — it can be **hard** for **start-ups** or other **risky businesses** to be approved for finance.

Peer-to-Peer Lenders

1) Peer-to-peer (P2P) lending companies operate online — examples are Zopa and Prosper.

2) They allow individuals to lend money to other individuals or businesses. Lenders say how much money they are willing to lend and indicate what sort of interest rate they want. Borrowers say how much money they want to borrow and give some information about why they need the money and how long they want the loan for. The lending company then assesses how risky the borrower is and matches them with appropriate lenders (more risky borrowers are charged a higher interest rate).

3) Peer-to-peer loans usually have a lower rate of interest than a bank loan and are an attractive option if a bank has refused to provide a loan.

Business Angels

1) **Business angels** are **wealthy individuals** who invest money into **new** or **innovative** businesses that they think have the **potential** to be **successful**. They usually offer the business owners **advice** and **guidance** too. In return, they ask for a **share** of the business.

2) An advantage is that a business angel might have lots of **business knowledge** and useful **contacts**.

3) However, it can be **difficult** and **time-consuming** trying to find a business angel willing to invest. Also, a **share** of the business has to be given up, which may mean that the business angel gains some **control** of the business and its **decisions**.

Crowd Funding

1) Crowd funding is raising money from a large number of people, usually via the internet. Typically each person only contributes a small amount but collectively enough can be raised to meet a large target. It's a common source of funding for start-ups, but can be used by established businesses too.

2) To be crowd funded, a business puts details of the new idea it needs money for onto a crowd funding website (e.g. KICKSTARTER). The details are made public so anyone can see them and contribute to the funding. Rewards are sometimes offered for donations, such as early access to a product or the product at a discounted price upon release.

3) A benefit of crowd funding is that the business raises awareness of its product or brand to people using the crowd funding website — this may increase sales, even from people who choose not to contribute.

4) However, as details of the business idea are made public, the business risks having its idea copied by someone else before they've got the idea up and running. Also, if the business idea fails, lots of people may be aware of it, which may negatively affect the reputation of the business.

Other Businesses

1) A business with a **large retained profit** might want to **invest** in another business rather than **save** their **profit**. They might want to do this if bank **interest rates** are **low**.

2) A business might want to offer finance to a firm that aids its **own success**. For example, a business might want to invest in its **supplier**. This can improve the **supplier-buyer relationship**.

3) However, the business offering the finance is likely to want **shares** in the other business. This may mean they gain some **control** of the business or have an **influence** in its **decision making**.

Sources and Methods of Finance

Some **Methods of Finance** are Suitable in the **Short-** or **Medium-Term**

1) **How long** a business needs finance for will affect the **method** of finance it chooses.

2) If a business only needs finance in the short- to medium-term (e.g. to buy **raw materials** or **assets**, **pay staff** or **rent office space**) then it might choose one of the methods below:

Overdrafts are Available From Banks

1) **Overdrafts** are where a bank lets a business have a **negative** amount of money in its bank account.

2) Overdrafts are **easy to arrange** and **flexible** — businesses can borrow as **little** or as **much** as they need (up to the overdraft limit) and they only pay **interest** on the amount of the overdraft they actually use.

3) The main **disadvantage** of overdrafts is that banks charge **high rates** of **interest** on them. There may also be a **fixed charge** for using an overdraft. So they're **unsuitable** for using in the **long-term**.

Expensive or not, Carlos loved getting an overdraft.

Leasing is Paying to Use Another Firm's Asset

1) If a business doesn't have **enough money** to **buy new assets** (e.g. machinery or property) they can **lease** the assets instead.

2) Leasing means paying **monthly sums** of money over a **set period** of **time**, in return for the use of the asset. After the lease period, the asset is often **returned** to the **leasing firm**.

> Hire purchase (HP) is a type of lease — the buyer pays an initial deposit and pays the rest of the balance over a set period of time, while they have use of the asset. At the end, the buyer owns the asset.

3) An **advantage** of leasing is that a business doesn't have to pay a **large up-front sum** of money to **buy** the asset. Also, the asset leased is often **up to date** and so **less likely** to become **faulty**, and sometimes **maintenance** and **repair** costs are **included** in the lease.

4) A **disadvantage** of leasing is that it can be **more costly** in the **long-run** than buying an asset outright.

Grants Don't Need to be Repaid

1) A **grant** is a **fixed sum** of money given to a business, often by a **government**. Grants are usually given to fund **specific projects** in a business.

2) A business needs to **apply** to get a grant — during this process it needs to supply **lots of information**, e.g. about its **financial position** and the **project** it would spend the grant money on (market research showing the project would be a success, financial forecasts, how many jobs the project would create, etc.).

3) The biggest **advantage** of a grant is that it **doesn't** have to be **paid back**. **No interest** needs to be paid and **no share of the business** has to be given up. Plus, the application process **forces** a business to **think thoroughly** about the project and how the money will be spent.

4) However, the application process can be **long** and **time-consuming** and there's a **risk** of not successfully getting a grant. Even if a firm is awarded a grant, it often doesn't get the money until the **end** of the project, so it has to find another source of finance in the meantime. There is usually strict **criteria** from the grant provider about how the money is **spent** — if the business fails to meet the criteria, any grant money it was offered may be **retracted**.

Trade Credit Gives a Firm More Time to Pay Money it Owes

1) **Trade credit** is when a business **buys** a good or service and **doesn't** have to pay **straight away** — the business pays within an **agreed time limit** (usually set between **30 and 90 days**) of receiving the product.

2) This can help a business with **cash flow**. For example, it could allow a builder to complete a job and **receive payment** before they have to **pay** their **supplier** for the materials they used.

3) A **disadvantage** is that using trade credit could mean missing out on **discounts** for paying **up-front**.

4) A **failure** to pay trade credit **on time** could result in **problems** for the business. The business will be charged **interest** on the credit by the **supplier** until it's all paid off and may also be **charged a fee**. They will also get a **bad credit rating**, making it **harder** to get credit from suppliers and finance providers **in the future**.

Sources and Methods of Finance

Businesses Might Use Long-Term Methods of Finance

Businesses Can Take Out Loans to Finance Their Projects in the Long-Term

1) **Loans** are where a **fixed amount** of money is borrowed and **paid back** over a **fixed period of time** with **interest** — the amount paid back depends on the **interest rate** and the **length of time** the loan is for.

2) Loans can come from **different sources**, such as **banks**, **family** and **friends**, or **peer-to-peer lenders**. **Security** may be needed for a loan, often in the form of **property**. This is in case the loan **isn't** **repaid** — the lender can **take possession** of the property as payment for the loan instead.

3) Loans are a good **long-term** source of finance for a **start-up** business and for paying for **assets** like machinery and computers. They are **not** a good way to cover the **day-to-day** running costs of the business.

Businesses can also get short-term loans, but this isn't done often. They're easier to get than long-term loans, but tend to have higher interest rates.

4) A **benefit** of a loan is that the business only has to pay back the loan and interest — the loan provider **won't own** any of the business and it doesn't have to give them a **share of the profits**.

5) However, loans can be **difficult to arrange**, as a loan provider will only lend a business money if they **think** they're going to **get it back**. If the business **doesn't own** any **property** or **assets** that can be used for **security**, they **might not** be able to get a **loan**.

Share Capital is a Method of Finance for Limited Companies

1) **Private and public limited companies** can be financed in the **long-term** using **ordinary share capital** — money raised by selling **shares** in the business (see p.51).

2) Using share capital to finance a business has its **advantages**. E.g. the money **doesn't** need to be **repaid** (unlike a loan) and **new shareholders** can bring additional **expertise** into a business.

3) The **drawback** of selling shares is that the original owner(s) no longer **owns** all of the business. Shareholders expect to get a **share of the profits** as **dividends** and (depending on how many shares they own) may also want a **say** in how the business is run.

4) Selling shares is a **costly** and **time-consuming** process and so is only used to **raise big sums** of money — it wouldn't be used as a short-term method of finance, e.g. to fund the purchase of raw materials.

Venture Capital Can be Used by Businesses with High Growth Potential

1) **Venture capital** is money that can be used as a method of finance for a business that is **high risk**, but has the **potential** to be **successful**. This could be a business that's just **starting up**, or an **existing business** that's wanting to **grow**.

2) Venture capital can be provided by **business angels** (see page 55) or by **professional employees** (**venture capitalists**) working on behalf of a **venture capital firm**. Venture capital firms are more likely to invest in an **established business** rather than a start-up and generally provide **much more money** than business angels (venture capital firms usually invest **more than £1 million** in a business).

3) In return for venture capital, a firm has to give up a **share** of their business and sometimes the investors want a **big say** in how the business is run. However, the money **doesn't** have to be **repaid** and the business may benefit from the **expert advice** that the investors can offer.

Warm-up Questions

Q1 Explain the pros and cons of these sources of finance: a) selling assets, b) crowd funding.
Q2 Give four methods of finance that a business could use in the short- or medium-term.

Exam Question

Q1 DwnTym Ltd is a small start-up firm. The two owners have recently graduated with degrees in computing-related subjects. They plan to sell a new computer game that they have designed but they need £500 000 to help them fund the production and distribution of the game. They are considering either using venture capital or a loan as a method of finance. Evaluate these two options and recommend which is most suitable for DwnTym Ltd. [20 marks]

"Doctor, I've swallowed my wallet" — a classic example of internal finance...

Sources and methods of finance might not be the most exciting topic, but they're really important for businesses...

Liability and Finance

You may remember from pages 50-51 that the type of legal ownership a business has affects whether it has unlimited or limited liability. Well if you enjoyed all that talk of liability then you're in luck — now you need to know how having unlimited or limited liability affects how a business is financed...

Liability to Pay Off Business Debts Can be Limited or Unlimited

Responsibility for **business debts** works differently for different types of **legal ownership** of a business. This is because of the **liability** they have:

Unlimited liability

1) If a business has unlimited liability, the **business** and the **owner(s)** are **seen as one** under the **law**. This is the case for **sole traders** and **partnerships**.

2) This means any **business debts** become the **personal debts** of the owner(s). Business owners can be forced to **sell personal assets** like their **house** to pay off business debts.

Limited liability

1) Limited liability means that the owners **aren't personally responsible** for the debts of the business.

2) The **shareholders** (owners) of both **private** and **public limited companies** have limited liability, because a limited company has a **separate legal identity** from its owners. The **most** the shareholders in a limited company can lose if the company fails is the money they have **invested**.

Liability Affects Sources and Methods of Finance

1) Businesses with **limited liability** usually find it much **easier** to encourage people (e.g. business angels and other businesses) to **invest** in their business than those with unlimited liability — people are more **willing** to become part owners of a business if they know they'll **only lose as much as they've put in** if the firm goes bust.

2) This means that **sole traders** and **partnerships** (that have unlimited liability) are likely to rely on **internal sources of finance** and **external sources** that **don't** involve the source of finance becoming a **part owner**. For example, they may use **methods** of finance such as **loans**, **overdrafts**, **leasing** and **trade credit**, from **sources** of finance such as **family and friends**, **crowd funding** and **banks**.

3) **Limited companies** can raise **lots of finance** via **share capital**. Businesses with **unlimited liability** aren't owned by shareholders so can't rely on this **method** of finance. They could still get people to invest in return for a share of the business (e.g. a business angel may invest and become a partner) but their unlimited liability status may **limit** the **amount of money** people are willing to **put in** and the **number of people** that they can persuade to invest.

4) However, in some cases it may be **easier** for firms with **unlimited liability** to **raise finance** than firms with **limited liability**. For example, if a business with unlimited liability becomes a **limited company**, firms offering finance (e.g. via a loan or trade credit) may be **wary** that the owners are trying to **protect themselves** as they know their business is very **risky** — this could make them **less willing** to offer finance. Although many businesses with unlimited liability may be **small** or **new** (which puts them at **high risk**), sources of finance know that even if the business goes **bust** there's still a good chance they'll **get their money back**, even if it means the owners have to sell everything they own to pay back the debt.

Warm-Up Question

Q1 What does it mean if a business has limited liability?

Exam Question

Q1 Pat and Shaliza own a plumbing business as a partnership. They are planning to expand their business but need £50 000 of finance. They are considering becoming a private limited company before they expand. Assess how becoming a private limited company could impact Pat and Shaliza's ability to raise finance. [10 marks]

I'm a bit of a liability really...

So unlimited liability is the risky one — the owners of unlimited liability firms are responsible for the full amount of any business debts, whereas shareholders in limited companies are only responsible for what they invested. Lucky things...

Business Plans

£2 million needed for an earth-shattering investment you say? No problem, I have a ~~cunning~~ business plan...

All Businesses Should Have a Business Plan

1) A **business plan** is a document that outlines **what** a business plans to achieve, and **how** it plans to achieve it. A business plan is really important for a **new** business, but it's also important for an **established** business, e.g. as a way of monitoring performance and keeping on track.

2) There are **no rules** saying what a business plan **needs to contain**, but a good plan for a new business would usually include a **business overview** (e.g. who is setting up the business and why, what products the business will sell, where the business will be located, etc.), the business's **aims and objectives**, the **marketing** and **sales** strategy, details of **who** will work in the business and **financial forecasts**.

3) The **financial forecasts** part of a business plan should include a **cash flow forecast** (see p.60-61), **sales forecast** (see p.62), **break-even analysis** (see p.64-65), **expenditure budget** (see p.66), **projected statement of comprehensive income** (see p.71) and **projected statement of financial position** (see p.74). These forecasts should be done for both the **short-term** (e.g. the first year) and the **medium-term** (e.g. the first 3-5 years).

The investors felt that Yestin's presentation of his business plan was a touch too dramatic.

A Business Plan Helps a Business to Obtain Finance

1) A **business plan** is really important for a business that's trying to get **external finance**.

2) A good plan proves that the business owners have done their **research**. It helps to **convince** potential investors that everything has been **well thought through** and there are **low risks** of the business failing.

> Businesses don't actually <u>need</u> a business plan. It makes getting external finance easier, but they could still get some finance without one, e.g. family and friends or people that contribute to crowd funding may not be so bothered about seeing a business plan.

3) It provides a good description of the **product** and the **people** running the business — some sources of finance (e.g. those that contribute to crowd funding and business angels) may be less concerned about getting **financial returns** for the money they offer, but could be encouraged to support the business owners if they **believe** in the **product**, see that the owners are **passionate**, and see that they have the **drive** to be successful.

4) A business plan can show how **profitable** the business expects to be and **when**, so potential investors know when they could start seeing **returns** on their investment.

5) Overall, a good business plan gives the business access to a **wider range** of **sources** and **methods** of finance, as **more people** may be willing to offer the business finance.

6) It can also help a business to get **cheaper** long-term finance. For example, if cash flow forecasts in the business plan show that **loan repayments** can be made **successfully** and **on time**, then the business could get a loan at a **lower rate** of **interest**. Also, if the business plan shows that the business will be **successful** and **highly profitable**, then investors (e.g. venture capitalists) may be happier to accept a **smaller share** of the business in return for their investment.

Warm-Up Questions

Q1 What is a business plan?

Q2 Give three things that should be included in a business plan.

Exam Question

Q1 Hold it Up is a business that specialises in producing stationery for people who have difficulty gripping objects.
It is planning to extend its range of products over the next year, but needs £25 000 of external finance.
It is hoping to get the finance in the form of a bank loan.
Explain how a business plan could help Hold it Up to get a bank loan.   [4 marks]

Fail to plan and you plan to fail...

There's a little life lesson for you right there. Producing a decent business plan can take ages, but it forces business owners to think things through properly and lets others feel confident when it comes to offering the business finance.

Cash Flow Forecasts

Cash flow forecasts are used to predict when money will come in and out of a business over a period of time. They're dead important, so you need to make sure you really focus on these pages. Here we go...

Cash Flow Forecasts Show Cash Inflows and Cash Outflows

1) Cash **inflows** are sums of money **received** by a business, e.g. from product sales or loans. Cash **outflows** are sums of money **paid out** by a business, e.g. to buy raw materials or pay wages.

2) The amount of **cash** that a business has available for **day-to-day spending** is called **working capital** (see p.77).

3) Businesses need to **pay out money** for the costs of producing an order, or for assets like machinery, **before** they **get paid** for that order. It's important to make sure there's always **enough working capital** available to make payments.

Maintaining enough working capital can be especially tricky for new businesses because they need money for start-up costs before they've made any sales at all.

4) When a customer **buys** a product, the business might not get the money for it **straight away**. This is because the customer might get the product on **credit** — this means the goods are **received** but the buyer has an agreed **period of time** before **payment** is **due**. People who owe the business money are called **debtors** and money that is owed to the business is known as **receivable**.

5) Similarly to customers getting credit, when a business **buys goods** it might use **trade credit**, meaning it doesn't need to pay straight away. People who are owed money by the business are known as **creditors**. Money that the business owes is known as **payable**.

6) With **lots of money** coming **in and out** of the business at **different times**, it's important that the business has a procedure in place to make sure that it doesn't **run out of cash**. This is where **cash flow forecasts** come in...

Businesses Make Cash Flow Forecasts to Help Them Make Decisions

1) **Cash flow forecasts** (also called cash budgets) show the amount of money that managers **expect** to **flow into** the business and **flow out** of the business over a period of time in the **future**. There's an **example** of a cash flow forecast on the next page.

2) **Established** firms base forecasts on **past experience**. **New** firms have no past data, so their forecast should consider the business's **capacity**, experiences of **similar firms** and customer trends shown by **market research**.

3) Managers use cash flow forecasts to **make sure** they always have **enough** cash around to pay **suppliers** and **employees**. They can **predict** when they'll be **short of cash**, and arrange a **loan** or **overdraft** in time.

4) Businesses include cash flow forecasts in their **business plans**. Sources of finance, such as **banks** and **venture capitalists**, will want to see the forecasts when deciding whether to give the business a **loan** or **other finance**. Cash flow forecasts prove that business owners have done their **research** and have an idea of where the business is going to be in the **future**.

5) Cash flow forecasts can also be used to check that a firm isn't holding **too much cash**, i.e. cash that could be invested in the business instead.

Cash Flow Forecasting Isn't Always Accurate

1) Good cash flow forecasting needs lots of **experience** and **research** into the market.

2) Businesses exist in **dynamic markets** where circumstances can **change suddenly** and **frequently**. For example, **costs** can go up or down, which affects a firm's cash **outflows**. **Competitors** can enter or leave the market and **consumer preferences** can change — both of these can affect a firm's **sales** and therefore its cash **inflows**.

3) A business needs to consider how any **changes** such as these will **affect** the **cash flow forecast** and **update** it accordingly. This may involve **making changes** to some business activities — for example, a hotel may encourage **payment** for **early bookings** to **bring forward cash inflow** at times when they predict they may run out of cash.

4) Because circumstances can change so often, it can be hard to make **accurate** cash flow forecasts. The **longer** the **time period** over which the forecast is made, the **less accurate** the forecast will be.

Take it from Percy — an inaccurate cash flow forecast can do a lot of damage.

5) An **inaccurate forecast** that isn't updated can have **disastrous** results. A business that **runs out of cash** could end up **insolvent** (unable to pay its debts) and have to **close down**.

Cash Flow Forecasts

You Need to be Able to **Interpret** a **Cash Flow Forecast**

1) The **table below** shows the **cash flow forecast** for a **new firm**.

2) It starts up with a **loan** of **£18 000** and **£5000** of **owner's capital**. It expects to sell **£5000** of goods in January, **£35 000** in February, **£35 000** in March and **£40 000** in April. All customers will get a **one month credit period**.

3) Fixed costs such as managers' salaries and rent will cost **£15 000** in total each month, and variable costs are expected to be **£5000** in January, **£8000** in February, **£2000** in March and **£2000** in April.

Fixed costs don't change with output, whereas variable costs do (see p.63).

This shows **cash going out** to pay for the firm's **costs**.

This shows cash coming in from **sales** and from the initial **start-up loan**.

There's a **one month** credit period, so each month's sales revenue isn't received until the following month.

Net cash flow = cash inflows – cash outflows

Figures in brackets are negative.

	Item	Jan	Feb	Mar	Apr
Cash in	Sales revenue		£5000	£35000	£35000
	Other cash in	£18000			
	Total cash inflows	**£18000**	**£5000**	**£35000**	**£35000**
Cash out	Fixed costs	£15000	£15000	£15000	£15000
	Variable costs	£5000	£8000	£2000	£2000
	Total cash outflows	**£20000**	**£23000**	**£17000**	**£17000**
Net monthly cash flow	**Net cash flow**	**(£2000)**	**(£18000)**	**£18000**	**£18000**
	Opening balance	£5000	£3000	(£15000)	£3000
	Closing balance	**£3000**	**(£15000)**	**£3000**	**£21000**

According to this, the business will have £21 000 in the bank by the end of April. **But** it'll still owe £18 000 from the start-up loan...

The **opening balance** is money in the bank at the start — for January it's £5000.

Closing balance = opening balance + net cash flow

The **closing** balance for **last month** is **this month's opening balance**.

4) In the cash flow table above, make sure you know **where** each number has **come from** and **how it's calculated**. In the exam, you could be given a **part completed** cash flow table and be asked to **fill in** the **missing figures**.

5) You might see cash flow tables that look a bit **different** to this — the **basic principles** will still be the **same** so you should be **comfortable** tackling any cash flow table you meet.

Warm-Up Questions

Q1 Give two examples of cash inflows and two examples of cash outflows.

Q2 Give two reasons why cash flow forecasting is useful to a business.

Q3 Explain why cash flow forecasting isn't always accurate.

PRACTICE QUESTIONS

Exam Question

Q1 Darn It! is a business that sells knitting materials and supplies for other crafts and hobbies. The table shows its cash flow forecast for three months last year. Calculate the closing balance of Darn It! in March. You are advised to show your working.

Answer on p.193.

	Item	January	February	March
Cash in	Sales Revenue	£0	£3000	£4500
	Other	£2000	£0	£0
	Total cash inflows	**£2000**	**£3000**	
Cash out	Fixed costs	£2500	£2500	£2500
	Variable costs	£500	£250	£500
	Total cash outflows	**£3000**	**£2750**	
Net monthly cash flow	**Net cash flow**	**(£1000)**	**£250**	
	Opening balance	£4000	£3000	
	Closing balance	**£3000**	**£3250**	

[4 marks]

If only you could do exams on credit — get the grade now and revise later...

Don't just revise the layout of the table on this page — make sure you really know what all the different parts mean. That way you'll be prepared for whatever cash flow table the examiners throw at you. (They don't actually throw anything at you.)

Sales Forecasts

Sales forecasts are pretty self-explanatory — they're about predicting (or forecasting) future sales. Simple.

Sales Forecasts Help Businesses Make Decisions

Sales forecasting is about **predicting** future **sales volume** and **sales revenue** based on **past sales data** and **market research**. Sales forecasting allows businesses to make **decisions** about:

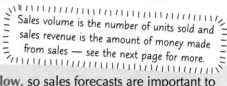 *Sales volume is the number of units sold and sales revenue is the amount of money made from sales — see the next page for more.*

1) **Finance** — **Sales revenue** is usually a firm's main source of **cash inflow**, so sales forecasts are important to be able to generate accurate **cash flow forecasts**. Cash flow forecasts help a firm to know when it might need **more finance** to prevent it **running out of cash** — see p.60-61 for more on cash flow forecasts.

2) **Marketing** — Firms use **different marketing methods** to drive sales, so sales forecasts and the actions of the marketing department are tightly linked. For example, if sales are forecast to **decline**, a business may decide to launch a **promotional campaign** to increase sales and cash inflow.

3) **Resources** (e.g. machinery, staff, stock) — **How much** of a product a firm sells affects how many **resources** it needs. For example, the more of a product that is made, the **more raw materials** that will be needed. Sales forecasts help to make sure the firm has **all the resources** it **needs** so that it can meet the predicted demand, but doesn't waste money on resources when sales are expected to be low. E.g. by identifying **seasonal peaks** in sales, a firm can increase its productive capacity during the **busy times** of the year (e.g. by hiring additional **temporary staff**).   *See p.84 for more on productive capacity.*

Lots of Factors Affect Sales Forecasting

Predicting future sales is a **tricky task** — there are lots of **external factors** that can affect sales, for example:

1) **Consumer trends** — Sometimes these are fairly **predictable** (e.g. more people want to buy fairy lights near Christmas) but sometimes they're much more **uncertain** (e.g. scientific research in the 2010s showing that butter isn't as bad for health as previously thought led to a rise in demand for butter).

2) **Economic variables** (e.g. **interest rates**, **inflation** and **unemployment levels**) — Changes in economic variables affect **how much money** consumers have and therefore **how many products** they buy. How a change in an economic variable affects a firm's sales depends on the **nature** of the firm and the **products** it sells. For example, a **rise** in the value of **domestic currency** could **reduce** the sales volume of a firm that usually sells a lot to **overseas buyers**. A **rise** in **unemployment** could **increase** the sales of a **budget** fast food takeaway business, but **decrease** the sales of an **expensive restaurant**.

3) **Actions of competitors** — For example, if a **competitor** decreases their **prices** or launches a **new product**, a firm's predicted sales may decrease.

Accurate sales forecasts are very hard to make, especially in **dynamic markets** when external factors that affect sales are **constantly changing**. It can be difficult to know **in advance** how the factors are going to change and even more difficult to **predict** the **knock-on effect** these will have on sales. Firms have to make their **best guess**, but it can be difficult to make accurate sales forecasts **very far** into the **future**.   *If you're doing the full A-level course, there's more on pages 116-118 about how firms forecast sales based on past sales data.*

Warm-Up Questions

Q1 Give examples of two economic variables and explain how each one could affect a firm's sales forecast.

Q2 Other than economic variables, give two external factors that could affect a firm's sales forecast.

Q3 Why can sales forecasting be inaccurate?

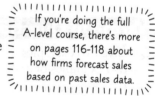

Exam Question

Q1 Zany's Big Top is a travelling circus business that has been operating for ten years. It travels around the country, putting on a circus show in different towns. As well as tickets to the performance, it also sells merchandise and refreshments to the audience. It spends about two weeks in each town before moving on, depending on demand. Assess why accurate sales forecasting would be important to Zany's Big Top.   [10 marks]

I broke both my arms and both my legs — I had to have four casts...

Make sure you know how a sales forecast can be used to help a firm make decisions and what factors affect a forecast.

Sales Volume, Sales Revenue and Costs

Calculators at the ready — prepare to learn how to calculate sales volume and sales revenue (or turnover)...
And no, I don't mean you can turn over the page if you don't fancy learning it. Turnover is just another term for sales revenue. Sorry.

Sales Volume Affects Sales Revenue

1) **Sales volume** is the **number of units sold** in a given time period.

2) **Sales revenue** is the **value of sales** in a given time period — it's sometimes just called **sales**, sometimes just called **revenue**, and can also be called **turnover**. It's the amount of money generated by sales of a product, **before** any deductions are made.

> The word revenue actually means any incoming money that a business has earned. A business can get revenue from sources other than sales (e.g. interest from savings accounts or money from selling assets) but normally most of a business's income comes from sales. That's why when you see the term 'revenue' or 'total revenue', it's usually just referring to sales revenue.

3) It's calculated like this: ➡ **Sales revenue = selling price × sales volume**

4) You can **rearrange** the formula above to calculate **sales volume**: ➡ $$\text{Sales volume} = \frac{\text{sales revenue}}{\text{selling price}}$$

> **Examples:** If a business sells 2000 teapots for £8 each, the sales revenue is £8 × 2000 = £16 000.
>
> If a business makes £70 000 from selling laptops that cost £400 each, then the sales volume is £70 000 ÷ £400 = 175 laptops.

Costs Can be Fixed or Variable

1) **Fixed costs** don't change with output. **Rent** on a factory, **business rates**, **senior managers' basic salaries** and the cost of **new machinery** are fixed costs. When output increases, a business makes more use of the facilities it's already got. The **cost** of those facilities **doesn't change**.

2) **Annual interest** on a **bank loan** is also a fixed cost. E.g. if a firm has a **£5000** loan at an interest rate of **15% per annum** (p.a.), then it will have to pay interest that year of 15% of £5000, which is (15 ÷ 100) × £5000 = **£750**.

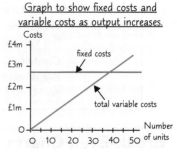
Graph to show fixed costs and variable costs as output increases.

3) **Variable costs** rise and fall as output changes. Hourly **wages**, **raw material costs** and the **packaging costs** for each product are all variable costs.

Total variable costs = average variable cost (AVC) × quantity produced

4) The **total costs** are just the fixed costs plus the variable costs:

Total costs = fixed costs + variable costs

Profit is the Difference Between Revenue and Costs

1) When you deduct a business's **total costs** from its **total revenue**, you're left with the **profit**.

Profit = total revenue – total costs

> There are also other ways of expressing profit — these are coming up on pages 70-73.

2) If a business's **total revenue** is **greater** than its total costs, then it will make a **profit**. If the **total costs** are greater than the total revenue, then the business will make a **loss**.

Warm-Up Questions

Q1 What is the equation for calculating sales revenue?

Q2 A firm made £50 299 from selling coats at a price of £89.50 each. How many coats did it sell?

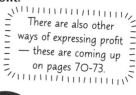

> Answers on p.193.

Exam Question

Q1 Años Calendars produces desk calendars. In 2018, it made 8200 calendars and sold 7800 of them, each with a selling price of £3.95. Años Calendars' annual fixed costs are £7400 and the average variable cost is £1.47. Calculate the amount of profit Años Calendars made in 2018. You are advised to show your working. **[4 marks]**

Not enough sales volume? Try cleaning your ears out...

Make sure everything here is clear before moving on — this stuff is pretty important for the rest of the section.

Break-Even Analysis

Break-even analysis is a great way of working out how much you need to sell to make a profit.

Breaking Even Means Covering Your Costs

1) The **break-even point** (or **break-even output**) is the level of sales a business needs to **cover** its **total costs**. At the break-even point, **total fixed costs + total variable costs = total revenue**.

2) When sales are **below** the break-even point, costs are more than revenue — the business makes a **loss**. When sales are **above** the break-even point, revenue exceeds costs — the business makes a **profit**.

3) **New businesses** should always do a **break-even analysis** to **find** the break-even point. It tells them how much they will need to sell to break even. Anyone thinking of **loaning** money to the business may want to **see** a break-even analysis as part of the **business plan** (see p.59). This helps them to **decide** whether to lend money to the business.

4) **Established businesses** preparing to launch **new products** use break-even analysis to work out how much **profit** they are likely to make, and also to predict the impact of the new activity on **cash flow** (see p.60-61).

Contribution is Used to Work Out the Break-Even Point

1) **Contribution per unit** is the difference between the **selling price** of a product and the **variable costs** it takes to produce it.

> **Contribution per unit = selling price – variable cost per unit**

2) **Total contribution** (contribution from all units sold) is used to pay **fixed costs**. The amount left over is **profit**. The break-even point is where **total contribution = fixed costs**.

3) If you know the **total fixed costs** and the **contribution per unit** you can calculate the **break-even point** using this formula:

$$\text{Break-even point} = \frac{\text{total fixed costs}}{\text{contribution per unit}}$$

> **Example:** Harry sets up a business to print T-shirts. The **fixed costs** are **£3000** and the **variable costs** per T-shirt are **£5**. Each printed T-shirt sells for **£25**.
>
> **Contribution per unit** = £25 – £5 = **£20**
> **Break-even point** = £3000 ÷ £20 = **150**
> So Harry has to sell **150** T-shirts to **break even**.

If you get a decimal for the break-even point, always round up to the nearest whole number to find the full number of units needed.

Break-Even Charts Show the Break-Even Point

1) Break-even charts show **costs** and **revenue** plotted against **output**. Businesses use break-even charts to see how costs and revenue **vary** with different levels of output.

2) This is a break-even chart for **Harry's business** (from the example above).

3) **Output** is shown on the **horizontal axis** and **costs** and **revenue** are shown on the **vertical axis**.

4) **Fixed costs**, **total costs** and **revenue** are plotted on the chart.

5) The **break-even point** is where the **revenue** line crosses the **total costs** line. On the diagram it's **150 units**.

6) You can use a break-even chart to identify the **profit** or **loss** that would be made at a specified level of **output**. You find the value for **total costs** and for **revenue** at your chosen level of output, then subtract the **total costs** from the **revenue**. If the answer's **negative** then it's a **loss**, and if it's **positive** then it's a **profit**.

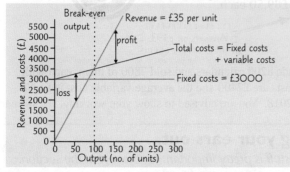

Changing either the **variable costs** or the **price** of the products will affect the break-even point.

This graph shows that if Harry **increased the price** of the T-shirts to £35 each, his break-even point would be **lowered** to 100 units.

When **prices increase**, the **revenue line** gets **steeper**, so the break-even point is **lowered** — if you **charge** more, you don't need to sell as **many** to break even.

Break-Even Analysis

The Margin of Safety is the Amount Between Actual Output and Break-Even

> Margin of safety = actual output – break-even output

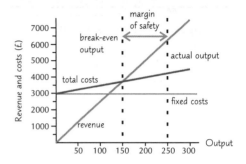

1) The diagram on the right shows the margin of safety for Harry's T-shirt business when his output is 250 T-shirts. If Harry sells **250** T-shirts, the **margin of safety** is 250 – 150 = **100**. He could sell up to 100 fewer T-shirts before he started losing money.

2) If his output changed to **300** T-shirts, the margin of safety would go up to 300 – 150 = **150**.

3) Knowing the break-even output and margin of safety allows businesses to make **important decisions** — if Harry's calculations show that his T-shirt business has a low margin of safety, he can take action to increase it by either **lowering his costs** or **increasing his revenue**.

4) This would **lower** his break-even output, so he'd have a **greater** margin of safety. A big margin of safety is useful for a business because it means **less risk**.

Break-Even Analysis Has Advantages and Disadvantages

Advantages of break-even analysis	Disadvantages of break-even analysis
It's easy to do. If you can plot figures on a graph accurately, you can do break-even analysis.	Break-even analysis assumes that variable costs always rise steadily. This isn't always the case — e.g. a business can get discounts for buying in bulk so costs don't go up in direct proportion to output.
It's quick — managers can see the break-even output and margin of safety immediately so they can take quick action to cut costs or increase sales if they need to increase their margin of safety.	Break-even analysis is simple for a single product — but most businesses sell lots of different products, so looking at the business as a whole can get a lot more complicated.
Break-even charts let businesses forecast how variations in sales will affect costs, revenue and profits and, most importantly, how variations in price and costs will affect how much they need to sell.	If the data is inaccurate, then the results will be wrong.
Businesses can use break-even analysis to help persuade sources of finance to give them money.	Break-even analysis assumes the business sells all the products, without any wastage. But, for example, a restaurant business will end up throwing away food if fewer customers turn up than they're expecting.
Break-even analysis influences decisions on whether new products are launched or not — if the business would need to sell an unrealistic volume of products to break even, they would probably decide not to launch the product.	Break-even analysis only tells you how many units you need to sell to break even. It doesn't tell you how many you're actually going to sell.

Warm-Up Questions

Q1 Describe how you could identify the break-even point from a break-even chart.

Q2 What is the formula for working out the margin of safety?

Exam Questions

Q1 Muneer Khan has a small restaurant. The average price per customer per meal is £13. The variable costs of materials and labour per meal are £5. The annual fixed costs of the restaurant are £15 000. Calculate the break-even number of customers per month. You are advised to show your working. *Answer on p.193.* [4 marks]

Q2 Bob is deciding whether to set up a business selling fishing equipment. Assess the value of break-even analysis in helping Bob to decide whether or not to go ahead with the business. [10 marks]

Ah, give us a break...

You might be asked to calculate the break-even point or identify it on a break-even chart, so check you can do both. Make sure you can give examples of how break-even analysis is used by businesses to make decisions and plans, and learn some advantages and disadvantages of break-even analysis. Then give yourself a pat on the back. Yippee...

Setting Budgets

Businesses set targets for how much money they're going to spend. Then they check to see how they've done...

A **Budget** is a **Financial Plan** For the Future

A **budget** forecasts **future earnings** and **future spending**, usually over a 12 month period. Businesses use different budgets to estimate different things. There are **three types** of budget:

1) **Income budgets** forecast the amount of money that will come **into** the business as revenue. To do this, the business needs to predict **how much** it will sell, and at what **price**. Managers usually estimate this using **sales figures** from previous years, as well as **market research**.

2) **Expenditure budgets** predict what the business's **total costs** will be for the year, taking into account both fixed and variable costs. Variable costs increase with output, so managers must predict output based on sales estimates.

No matter how hard she tried, Marsha just couldn't budge it.

3) The **profit budget** uses the **income budget** minus the **expenditure budget** to calculate what the expected **profit** (or **loss**) will be for that year.

Budgets are a good **communication tool** — they help everyone interested in the firm (e.g. employees, sources of finance) see what **needs to be achieved**, in terms of **sales** and **expenditure**, for the firm to reach its **profit targets**.

Budgets Affect **All Areas** of the Business

1) The **expenditure budget** is often broken down into **department** expenditure budgets — each department is allotted a certain amount of money to spend.

2) **Budget holders** are people **responsible** for spending the money for each budget. For example, the budget holder of the expenditure budget for marketing could be the head of the marketing department.

3) Department expenditure budgets are broken down into budgets for **specific activities** within the department. These help local managers control and coordinate their work.

The **Budget Setting** Process Involves **Research** and **Negotiation**

1) To set the **income budget**, businesses **research** and **predict** how sales are going to go up and down through the year, so that they can make a good prediction of **sales revenue**.

2) To set the **expenditure budget** for **production**, businesses research how labour costs, raw materials costs, taxes and inflation are going to go up over the year. They can then figure out the **costs** of producing the volume of product that they think they're going to sell.

3) **Budgets** are **influenced** by a business's **objectives** — e.g. if they aim to increase sales, this will affect their predicted sales revenue and cost of sales, and they might allocate more of the expenditure budget to marketing.

4) Annual budgets are usually agreed by **negotiation** — when budget holders have a say in setting their budgets, they're **motivated** to achieve them.

5) Budgets should **stretch** the abilities of the business, but they must be **achievable**. **Unrealistically** high income budgets or low expenditure budgets will **demotivate** staff. No one likes being asked to do the **impossible**.

6) Once a budget is agreed, budget holders **check** performance against the budget using **variance analysis** (p.68-69).

Budgets Have **Advantages** and **Disadvantages**

Benefits of budgeting

- Budgets can be **motivating** — they give employees **targets** to work towards.
- Budgets help **control** income and expenditure.
- Budgeting helps managers to **review** their activities and make decisions.
- Budgeting helps focus on the **priorities**.
- Budgets can be used as a **communication tool** to share information, e.g. about how money is being spent.
- Budgets let departments **coordinate** spending.
- Budgets help persuade **investors** that the business will be successful.

Drawbacks of budgeting

- Budgeting can cause **resentment** and rivalry if departments have to compete for money.
- Budgets can be **restrictive**. Fixed budgets stop firms responding to changing market conditions.
- Budgeting is **time-consuming**. Managers can get preoccupied with setting and reviewing budgets, and forget to focus on the real issues of **winning business** and **understanding the customer**.
- **Inflation** is hard to predict — some prices can change by levels much **greater** than average.
- Start-up businesses may struggle to get data from other firms, so the budget may be **inaccurate**.

Setting Budgets

Budgets Can be **Updated Every Year** or Developed From **Scratch**

1) **Start-up businesses** have to develop their budgets **from scratch** (known as **zero-based budgeting**). This is difficult to do because they don't have much information to base their decisions on — they can't take into account the previous year's sales or expenditure. This means that their budgets are likely to be **inaccurate**.

2) After the first year, a business must decide whether to follow the **historical budgeting** method, or to continue using the **zero-based budgeting** method.

Historical budgets are updated each year

1) This year's budget is based on a **percentage increase** or **decrease** from last year's budget. For example, a business expecting **10% revenue growth** might add 10% to the advertising, wages and raw materials purchasing budgets.

2) Historical budgeting is **quick** and **simple**, but it assumes that business conditions stay **unchanged** each year. This isn't always the case — for instance, a product at the introduction stage of its **life cycle** (see p.26) needs more money spent on advertising than one in the growth or maturity stages.

Zero-based budgeting means starting from scratch each year

1) Budget holders **start** with a budget of **£0**, and have to **get approval** to spend money on activities.

2) The figures used in the budget are based on **potential performance**. Budget holders have to **plan** all the year's activities, ask for money to spend on them, and be prepared to **justify** their requests to the finance director. Budget holders need good **negotiating** skills for this.

3) Zero-based budgeting takes much **longer** to complete than historical budgets.

4) If zero-based budgeting is done properly it's **more accurate** than historical budgeting.

Budgets Can be **Fixed** or **Flexible**

1) **Fixed budgeting** means budget holders have to **stick** to their budget plans throughout the year — even if market conditions change. This can **prevent** a firm reacting to **new opportunities** or **threats** that they didn't know about when they set the budget.

2) However, **fixed budgets** provide **discipline** and **certainty**. This is especially important for a business with **liquidity** problems — fixed budgets help control **cash flow**.

Liquidity is the ability of a firm to pay its short-term debts — see p.76.

3) **Flexible budgeting** allows budgets to be altered in response to significant changes in the market or economy.

4) **Zero-based budgeting** gives a business more **flexibility** than **historical budgeting**.

Warm-Up Questions

Q1 What is a budget?
Q2 Explain why having a budget may help to motivate employees.
Q3 What is historical budgeting?

Exam Questions

Q1 Flo's Flowers is a new business. Flo has a target to keep costs as low as possible to help her business survive the first few months. Assess two possible disadvantages to Flo of setting an expenditure budget. [8 marks]

Q2 memARY is a business that produces computer software. Its main aim is to maximise profits. Overall, memARY has seen a 10% increase in sales over the last 5 years, but sales have fluctuated year on year. Each year, memARY spends a lot of time producing a zero-based budget for the following year.
Assess the importance to memARY of investing time in producing a zero-based budget each year. [12 marks]

I set myself a word budget today and I'm just about to run out...

Budgets are multi-purpose — they help businesses to forecast and plan their future spending as well as being a good way to communicate financial information and motivate employees. Just four words left... and... now... I'm... done.

Analysing Budgets

Budgets are often reviewed using variance analysis. Variance is the difference between actual and budgeted amounts. Understanding variances helps managers make decisions and fix problems, and it'll help you sail through your exams.

Variance is the Difference Between Actual Figures and Budgeted Figures

1) A variance means the business is performing either **worse** or **better** than expected.

2) A **favourable variance** occurs when a firm is performing **better** than expected. A favourable variance is a **good thing**, so it can be called a **positive** variance. If **revenue** or **profit** is **more** than the budget says it's going to be, that's a favourable variance. If **costs** are **below** the cost predictions in the budget, that's also a favourable variance.

3) An **adverse variance** occurs when a firm is performing **worse** than expected. An adverse variance is a **bad thing**, so it can be called a **negative** variance. **Selling fewer items** than the income budget predicts or **spending more** on an advert than in the budget are examples of adverse variance.

4) The formula for calculating a variance is: **variance = actual figure – budgeted figure**. Once you've got your answer, you need to **think about** whether its favourable or adverse. E.g. £10 000 is spent on raw materials when the budget was £6000. Variance = £10 000 – £6000 = £4000 — this is an **adverse** variance of **£4000**, as the firm has **overspent** by that amount.

5) Variances **add up**. For example, if actual sales exceed budgeted sales by £3000 and expenditure on raw materials is £2000 below budget, the variance is £3000 + £2000 = £5000, so there's a combined **favourable variance** of £5000. This is called **cumulative variance**.

6) Variances can be calculated for each budget **each month**, for each budget as a **running total**, and for **groups of budgets** as a monthly or running total variance:

	January			February			Cumulative Variance
	Budget	**Actual**	**Variance**	**Budget**	**Actual**	**Variance**	
Revenue	£100k	£90k	£10k (A)	£110k	£110k	£0	£10k (A)
Wages	£40k	£30k	£10k (F)	£40k	£41k	£1k (A)	£9k (F)
Other costs	£15k	£16k	£1k (A)	£15k	£17k	£2k (A)	£3k (A)
Total costs	£55k	£46k	£9k (F)	£55k	£58k	£3k (A)	£6k (F)

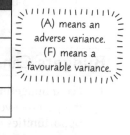
(A) means an adverse variance. (F) means a favourable variance.

Variances Can be Bad — Even if They Say You're Doing Better Than Expected

1) When variances occur, it means that what has happened is **not** what the business was expecting. Businesses need to **know** about variances so that they can find out **why** they have occurred.

2) It's extremely important to spot **adverse** variances as **soon** as possible. It's important to find out which budget holder is responsible — and to take action to fix the problem.

3) It's **also** important to **investigate favourable variances**. Favourable variances may mean that the budget targets weren't **stretching** enough — so the business needs to set more **difficult targets**. The business also needs to understand **why** the performance is better than expected — if one department is **doing something right**, the business can **spread** this throughout the organisation.

Variances are Caused by Several Factors, Both External and Internal

External
1) **Competitor behaviour** and changing **fashions** may increase or reduce **demand** for products.
2) Changes in the **economy** can change how much workers' wages cost the business.
3) The cost of **raw materials** can go up — e.g. if a harvest fails.

Internal
1) Improving **efficiency** (e.g. introducing automated production equipment) causes **favourable** variances.
2) A firm might **overestimate** the amount of money it can save by streamlining its production methods.
3) A firm might **underestimate** the **cost** of making a change to its organisation.
4) Changing **selling price** changes revenue — this creates variance if it happens after the budget's set.
5) Internal causes of variance are a **big concern**. They suggest internal **communication** needs improving.

Analysing Budgets

Variance Analysis Means Identifying and Explaining Variances

1) Variance analysis means **spotting** variances and figuring out **why** they've happened, so that action can be taken to fix them.

2) **Small** variances aren't a big problem. They can actually help to **motivate** workers. Staff try to **catch up** and sort out small **adverse** variances themselves. Small **favourable** variances can motivate staff to **keep on** doing whatever they were doing to create a favourable variance.

3) **Large** variances can **demotivate**. Staff don't work hard if there are large favourable variances — they **don't see the need**. Staff can get demotivated by a large **adverse** variance — they may feel that the task is **impossible**, or that they've **already failed**.

Mary planned to buy her team a cake a day to sort out the adverse cost variance. Jolly good show, Mary.

Businesses Have to React to Variances

When variances occur, businesses need to act on them. They can either change what the **business** is doing to make it fit the budget, or change the **budget** to make it fit what the **business** is doing. There are **three factors** that they need to take into account to make this decision:

1) Businesses need to **beware** of chopping and changing the budget **too much**.

2) Changing the budget **removes certainty** — which removes one of the big benefits of budgets.

3) Altering budgets can also make them **less motivating** — when staff start to expect that management will change targets instead of doing something to change performance, they don't see the point in trying any more.

Decisions based on Adverse Variances

1) They can change the marketing mix. Cutting prices will increase sales — but only if the demand is price elastic (see p.15). Updating the product might make it more attractive to customers. Businesses can also look for a new market for the product, or change the promotional strategy — e.g. by advertising the product more.

2) Streamlining production makes the business more efficient, so this reduces costs.

3) Try to motivate employees to work harder.

4) Businesses can try to cut costs by asking their suppliers for a better deal.

5) Businesses may need to do additional market research to improve forecasts in the future.

Decisions based on Favourable Variances

1) If the favourable variance is caused by a pessimistic budget, they can set more ambitious targets next time.

2) If the variance is because of increased productivity in one part of the business, they can try to get everyone else doing whatever was responsible for the improvement, and set higher targets in the next budget.

3) A favourable variance could indicate more sales than predicted, so a business may need to increase the production of a product or take on additional staff to meet demand.

Warm-Up Questions

Answer on p.193.

PRACTICE QUESTIONS

Q1 Define variance.

Q2 If a business sets an expenditure budget of £15 000 for marketing and the actual expenditure for marketing is £18 000, how much is the variance and what type of variance is it?

Exam Question

Q1 The owners of Happy Mugs Ltd analysed the business's budgets for 2018.
They found that there was a highly favourable sales variance but an adverse profit variance.
a) Explain why the owners may be concerned about a highly favourable sales variance. [4 marks]
b) Assess two ways that the owners of Happy Mugs Ltd could improve their budgets going forwards. [8 marks]

Variance is one of those words that looks odd if you stare at it enough...

Variance variance variance... anyway. As well as knowing what firms do when budget-setting, you need to know what they do when the results and the budget don't match. And remember, if a variance is described as being positive or negative, it means whether it's good or bad for the firm — not whether the numerical figure is positive or negative.

Reporting Profit

You might think that measuring profit is as simple as working out how much money's been made once costs have been accounted for. But of course (*heavy sigh*) it's not that simple. Profit can be measured in different ways...

Businesses Usually Want to Maximise Their Profits

1) Most businesses exist to make a **profit** — if a business makes large profits then it is **successful**. Even successful businesses want to **increase profits** and become **more successful**.

2) Businesses **measure** their profits on a regular basis. They **compare** their profits from the current period (usually a year) to the profits from previous periods to measure their **progress**.

3) If profits go **down**, this is **bad news**, even if the business is still making large profits. For example, if a business makes a profit of £100 million in a year, this might sound like good news, but if the previous year's profit was £125 million then it's a **bad sign**.

4) This is why businesses work out the **percentage increase** or **decrease** in their profits from year to year — it makes it easy to see how well they're performing in comparison with other years.

5) If profits are decreasing, the business needs to investigate **why** this is happening and **take action** to fix it.

6) The formula for measuring the **percentage change in profit** is:

$$\text{Percentage Change in Profit} = \frac{\text{Current Year's Profit} - \text{Previous Year's Profit}}{\text{Previous Year's Profit}} \times 100$$

There are Three Different Measures of Profit You Need to Know About

Profit is basically the **difference between total revenue and total costs** (see p.63), but there are different ways of looking at it:

Remember, 'total revenue' can also be called revenue, sales revenue, sales or turnover.

1) **Gross profit** is the amount left over when the **cost of sales** is **subtracted** from **total revenue**. Cost of sales is the costs **directly related** to making the product, e.g. the cost of raw materials.

Gross Profit = Total Revenue – Cost of Sales

2) **Operating profit** considers both the **cost of sales** and **operating expenses**, such as administrative expenses. If a business's **gross profit** is **increasing** but its **operating profit** is **decreasing**, it usually means the business is **not controlling** its **costs**.

Operating Profit = Gross Profit – Other Operating Expenses

3) **Profit for the year** (also called **net profit**) takes into consideration the cost of any **interest** the business has to pay for **borrowing money**.

Profit for the Year (Net Profit) = Operating Profit – Interest

This equation for profit for the year gives a pre-tax figure. All businesses need to pay a percentage of this figure as tax (as long as the figure's not negative).

If the business has made any profit (or losses) from **one-off events** throughout the year (e.g. money made from investments), these would be taken into account when calculating profit for the year.

Example: Hannah's Hammers is a small business selling hammers with an easy-grip handle. The cost of producing each hammer is **£2**, and they are sold for **£5** each. Hannah has operating expenses of **£9000** a year and pays **£600** a year in interest repayments.

If Hannah sells **10 000** hammers in a year, her **sales revenue** is 10 000 × £5 = **£50 000**.

Gross profit is £50 000 – (£2 × 10 000) = **£30 000**.

Operating profit is £30 000 – £9000 = **£21 000**.

Profit for the year is £21 000 – £600 = **£20 400**.

If Hannah doesn't sell 10 000 hammers in a year, run away.

Reporting Profit

Profit Can be Shown on a Statement of Comprehensive Income

1) A **statement of comprehensive income** (also known as a **profit and loss account**) shows how much money has been **coming into the business** (**revenue**) and how much has been **going out** (**expenses**) over a period of time.

2) These figures can be used in **assessing** a business's **financial performance** — e.g. if **revenue** has **increased** by **more than** the rate of **inflation** (see p.90) since the business published its last statement of comprehensive income, it's often a sign that the business is **healthy**.

3) A statement of comprehensive income also shows the **three different measures** of profit from the previous page in a simple format.

4) Statements of comprehensive income should cover one whole accounting year — one that covers **less than 12 months** can be **misleading**. High street retailers can generate **half their annual revenue** in the lead-up to **Christmas** — a statement of comprehensive income ignoring this period won't give an **accurate picture**.

5) Statements of comprehensive income can also contain the **previous year's data**, for **easy comparison**, to see what's **changed**. Some businesses provide the previous five years' data. It's useful for spotting **trends** in revenue, expenses and profits, and helps whoever's looking at the accounts to see what kind of a **financial position** the business is in.

6) **PLCs** (public limited companies) have to **publish** their accounts so that they're available to **anyone** who wants to look at them — that includes shareholders, other investors and competitors.

Here's What a Statement of Comprehensive Income Looks Like

Here's a part of a statement of comprehensive income. Sometimes the costs and expenses will be **broken down** into different categories, but I've lumped them all together so you can see what's going on. You need to be able to **calculate** the **three measures of profit** from a statement of comprehensive income.

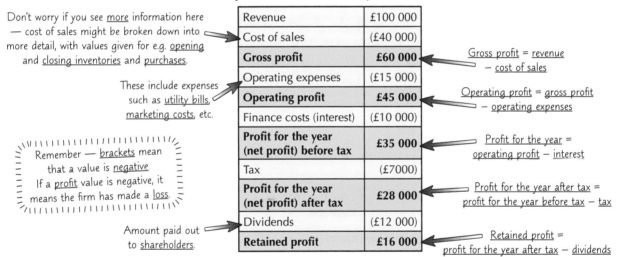

Horwich Designs Ltd
Statement of Comprehensive Income for year ended 31st March 2017

Don't worry if you see <u>more</u> information here — cost of sales might be broken down into more detail, with values given for e.g. <u>opening</u> and <u>closing inventories</u> and <u>purchases</u>.

These include expenses such as <u>utility bills</u>, <u>marketing costs</u>, etc.

Remember — <u>brackets</u> mean that a value is <u>negative</u>. If a <u>profit</u> value is negative, it means the firm has made a <u>loss</u>.

Amount paid out to <u>shareholders</u>.

Revenue	£100 000
Cost of sales	(£40 000)
Gross profit	**£60 000**
Operating expenses	(£15 000)
Operating profit	**£45 000**
Finance costs (interest)	(£10 000)
Profit for the year (net profit) before tax	**£35 000**
Tax	(£7000)
Profit for the year (net profit) after tax	**£28 000**
Dividends	(£12 000)
Retained profit	**£16 000**

Gross profit = <u>revenue</u> – <u>cost of sales</u>

Operating profit = <u>gross profit</u> – <u>operating expenses</u>

Profit for the year = operating profit – interest

Profit for the year after tax = profit for the year before tax – tax

Retained profit = profit for the year after tax – dividends

Warm-Up Questions

Q1 Give the formula for calculating gross profit.
Q2 Describe the difference between gross profit and operating profit.
Q3 What can a statement of comprehensive income also be called?

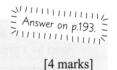

Exam Question

Q1 In the year ending 31st March 2018, a haulage company had a profit for the year of £650 000. Its interest payments were £100 000 and its operating expenses were £250 000. Calculate the gross profit of this haulage company. You are advised to show your working. [4 marks]

Answer on p.193.

I'd definitely spend all my profits on ice cream...

This might all look a bit confusing, but you should be able to extract figures from a statement of comprehensive income to calculate the three different types of profit, so make sure you're confident with them before moving on...

Profit Margins

Time for some more profit-related calculations now. Woo. Make sure you're confident with the three different measures of profit covered on the last two pages before you get stuck in...

Profit Margins Show How Profitable a Business is

1) As well as measuring profits, businesses are interested in measuring **profitability** — the amount of profit **relative** to **revenue** or **investment**.

2) Profitability can be measured using **profitability ratios**, such as **profit margins**. Profitability ratios are a type of **accounting ratio** — a ratio that's calculated from a firm's **financial statements** and used to **evaluate** its financial performance.

3) **Profit margins** measure the relationship between the **profit made** and the **revenue**. They tell you what **percentage** of the selling price of a product is actually **profit**.

(Return on capital employed (ROCE — see p.141) is also a profitability ratio.)

Gross Profit Margin

1) The **gross profit margin (GPM)** measures gross profit as a percentage of revenue:

$$\text{Gross Profit Margin (\%)} = \frac{\text{Gross Profit}}{\text{Revenue}} \times 100$$

2) What counts as a good GPM depends on the **type of business**, but a **higher** percentage is usually better. A business with **high sales volume** (e.g. a bakery) can afford to have a low GPM.

3) The GPM can be **improved** by **increasing prices** or **reducing** the direct **cost of sales**.

Operating Profit Margin

1) **Operating profit margin (OPM)** takes into account all the costs of regular trading:

$$\text{Operating Profit Margin (\%)} = \frac{\text{Operating Profit}}{\text{Revenue}} \times 100$$

2) It's best to have a **high** OPM, although it does depend on the type of business. OPM can be **improved** by **increasing prices** or **reducing** the **cost of sales** or **operating expenses**.

3) It's useful to **compare** a business's OPM with its GPM over a **period of time**. A business with a **decreasing OPM** compared to GPM is **struggling** with operating expenses. A business with an **increasing OPM** compared to GPM is **controlling** operating expenses well.

Profit for the Year (Net Profit) Margin

1) The **profit for the year margin** measures the profit for the year as a percentage of revenue:

$$\text{Profit for the Year Margin (\%)} = \frac{\text{Profit for the Year}}{\text{Revenue}} \times 100$$

2) This margin takes into account **most expenses** (apart from tax) so gives the best **overall impression** of how profitable a business is.

3) A high profit for the year margin is **attractive** to **shareholders**, because it can indicate that they may receive **high dividends**.

Alice's net profit was just a few tadpoles and a bit of pondweed.

Businesses Use Different Methods to Increase Profit Margins

1) Businesses can **improve** all of their **profit margins** by **increasing** their **revenue**. They could do this by increasing their **prices** (if the demand for their products is price inelastic — see p.15) or **reducing** their prices to increase **demand** (if demand is price elastic). They could also try to **improve product quality**, which could lead to a greater sales volume and possibly a higher selling price, both of which could increase revenue.

2) **Reducing costs of sales** is another way businesses could improve their profit margins. For example, they could find a cheaper supplier of materials. However, changing the way a product is produced may lead to a **lower quality product**, which could reduce the sales volume and therefore the revenue.

3) To increase their **OPM** and **profit for the year margin**, they could **reduce operating expenses**, e.g. by finding cheaper premises to rent and by cutting out unnecessary administrative tasks.

Profit Margins

You Need to Know How to **Interpret Profit Margins**

To **interpret** profit margins you usually need to **compare** them with something, e.g. with the firm's **previous** profit margins or the profit margins of a **similar firm**. You could also compare one type of profit margin **against another**.

> **Example:** In **2015**, a fast food restaurant had a **revenue** of £1.2m and **cost of sales** of £0.6m. This meant its **gross profit** was £1.2m – £0.6m = **£0.6m**, and its **GPM** was:
>
> $GPM = \frac{\text{gross profit}}{\text{revenue}} \times 100 = \frac{0.6}{1.2} \times 100 = 50\%$. In **2014**, its GPM was **40%**.
>
> A **50%** GPM may sound good, especially as the GPM was **40%** the **previous year**, but the firm would need to **compare** itself against **other fast food restaurants** to see whether this profit margin is good. Other fast food restaurants might have GPMs of **higher** than **50%**, suggesting that the firm could be more profitable if it **increased** its **revenue** or **decreased** its **cost of sales**. However, the firm's **other profit margins** should also be considered...
>
> In **2015**, in order to **increase revenue**, the fast food restaurant started offering a delivery service and ran an advertising campaign. Its **operating expenses** increased from £0.3m to £0.5m a year. This meant its **operating profit** in 2015 was £0.6m – £0.5m = **£0.1m**, and its **OPM** was:
>
> $OPM = \frac{\text{operating profit}}{\text{revenue}} \times 100 = \frac{0.1}{1.2} \times 100 = 8.3\%$. In **2014**, the OPM was **10%**.
>
> Although the **GPM increased** between 2014 and 2015, the extra operating expenses in 2015 led to a **decrease** in the OPM. This is likely to mean that their **profit for the year margin** would have decreased too (assuming the firm's interest payments stayed the same and they had no other one-off events that would affect the profit for the year). A fall in these profit margins could make investors **wary**, despite the rise in GPM.

Don't Confuse **Profit** and **Cash** as Being the Same

1) You should have got the message by now that **profit** is the money that a business has left from its revenue once costs have been paid. But **don't** ever think that **profit** is the **same as cash** — it's **not**.

2) **Cash** is what a business has **now** to pay its bills. Cash is constantly **flowing in and out** of a business (pages 60-61 are all about cash flow). A business **doesn't get** the **profit** it makes **straight away** — customers may not **pay for their goods** straight away or the business may not have to **pay its costs straight away**.

3) So a business that's making **lots of profit** might still **run out of cash**, and a business that has **lots of cash** might still end up **not making a profit**.

> **Example:** A window fitter makes an average of **£20 profit** for every window he fits. Depending on demand, he earns around **£1500 profit a month**. However, he needs to **pay** for his materials in **advance** and gives customers a **one-month credit period**. If he has a particularly **expensive month** (e.g. his van needs repairs costing £1000) he might **run out of cash**, although his business is still making a **profit**.

Warm-Up Questions

Q1 Give the formula for calculating a gross profit margin.

Q2 Explain why cash is not the same as profit.

Calculation answers are on page 193.

	2017 (£000)
Turnover	85
Gross profit	43
Operating profit	12
Profit for the year	7

Exam Question

Q1 Sur-weet Ltd is a confectionary firm. Part of Sur-weet's statement of comprehensive income for 2017 is shown on the right. The firm has compared its profit margins with those of its main competitor. The competitor is a much larger firm but has an operating profit margin of 16%. Sur-weet is considering taking out a loan in 2018, for which the annual interest payments would be £1000. The loan will pay for new machines to improve the firm's efficiency and the quality of its products. However, some shareholders are opposed to the plan as they are dissatisfied when the profit for the year margin is below 5%. Using the data in the statement of comprehensive income, calculate appropriate profit margins for Sur-weet and evaluate whether or not it should go ahead with its investment plan. You are advised to show your working. [20 marks]

I'm just about 100% fed up with all these percentage calculations...

Make sure you know how to calculate profit margins and understand how to interpret what they mean for a business.

Statements of Financial Position

At any time, a firm usually has lots of different people that owe it money, plus it usually owes money to lots of different people. It usually has money tied up in assets and may have a big loan it needs to pay off. So working out what a firm is worth at any point in time is tricky — this is where statements of financial position come in handy....

Statements of Financial Position are Lists of Assets and Liabilities

1) **Statements of financial position** can also be called **balance sheets**. They are a **snapshot** of a firm's finances at a **fixed point in time**.

2) They show the value of all the business's **assets** (the things that belong to the business, including cash in the bank) and all its **liabilities** (the money the business owes). They also show the value of all the **capital** (the money invested in the business), and the source of that capital (e.g. loans, shares or retained profits) — so they show where the money's **come from** as well as what's being **done** with it.

3) The '**net assets**' value (the total fixed and current assets minus total current and non-current (long-term) liabilities — see next page) is **always the same** as the '**total equity**' value — the total of all the money that's been put into the business. That's why they can also be called balance sheets — because they **balance**.

Sally only wished that balancing her statement of financial position was this easy.

Here's an Example of a Statement of Financial Position

There's more info on the next page about the different things you'll find on a statement of financial position — but here's one for you to have a look at first:

The value of <u>raw materials</u> and <u>finished products</u> — this is how much they're worth in their <u>current state</u>, not what the business paid for them.

Value of products <u>sold</u> but <u>not paid for</u> yet. Money <u>owed to</u> the business.

You might also see <u>cash equivalents</u> included with the cash entry. These are things that will <u>definitely</u> be turned into cash soon, e.g. money from an investment that the business will be getting back within 3 months.

Dividends <u>not yet paid</u> to shareholders.

This is the <u>working capital</u> available to pay for day-to-day spending. See p.77.

<u>Reserves</u> are <u>retained profits</u> — the amount of profit that is <u>reinvested</u> back into the

A statement of financial position shows the financial state of affairs on <u>one particular day</u>.

The value of non-current assets includes <u>depreciation</u> (see next page) — it's what they're worth <u>now</u>, not when the business bought them.

Payables are money <u>owed by</u> the business.

Net current assets = <u>current assets</u> − <u>current liabilities</u>

Net assets = <u>net current assets</u> + <u>non-current assets</u> − <u>non-current liabilities</u>.

These two figures ALWAYS balance.

Abaythay Ltd
Statement of Financial Position on 30 March 2018

Premises			£100000
Machines			£10000
Vehicles			£15000
Total non-current assets			£125000
Inventory (stock)		£20000	
Receivables (debtors)		£10000	
Cash in the bank		£5000	
Total current assets		£35000	
Payables (creditors)	(£20000)		
Overdraft	(£2000)		
Dividends	(£10000)		
Unpaid tax	(£1000)		
Total current liabilities		(£33000)	
Net current assets			£2000
Non-current liabilities (long-term loans)			(£55000)
Net assets			£72000
Share capital			£60000
Reserves			£12000
Total equity (shareholders' funds)			£72000

business. If the figure here is <u>negative</u>, it means the business has an <u>accumulated loss</u> — the amount of share capital will have to exceed the accumulated loss otherwise the firm will face bankruptcy. The figure for reserves takes into account <u>depreciation</u> (see next page). Depreciation is taken into account in '<u>net assets</u>', so if it wasn't included here, the figures <u>wouldn't balance</u>.

Statements of Financial Position

Assets Can be Non-Current or Current

1) Businesses can use **capital** to buy **assets** that will generate more revenue in the future — this is **investment**.

2) Assets (like machinery and stock) provide a **financial benefit** to the business, so they're given a monetary value on a statement of financial position. Assets can be classed as **non-current assets** (fixed assets) or **current assets**.

3) **Non-current assets** are assets that the business is likely to keep for **more than a year**, e.g. property, land, production equipment, desks and computers. The '**total non-current assets**' value on the statement of financial position is the **combined value** of all the business's non-current assets.

4) Non-current assets often **lose value** over time (e.g. because they become less reliable or outdated), so they're worth less every year. This is **depreciation**. Businesses should factor in depreciation to give **realistic** values of their non-current assets on the statement of financial position.

5) **Current assets** are assets that the business is likely to exchange for cash **within the accounting year**, before the next statement of financial position is made. All the current assets are added together to give the '**total current assets**' value on the statement of financial position.

> Current assets include **receivables** (money owed to the business by other businesses and individuals) and **inventory** (or **stock** — products, or materials that will be used to make products, that will be sold to **customers**).

6) The business's **current and non-current assets** are added together, then current and non-current liabilities (see below) are deducted to give the figure for '**net assets**' on the statement of financial position.

Liabilities are Debts the Business Owes

1) **Current liabilities** are **debts** which need to be paid off within a year. They include **overdrafts**, **taxes** due to be paid, **payables** (money owed to **creditors**) and **dividends** due to be paid to shareholders. **Total current liabilities** are **deducted** from total non-current and current assets to give the value of 'assets employed'.

2) **Non-current liabilities** are debts that the business will pay off over several years, e.g. mortgages and loans.

Bad Debts are Debts that Debtors Won't Ever Pay

1) **Ideally**, every debt owed by debtors to the business would be paid. **Unfortunately**, the **real world** isn't like that. Most debts get paid eventually, but some debtors **default** on their payments — they **don't pay up**.

2) Debts which don't get paid are called "**bad debts**". These bad debts **can't** be included on the statement of financial position as an **asset** — because the business isn't going to get money for them.

3) The business **writes off** these bad debts, and puts them as an **expense** on the statement of comprehensive income (see p.71). This shows that the business has **lost money**.

4) It's important to be **realistic** about bad debts. The business shouldn't be **over-optimistic** and report debts as **assets** when they're unlikely to ever be paid. On the other hand, they shouldn't be **too cautious** and write debts off as **bad debts** when they could make the debtors pay up.

Warm-Up Questions

Q1 What's the difference between current and non-current assets?

Q2 What are liabilities?

Exam Question

Q1 Padma's Pasties is a nationwide bakery. It takes out a £4000 overdraft to buy a new oven. Explain what effect (if any) this will have on the net current assets figure of the statement of financial position. [4 marks]

All this revision's making me feel a bit unbalanced...

Not all statements of financial position look like the one on the previous page (e.g. they don't all have three columns). It's really important that you understand how the different figures are calculated so you're ready to interpret any statement of financial position you might see in the exams. And remember the golden rule — it's got to balance.

Liquidity and Working Capital

Now that you've learnt all about the wonders of statements of financial position, it's time to see what they can be used for. You can extract information from the statements to calculate liquidity — prepare for some equations...

Liquidity Ratios Show How Much Money is Available to Pay the Bills

1) The **liquidity** of an asset is how easily it can be turned into **cash** and used to **buy** things. **Cash** is **very** liquid, **non-current assets** such as **factories** are **not liquid**, and **inventory** (**stock**) and money owed by **debtors** (**receivables**) are in between.

The money a business has available to pay its day-to-day bills is called working capital (see next page).

2) A business that doesn't have enough **current assets** to pay its liabilities when they are due is **insolvent**. It either has to quickly **find the money** to pay them, ask **creditors** if it can pay its debts over a **longer time period**, or go into **liquidation** (cease trading and sell all of its assets to pay off its debts).

3) **Liquidity** can be **improved** by decreasing stock levels, speeding up collection of debts owed to the business, or slowing down payments to creditors (e.g. suppliers).

4) An accounting ratio called a **liquidity ratio** shows how **liquid** a firm is (how able it is to pay its short-term debts). There are **two** liquidity ratios you need to know about:

Current Ratio = Current Assets ÷ Current Liabilities

$$\text{Current ratio} = \frac{\text{current assets}}{\text{current liabilities}}$$

1) The **current ratio** (also called the working capital ratio) compares **current assets** to **current liabilities**.

> **Example:** A business has **£30 000** of **current assets** and **£32 000** of **current liabilities**.
>
> The current ratio is: $\frac{£30\,000}{£32\,000} = 0.9375$
>
> This means that for £1 of liabilities, the business only has £0.9375 (or 93.75p) of current assets, which isn't great, as it means there **aren't enough assets** to **cover** the **liabilities**.

You could write this in ratio form as 0.9375:1 — see p.186 for more on writing ratios.

2) In reality, a business probably couldn't **sell off** all its inventory. It'd also need **additional capital** to **replace** inventory — the current ratio should be **higher** than 1 to take account of this. 1.5 to 2 is considered ideal.

3) A value much below 1.5 suggests a **liquidity problem** and that it might struggle to meet its current liabilities.

4) A value much higher than 2 suggests that the firm has **more current assets** than it **really needs** — the money **tied up** in these assets could be **reinvested** into the business to make **more profit**. So a high ratio could put **potential investors** off, as it suggests the business is **not focused** on maximising profit.

Acid Test Ratio = (Current Assets – Inventory) ÷ Current Liabilities

1) The **acid test ratio** (also called the liquid capital ratio) is a **tougher measure** of liquidity than the current ratio as it **accounts for the inventory**.

2) **Inventory** can take a **long time** to sell or it might **not sell at all**. By **removing inventory** from the current assets, the acid test ratio gives a more **accurate** measure of the ability of a firm to pay its current liabilities.

$$\text{Acid test ratio} = \frac{\text{current assets} - \text{inventory}}{\text{current liabilities}}$$

> **Example:** A business has **£20 000** of **current liabilities** and **£30 000** of **current assets**, **£5000** of which are **inventory**.
>
> The acid test ratio is: $\frac{£30\,000 - £5000}{£20\,000} = 1.25$
>
> This means that for £1 of liabilities, the business has £1.25 of current assets that **aren't inventory** — this is good, as the business has **enough assets** to **cover** its **liabilities**, even **without** selling its inventory.

3) Most businesses should have an acid test ratio **higher than 1**. However, businesses with a **high stock turnover**, such as supermarkets, might have a **very low** acid test ratio and **still survive** (because they can easily generate cash from their inventory, which the acid test ratio ignores).

4) A high acid test ratio may indicate cash is **lying idle** in inventory rather than being **reinvested** to make **profit**.

Liquidity and Working Capital

Working Capital is the Finance Available for Day-to-Day Spending

1) **Working capital** is the amount of **cash** (and **assets** that can be easily turned into cash) that the business has available to pay its **day-to-day debts**. The more working capital a business has, the more **liquid** it is.

2) Working capital is the same as **net current assets** on the statement of financial position (see p.74) — it's the amount left over when you subtract **current liabilities** from **current assets**:

> **Working capital = current assets – current liabilities**

3) Businesses **can't survive** if they don't have **enough working capital** because they can't **pay their debts** when they're due.

4) A business's working capital goes through a cycle as the business **buys raw materials**, **makes** their products and **sells** their products. The time it takes a business to do this is called the **working capital cycle**:

5) In other words, the working capital cycle is the **length of time** between buying **raw materials** and getting **cash** from **sales** of the finished product. It's usually measured in **days**.

6) The **length** of the working capital cycle depends largely on the **nature** of the **product** — this affects how long it **takes to produce** and how long it's **held as stock** before it's sold.

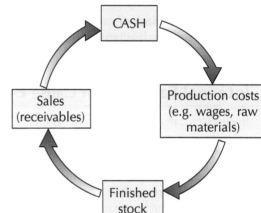

7) The **length** of the cycle also depends on the **credit periods** the business gets from its suppliers and gives to its customers — e.g. a business that gives its customers **a month** to pay for their goods would have a **shorter** working capital cycle if it demanded payment within **a week**.

Businesses Need Enough Cash but Not Too Much

1) Businesses need **just enough** cash to pay short-term debts, but they **shouldn't** have **too much** cash — spare cash is great at paying off debts, but **lousy** at **earning money** for the business.

2) **Different factors** affect **how much cash** a business needs. For example:

- A business with a long working capital cycle needs more cash than a business with a short working capital cycle, as it has to wait longer for money to come in.

- Inflation increases the costs of wages and buying or holding stock, so businesses need more cash when inflation is high.

- When a business expands, it needs more cash to avoid overtrading. Overtrading means producing so much that the business can't afford to pay its suppliers until it gets paid by its customers.

Stuart was happy to hold a bit of extra cash — he'd be expanding soon.

Warm-Up Questions

Q1 Write down the formula for: a) the current ratio, b) the acid test ratio.

Q2 What is a working capital cycle?

Exam Question

Q1 Ski Turtle is a business that sells skiwear. Ski Turtle has recently been bought by new owners who have been analysing the business's financial state, including its liquidity. They found that Ski Turtle has a current ratio of 1.4 and an acid test ratio of 0.9. The new owners plan to make some big changes to the business, including selling one of its warehouses in order to reduce the amount of stock held by 50%.

a) What is meant by liquidity? [2 marks]

b) Assess how selling the warehouse will affect the liquidity of Ski Turtle. [10 marks]

Eurgh — liquidity ratios are a real pain in the assets...

...I'm just trying to be honest. It's easy to get the two liquidity ratios mixed up, so make sure you learn them properly. You need to be able to extract data from a statement of financial position and use it to calculate both of the ratios, so perhaps go back to page 74 to solidify your knowledge on statements of financial position.

Business Failure

Unfortunately, not all businesses are successful, and there are loads of reasons why a business can fail.
Business failure can be down to internal factors, external factors, financial factors and — oh just read the page...

A **Business Fails** When it Can't Cover its **Expenses**

Stan may have known nothing about business failures but he knew a lot about fashion failures.

1) **Business failure** is when a business can no longer **stay open** because it isn't making **enough money** to **cover** its **costs**. The business isn't able to **continue trading** and shuts down while still **owing** people money.

2) A business usually fails because it doesn't have enough **cash** to pay its **current liabilities**.

3) A business's **lack of cash** (and therefore failure) can be due to factors **inside** or **outside** the business, and these factors can be **financial** or **non-financial**.

Internal Factors Can Cause **Business Failure**

Businesses can fail due to problems that occur **inside** the business, for example:

Financial factors

- **Bad management** of working capital can cause business failure (it's kind of obvious, really). This can result in a business not having enough cash available to pay its day-to-day running costs, such as paying suppliers and employees. If it can't pay these costs, then the business will quickly fail. To ensure that the business has good management of working capital, it needs to make sure that it has accurate cash flow forecasting (see page 60).

- **Poor efficiency** can lead to business failure. This is because a business with poor efficiency has costs that aren't as low as they could be. This could mean that they need to charge higher prices than their competitors to still make a profit, which could lead to them not generating the revenue needed to keep operating.

- **Bad decisions** about how a firm is financed can lead to business failure. For example, a firm may rely on expensive forms of finance such as overdrafts in the long term, meaning its costs are very high. It may also take on too much debt at once and retain very little profit — if it needs more finance in the future to prevent it from failing, it may find it very difficult to find a source of finance willing to lend it money at an affordable interest rate.

Non-financial factors

- **Poor communication** can result in business failure because it can mean that the **different departments** of the business aren't **working well together**, which reduces the **efficiency** of the business. It also means that messages about **problems** that arise and strategies to **fix** them aren't passed on effectively between managers and workers or different departments, meaning that problems don't get **solved quickly**.

- Inadequate **market research and analysis** means the business fails to monitor **changes** in the **market** that could affect it, such as a change in customers' **needs** and **preferences**. If a business doesn't sell products that people **want to buy**, then there will be **low demand** for its products. This may lead to a **lack of revenue** for the business, which could mean it runs out of money needed to pay its expenses.

- **Marketing** is used to **drive demand** for products. If marketing isn't done **well** (e.g. at the right time or strongly enough) then sales might not be high enough to generate enough **sales revenue** to cover the business's costs.

- **Failure to innovate** can cause business failure. If a business fails to keep up with **consumer preferences** by lacking **innovative new products**, it is likely to fail.

> **Example:** Before the internet was introduced, **video rental stores**, where people could rent **physical copies** of films, were widely popular. However, as the internet grew, these businesses faced **competition** from firms such as **NETFLIX** that let customers **stream** films from **home**. Businesses that focused on physical copies of films and **failed to innovate** into **digital** film streaming services saw demand fall so low that many **failed** and **ceased trading**.

Business Failure

External Factors Can Also Cause Business Failure

Financial factors

1) **Economic recession** can result in consumers having **less money to spend**. This can cause a **fall in sales**, especially for luxury items (items with a positive **income elasticity of demand** greater than 1 — see page 16), which may **reduce sales** so much that a business fails.

2) A change in **exchange rates** can also have huge effects on demand for a firm's products. For example, if the **pound strengthened** (see p.92), then **foreign firms** exporting goods to the UK would offer **cheaper prices** than firms inside the UK. This would mean that the demand for imports would increase, which could lead to a **fall in the demand** for **domestic products**. Also, the demand for **exports** from the UK by other countries would **decrease**, as they would be more expensive. This could lead to UK firms having to close if they couldn't compete in the long term with **cheaper rivals**, or if they lost too many **overseas customers**.

Non-financial factors

1) The **actions of competitors** are a common cause of business failure. If competitors are able to offer **similar products** at a **lower price** or develop **new products** that are **more desirable** than the ones a firm currently offers, then customers may buy from the firm's competitors. This could cause the firm's **sales to fall**, which would lead to a **loss of revenue** that may put the firm out of business.

2) A change in **consumer trends** could also lead to business failure. For example, if customers suddenly **stop wanting** a product then this will cause a sudden **drop in revenue** for a business selling this product — unless it has a **wide range** of products or can **react quickly** to this change, then the business may fail.

3) **Poor communication** outside of the business can cause failure. If a business fails to communicate well with **suppliers**, it could **lose suppliers** and may not be able to keep up production of products. Also, if communication with **customers** is poor, the business may get a reputation for **poor customer service**, which may result in a loss of revenue and potentially business failure.

How Important Different Causes of Failure are Depends on the Business

1) The **factors** that are **most likely** to cause a **particular business** to fail depend on lots of things, such as the **experience** of the **owners**, the **size** of the business, the **product** it sells and the **market** it's in.

2) For businesses that operate in a **dynamic market**, such as in the **technology** market, a lack of **innovation** can be a big cause of business failure. For example, when a mobile phone business releases a phone with a **new** and **innovative feature**, other businesses might just **stick** with the current features they use. The **lack of innovation** shown by those businesses could contribute to **declines in sales** for them.

3) For businesses that sell very **price elastic** products, economic changes that **increase** the **relative price** of their products (e.g. the availability of cheaper imports) can have a big effect on **demand**.

4) **Large** and **fast-growing** businesses are more likely to fail due to **communication** problems compared to smaller or slower-growing firms.

Warm-Up Questions

Q1 Describe three internal financial factors that may cause business failure.
Q2 Describe two external financial factors that may cause business failure.

Exam Question

Q1 Musik World was a small independent high street music shop that sold CDs in store. In 2017, the business failed.
   a) What is meant by business failure? [2 marks]
   b) Assess two non-financial factors that could have caused Musik World to fail. [8 marks]

I saw a poorly bumblebee on the ground today — buzzzzziness failure...

There're loads of reasons why a firm might fail, but ultimately it comes down to not having enough money to cover costs. So if you're asked in the exam why a particular firm may fail, think about things that could cause its revenue to fall or its costs to increase and consider how able the firm would be to respond to those changes.

Production Methods and Productivity

Production is needed to make the things you're going to sell. Makes sense — you can't sell something you don't have...

There are **Four Methods of Production** You Need to Know About

Job Production

1) **Job production** is used for **one-off** items produced by **skilled workers**, e.g. made-to-measure wedding dresses.

2) Each product can take a **long time** to make, so **fewer products** are made in a given time period compared to other production methods, meaning **productivity** is **lower**.

3) Skilled workers will need to be paid **higher wages** than unskilled workers, which **increases costs**.

4) The firm is **less able** to take advantage of **economies of scale** (see p.49) because the products are **unique** and **can't be made in bulk**. This means that the **unit costs** can be **high**.

5) Higher unit costs can mean that a firm needs to charge **higher prices** for its products. However, customers are often **willing** to **pay higher prices** for a product that is **unique** or **handmade**.

There's more about productivity on the next page.

Flow Production

1) **Flow production** uses an **assembly line** to produce **lots** of **identical** products, e.g. televisions, chocolate bars, mobile phones. **Each worker** within the 'flow' completes a task before the product is **passed on** to the **next worker**, who completes a **different task**.

2) To be most **efficient**, production can be **continuous with no stoppages** — many flow production factories operate **24 hours** a day using **machines** and/or **human workers** rotating in **shifts**.

3) Flow production allows a firm to **benefit** from **economies of scale** as they can buy **raw materials in bulk**. This **reduces unit costs** and allows the firm to charge **lower** and more **competitive prices** for their products.

4) Firms in a **mass market** are likely to use flow production, as they produce (and sell) **large volumes** of **identical products**.

Batch Production

1) **Batch production** is when much of the **same equipment** is used to make **small batches** of **different products**. The products made **in each batch** are **identical** to each other.

2) When one batch of products has been made, production is **stopped** and the equipment is **adjusted** and **cleaned** (if necessary), and the **next batch** of products is made. E.g. a **clothes factory** might produce lots of **identical T-shirts** in one batch, before **switching** production to produce a **batch of dresses**.

3) This production method is used for businesses that have a **small product mix** (see p.27) that they sell in **limited quantities** or for a **limited time**. For example, businesses producing **clothes** or **furniture**. It allows businesses to be **flexible** with their output, e.g. if demand for a certain variation of a product suddenly increased, they could **increase** the **quantity** they produce in the **next batch**.

4) Because each product in a batch is identical, the **productivity** of a business using batch production is **higher** than one using **job production**. However, because production needs to be **stopped** to change between batches, **productivity** is **lower** than if **flow production** was used.

5) A business using batch production can buy **raw materials** in **larger quantities** than one using job production, so it can benefit from **economies of scale** and potentially sell products at lower **prices**.

6) However, it means they have the **cost** and **inconvenience** of having to **store** lots of raw materials.

Cell Production

1) Cell production is when a **flow** is **divided** into **sets of tasks**, with each set of tasks being completed by a **work group**. E.g. rather than a car being produced in one long stream with each worker adding a different part, each work group might be responsible for assembling a different part of the car.

2) This means that **individual workers** are not carrying out **repetitive** tasks on their **own** within a flow (as they would in flow production). This could **increase** a worker's **productivity**, as they **feel happier**.

3) Because each work group is **responsible** for a **large chunk** of the assembly process, workers may take more **pride** in their work. This could result in **higher quality** products.

4) Having the production process clearly **split into stages** means that it's easier to **alter** or **customise** certain parts of the product to **meet customer needs**, which may help to **boost sales**.

5) **Productivity** is **higher** than it is when using **job production**. However, because the product is **removed from the flow** at each cell, productivity can be **lower** than when using **flow production**.

Production Methods and Productivity

Firms Try to Have **High Levels** of **Productivity**

1) **Productivity** is measured as the **output per unit of input, per unit of time**.
   It's the **rate of production** from **each input** (**human worker** or **automated machine**).

2) It shouldn't be confused with **production**, which is the **total output per unit of time**.

3) Improved productivity can be associated with a **lower unit cost**, as **less input**
   is required to produce the same amount. Lower **unit costs** can allow a firm to
   charge lower prices and still make a **profit**. If prices are **lower** than for **similar
   products** from competitors, the firm will have a **competitive advantage**.

22 fairy sleeping bags made in one hour. Boom.

The Use of **Machinery** Can **Increase Productivity**

1) **Machines** can often be used to complete some of the **tasks** done by a **human workforce**.

2) Although the **initial cost** of the machinery can be **high**, once it's **up and running** the use of machines often
   increases a firm's **productivity** — this is largely because machines can carry out tasks **faster** than humans
   and they can work for **more hours each day** (some automated machines operate 24 hours a day, e.g. robot
   technology in a car factory).

3) Firms may **regularly invest** in machinery to boost productivity further, e.g. to **replace** old machinery that
   often **breaks down**, to **upgrade** existing machinery (e.g. by installing new software), or to **take over more
   tasks** currently done by humans.

4) However, there are **drawbacks** to a firm relying heavily on machinery to increase productivity. E.g. as
   machinery gets **old**, the level of **maintenance** required to keep it running can increase, which can result in
   production stoppages. This can **reduce productivity** because it **increases** the **time taken** to make products.

5) Also, if a business **alters production**, machinery may need to be **reprogrammed** or have new software
   installed, whereas **humans** would be more able to **quickly adjust**, which could **maintain productivity**.

The **Human Workforce** Can Also be Used to **Increase Productivity**

1) **Training** a human workforce so that staff know the **best** and **quickest** methods to make a product can **improve
   productivity**. Training may also **motivate** staff to **work harder**, because they may feel **more valued** and so
   want to **contribute** to the **success** of the business. However, there may be an **initial drop** in productivity
   while the workforce **takes the training** and gradually becomes **accustomed** to the new way of working.

2) The workforce could also just be **instructed** to increase its productivity. An example might be in a packing
   warehouse where managers set the workforce **higher targets** to meet during the day. However, if the targets
   are **too ambitious** then this may **demotivate** the workforce as well as reduce
   the **quality** of the work. This could mean that **more time** and **money** may
   need to be spent on **quality management**.

> There are loads of methods of motivation that can increase productivity — see pages 38-41.

3) **Piecework** could also be used to increase productivity — this is where workers
   are **paid only** for the **units** they **produce**, so they're motivated to **work faster**.
   However, this can also lead to a **reduction** in **product quality**.

4) **Hiring a key worker** may improve productivity. For example, the addition of a production line
   supervisor to a workforce could help to **motivate** and **monitor** the workforce, and increase productivity.
   However, the **additional cost** of extra employment should be **compared against** the **productivity gains**.

Warm-Up Questions

Q1 What is productivity?

Q2 Describe three ways in which a firm could improve its productivity.

Exam Question

Q1 Acheeles is a firm that makes three types of specialist shoes. It employs 20 skilled workers who make shoes as
and when they receive orders, in the colour and size the customer requests. It has recently experienced a four-fold
increase in its sales volume, and as such is planning to change its production method to meet its output demands.
Evaluate whether moving to a flow production or batch production method would be better for Acheeles. [20 marks]

I've heard that cell production is the preferred choice of prisons...

Make sure you know the difference between production and productivity. It'd be a silly mistake to make in your exam.

Efficiency

It might seem productive to revise these pages in 30 seconds flat, but if you forget half of it you're not being efficient.

Production at the **Minimum Average Cost** is **Efficient**

1) **Efficiency** is when production happens at an overall **minimum average cost**.

2) Being efficient is essentially about getting **more output** from a given amount of inputs and **reducing the waste** of **all the inputs**, e.g. time and materials. Greater efficiency should **decrease unit costs** and **increase profits**.

3) Efficiency is **not the same** as productivity (remember productivity is how much is produced by a worker or machine in a given time, see p.81). It's possible for a firm to have **high levels of productivity** but not be very **efficient**...

> **Example:** A furniture business makes 50 wooden tables a day — its productivity levels are quite high. However, it uses twice as many nails as are really needed and wastes lots of wood, so it's not very efficient.
>
> A rival furniture business makes 10 tables a day, so its productivity is lower than that of the first business. However, it uses just the right amount of nails needed and wastes no wood — so it's more efficient than the first business.

There are **Many Ways** a Business Can **Increase Efficiency**

1) **Increasing productivity** can increase efficiency.

> **Example:** If the rival business mentioned in the example above increased output to 20 tables a day, without making other changes (e.g. hiring more staff, wasting more, etc.), then its efficiency would increase. This is because the input costs (e.g. staff wages, costs of raw materials, etc.) are now spread over more tables.

2) Businesses can improve their efficiency by **cutting the costs** involved with the production of a product. These could be **variable** costs, such as **materials** or **wages**, or **fixed costs**, such as **rent**.

3) Businesses may also reconsider a product's **design mix** (see page 18) so that it's **easier** or **cheaper** to make.

4) A business may adopt a **lean production** approach — this is when they focus on **minimising waste** to **reduce** the **costs** of making a product (see page 87).

5) How a business increases its efficiency is partly dependent on whether it's **labour-** or **capital-intensive**...

Labour-Intensive Firms are Very **People-Heavy**

1) A **labour-intensive** firm uses more **workers** and less **machinery**. For example, the NHS is very **labour-intensive**. This is mainly because the NHS needs **skilled workers** that can **solve problems** relating to patient health — there **isn't the technology** that would allow **machines** to carry out this work at the moment.

2) In countries where labour is relatively **cheap** (e.g. China), **labour-intensive** production is common.

There are **Advantages** of Labour-Intensive Production...

1) For a firm that only produces on a **small scale**, it might **not** make **financial sense** to buy expensive machines to do jobs that humans could do.

2) Humans can be **retrained** if they need to carry out a **new task**, whereas machines may need to be **replaced**.

3) Also, human workers can **solve** any **problems** that arise during production and suggest ways to **improve quality**.

Joan found her job as a midwife to be quite labour-intensive.

...as well as **Disadvantages**

1) It's **harder** to **manage** people than machines.

2) Also, people can be **unreliable** (e.g. they can get sick) and they can't work without **breaks** or **holidays**.

3) **Wage increases** mean that the cost of production can **increase** over time.

Efficiency

A **Capital-Intensive** Firm has **Lots** of **Machinery**

1) A **capital-intensive** business uses more **machinery** and relatively few **workers**.

> **Example:** BMW makes a **large number** of **identical** cars at any one time, so it uses lots of **robots** and **machinery** — it's **capital-intensive**. In contrast, the Morgan Motor Company makes a **small number** of **hand-built** sports cars using a **human workforce**, so it's more **labour-intensive** than BMW.

2) **Larger** firms tend to be more **capital-intensive** than smaller firms.

3) A rise in the **cost** of **labour** can also cause firms to **switch** to a **capital-intensive** method of production.

Capital-Intensive Production has **Advantages**...

1) Despite the **high initial investment**, in the **long term** machines can be **cheaper** than using lots of manual labour.

2) Machinery is often **more precise** than human workers, which might lead to more **consistent quality** levels.

3) Machinery is able to work **24/7** and is **easier** to **manage** than people.

...as well as **Disadvantages**

1) Machinery can be **very expensive** to **buy** and **maintain**, meaning it can be difficult for **small** or **start-up** firms to be very capital-intensive.

2) Machines are usually only suited to **one task**, which makes them **inflexible**.

3) If machinery **breaks down**, it can lead to long **delays** in production, which could mean the firm **misses out** on **sales** and risks its **reputation** being **damaged**.

4) The fear of being replaced by a machine can cause workers' **motivation** to **decrease**, which can lead to a decrease in the productivity of the workforce.

Businesses Need to Have the **Right Balance** of **People** and **Machines**

1) Businesses should try to **optimise** the amount of **machinery** and **people** that they have in order to meet their business needs. How hard it is to get this right depends on the **complexity** of the product and the number of **production stages**. A business needs to strike the right **balance** between **labour-** and **capital-intensity** at each stage of production.

2) The **design** of the product affects the balance — e.g. freshly squeezed orange juice has just one component (oranges), but a car has hundreds. The **higher** the number of **components**, the more **complicated** the product is to produce, so the **harder** it is to get the **correct mix** of people and machines.

3) Businesses can have problems getting the right mix if there's a **shortage** of suitably skilled **labour**.

4) Businesses are also limited by their **finances**. Most firms would have the **latest technology** if they could **afford** it, but in reality **smaller firms** can rarely afford to keep updating their machinery.

Warm-Up Questions

Q1 Give three ways that a business can increase efficiency.

Q2 Give one benefit and one drawback of switching from labour-intensive to capital-intensive production.

Exam Question

Q1 Voiture is a labour-intensive car manufacturer that uses a lot of water during production. Currently, the business is charged for the water they use through a water meter. Voiture wants to increase its efficiency and is considering installing new technological systems to allow it to use rainwater as a supply and to re-use its wastewater.
a) What is meant by labour-intensive production? [2 marks]
b) Assess two implications of installing the new systems on the efficiency of production for Voiture. [8 marks]

THIS SENTENCE IS VERY CAPITAL-INTENSIVE...

When we talk about efficiency and cost, we don't just mean the cost of any raw materials. We also need to think about cost in terms of time. Wages are essentially the business paying staff for their time. They do say time is money...

Capacity Utilisation

Businesses need to analyse capacity utilisation data before making important decisions about production...

Capacity is Maximum Output with the Resources Currently Available

1) The **capacity** of an organisation is the **maximum** output that it can produce in a given period without buying any more fixed assets — machinery, factory space, etc.

2) Capacity depends on the **number of employees** and how skilled they are.

3) It also depends on the **technology** the business has — what **machinery** it has, what state it's in, what kind of computer system it has, etc.

4) The kind of **production process** the business uses will also affect its capacity.

5) The amount of **investment** in the business is also a factor.

Capacity can also be called productive capacity.

Capacity utilisation is how much **capacity** a business is **using**. This is the formula used to calculate it:

Examples: a hotel with half its rooms booked out has a **capacity utilisation** of 50%. A clothing factory with an output of 70 000 shirts per month and a potential to do 100 000 shirts per month is running at **70% capacity utilisation**.

$$\text{Capacity Utilisation (\%)} = \frac{\text{Current Output}}{\text{Maximum Possible Output}} \times 100$$

Increasing Utilisation Too Much Can Lead to Over-Utilisation

High capacity utilisation is better than low capacity utilisation.
However, **100% capacity utilisation** has drawbacks and can be known as **over-utilisation**:

1) Businesses have to consider all their **objectives** when they plan their capacity usage. **Cost** isn't the only thing to think about — it might not be possible to operate at 100% capacity and keep **quality** levels high.

2) The business may have to **turn away** potential **customers** because it can't increase output any more.

3) There's no **downtime** — machines are on **all the time**. If a machine **breaks down**, it'll cause **delays** as work piles up **waiting** for it to be fixed. There's no time for equipment **maintenance**, which can reduce the life of machinery.

4) There's no **margin of error**. Everything has to be perfect first time, which causes **stress** to managers. **Mistakes** are more likely when everyone's working flat out.

5) The business can't **temporarily increase output** for seasonal demand or one-off orders.

6) If output is greater than demand, there'll be **surplus stock** hanging about waiting to be sold. It's not good to have valuable **working capital** (see p.77) tied up in stock.

Businesses should plan production levels to achieve almost full capacity utilisation.

Firms with Over-Utilisation Can Increase Their Capacity

Firms that are operating at close to 100% capacity utilisation don't just stop accepting new orders. They have ways of **increasing** their **capacity** so that they can **match** their **output** to **demand**. The best way to do this depends on whether the rise in demand is expected to be **temporary** or **long-term**.

1) Businesses can **increase capacity** by using their facilities for **more** of the **working week**. They can have staff working in two or three **shifts** in a day, and on weekends and bank holidays.

2) Businesses can buy **more machines**, if they can afford them (and the staff needed to operate them).

3) Businesses can **increase** their **staff levels** in the long run by recruiting new permanent staff. In the short run they can employ **temporary staff**, **part-time staff**, or get their staff to work **overtime**.

4) Businesses can also increase their capacity by increasing **productivity**. They can reorganise production by reallocating staff to the busiest areas, and they can increase employee **motivation**.

5) If the rise in demand is **temporary** then businesses might choose to **outsource** work:

- **Outsourcing** is when a business uses another firm to do some work on its behalf. E.g. a manufacturer of detergent might make detergent for a **supermarket** and package it with the supermarket's own label.

- Firms can **outsource** work to other businesses in **busy periods**. This means they can meet **unexpected increases in demand** without increasing their own capacity and having the costs of extra staff and facilities all year round.

There's more on outsourcing on p.165 if you're doing the full A-level course.

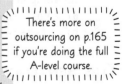

Capacity Utilisation

Under-Utilisation is Inefficient and Increases Unit Costs

Low capacity utilisation is called **under-utilisation**. It's **inefficient** because it means
a business is **not** getting good **use** out of **machines** and **facilities** that have been paid for.

1) **Fixed costs** have to be spread over fewer units of output, so unit costs increase.
   An increase in unit costs may mean a firm needs to increase prices.
   This could make it less competitive, which may reduce sales and profits.

2) Under-utilisation can lead to a negative brand image being perceived by consumers.
   E.g. if a supermarket didn't use all of the shelving space it had, then the appearance of
   all the empty shelves may give customers a negative impression of the supermarket.

3) It can also reduce employee motivation as there may be long periods when there's not enough work
   for them to do. There'd be less need for supervisory roles compared to if capacity utilisation was high
   — this means there would be less opportunity for promotion, which could also reduce motivation.

However, there may be **benefits** from under-utilisation. For example, the firm may be able to **accept new orders**, e.g.
from increases due to seasonal demand. Also, organising machine **maintenance** and **staff training** could be easier.

Businesses Deal with Under-Utilisation in Two Ways

Under-utilisation can occur when firms have **too much capacity** and **not enough demand** for their product.
When this happens, they'll **first** try to **increase demand**, but if that doesn't work, they need to **reduce capacity**.

1) Businesses stimulate demand by changing their marketing mix (see p.18).
   E.g. they can change the promotion of a product, or change its price or its distribution.

2) Changing the marketing mix might take customers away from competitors — if a competitor
   exits the market, it may cause demand for the remaining businesses to increase.

3) Businesses can also fill spare capacity by accepting outsourced work from other firms. It's often better
   to make goods for a competitor and make some money than it is to leave machinery doing nothing.

4) If a business can't increase demand for their product, they need to reduce their capacity by closing
   part of their production facilities. This is called rationalisation (or downsizing).

5) Businesses can reduce capacity in the short term by stopping overtime or reducing the length of the
   working week, allocating staff to other work in the business, and by not renewing temporary contracts.

6) Businesses can reduce capacity in the long term by not replacing staff as they retire (natural wastage),
   making staff redundant, and by selling off factories or equipment.

Businesses Have to Consider How Their Capacity Needs Will Change

1) **Demand changes** over time, so firms must think about demand in the **future** as well as the current demand.

2) The key to **long-term** success is planning **capacity** changes to match long-term changes in demand. You can
   use **market research** to help **predict** future demand, but it's not 100% certain. There's always some **risk**.

3) **Short-term** changes in **capacity utilisation** provide **flexibility**. Firms should be flexible and **temporarily**
   increase existing capacity utilisation if an increase in demand isn't expected to continue **long-term** — e.g. with
   seasonal goods like sun cream, goods heading towards **decline** in their life cycle, and **one-off** special orders.

4) **Long-term** solutions end up giving **lower unit costs** — as long as **predictions** of demand turn out to be **true**.

Warm-Up Questions

Q1 What is the formula for calculating capacity utilisation?
Q2 Give four ways in which a firm can increase its capacity.

Exam Question

Q1 A cinema with 300 seats shows 3 films a day. It gets about 315 customers a day.
Explain how the cinema could improve its capacity utilisation. [4 marks]

She cannae take any more, Jim...

*When a business launches a product, capacity utilisation can start out low and then build up as demand for the new
product increases. It's really worth knowing how businesses should deal with high and low capacity utilisation...*

Managing Stock

If this section was about stock cubes, I'd tell you that beef stock makes a great French onion soup. But it's not, so I won't...

Stock is the Store of **Raw Materials**, **Work-in-Progress** or **Finished Goods**

1) A business's **stock** (or 'inventory') includes the **raw materials** needed for making a product, the materials being used for **work-in-progress**, and the store of **finished goods** that a business holds to supply to customers.

2) Most businesses try to **minimise** the level of stock they're holding because of the **costs** involved (see below). The **maximum** level of stock a business wants to hold usually depends on the **size** of their **warehouses** or **stockrooms**, on **opportunity cost** (see below), and their **production method**.

3) Businesses that use **flow production** need a **large stock** of **raw materials**, whereas **batch production** leads to large stocks of **work-in-progress**. **Job production** often means there is **no stock** of **finished goods** to be stored, and **cell production** usually relies on **just-in-time** stock control (see the next page).

Stock Control Diagrams Help Businesses Keep Levels of Stock **Just Right**

1) A business needs a **minimum** level of stock so that it **won't run out** of raw materials or finished goods. This minimum stock level is called **buffer stock**.

2) The **amount** of buffer stock needed depends on the storage **space** available, the kind of product (**perishable**, or something that keeps), the **rate** at which stocks are used up, and the **lead time**.

3) The **lead time** is the time it takes for goods to **arrive** after ordering them from the supplier. The **longer** the lead time, the **more buffer stocks** you need to hold — if customer demand suddenly went up, you wouldn't want to wait a long time for stocks to arrive from the supplier.

4) The **re-order quantity** is the amount the business orders from its supplier. The stock level at which this re-order is placed is called the **re-order level**.

5) **Stock control diagrams** allow managers to **analyse** and **control** stock over a period of time — as shown below.

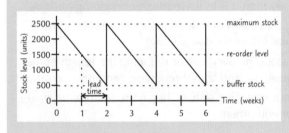

1) The **buffer stock level** is **500 units**. The **lead time** is **1 week**, and the business uses **1000 units** a week. 1500 units is the **re-order level**.

2) The **re-order quantity** is **2000 units**. This takes them back to their **maximum stock level** of 2500 units.

It Can be **Beneficial** for a Business to **Hold Buffer Stock...**

1) Buffer stock is needed to avoid **running out** of stock. This is beneficial for a business in a **mass market** where they need to be able to **consistently** meet customer demand or risk losing loyal customers to rival firms. For example, a clothing retailer might hold a **buffer stock** in case there is a **sudden increase** in **demand** or a sudden **reduction** in **supply** from the manufacturers. This will help it to retain customers.

2) If they can afford to, it may be **beneficial** for firms to hold a **large** amount of **buffer stock**. Businesses can be offered a **discount** for **bulk buying** stock, which gives them **purchasing economies of scale** (see p.49) — this **lowers** the **unit cost**. Firms can pass these savings on to customers by **lowering prices**. E.g. this is how a supermarket in a **mass market** will gain a **competitive price advantage** over smaller stores in a **niche market**.

...But it Can Also Have **Drawbacks**

1) Firms need to consider **how much** buffer stock to hold as there are **costs involved**.

2) **Storage costs** are the most **obvious cost** of holding buffer stock. Storage costs include **rent** for the warehouse and also the non-obvious costs of **heating**, **lighting**, **refrigeration**, **security**, etc.

3) **Wastage costs** are the costs of **throwing away** useless stock. The longer a business holds stock, the more likely it is to create waste. Stock gets **physically damaged** or **perishable food spoils** as time goes on. In dynamic markets there could be high wastage as things change very quickly and can go **out of fashion**.

4) Capital tied up in stock is **unproductive** and could be used more productively elsewhere. Deciding to hold lots of stock has an **opportunity cost** — this is the **benefit** that could be **gained** if the money was **spent elsewhere** (see p.53 for more on opportunity costs).

Managing Stock

Poor Stock Control Can Result in Stock-In and Stock-Out Costs

1) If a business **doesn't control stock** properly then it could end up with **high stock-in costs** (the costs associated with holding too much stock). This could be particularly **bad** for **small businesses** with **little money**, or those in a **dynamic market** where there is a high chance that **demand may change** before stock gets used up.

2) Poor stock control could also lead to high **stock-out costs** (the costs associated with running out of stock). For example, in a manufacturing firm, running out of stocks of raw materials would mean that **production had to stop** but workers and expenses would still need to be **paid**. This could also be **demotivating** for staff as they wouldn't have any work to do.

3) Also, if a business is a **supplier** for other businesses, then running out of stock could affect the whole **supply chain**. If a supplier **loses a contract** with a **big buyer** then it could **ruin** the supplier business.

4) Stock-out costs can also be associated with **lost sales** from **losing customers** to a **competitor**, as the customers become tired of waiting for new stock to arrive. This can also damage the firm's **reputation**. A firm may also have to **compensate** customers for delayed or missing orders, which **increases costs**.

Lean Production Can Mean a Business Holds Very Little Stock

1) **Lean production** is an **efficient** form of production that focuses on **waste minimisation**. Waste minimisation means using as **few resources** (e.g. **time**, **money**) as possible to make products of a **given quality**. It can also involve **recycling** or **re-using** materials **in-house** to minimise waste.

2) Firms using lean production aim to minimise waste whilst **maintaining** or **improving** the rate of **output** and **quality** of the finished products.

3) If there's **less waste** then the firm is **more efficient**, which results in **lower costs**. This can lead to **lower prices** for customers, which can give the firm a **competitive advantage**.

4) One method of lean production is to hold **very little stock**...

Amir was very good at producing while leaning.

Just-In-Time (JIT) Management Keeps Stock Levels Very Low

1) **Just-in-time** stock management is a method of lean production. It aims to **reduce waste** of materials and products by having as **little stock** as possible — products are available just in time for when the customer needs them. For example, in a manufacturing firm, all **raw materials come in** one door, are **made into products** and go **straight out** another door — all **just in time** for delivery to customers.

2) JIT has **advantages** — **storage costs** are reduced and **cash flow** is improved as money isn't tied up in stock. There's **less waste** because there's less out-of-date or damaged stock lying around. The business is more **flexible** so it can cope with changes in **demand** and easily **adapt its products** to suit changing demand.

3) By removing the **cost of storage** and **reducing waste**, a business can price their products **lower** and gain a **competitive advantage** as a result. For example, Lidl stocks a **narrow range** of everyday, **fast-moving** items, which is part of the reason why they can **charge less** than their competitors for the products that they sell.

4) There are **disadvantages** of JIT too — having very little stock means that firms rely on lots of **frequent deliveries** from suppliers. These can be **hard to organise** and can be **stressful** for staff. If the supplier is **unreliable** then the firm may run out of stock and have to **stop production**. Having **smaller, more frequent** deliveries also means that the firm **can't benefit** from **purchasing economies of scale** from buying in bulk.

Warm-Up Questions

Q1 Give three disadvantages of holding buffer stock.
Q2 Describe what just-in-time stock management is.

Exam Question

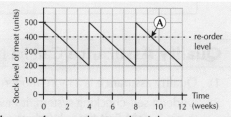

Q1 The diagram shows the stock control diagram for a butcher's firm.
a) Using the data in the diagram, calculate the maximum stock level if the re-order quantity at point A is 10% greater than in previous re-orders. You are advised to show your working. Answer on p.193. [4 marks]
b) Assess the implications for the business if the lead time (the length of time it takes stock to arrive) decreased on a long-term basis. [10 marks]

Just-in-time stock management is a good idea — just-in-time revision isn't...

Hopefully you're reading this a good few weeks before the exams and you've got time to read and scribble until it's properly embedded in your memory. If you are tight for time though, don't panic. Just do as much as you can.

Quality Management

Quality management is basically someone telling you off if your work's not up to scratch. Sounds just like a teacher...

A **High Quality Product** Can **Increase Profits** but May Have **Drawbacks**

1) Quality refers to **meeting** or **exceeding** consumer **expectations** of what a product should do.

2) The importance of quality will **differ** from business to business. For example, a business in a **competitive market** may focus more on quality than one in a less competitive market, as consumers can easily choose to **buy from elsewhere** if the quality of the business's products is poor. A business that produces **high-priced**, **luxury** items will focus more on quality than one that produces **cheap**, **disposable** items.

3) A business will use **quality management** to ensure that their products are of a **good quality**.

4) A business focused on improving quality can **reduce its costs** and **increase its revenue**:

   - Less **raw material** and less **worker** and **machinery** time get used up by **mistakes**.
   - Less **advertising** and **promotional** material is needed to persuade **shops** to stock high quality goods.
   - There are **fewer complaints** and **refunds** so employees can spend their time on other things.
   - Quality can function as a **unique selling point (USP)** for a product.
   - High quality products improve the **image** and **reputation** of the business and mean that the **customers** will be willing to **pay more** for the products.
   - Quality can be associated with **consistency**, so quality products make it easy to keep **existing customers** and **attract new customers**.

5) Being known for producing good quality products can give a firm a **competitive advantage** — customers are **more likely** to **buy** the firm's products rather than a competitor's, and may be willing to pay a **higher price**.

6) However, it can be **difficult** for businesses to improve the quality of their products **efficiently**.

7) There's a **limit** to how much quality can be improved — workers have to know when the quality is **good enough**. Trying to make every single product 100% perfect could prove **costly** to the business.

Quality Control and **Quality Assurance** are Methods of **Quality Management**

1) **Quality control** means **checking goods** after you've made them or when they arrive from suppliers to see if anything is wrong with them. It's often done by specially trained **quality inspectors**.

2) **Quality assurance** means introducing measures into the **production process** to try to ensure things don't go **wrong** in the first place. It assumes you can **prevent errors** from being made, rather than **eliminating faulty goods** once they've been made. It means that a product is tested at **each stage** of the **production process**.

Quality Control (QC)	Quality Assurance (QA)
• Assumes that errors are unavoidable.	• Assumes that errors are avoidable.
• Detects errors and puts them right.	• Prevents errors and aims to get it right first time.
• Quality control inspectors check other people's work, and are responsible for quality.	• Employees check their own work. Workers are responsible for passing on good quality work to the next stage of the production process.

Quality Assurance Can be More **Motivating** Than **Quality Control**

1) **Quality assurance** is a more modern approach to quality control.

2) Under a self-checking system, it's **everyone's responsibility** to produce good work. Everyone should try to get it **right first time**. Workers can **reject** components or work in progress if they're not up to standard. They don't pass the poor quality off as **someone else's problem**.

3) **Empowering** employees to **self-check** the quality of their work can be highly **motivating**.

4) **Training** is important for quality assurance. Workers have to be trained to produce good quality products. New recruits get this as part of their **induction**. Experienced workers might need to be **retrained**.

5) Workers must be **motivated** and **committed** to quality for quality assurance schemes to work.

6) Both methods have their **drawbacks** — unless **all products** are tested during quality control, some **faulty** products will slip through. Quality assurance can result in products only being '**acceptable**', not of a **high standard**.

Quality Management

Total Quality Management Assures Commitment to Quality

1) **Total Quality Management** (TQM) means quality is at the centre of everything a business does — it's a big part of the business's **culture**. The idea is that **every employee** in **every department** focuses on quality in order to improve the **overall quality** of the products.

2) With TQM, every employee has to try to **satisfy customers** and **co-workers** — customers need to be happy with products they are being sold, and co-workers need to be happy with work being passed on to them.

Advantages of TQM	Disadvantages of TQM
• As all employees are involved with improving quality, TQM can help them to bond as a **team**. • TQM boosts a company's **reputation** for providing quality services or products. • TQM usually leads to fewer **faulty** products being made — so the business creates less **waste**.	• It can take a **long time** to introduce TQM. Firms might not see immediate improvements in quality. • TQM can **demotivate staff** — it can seem like a lot of effort to consider quality in all parts of the firm. • TQM is usually **expensive** to introduce — it often means investing in **training** for all employees.

Quality Circles and Kaizen are Other Methods of Quality Management

Quality Circles

1) **Quality circles** meet at regular intervals to discuss quality control issues.
2) They use the knowledge of employees from **various departments** and **all levels** of the organisation.
3) Quality circles aim to **identify** and **solve** specific quality problems that arise.
4) They're a great way to get staff **involved** and can lead to increased **motivation** and **productivity**.
5) However, suggestions can often be **unrealistic** and management may **not listen** to the floor staff.

Kaizen (continuous improvement)

1) The **kaizen** approach is a **lean production method** (see p.87) — employees should be **improving** their work slightly **all the time**, instead of just making one-off improvements. This **reduces waste** as employees are **constantly evaluating** the way they work and finding ways to be **more efficient**.

2) To have a **culture** of **continuous improvement** in a business, employees need to know **how** to **suggest improvements** — there needs to be appointed people who will **listen** to workers and help to **implement** any ideas they have.

3) Employees need to be **encouraged** to question **why** a problem has occurred and even employees at the bottom of the hierarchy have to be given some control over **decision-making**.

4) **Kaizen** helps workers feel involved in **quality assurance**. It's also **cheap** for the business to introduce.

5) The downside of **kaizen** is that, because it makes **small changes** over time, it's not great for **urgently** improving quality. It needs the business to be willing to commit to the method in the **long term**.

Holidaying in the Lake District always left Kai feeling pretty Zen.

Warm-Up Questions

Q1 Give two reasons why quality management gives a business a competitive advantage.

Q2 What's the difference between quality control and quality assurance?

Q3 How does a total quality management approach improve quality within a business?

Q4 How does the kaizen approach help to reduce waste?

Exam Question

Q1 Lightoptic manufactures table lamps. Recently a large number of customers have been complaining about the quality of the lamps. Assess the likely effects for Lightoptic of using quality circles to address this. [10 marks]

Examiners — the ultimate quality control inspectors...

Poor quality products can have huge impacts on a business. Good quality management can help businesses to get it right first time. Just like in your exam really — get it spot on first time and bathe in the glory of your achievements.

Interest and Inflation Rates

Now there's a title that'll put you to sleep. I'm not inflating things when I say my interest rate has already declined...

Interest Rates Determine the Cost of Borrowing or Saving

1) **Interest rates** tell you the **cost of borrowing** or the **return on savings**:
   - The interest rate for borrowing money is the **money charged** for doing so — it's calculated as a **percentage** of the amount borrowed. For example, if you borrow £100 with a 10% interest rate, you'll actually pay back £110. A **fall** in interest rates means a **decrease** in the **cost of borrowing** for businesses. A **rise** in interest rates leads to an **increase** in the cost of borrowing.
   - The interest rate on **savings** is the amount of money **paid** into a savings account **by the bank**, based on **how much** the customer has **saved in the account**. For example, if you save **£1000** in a savings account with a **2.5%** interest rate, the bank will pay you **£25 in interest**, so you'll have **£1025**. A **fall** in interest rate means a **decrease** in the **return on savings** and a **rise** in interest rate leads to a **greater return**.

2) The **Bank of England base rate** influences other banks' interest rates (although banks can choose to set the interest rates **higher** or **lower** than the base rate).

3) **Changes in interest rates** will affect a business's **costs** if it has a loan or a mortgage.

4) Interest rates also affect **consumer spending**, and therefore businesses. **High interest** rates mean most consumers have **less money** to spend — people with existing **borrowing** (like mortgages) have to pay more money back in **interest**, so they have less **disposable income** (the money left over after essential payments like tax), and so market **demand** goes **down**. People might also decide to **save more** to take advantage of the interest earned on their savings, **reducing demand**. **Low interest** rates mean consumers have more disposable income and there is less reward for saving, so **demand** goes **up**.

5) The effect of interest rates on demand depends on the **product**. Products that often require **borrowing** (e.g. cars and houses) are more **sensitive** to interest rate changes. When interest rates **go up significantly**, firms can **change strategy** to **diversify** away from these products and into **cheaper ones**.

Inflation Can Happen Because Demand or Costs Rise for Businesses

1) **Inflation** is an **overall increase** in the **price of goods and services** within an economy. There are two types:
   - Demand-pull inflation is when there is **too much demand** (more than the economy can supply). It happens when there's an **increase** in **disposable income** so people buy more and businesses **can't supply goods** quickly enough, so **increase** their **prices**. **Demand-pull inflation** can make **profit margins** go **up**. Businesses can put up prices in response to **high demand** without their **costs** going up by as much.
   - Cost-push inflation is when **rising costs** push up **prices**. **Employee wage rises** can make prices go up — especially if productivity isn't rising. **Cost-push inflation** can make **profit margins** go **down** if businesses decide not to put up their prices.

2) The **rate of inflation** is the **percentage change** in the price of goods and services within an economy, in **one year compared** to the **previous year**.

3) **Expectations** of inflation can make inflation worse. A business which expects its **suppliers** to put their prices up will put its **own** prices up to cover the expected increase in costs. These rising prices cause people to demand **higher wages**, which can cause prices to go up further due to **increased labour costs** for the employing businesses. As wages go up, there's an **increase in demand** as people can **afford more**, which also causes prices to go up. This is the **wage-price spiral** — it's a big cause of cost-push inflation.

4) When inflation is **high**, spending goes **up** temporarily — people rush to buy more before prices go up further. If **wages** don't go up in line with inflation, however, spending goes **down** as people can afford less.

5) When **inflation** in the UK is **high**, it makes UK **exports** expensive abroad. UK businesses become **less competitive** globally. When inflation in the UK is **low**, UK businesses have a **competitive advantage** globally.

6) Inflation that's **too high** is bad for the economy. The Bank of England aims to keep the rate of inflation within a **target range** set by the government — they do this by changing the Bank of England **base rate**.

Deflation
1) **Deflation** is an overall **decrease** in the **price of goods** and **services within an economy**.
2) **Deflation** is the **opposite** of inflation — there's **not enough demand**, so businesses **reduce their prices**.
3) Deflation causes a **fall** in **productivity** because businesses won't keep endlessly supplying the market with goods that nobody wants. **Lower productivity** usually means firms don't need as many workers — so deflation often leads to a **rise** in **unemployment**. This makes **demand drop** more and causes firms to **lower prices** further.

Interest and Inflation Rates

Inflation Can be Tracked Using the Consumer Prices Index

1) The **Consumer Prices Index** can be used as a measure of inflation in a country — it uses **index numbers** to track the **changes** in the **average cost** of a 'basket' of hundreds of goods and services that an **average household** would **regularly buy**.

There's more on index numbers on page 185.

2) The **graph** on the right shows the **Consumer Prices Index** over 10 years, from March 2008 to March 2018, for the country **Fakeland** which uses **dollars** as its currency.

3) A graph line **going up** between **two consecutive years** shows **inflation**. A line going **down** shows **deflation**.

4) In 2008, the **average value** of the 'basket' in Fakeland was **$863.42** — this is the **base value** for this graph. As 2008 is the **base year**, the average value of the 'basket' is given the **index number** of **100**.

5) The index numbers for the other years are calculated with the **equation**:

index number = $\dfrac{\text{average value of the 'basket'}}{\text{base value of the 'basket'}}$ × 100

For example, if by 2015 the average value of the 'basket' was **$847.88**, the index number is calculated as: index number = $\dfrac{847.88}{863.42}$ × 100 = **98.2** (to 1 decimal place).

This means the average value of the basket went down by **1.8%** between 2008 and 2015.

6) You can also **use** a given **index number** to find the **average value of the 'basket'** in a year, using the equation:

average value of the 'basket' = $\dfrac{\text{index number}}{100}$ × base value of the 'basket'

For example, in **2018** the index number was **101.8**, so the **average value of the 'basket'** can be calculated:

average value of the 'basket' = $\dfrac{101.8}{100}$ × 863.42 = **$878.96** (to 2 decimal places).

Inflation Affects Business Strategy

"No, Dave, I can't inflate it any more."

1) Businesses producing **premium goods** are the **most** likely to be **affected** by inflation because if customers have less to spend they start to look at **cheaper** alternative **products**. Manufacturers of premium products can react by **reducing prices** (although they have to be careful not to reduce them so far that the product loses its premium image) or by investing heavily in **advertising**.

2) Periods of high inflation can be a **good time** for firms to **expand** — if **interest rates** are **lower** than the rate of **inflation** it's **cheap** for them to **borrow money** to invest in **new premises** or **machinery**. The **interest** they'd earn on their savings would be **less** than the amount prices would have gone up by in the same time, so it makes sense to **spend** rather than save. However, the Bank of England often **raises** its base rate in times of high inflation to encourage saving, so businesses don't always benefit from high inflation.

3) Businesses compare **UK** and **foreign** interest rates. When the UK interest rate is high or fluctuating, firms tend to expand into **countries** with low, stable interest rates, as it's **cheaper** to borrow money for expansion there.

4) It's hard for a business to **plan** when inflation is **high**. It needs **stable prices** to make **accurate forecasts** (p.62).

Warm-Up Questions

Answer on p.194.

Q1 Explain why higher interest rates can reduce demand.

Q2 Using the graph above, find the average value of the 'basket' in Fakeland in 2011. The base value is $863.42.

Q3 What type of goods are most likely to be affected by inflation? Why is this?

Exam Question

PRACTICE QUESTIONS

Q1 The Bank of England base rate was 0.75% in October 2018. At this time, the UK Consumer Prices Index was 2.4% and UK wages had increased by an average of 3.3% since October 2017. In 2018, the UK had a target to keep the rate of inflation at 2%. Scrubbed Up! is a business that sells expensive, luxury soaps. Currently it only operates in the UK, but its owners are deciding whether to remain solely in the UK or to expand abroad. Evaluate these two options and recommend which is more suitable for Scrubbed Up! [20 marks]

I was only showing an interest, now you're trying to charge me for it...

This stuff's pretty complicated, so I'd say you should make sure you really understand these pages before moving on.

Exchange Rates

Exchange rates tell you how much of one currency you can buy with another. Easy peasy. Except, well, changes in exchange rates affect businesses and you might need to use index numbers too... OK, maybe it's average paverage.

Exchange Rates Affect the Price of Imported and Exported Products

1) An **exchange rate** is the **value** of **one currency** in terms of **another currency**.

2) For example, **£1** might be **worth $1.20**. If this **increased** so that £1 was worth $1.60, it's said that the **pound** has **appreciated against** the **dollar**. The pound **depreciates** against the dollar if the **amount of dollars falls**.

3) You can also talk about the **strength** of one currency against another. For example, if the pound changed from being worth **$1.20** to being worth **$1.60**, then it's said that the pound has **strengthened against the dollar**.

4) Moving exchange rates affect the **price of products**:

> 1) When the exchange rate increases (e.g. the **pound appreciates** against the **dollar**), UK **exports** become more **expensive** abroad, which is **bad** for UK exporters because their products become **less competitively priced** abroad. This means that UK exporters may need to **reduce their prices**, which will affect their **profits**. They may also **alter** their **marketing strategy** and market to **UK customers** instead.
>
> 2) An increase in the exchange rate is good for UK importers because **imports** become **cheaper**.
>
> > **Example:** Over the Moon Spoons (OMS) is a **UK business** that makes cutlery.
> > They **import** the **steel** they need from a **US supplier** at **$1.79 per 500 g**.
> > At the current exchange rate of **£1 = $1.28** this would cost OMS:
> > **$1.79 ÷ 1.28 = £1.40 per 500 g**
> > If the **exchange rate increased** to **£1 = $1.63**, then 500 g of steel
> > would only cost OMS **$1.79 ÷ 1.63 = £1.10**, which is cheaper than before.
> >
> > *There's more on converting between currencies below.*
>
> **Cheaper imports** mean **higher profitability**, which can lead to higher profits. This money can then be **reinvested elsewhere** within the business.

> 1) When the exchange rate decreases (e.g. the **pound depreciates** against the **dollar**), UK **exports** become **cheaper** for other countries. This is **good** for **UK exporters** because their products become **more competitively priced** abroad, and so may be **cheaper** than **similar products** offered by businesses in other countries. UK exporters might **keep the same price** in pounds, which could increase **demand** as the price abroad decreases, or they might **increase their price** in pounds, which will increase their **profitability** but won't increase **demand**.
>
> 2) A decrease in the exchange rate is **bad** for UK importers because **imports** become **more expensive**. UK importers might **change suppliers** so that they buy from **UK suppliers** instead. They may also **increase their prices** to customers to **cover** the **extra costs** of buying from their suppliers.

Make Sure You Can Convert Between Currencies

1) Exam questions might ask you to use an **exchange rate** to **convert** between **two currencies**.

2) You'll be given how much of one currency is equal to a **unit of the other** — this is the exchange rate. To convert **from** the **single unit** currency to the other, you need to **multiply** by the **exchange rate**:

> **Example:** Using an exchange rate of €1.41 to £1, convert £47 into euros.
> Multiply: £47 × 1.41 = €66.27

Iona and Mike realised they might not have a very fair gift exchange rate.

3) If you have to convert the other way, you have to **divide** by the **exchange rate**:

> **Example:** Using an exchange rate of €1.41 to £1, convert €320 into pounds.
> Divide: €320 ÷ 1.41 = £226.95
>
> *Round your answer to 2 decimal places.*

4) **Check** that your answers are **sensible**. For the exchange rate in the examples above, the number of **euros** will always be **higher** than the equivalent number of **pounds**.

Exchange Rates

Exchange Rates Can be Compared Using a Currency Index

1) You can use currency indices to **compare** the **exchange rates** for two different currencies. Each currency will have a **different base rate**, but using currency indices means that they will **both change** in relation to a starting value of **100** — this makes it easier to compare the exchange rates of different currencies.

2) The **exchange rates** for the pound (GBP) to euro (EUR) and the pound to Canadian Dollar (CAD) for 2008 to 2011 are shown in the **table** on the right. From this it's difficult to determine against which currency the pound has **appreciated** or **depreciated** the **most**.

Year	GBP	EUR	CAD
2008	1.00	1.36	1.98
2009	1.00	1.04	1.78
2010	1.00	1.13	1.70
2011	1.00	1.16	1.55

3) A **better way** to **compare** them is to **calculate currency index numbers** and **plot** them on a graph. They're calculated using this **equation:**

$$\text{currency index number} = \frac{\text{exchange rate}}{\text{base exchange rate}} \times 100$$

1) In 2008 (the base year), the **pound** to **euro** exchange rate was **1.36** — this is the **base exchange rate** and has a currency index number of 100. The exchange rate **decreased** to 1.04 in 2009 (the **pound depreciated** against the euro). So the **currency index number** for 2009 is: $\frac{1.04}{1.36} \times 100 = \textbf{76.5}$.

Indices came up earlier on page 91 and are also covered in the Maths Skills section, on page 185.

2) This shows that the exchange rate for pounds to euros **decreased** by **23.5%** (100 − 76.5 = 23.5).

3) In 2008, the **pound** to **Canadian dollar** exchange rate was **1.98**. This **decreased** to 1.78 in 2009. By doing similar calculations as those done above, this gives the **currency index number** for 2009 as **89.9**.

4) This shows that the exchange rate for pounds to Canadian dollars **decreased** by **10.1%**.

5) So the **index numbers** show that the **pound depreciated** against the **euro more** than it depreciated **against** the **Canadian dollar** from 2008 to 2009.

6) The currency index numbers for 2008 to 2018 have been **plotted** on the **graph on the right**. Currency index graphs can be used to see **trends** over **several years**. So the graph on the right shows that the **depreciation** of the **pound** against the **euro** was **23.5%** by 2009. The pound then appreciated, so that **by 2016** the exchange rate was the same as in 2008. It then depreciated again to be **17% lower** than in 2008 **by 2018**.

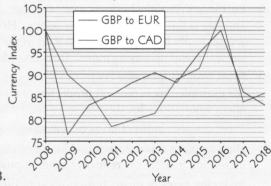

7) You can also **use the graph** to **work out** the **exchange rate** for any given year, if you know the base exchange rate, by using the equation: $\text{exchange rate} = \frac{\text{currency index number}}{100} \times \text{base exchange rate}$.

For example, in 2011, the pound to Canadian dollar exchange rate had a **currency index number** of about **78**, so you can calculate the exchange rate: $\text{exchange rate} = \frac{78}{100} \times 1.98 = \textbf{1.54}$.

Warm-Up Questions

Answers to warm-up Qs 1-3 are on page 194.

Q1 If 1 Australian dollar = £0.55, convert £80 into Australian dollars.

Q2 In January 2017 (the base year), the exchange rate for the pound (GBP) to South Korean won (KRW) was £1 = 1480 KRW. In January 2018, it was £1 = 1441 KRW. Calculate the currency index number in 2018.

Q3 Using the graph above, calculate the 2015 exchange rate for pounds to euros. The base exchange rate is 1.36.

Exam Question

Q1 What is meant by the depreciation of the pound against the euro? [2 marks]

Q2 Biznom imports components from Russia and exports its finished products to Germany. The pound is forecast to appreciate against both the Russian ruble and the euro. Assess how this will influence the business decisions of Biznom. [10 marks]

I traded a cup of honey for a bushel of wheat...

...a pretty sweet exchange rate. Keep going over these pages until you really understand them — they're pretty tricky.

Government and the Economy

Nothing exciting ever started with the words "Government and the Economy". If it said "A Red Velvet Cupcake and Vanilla Ice Cream", well, that would be a different story... Maybe treat yourself to one after revising these two pages.

Government Spending Influences the Economy

1) **Government spending** is one way that the government influences the economy.

2) **Government spending** on things like social services, health and education pumps money into the economy. **Changes** in government spending **affect firms** within the economy controlled by that government. For example:

   - Changing government expenditure on **welfare benefits** has a **quick** impact on the economy, because people who receive benefits will instantly have **more** (or less) **money** available to spend, which means that businesses may see **demand** for their products **go up** (or down).

   - Government spending on **infrastructure** such as roads has a **slower** effect on the economy. This spending can improve **supply routes** for businesses so that they can get things like **raw materials faster** and **more cheaply**. It can also increase **customer access** to businesses, so **demand** could **increase**.

Taxation Rates Affect Economic Activity

1) The **government taxes people** and **businesses** and can **change taxation rates**.

2) **Income tax** taxes **individuals** on their **income**. **High** tax rates for individuals reduce consumers' **disposable income**, so people tend to **spend less** — this is bad news for businesses because it's likely to **reduce** their **turnover**. **Low** tax rates encourage people to spend, so businesses make **bigger profits**.

3) Businesses are taxed on **profits** — sole traders and partnerships pay **income tax**, and limited companies pay **corporation tax**. These are **direct taxes**. **High** tax rates for **businesses** mean that **profits after tax** are **reduced**.

4) Businesses also pay **business rate** tax based on the **value** of their **premises**. The rate is the same all over the country. However, because **property values** are generally **higher** in the **South** than in the North, **businesses** in the South generally end up **paying more**. This can **reduce** their **competitiveness**.

   Businesses that operate in more than one country can strategically locate their operations in countries with low tax rates — this can be controversial as many people see it as the business dodging taxes.

5) Firms want to **minimise** costs, so tax rates affect their **decisions**. For example, **tax** is paid on **properties** and **vehicles**, so this can affect where firms **locate** themselves and whether to **hire** or **buy** vehicles.

6) There are also **indirect taxes on spending**, e.g. VAT, and taxes on pollution, tobacco and alcohol.

7) **High** tax rates **discourage** individuals from **spending**, and businesses from **expanding**. Increasing income tax **reduces spending power**, **cuts demand** and **lowers economic activity**.

8) **Reducing taxes** or giving businesses **subsidies** (financial assistance) encourages businesses to expand.

9) The effect of a tax cut or tax rise depends on the **income elasticity** (p.16) of the good or service. Rises in income tax hit **luxury goods** (e.g. expensive kitchen appliances) harder than **staple goods** (e.g. petrol or bread).

A Business Cycle Diagram Shows Changes in the Economy

Very high rates of growth are usually followed by **recession**, so governments try to keep growth at a **sustainable level**, by changing the Bank of England base rate, taxation and government spending.

1) In a **boom**, GDP is high. As production reaches **maximum capacity**, there are **shortages** and price increases. Shortages of skilled labour mean **wages rise**.

2) In a **recession**, incomes start to go down, and **demand** goes down. Business **confidence** is reduced.

3) In a **slump**, GDP is at a **low**. Businesses close factories and there are a lot of **redundancies**. **Unemployment** is **high**. A lot of businesses become **insolvent** (p.76) or go **bankrupt**.

4) In a **recovery** or upswing period, **production increases**, and **employment** increases. People have more money to spend.

Gross domestic product (GDP) is a measure of the value of all final products in a country.

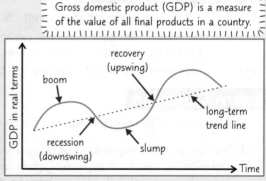

5) Like changes in taxation rates, how much a business is **affected** by this cycle depends on the **income elasticity of demand** of its products. Businesses selling **income elastic** products such as luxury holidays find that demand shoots **up** in a **recovery**, and dives **down** in a **recession**. Firms selling **income inelastic** products such as staple foods **aren't affected** all that much by these changes.

Government and the Economy

Changes in the Business Cycle Affect Businesses

1) Businesses will need to be able to **react** to changes in the **business cycle**.

2) The **state** of the **economy**, whether local or global, influences the **decisions** that businesses make:

> 1) During **booms**, businesses can **raise prices**. This **increases profitability**, and it **slows down demand** a bit.
>
> 2) In a long-lasting boom, businesses **invest** in **production** facilities to increase capacity. They may come out with **new products** to take advantage of increased consumer income.
>
> 3) During **recessions**, businesses may make workers **redundant** to **save wage costs** and **increase capacity utilisation** (see p.84-85).
>
> 4) During a **local recession**, businesses can **market** their goods elsewhere in the country — a local shop could market online. In a **national recession**, businesses can **market** their products **overseas**.
>
> 5) When a national recession or slump lasts a long time, some businesses choose to **relocate** abroad.
>
> 6) In general, **global upswings** provide growth opportunities for **everyone**, and **global recessions** are bad for **everyone**.

The Business Environment can be Affected by Economic Uncertainty

1) A **microeconomy** is a part of the economy that consists only of the **individual consumers** and **firms** that **make up** a specific **market**.

2) The **macroeconomy** is the economy as a **whole** (including **all businesses and consumers**).

3) The business environment can be affected by **microeconomic** and **macroeconomic uncertainty**.

The business environment includes all of the factors that can affect a business and its day-to-day running.

He'd made it, but Abbas was uncertain about getting down.

4) **Examples** of **microeconomic uncertainty** can include:
   - A **new competitor** entering a market that a business is in can lead to **uncertainty** over the **number of customers** that the original business will have in the future.
   - A **shortage** in a **raw material** can lead to uncertainty for a business that needs it, as their **suppliers** might change their prices, which will affect the business's **costs**.

5) Examples of **macroeconomic uncertainty** can include:
   - A **change in government** may lead to **uncertainty** over the **availability of government spending** in the future.
   - The decision of a **country** to **leave a trade agreement** with another country could lead to **uncertainty** over **future exchange rates**.
   - Changes to **business or employment legislation** by the government can lead to **uncertainty** over exactly how the **legislation** will **affect** things like **customers**, **sales** and **profits** when the legislation comes into effect.

6) A business could use **economic forecasting** or **scenario planning** (see p.152 if you're doing the full A-level course) to try to **predict** the **effects** of uncertainty or to **create plans** to help deal with it.

Warm-Up Questions

Q1 Give one way that government spending could change and what effect this could have on a business.

Q2 Give one way that an increase in corporation tax could affect a company.

Q3 What is the business cycle?

Q4 Give two examples of how the business environment could be affected by economic uncertainty.

PRACTICE QUESTIONS

Exam Question

Q1 A car manufacturer imports steel to be used in the production of cars. It then exports its finished cars abroad.
   a) The manufacturer's country is currently experiencing a boom.
      Explain one action the manufacturer should take to ensure it is able to continue to meet demand. [4 marks]
   b) Assess two impacts on the manufacturer if the government increases tax rates on steel imports. [8 marks]

Toadstools and gemstones are important parts of the eco-gnomey...

Nice and simple — businesses are affected by changes in government spending, tax rates and the business cycle. And economic uncertainty can affect the business environment. Throw some fish in a barrel and have a piece of cake.

Business Legislation

Legislation is just a fancy word for a law, or a set of laws. That's about as fun as these pages get, I'm afraid...

The **Law** Protects **Customers** and **Consumers**

Certain laws protect customers and consumers — these laws affect the **functional decisions** made by the different departments of a business. For example, the research and development, manufacturing and marketing departments need to bear the laws in mind when **developing**, **making** and **marketing** products.

- The **Trade Descriptions Act (1968)** requires that businesses don't **mislead** consumers with **false descriptions** on **packaging** or **advertising materials**.
- The **Sale of Goods Act (1979)**, the **Sale and Supply of Goods Act (1994)**, and the **Sale and Supply of Goods to Consumers Regulations (2002)** set out the **rights** of customers. These laws mean that goods must be **fit for their purpose** and of **satisfactory quality**.
- The **Consumer Protection Act (1987)** says that **new consumer goods** must be **safe**. There are also other, **more specific regulations**, e.g. sofa and chair cushions must be made of **fire resistant** materials.
- The **Data Protection Act (2018)** stops the **misuse of data**. Amongst other things, it stops firms **holding on to customer data** beyond the point it's needed, and ensures data is only used for its **specified purpose**.

The **Law** Protects the **Community** and the **Environment**

1) The **Environment Agency** is sponsored by the government to protect and improve the environment. One of its responsibilities is to **regulate businesses** that release pollutants into water or onto the land. Industrial processes which only release pollution into the **air** are regulated by **local authorities**.

2) Businesses have to ensure their **production processes** don't cause **unnecessary pollution**, or risk **heavy fines**.

3) Businesses must get **authorisation** from the local council before carrying out processes which create **smoke** or make **noise**. **Environmental health officers** can force factories to **stop making noise** at night if it's disturbing **local residents**.

4) Here are some examples of specific laws and directives that affect businesses:

- The EU directive on **Waste Electrical and Electronic Equipment (WEEE)** forces businesses to increase recycling of waste electrical and electronic equipment, much of which previously ended up in landfill sites. Since August 2005, manufacturers have had increased responsibility for ensuring that goods such as computers, TVs and VCRs are recycled once they've come to the end of their useful life.
- The Landfill Tax was introduced in 1996 to reduce the amount of waste being dumped in landfill sites.
- The EU Packaging Waste Directive forces businesses to increase the recycling of packaging. There are targets for the percentage of wood, paper, glass and plastic that must be recycled.
- The Climate Change Act requires UK PLCs to report greenhouse gas emissions in their annual reports. The idea is that if these are made public, businesses are more likely to try to reduce them.
- The government also has some 'green subsidy schemes'. For example, the Renewable Heat Incentive pays businesses that use renewable energy to heat their buildings.

5) Businesses must factor in the **cost** of complying with these laws in any **decisions** they make. Decisions about the **materials** or **processes** used might also be influenced by environmental laws.

6) Businesses breaking laws will be **fined** or **prosecuted**.

7) A business that follows the government's **ethical** or **environmental initiatives** can be appealing **to consumers**. Some businesses are even able to turn environmental **restrictions** into **unique selling points** of their products — e.g. by being the most **environmentally friendly** business in the market.

8) The government **funds organisations** that encourage more efficient use of raw materials, such as the **Waste and Resources Action Programme (WRAP)**. WRAP works with businesses to achieve a '**circular economy**' which keeps resources in use for as **long as possible**. As well as protecting the **environment**, it helps businesses **save money** and appeals to customers concerned about the environment. For example:

Through a **WRAP initiative**, Britvic™ launched **Robinsons Squash'd®** in 2014. These are **ultra-concentrated** tiny bottles of squash. **Less packaging** means **less environmental impact** and also reduced transportation costs.

Business Legislation

There are **Policies** About **Competition**...

1) **Fair competition** means businesses are motivated to provide **good quality products** for **reasonable prices**. If they don't, customers will simply go **elsewhere**. Competition also encourages businesses to **innovate** and develop **new products**, as well as provide customers with **choice** by **product differentiation** (see p.11).

2) **Competition policies** encourage fair competition. In the UK, the **Competition Act 1998** sets out the laws on competition and what constitutes unfair business practices. It's the job of the **Competition and Markets Authority (CMA)** to prevent businesses breaking competition laws. **EU competition law** also regulates competition across the EU. Businesses breaking these laws can be given **big fines** or be criminally prosecuted.

3) Businesses need to understand competition laws so they **don't break them** and also so they can watch out for **competitors breaking them** — they'd want to report them so the authorities could **investigate**.

4) **Competition law** means that, amongst other things:

Deciding not to divide up the cakes led to some fierce competition.

- Businesses can't conspire to **fix prices** — where an agreement is made to keep the price of a product above a fixed amount. For example, in the early 2000s several sportswear retailers were fined for fixing prices of football shirts.
- Businesses can't conspire with competitors to **limit production** so that higher prices can be charged due to a **shortage**.
- Businesses can't **divide up the market** to avoid having to compete. For example, one business sells only in Europe if another sells only in Asia.

...and About **Abusing** a **Dominant Position**

1) Businesses have a **dominant position** if they have a market share of **at least 50%**.

2) Some **laws** to stop businesses **abusing** this position are:

- Dominant businesses can't demand '**exclusivity**' — that wholesalers or retailers **only** buy from them.
- They can't demand that retailers must buy a **second type of product** in order to buy the popular product they actually want (known as **tying**).
- Businesses can't sell goods at a **loss** to force smaller competitors **out of the market** (**predatory pricing**).

Warm-Up Questions

Q1 Explain how consumer protection laws can affect the decisions made by a business when marketing a product.

Q2 Give two advantages to businesses of following environmental laws.

Q3 What is the purpose of competition policies?

Exam Question

Q1 Ados Soda is a UK manufacturer of soft drinks that has set up its production plant in a residential area. Ados Soda faces a lot of competition in the soft drinks market so it has developed a new type of soft drink that isn't available from any of its competitors. However, the production processes for this new product are very different to those used to produce its regular soft drinks, and produce more smoke and noise. The production processes also create a lot of waste water that Ados Soda needs to buy a permit to be able to dispose of. The UK government has made changes to environmental legislation that reduce the amount of smoke and noise pollution that businesses are allowed to produce, and increase the price of permits for waste disposal. Assess how these changes to environmental legislation could affect the success of Ados Soda.

[12 marks]

I fought the law and the law took my profits and stopped me from trading...

Most businesses comply with the law, but there'll always be some who try to get away with cheating customers, selling dangerous tat or polluting the environment. The law's there to make sure that firms obey the rules or face the music.

Employment Legislation

Employment legislation aims to make things fairer for workers, and stop employers taking advantage of employees. Employers that are found to be breaking employment legislation can be fined or prosecuted.

Labour Legislation Controls What Rights Employees Have

1) An employee has a legal right to **fair treatment** while at work, as does anyone looking for employment.

2) The **Equality Act 2010 protects** employees from **discrimination** based on age, gender, race, sexual orientation, religion, disability, pregnancy, etc. These things are known as '**protected characteristics**'.

3) This Act **simplified** things by **replacing** several previous anti-discrimination acts, such as the **Race Relations Act (1976)** and the **Sex Discrimination Act (1975)**. It reflects the content of the **EU's Equal Treatment Directive**.

4) There are **two types** of discrimination — **direct** and **indirect**:

- **Direct discrimination** is treating someone **less favourably** because they have a protected characteristic, e.g. not employing someone because of a **disability**, or paying women **less** than men doing the **same job**.

- **Indirect discrimination** is when everyone is **treated the same** but it has a **worse effect** on one group of people than on others. For example, a rule that employees must **not wear head coverings** could be indirect discrimination against some **religions**.

5) Employers have to make '**reasonable adjustments**' for workers with **disabilities**, such as installing ramps.

6) **Parents** can ask to **work flexibly** (see p.31), and employers can only refuse for a **good business reason**. **Men** with young children who are **refused** flexible working could claim that it is **direct sex discrimination** if **women** with young children have had flexible working requests **approved**.

Discrimination Laws Affect Businesses

Recruitment

1) Employers aren't allowed to **state** in job adverts that candidates must be a particular age, race, gender, etc. They can't use **discriminatory language**, e.g. advertising for a "waitress" excludes men.

2) Businesses are only allowed to advertise for someone of a specific age, gender, etc. if it's a **genuine requirement** of the job — e.g. a female toilet attendant for ladies' toilets.

3) Businesses have to make **decisions** about who to employ without discriminating. They have to be able to **justify** why they gave a job to a particular candidate, in case an unsuccessful candidate takes them to a **tribunal** (see below).

4) **Avoiding discrimination** when recruiting means that businesses will recruit a more **diverse workforce**. This means they'll have a wider range of **skills**, **talents** and **experiences** to draw upon.

Pay

1) Businesses have to give male and female employees the **same pay** for work of **equal value**. They're entitled to the same **benefits** too (e.g. a company car).

2) Not paying fairly can result in a fall in the **quality of work** and poor **staff retention**, as well as having to pay **compensation** and **legal fees** if taken to tribunals.

Promotions and Redundancies

1) Discrimination laws mean everyone should have the **same opportunity** to get **promoted**. For example, businesses can't just **promote older people** because they think **young people** are likely to change jobs.

2) If businesses need to make **redundancies**, they can't **deliberately** **select** staff who are, for example, older or disabled.

Employment Tribunals Can Settle Disputes

1) If employees feel that they've been treated **unfairly** by their employers they can make a claim to a **tribunal**.

2) At a tribunal, representatives of the employer and the employee put forward their cases, and a **tribunal judge** (or sometimes a tribunal panel) decides who's in the right.

3) The employer might have to pay **compensation** or give the employee their job back in an **unfair dismissal** case.

Employment Legislation

Employers Have to Pay Staff a Minimum Amount

1) The **National Minimum Wage** and **National Living Wage** (you met these on page 30) prevent employees from being paid unfairly low wages.

> The National Living Wage is **controversial** because it's **lower** than the **independently calculated** living wage. Some employers **voluntarily** pay employees the independently calculated living wage — this can **increase motivation**, **reduce absenteeism** and allow the business to market themselves as an **ethical employer**.

2) Employers who are found to have underpaid their staff have to **reimburse** their staff with the total amount that they've been underpaid and can also be 'named and shamed', **fined** up to **£20 000** or even prosecuted.

An Employment Contract Sets Out the Conditions of Employment

1) A **new employee** will receive an **employment contract** (see page 30) when they start working for a **new employer**. This contract sets out the **various duties and rights** of both the employee and the employer.

2) Employees are entitled to receive a **written statement** of employment within **two months** of starting work.

3) There are some **responsibilities** that are **common** to all employers and employees, for example:

- Employees are entitled to paid holiday. In April 2009, the European Working Time Directive gave full-time workers the right to 28 days of paid holiday per year, including bank holidays.
- Employees have the right to paid maternity or paternity leave, although usually not on full pay.
- Employees have to attend work when they're supposed to, and be on time.
- Employees must be willing to carry out any reasonable task that's asked of them.

Businesses Must Follow Health and Safety Laws

1) Employees have the right to a **safe** working environment. **Health and safety legislation** is there to ensure that this happens.

2) The **Health and Safety at Work Act (1974)** states that the employer must ensure the working environment is **safe**. For example, they may need to make sure that any electrical equipment or machinery are safe **to use** and **work around**.

3) The Health and Safety Executive (HSE) is responsible for **inspecting businesses** and **enforcing** health and safety **laws**. For example, a construction company could be **fined** if it doesn't **provide safety barriers** to prevent people from falling from scaffolding.

4) Businesses must **select someone** to help them **keep** to health and safety **laws** — they may be someone from **inside** or **outside** the business. This can **increase costs** for the business if it needs to **train** an employee or **hire someone new**.

5) Some businesses might try to **ignore** health and safety laws to **cut costs**. However, HSE **encourages workers** to **let them know** if their employer is breaking the law.

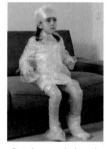

Rosa's grandad took health and safety a bit too far.

Warm-Up Questions

Q1 Give two ways that employment legislation protects employees' rights to fair treatment at work.

Q2 What is the purpose of health and safety legislation?

PRACTICE QUESTIONS

Exam Question

Q1 FrankenZ is a UK business that manufactures and sells computer parts, including electrical components and computer accessories. It employs 35 skilled staff that design the electrical components, and 60 unskilled staff to make all of FrankenZ's products. The UK government has recently announced that the National Minimum and National Living hourly wages are to increase by 3%. Assess two changes that FrankenZ may make following this change. **[8 marks]**

Can tribunals settle disputes about whose turn it is to make the tea?...

Businesses have to take all these laws into account when making decisions. For example, an employer may try to save money by only recruiting under 18s, as they have a lower minimum wage. However, if an older applicant takes the employer to a tribunal and they're found guilty of age discrimination, they might have to fork out loads of money.

Competition

Competition is when two or more businesses compete for something (kinda obvious, really).
Like last night at the supermarket, when Susan and I squabbled over the last punnet of raspberries...

Businesses in a Market **Compete** With Each Other

1) A highly competitive market has a **high number** of businesses that are offering **similar goods or services**.

2) An **increase in competition** means that businesses might lose customers. In order to avoid this, they might **increase** their **marketing costs** or spend more on **improving** or **diversifying** their products. Alternatively, businesses might **cut** costs to keep the price of their products lower than their competitors' to **increase demand**.

Competition between the business owners for more customers took a pretty unusual turn.

3) This can **benefit** the consumer as it results in businesses bringing **new** and **innovative products** to the market. It can also **reduce** the **prices** of existing products within the market.

4) Competition amongst a business's **suppliers** can **reduce costs** for the business, for example if the price of its raw materials decreased. These **savings** can be **passed** on to **consumers** in the form of **cheaper products**.

5) However, **heavy competition** can have **negative effects** on consumers as it can lead to businesses failing.

6) For example, **airlines** are in **fierce competition** with one another. In 2017, the airline Monarch **closed down**, partly because **competition** was so **fierce** and Monarch **couldn't match** its **competitors** so began making large losses. This led to customers having their **flights cancelled**.

7) Firms in competitive markets need to **monitor** their **rivals** and their **costs** (such as **marketing costs** or **production costs**) to prevent themselves losing money.

Different Markets Have Different Types of Competition Between Businesses

Perfect

1) **Perfect competition** is a theoretical type of competition where there are lots of firms in a market and they all compete on an **equal** basis — their **products** are pretty much **identical**, and they all charge a similar price.

2) Businesses would need to **keep costs low** to keep prices low, otherwise demand would be taken by the competition.

3) However, they would also need to keep a **high quality** of product to keep a good level of demand.

Oligopoly

1) In an **oligopoly**, a small number of large firms **dominate** the market and charge similar prices. For a business to get ahead, they will focus on **marketing** and **brand image** to increase demand, so **marketing costs** will be **high**.

2) Oligopoly firms tend to behave in a competitive environment by **improving** their **customer service** or by improving the **quality** of the **product** offered.

3) For example, the **mobile phone operating system** market is dominated by Apple®'s iOS® and Google™'s Android™. The two businesses are in **close competition** with one another and so charge **similar prices** to ensure that they don't lose customers simply because they're **more expensive**. Instead, the businesses compete on **branding** and **marketing**. It's extremely difficult for **new businesses** to **enter** this market as Apple® and Google™ have **established brands** and **marketing**, as well as **loyal customer bases**.

Monopoly

1) A monopoly is where one business has complete control over its market (p.97). There's no competition. A business with a monopoly can usually increase its prices without too much concern of the demand decreasing, and they are able to keep marketing costs low.

2) A monopoly will risk being fined if they act against the consumers' interests. For example, in 2017 Google™ was fined £2.1 billion by the EU for abusing its monopoly on internet searching by promoting its own online shopping comparison service rather than other similar services.

Competition

A **Large Market** Usually has a **High Number** of **Competing Businesses**

1) **Market size** is the **number of buyers** and the **number of sellers** within a market.

2) Because **larger markets** have **more potential customers**, **more businesses** are **attracted** to these markets. That means that **larger markets** tend to have **higher levels of competition** than smaller markets, as there are **more businesses** or suppliers operating in the market.

3) Before entering a market, a business will need to **conduct market research** to determine the **size** of the market and estimate **how many customers** would **actually be willing to buy** its product.

4) Carrying out market research means that a business is better able to **make decisions** on how to **market its product** successfully. For example, if entering a **small market**, a business might decide to use more **direct advertising**, such as **targeted online advertising**.

See page 19 for more ways to promote products.

5) Market research will also tell a business the **level of competition** within a market.

6) The **number of competitors** in a market will affect the business's **marketing strategy**. For example, if there are **lots** of **competing firms** in a market then a business might **invest heavily** in **promotion** and sell at **low prices**.

7) The level of competition in a market and the size of the market will also affect a business's **strategy** for **launching a new product** into the market. For example, if there's a **lot of competition** in a market then a business would need to **make sure** it has **enough stock** of the new product so that it can **meet initial customer demand**, otherwise it may **lose customers** to those competitors who were able to **copy** the product quickly **following the launch**.

Jörgen was going to launch his products into brave new markets, far away from all the competition.

The **Level of Competition** within a Market can **Change**

1) Businesses will often try to **leave small** or **shrinking** markets and move into **growing** or **large**, **mature** markets.

2) Businesses will move from smaller to larger markets because a **larger** market size allows for more **potential** for **growth**, which could lead to **increased profits** for the business. However, because of this, a large or growing market may **attract** other **new entrants**, resulting in **increased competition**.

Warm-Up Questions

Q1 What is meant by a highly competitive market?
Q2 Why might a large market have a lot of competition?

Exam Questions

Q1 What is meant by market size? [2 marks]

Q2 Riteo Ltd is an established company in the technology market.
Gyreo Ltd is a new company that competes with Riteo Ltd.
Explain how the arrival of Gyreo Ltd could affect the business costs of Riteo Ltd. [4 marks]

Q3 Puff! is a popular, established bakery that has existed in a small town for 20 years.
A new bakery called Choux is due to open in the same town as Puff! and looks set to offer similar products.
Assess what business decisions Puff! might need to make due to the arrival of Choux. [12 marks]

Ol' Suse won, of course — I had to settle for blackberries instead...

Market size can have a big impact on the level of competition. Many businesses would prefer to be in a large market, so they've got plenty of customers and profits. However, we all know that when someone sees you with something great, they want it too. This means that other businesses will be attracted to larger markets, increasing competition.

Corporate Objectives

Businesses need to have aims to give them something to work towards. Otherwise they could end up not selling anything, wandering around bumping into walls... that kind of thing. My aim was to make these pages the most interesting pages ever to be found in a book. If I'd have set more realistic objectives, I might have achieved it... sigh.

A Mission Statement Tells You About a Business's Intentions

1) The **mission** of a business is its **overall purpose** or **main corporate aims**. The **mission statement** is a written **description** of these aims. Mission statements are intended to make all **stakeholders** aware of what the business does and why, and to **encourage** all employees to **work towards** its aims.

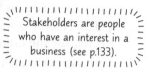
Stakeholders are people who have an interest in a business (see p.133).

2) Mission statements tell you the **purpose** of the business, and can include information such as its **values**, its **standards**, how it will **achieve** its mission, who the **customers** are and what makes the business **unique**.

3) Mission statements can give clues about the business's **beliefs**. For example, a mission statement that mentions **ethics** and **principles** gives a big hint that **ethical practice** is important as well as **profitability**.

4) Mission statements can give staff a sense of **shared purpose**, and encourage them to work towards **common goals** — having the **cooperation** of all the staff makes it more likely that a business will achieve its aims.

Geraldine didn't need a mission statement to achieve her aim.

5) On the other hand, businesses **don't** have to prove that what's in their mission statement is **accurate**, so they can say what they think consumers want to hear, without having to do anything about it. But this is **bad practice**, and a business's **reputation** will be **damaged** if consumers find that its actions don't reflect its stated values.

6) A mission statement's use is **limited** as it doesn't go into detail about **how** the mission will be **achieved** — it doesn't set out any **corporate strategies** or **tactics** (p.104).

A Business's Mission Statement Needs to be Clear and to the Point

You **need** to be able to **critically appraise** (assess the **effectiveness** of) a business's **mission statement**.

> **Example:**   Golden Hour is an **adult tutoring** business with a mission statement that reads:
>
> > *"To empower our customers to have individual pride in their personal growth."*
>
> 1) The **purpose** of the business **isn't very clear** from the mission statement and it would be **difficult** to measure whether it had achieved its aims.
>
> 2) The mission statement doesn't include **how** Golden Hour will **achieve** its aims. So stakeholders might be **sceptical** about the mission statement and might not have much **confidence** in the business.
>
> 3) The mission statement is clearly **aimed** at **customers** more than other stakeholders. This could have a negative effect — for example, investors might not feel **confident** enough about whether the **business can succeed** and so may decide **not to invest** in the business.
>
> 4) It's clear from the mission statement that Golden Hour **values** its **customers**.
>
> 5) The choice of **language** might put some customers off. It may be better to use, for example, **'you'** instead of **'our customers'** as this would make the mission statement feel more **targeted** and **personal**.

Corporate Objectives

Businesses Set Objectives at Different Levels

1) Businesses set **objectives** to enable them to achieve their mission. Objectives turn the corporate aims of a business into **specific goals** that must be met in the **short-** to **medium-term**.

2) The diagram on the right shows the hierarchy of objectives. They can be set at the **corporate** or **departmental** level.

Mission Statement

↓

Corporate Objectives

↓

Departmental Objectives

3) **Corporate objectives** are the goals of the business as a **whole**. The corporate objectives will depend on the **size** of the business. A new shop owner might focus on trying to **survive** (p.48), while a big international company will want to **grow bigger** and **diversify** its product range.

4) **Departmental objectives** (sometimes called **functional objectives**) are the objectives of each **department**. They're more **detailed** than corporate objectives, and they are **specific** to each department. Businesses need to set **departmental objectives** that will help them **achieve** their **corporate objectives**. Whenever a corporate objective is set, managers in the business have to look at how their department can help to achieve the objective, and set **departmental objectives** that will **contribute** to achieving the corporate objective.

5) Businesses set objectives for lots of reasons. If an objective is agreed upon, managers can make sure that **everyone** is working towards a **goal**, and **coordination** between departments should improve. Working towards an objective can also be **motivating** for employees. Objectives are really useful in **decision-making**, as they make it easier to see what the business is trying to achieve.

6) **Any objectives** that are set should be **aligned** with the **mission statement**, otherwise the business can **lose credibility** with its **stakeholders**.

7) Managers can **compare performance** with their **objectives** to **measure** the success of the business and **review** their decisions.

Objectives should be Specific, Measurable, Agreed, Realistic and Timely

To be effective, an objective should be '**SMART**' — specific, measurable, agreed, realistic and timely.

Specific   **Vague objectives** like "to improve quality" **don't** really tell staff what they're supposed to be aiming for. Making them more **specific**, e.g. "to reduce the number of items produced that have defects", means that the business is more likely to **achieve** them.

Measurable If the objective **isn't measurable**, the business **won't know** if it's achieved it or not. E.g. "to increase profit by 5%" is a measurable objective, but "to improve the business" isn't.

Agreed   Everyone who's going to be involved in **achieving** the objective needs to **know** about it and **agree** to it. E.g. if the objective is to increase sales, the sales manager and salespeople will all need to agree to it.

Realistic   There's no point setting objectives that are **too ambitious**, e.g. tripling sales within 12 months, or achieving a 95% market share. **Impossible objectives** just **demotivate** staff.

Timely   There should be a **specific timeframe** that the objective has to be achieved in. E.g. the objective might be to increase revenue by 5% within 12 months. If there's **no time limit**, staff won't see the objective as **urgent** — they might think they don't need to worry about achieving it because as long as it gets done at some time in the future then it doesn't matter.

Warm-Up Questions

Q1 State what a mission statement is and give one limitation of mission statements.

Q2 What does SMART stand for in the term 'SMART objectives'?

PRACTICE QUESTIONS

Exam Question

Q1 Fabia's Frocks owns 200 stores across the UK. None of its current products contain any recycled materials. One of its corporate objectives is "To increase the number of products made from recycled materials to 80%, in half of our stores, within the next five years." Assess how effective this objective is for Fabia's Frocks.   [10 marks]

Your mission, should you choose to accept it, is to revise these pages...

OK, mission statements — make sure you know what they are and how to assess them. Objectives — think SMART.

Corporate Strategies

You should be familiar with business objectives now — these pages are about how they're linked to strategy. How fun.

Strategies are Plans for Achieving Objectives

1) A **strategy** (or strategic decision) is a more long-term **plan of action** (compared to tactics, see below) developed to achieve a business's **objectives**. A **corporate strategy's** based on achieving **corporate objectives**.

2) A strategy can only be put in place once an organisation has **outlined** its aims and objectives (see p.102-103).

3) All businesses need to have a strategy. In **small firms**, these plans may not be **formally** written down. Strategies can simply be a **sequence** of business decisions made over time with the aim of reaching a particular **goal**, e.g. expanding into a new market segment. In **larger firms**, strategy is usually more **clearly defined** because it will influence the plans of **individual departments**, such as marketing and HR.

4) **Tactics** (or tactical decisions) are **short-term plans**. They're the **techniques** that a business will use to achieve its **overall strategy**.

5) For example, a business's **strategic decision** might be to **expand** its **production capacity** — a **tactical decision** to help achieve this could be to **recruit more staff**.

6) Tactics can sometimes be used to **react** to an **opportunity** or **threat**, which means they may **not always match** the business's **strategy**. For example, after a competitor **cuts** its **prices**, a business's tactic might be to **cut its own** prices, even if its strategy is to **increase profit**.

7) The **distinction** between **strategic** and **tactical decisions** can be **important**, especially for **managers**, as it gives a rough **time frame** for the decision. It also indicates how likely it is that the decision will **change** — a **tactical** decision is more likely to change in response to external influences.

8) Strategic and tactical decisions can impact **different resources** in a business, such as **human**, **physical** and **financial** resources:

Human	A business might need to consider whether its **staff** are **skilled** enough to carry out the **work needed** for the new strategies or tactics. For example, a **long-term strategy** to **improve productivity** might require **recruitment** of new staff, or it may require **investment** in **new technologies**, which could lead to **redundancies** as certain jobs are **no longer required**.
Physical	A business might need to **invest** in **new** or **updated** physical resources. For example, a **tactical decision** to **increase production** might mean the business needs to invest in another machine used in the **production** line.
Financial	A business would need to consider how to **fund** its **decisions**. For example, a **long-term strategy** of **growth** and **expansion** may need to be **financed** through a **change of ownership** from a **Ltd company** to a **PLC** (see page 51).

Ansoff Suggested Four Different Options for Strategic Growth

Ansoff suggested **four** corporate **strategies** that a business can use to set its **direction** for growth and development.

1) **Market penetration** means trying to **increase** your **market share** in your **existing market**. E.g. if a company makes washing powder and currently has a 25% market share, it might try to achieve a 30% market share using **sales promotions**, **pricing strategies** and **advertising**. This strategy works best in a **growth market**. It **doesn't work well** in **saturated markets**, where demand for the product has stopped growing.

2) **New product development** is selling **new products** in your **existing markets**. It's best when the market has good **growth potential** and the business has a high market share, strong R&D (research and development) and a good **competitive advantage**.

3) **Market development** (or **market extension**) is selling **existing products** to **new markets**. It can be done through **repositioning** — this means that a business focuses on a **different segment of the market**. It needs to **research** the target market segment and work out how it can **adapt** its product or promotion to suit the needs of a different set of consumers. This might involve creating **new promotions** which **target** a different audience. Businesses can also target different market segments by using **new channels of distribution**, e.g. using **e-commerce** to sell **directly to consumers**. **Market development** can also be done by **expanding** into new geographical markets to exploit the same market segment (e.g. in a different country — see p.162).

4) **Diversification** means selling **new products** to **new markets**. Diversification is a **risky** strategy, as it involves moving into markets that the business may have **no experience** of. It's used when a business really needs to reduce their dependence on a **limited product range** or if **high profits** are likely, which **reduces** the **risk**.

Corporate Strategies

Ansoff's Matrix can be Used to Look at Different Growth Strategies

1) **Ansoff's matrix** is a tool for comparing the **level of risk** involved with the different growth strategies. It helps **managers** to decide on a direction for **strategic growth**.

2) The **advantage** of Ansoff's matrix is that it doesn't just lay out potential strategies for growth — it also forces managers to think about the **expected risks** of moving in a certain direction.

3) One **disadvantage** of the matrix is that it fails to show that **market development** and **diversification** strategies also tend to require **significant change** in the **day-to-day workings** or **tactics** of the business.

4) **Product development** is less risky than diversification, and it works best for businesses that already have a strong **competitive advantage**.

5) **Market penetration** is the **least risky** strategy of all — so **most businesses** opt for this approach to start with.

6) Some people believe that Ansoff's matrix **oversimplifies** the **options** available for growth. For example, **diversification** doesn't have to be **completely unrelated** to what the business does currently. For example, in 2017, **IKEA®** bought **TaskRabbit**, an **online platform** for people such as **freelance decorators** and **furniture assemblers** to find jobs.

7) Ansoff's matrix isn't a **dynamic tool** as it doesn't take account of what a business's **competitors** are **doing** or how they may **react** to a business's chosen strategy.

8) Ansoff's matrix **isn't** as **useful** for **large**, **multinational** businesses. This is because it's likely they'll already be **operating** in each of the **four quadrants**. It's **more useful** for **small-** or **medium-sized** businesses that are established in a market and are **looking to grow**.

> SWOT (p.108) and PESTLE (p.109) analyses can be used alongside Ansoff's matrix to help choose a corporate strategy.

	Products	
	Existing	New
Existing (Markets)	Market penetration	Product development
New (Markets)	Market development or extension	Diversification

Increasing Risk →

Example: KFC®'s expansion from the USA market to the UK market is an example of market development. KFC® began operating in the USA in 1952 and extended its market by opening an outlet in Preston, UK, in 1965. This was the first American fast food chain to open in the UK. There are now over 750 outlets across the UK and Ireland. These outlets were run as a franchise by an independent company, KFC GB Ltd, until it was bought by PepsiCo in 1986.

KFC®'s market development strategy is the result of taking an existing product, its fast food business model, and developing it in a new market, the UK. Ansoff's matrix shows that this is a safer option than diversification.

Porter Suggested Three Generic Strategies to Gain Advantage

The three **generic corporate** strategies suggested by Porter are **competitive strategies**. They're based on giving a business an advantage through **low production costs** or **product differentiation**.

Cost Leadership
1) Cost leadership strategy calls for the lowest cost of production for a given level of quality. Big firms with large and efficient production facilities, benefiting from economies of scale, can use this strategy.
2) In a price war, the firm can maintain profitability while the competition suffers losses. If prices decline, the firm can stay profitable because of its low costs.

Differentiation
1) Differentiation strategy requires a product with unique attributes which consumers value, so they believe it's better than rival products. Unique products allow businesses to charge premium prices.
2) Businesses that are innovative, have strong branding and quality products can benefit from this strategy.
3) Risks include imitation by competitors and changes in consumer tastes.

Focus
1) Focus strategy concentrates on niche markets and either minimising costs or showing differentiation.
2) This strategy suits firms with fewer resources who can target markets with specific needs. A firm using this strategy usually has loyal customers, making it very hard for other firms to compete.

Corporate Strategies

Porter's **Generic Strategies** can be Put in a **Matrix**

1) Porter's **strategic matrix** shows the strategy a business is best placed to use based on its **competitive advantage** and its **market scope**. A business can be placed in a particular section depending on whether it's aimed at a **broad** or **narrow market** (also known as a niche market, see p.2), and whether it offers **cheaper** products than competitors or **unique**, **quality** products.

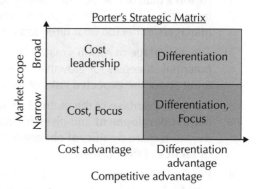

Porter's Strategic Matrix

2) For example, in the jewellery market, Accessorize sells products to a broad market at relatively low prices, so it would be placed in the **cost leadership** section of the matrix. Tiffany & Co.® sells high-quality products at premium prices, focusing on a narrow market, so it would fit into the **differentiation and focus** section.

3) Porter's strategic matrix may help **identify** a business that **hasn't got** a **clear focus** and is therefore **'stuck in the middle'** and at **risk of failure**. It could help to steer the business in a more **channelled direction**.

4) However, Porter's strategic matrix **oversimplifies** the **market structure**. It has a **narrow focus** on either **cost leadership** or **differentiation**, and doesn't account for businesses that **successfully achieve both**. Some businesses **successfully offer** a **range** of products. For example, Debenhams stocks **differentiated** brands **alongside cost leadership** brands.

5) Another disadvantage is that it only tells a business where it **currently sits** in the matrix and **doesn't** give **any information** on how to **improve**. For example, it doesn't help a business in a **dynamic market** where there are **fast-moving trends** and the business needs to be **quick** at **responding** to these changes.

Kay's Model Identifies **Three Capabilities** for a Business's Success

1) According to **Kay's model**, a **successful business strategy** for a business is one that's built on the **business's distinctive capability**.

2) A distinctive capability is something that a business is **good at** — it's something that **other businesses don't do**, that **sets it apart** from its competitors.

3) If a business successfully takes advantage of its distinctive capability, it will create **added value** for the business and therefore give it a **competitive advantage**.

Kay wasn't sure if her new cape was distinctive enough.

4) The **three distinctive capabilities** outlined by Kay are **architecture**, **reputation** and **innovation**.

5) Architecture describes the **relationships** a business has with its main **stakeholders** (p.133). If a business can maintain **strong** and **stable relationships** with its stakeholders then it's **more likely** to be **successful**. This is because the business will be better at **communicating** product and marketing information to the **relevant people**. This could **increase sales** for the business and save time during the production process.

6) A business can build a **reputation** by keeping **customers satisfied**. This can be through **good customer service** or by creating a **product** that is always of a **high quality**. Satisfied customers are likely to be **loyal** to the brand (p.49), which makes it **hard** for a **new business** to **compete** with it. Customers are also **more likely** to **recommend** a product to their family and friends, and this **word-of-mouth** advertising helps build a **strong brand** and give a business a **good reputation**.

7) A business that **invests resources** into **research** and **development** will be bringing **new** and **innovative** products to the market. The **USPs** of these products will give the business a **competitive advantage** (p.11).

> **Example:** Apple® has shown that it's **achieved all three** of Kay's distinctive capabilities.
>
> It has good **architecture** — for example, it has **stores** where customers can **try new products** and attend **workshops** with **employees** who are **motivated, informed** and have a **reputation** for **effective customer service**. This helps to build good **relationships** with the **customers**.
>
> It also has a **reputation** for **producing quality** mobile phones, tablets and computers. For many people, Apple® is the most **desired brand** of these products.
>
> Apple® shows **innovation** as it **invests** heavily in **product development** and it's often a **market leader** in **launching** a product with a **new feature**. For example, the iPhone® 8 has a wireless charging facility.

Corporate Strategies

Capabilities Need to be Sustainable and Appropriable

It's not enough for a business to have **distinctive capabilities**
— its capabilities also need to be **sustainable** and **appropriable**:

1) **Sustainable** means that once a business has **achieved** one of Kay's three capabilities, it needs to **maintain** this competitive advantage **over time**.

2) **Appropriable** means that one business is not able to **copy** the **distinct capability** that another business has **achieved**. New **ideas** and **inventions** can be protected through **trademarks** and **patents**, and **advertising slogans** and **logos** can be protected through taking out a **copyright**.

Charlie was annoyed that someone had already copied his hairstyle.

> **Example:** The distinctive glass bottle of Coca Cola® was patented in 1915 and is a good example of how this innovative design has been both sustainable and appropriable. The design is sustainable as it has lasted over 100 years and it can't be copied by anyone else, making it appropriable.

The Boston Matrix Helps Choose Which Products to Invest In

1) You met the **Boston matrix** on page 27. This **product portfolio analysis** is useful in helping a business **assess** where its individual **products** are in terms of their **market growth** and their **market share**.

2) It can help businesses come up with strategies about **product investment**, for example which products may need **more investment** to help them achieve their potential, and which products are **reaching the end** of their **lifetime**. However, the matrix does have its **limitations**:

    1) It's a simplified model as it only shows high and low market share and growth — it doesn't account for products that may have a medium market share or growth.

    2) Just because a product has a high market share, it doesn't mean that it's highly profitable, as it may have high costs too. This is also true of a product with high market growth, as the growth stage can be very costly, for example due to the need for investment in increased production.

    3) Growth rate and relative market share aren't the only indicators of profitability — profitability may be influenced by other factors that aren't covered by this model.

Warm-Up Questions

Q1 Define the term 'strategy'.

Q2 Which growth strategy shown in Ansoff's matrix has the lowest risk?

Q3 Describe Porter's generic strategies.

Q4 What is meant by a business's capability being described as appropriable?

Q5 Give two limitations to a business of using the Boston matrix to come up with business strategies.

Exam Questions

Q1 Rhubarb is a manufacturer of smartphones. It has just developed a smartphone with a unique feature and is ready to release the product to market. Rhubarb has decided not to trademark the feature due to the expense of doing so.
   a) Explain one effect on Rhubarb's financial resources when it releases the new phone to market. [4 marks]
   b) Assess two implications for Rhubarb of releasing its innovative product without a trademark, using your knowledge of Kay's model of distinctive capabilities. [8 marks]

Q2 Nice Noises is an established company in a niche market, specialising in making Wi-Fi home speakers and sound systems. Its main customer base is in England, where it currently has one manufacturing plant that employs around 500 staff. Nice Noises is looking to grow and has identified that it wants to either expand into other areas of the UK, such as Northern Ireland, Scotland and Wales, or that it wants to begin selling Bluetooth® portable speakers. Evaluate these two options and recommend which is best suited for Nice Noises. [20 marks]

The Matrix — helps me to choose between the red pill and the blue pill...

It's important that you understand what the different models mean, how they can be used and what their limitations are. You might have to apply any one of these models to any business in your exam. I bet you simply can't wait.

Choosing a Strategy

Businesses can use a couple of different analyses to decide on a corporate strategy — SWOT and PESTLE.

SWOT Analysis can be Applied to Any Business

Strengths
Weaknesses
Opportunities
Threats

1) A **SWOT analysis** is a four-factor model that details the **strengths, weaknesses, opportunities** and **threats** facing a business.

2) The **strengths** and **weaknesses** are **internal** factors that the business **can influence**.

3) **Internal factors** are **people** (e.g. employees), **marketing**, **finance** and **operations**.

4) The **opportunities** and **threats** are external factors that are **beyond the control** of the business. The business has to **understand** them in order to react appropriately.

5) **External factors** that might pose opportunities or threats include **political, economic, social, technological, legal** and **environmental** factors (**PESTLE** — see next page) and competitor behaviour.

Example A: Beasel's Tea Room is a small **tea shop** in a town-centre location. In 2014, it won an **award** in a local newspaper for "the best toasted teacake in the county". The tea shop only seats **22 customers**, but the owners have decided not to move to bigger premises because its current **location**, on a main shopping street, attracts **passing trade**. Instead, the manager has suggested that it starts selling **takeaway** drinks and cakes to take advantage of its popularity. The owners are concerned about reports that a big **coffee shop chain** is planning to open a branch nearby, as they don't think Beasel's Tea Room will be able to **compete** on price and may **lose business**.

> **Strengths:** Good reputation, good location, good quality products.
> **Weaknesses:** Small premises, cannot compete on price with chain stores.
> **Opportunities:** Selling cakes and drinks to take away could increase its market size.
> **Threats:** Possibility of a new competitor with lower prices.

Example B: Screen-it Cinemas is a **national cinema chain** that was recently **praised** for its **excellent customer service**. It has also recently released a very successful **ad campaign** that has gone **viral**. To **maintain** its high levels of customer service, Screen-it Cinemas **invests heavily** in its staff, which means that its **ticket prices** are slightly **higher** than other cinema chains. Despite this, **profits** have been **high enough** that Screen-it Cinemas could **invest** in new, so-called **"4D" technology**, which is "an immersive cinema experience using sounds, smells, air and vibrations". After several other cinema chains have **failed** due to the **rise** of **online film streaming** and a **reduction** in **customers**, the owners of Screen-it Cinemas are **concerned** for the future.

> **Strengths:** High quality customer service, well-known brand.
> **Weaknesses:** Prices are high so may be less attractive than competitors.
> **Opportunities:** "4D" technology may appeal to customers and increase ticket sales.
> **Threats:** There may be fewer customers as more people choose to stream films online.

SWOT Analysis Helps Businesses to Plan Strategies

1) **SWOT analysis** is a very useful tool in helping managers to make strategic and tactical decisions. It considers the business's **individual circumstances**, and is done in a **factual** and **objective** way.

2) In planning a strategy, managers will focus on **opportunities** that build on the business's **strengths**, on **converting weaknesses** into **strengths** and on **managing threats**.

3) For example, if a business has the **capacity** for **increased production**, this would be a **strength** in enabling it to **grow**. Or if a business's **strength** is making **high quality** products, it could develop a strategy for building its **brand** around quality.

4) One advantage of SWOT analysis is that it can easily be **redone** to take into account **changing conditions** (e.g. a changing economy or unforeseen events such as floods). This means that a business can **adapt** its strategy using the new SWOT analysis.

Keith was ready to do some swat analysis of his own.

5) SWOT analysis also lets the business know where it has a **competitive advantage** over its rivals — the business can change its **strategy** to focus on these elements.

Theme 3: Section 11 — Business Objectives and Strategy

Choosing a Strategy

PESTLE Analysis Looks at the External Influences on a Business

PESTLE analysis can look in more depth at the **political**, **economic**, **social**, **technological**, **legal** and **environmental** factors that present **opportunities** or **threats** to a business, to help managers make strategic and tactical decisions.

Political

Governmental **policy** on **taxation** and industry regulations can affect businesses. For example, a government that wants to **encourage new businesses** could introduce **lower rates** of **corporation tax** (tax on profit) which could help **smaller businesses grow**. It may also offer incentives for new businesses, such as **subsidy payments** to help with **start-up costs**. On the other hand, the government may **introduce taxes** on **unhealthy products** such as cigarettes, alcohol and sugar, to try to improve the **health** of the nation, **reducing** the **profits** for businesses involved in selling these products.

Economic

Economic influences can include changes in **consumer spending**, **interest rates**, **exchange rates** and **economic growth**. For example, a **strong economy** may have **low levels** of **unemployment**, meaning that many consumers would have a **steady income**, which would give them **confidence** in **spending** money on **non-essential goods** or **services**. In a **weak** or **uncertain** economy, consumers are more likely to **save rather than spend**. Changes in **exchange rates** can affect the **final price** of a product bought from **abroad**. For example, shortly after **deciding to leave** the EU in 2016, the **value** of the **Great British Pound fell**. One result was that some businesses **paid more** than they had been for **raw materials** from **abroad**.

Social

Changing social trends can result in changes in demand. For example, as people become more concerned with the health effects of consuming too much sugar there could be a fall in demand for sugary drinks and sweets. This could mean that businesses selling these products would reconsider their design mix (see page 18). Population changes will also have an impact on demand for certain products. For example, increased life expectancy means that there may be increased demand for residential care homes and mobility aids in the future.

Technological

Technological change can influence business decision-making. For example, **decisions** to **invest** in new machinery may be **delayed** if better and **more efficient technology** is **emerging**. However, **new technology** is often **expensive** and this can leave businesses at a **disadvantage** if they **can't afford** the newest technologies. Technological development may also mean that **production processes** or **products** that were previously **not possible** are **now available**. Businesses may therefore reconsider a product's **design mix** (p.18) as technology advances.

Legal

Changes in the law can have an impact on a business's activities. For example, there is global concern over the environmental effects of pollution. Some governments have introduced legal deadlines for the banning of diesel and petrol engines. This will result in a fall in demand for new petrol and diesel engines. Many car manufacturers are now instead focusing on hybrid cars, which are less polluting.

Environmental

Consumers are becoming more concerned with **protecting** the **environment**. To make sure they don't **lose customers**, businesses should make any changes needed to **reduce their environmental impact**. For example, in 2009 Greenpeace began their **#clickclean** campaign aiming to get **digital platforms**, such as Facebook®, to **commit** to using **renewable energy**. Some customers might **choose** to **only use** those digital platforms that can **show** they've made changes in response to Greenpeace's campaign.

Warm-Up Questions

Q1 Which of the four factors in a SWOT analysis are internal factors?

Q2 What do the letters P, E, S, T, L and E stand for in a PESTLE analysis?

Exam Question

Q1 Mo's Motors specialise in car insurance for young drivers under the age of 25.
Using PESTLE analysis, assess the external influences that could impact Mo's Motors. [10 marks]

These business folk are strange — I use a pestle to grind up peppercorns...

... it's a great stress reliever and you can use the ground up peppercorns to make a tasty Diane sauce. It's win win.

More on Choosing a Strategy

Michael Porter came up with a model that businesses could use to analyse the level of competition in an industry. As Prof Porter is considered to be the leading authority on competitiveness, he's probably worth listening to.

Porter's **Five Forces Model** Shows **Influences** on an Industry

1) Porter's **Five Forces model** shows an industry being influenced by **five competitive forces**.
2) It analyses the state of the market and helps managers of existing businesses to figure out the **best strategy** to gain a **competitive advantage** — it is a **decision-making** tool.
3) It can show potential market entrants how **profitable** the market is likely to be and whether it is worth getting into — and if it is, where best to **position** themselves.

Don't confuse Porter's Five Forces model with Porter's strategic matrix on page 106.

1) **Barriers to Entry** — How **Easy** it is For **New Firms** to Enter the Market

1) New entrants to the market will want to compete by selling similar products — it's in the **interests** of existing firms in the market to make it **hard** for new firms to get in.
2) **High start-up costs** (e.g. **expensive equipment**) might deter new firms from entering the market.

Strategies to raise barriers to entry:
- Patents or trademarks (see p.107) can be used to make it harder for new entrants to sell similar products.
- Established businesses may take control of distribution channels. This is known as 'vertical integration' (see p.113). It makes the channel unavailable to new entrants and makes the market less attractive. E.g. an outdoor clothing manufacturer which buys out or merges with an outdoor clothing retailer.
- Threatening new entrants with a price war. Large existing businesses are likely to be benefiting from economies of scale (see p.49), so can undercut the prices of new entrants (predatory pricing — p.23). However, selling goods at a loss to force competitors out of the market is against EU competition law.

2) **Buyer Power** — Buyers Want Products at as **Low a Price** as Possible

1) **Buyers** have **more power** when there are **few buyers** and many sellers.
2) Buyers have **more power** when products are **standardised** — it's easier for firms to charge a premium price for differentiated goods and services.
3) A supplier's **main customer** can **negotiate special deals** and lower prices.

Buyers can include business customers, wholesalers and retailers, as well as the general public.

Strategies to influence buyer power:
- If a buyer **increases the quantity** of a product that they're buying from a seller, their **buyer power has increased**. This is because the seller could **lose a large source of revenue** if the buyer decides to buy from somewhere else and so the buyer can be **more demanding** over **price** or **quality**.
- Similar businesses could come together to form a **buying group**. They'll be buying **bigger volumes** so will be able to demand a **better deal** and so increase their profits. Buying groups help **smaller businesses compete** with large businesses.

3) **Supplier Power** — Suppliers Want to Get as **High a Price** as Possible

1) **Suppliers** have **more power** when there are **few suppliers** and lots of customers buying from them.
2) If it costs customers to **switch suppliers**, then this gives suppliers more power.

Strategies to influence supplier power:
- Businesses can try to tie buyers into **long-term contracts** to make it harder for them to switch suppliers. E.g. mobile phone companies often have **2-year contracts** and lock handsets to their network.
- Businesses could **develop new products** and protect them with **patents** to gain supplier power. They'll be the **only ones** selling the product, so will be able to charge a **premium** if it's a hit.

More on Choosing a Strategy

4) Threat of Substitutes — How Likely Customers Are to Buy an Alternative

1) The **willingness** of customers to **substitute** is a factor affecting competitiveness.

2) Relative **price** and **quality** are important — buyers are unlikely to change to a poor value product.

3) For products with **very little differentiation**, e.g. milk, the threat is higher than for **unique products**.

Strategies to reduce the threat of substitutes:

- Businesses can make it **expensive** or **difficult** for customers to switch to a substitute (although they have to be careful not to annoy them). E.g. if you buy an Amazon Kindle®, you'll usually buy Amazon® products to read on it as it's tricky to convert other products to the correct format.

- Customers are often **loyal to a brand** that they perceive as better. If businesses can **differentiate** their product and create **brand loyalty**, they'll reduce the threat of substitutes.

- Businesses can **identify** a group of customers whose **needs** aren't quite being met and market a product designed to meet their needs **exactly**, e.g. environmentally-conscious disposable nappy users. There **won't** be any substitutes for them to buy (until other businesses notice anyway).

5) Rivalry Within the Industry — How Much Competition There is

1) Rivalry is **intense** in a market with lots of **equal-sized competitors**.

2) Industries with **high fixed costs** are **very competitive**, e.g. parcel delivery companies which have invested in vehicles. Firms have to sell **a lot** to even cover their fixed costs. So in competitive environments, they **cut prices** to **raise demand**. If they're not making a **profit**, it's often hard for them to **get out** of the market as their **expensive equipment** is **hard to sell on**. This means that businesses in the market are **unlikely to leave**, so there's always a high number of competitors — this **increases rivalry** even more.

3) Industries producing **standardised** goods (e.g. steel, milk, flour) have **intense** rivalry.

4) Rivalry is also **intense** in **young industries** where competitors are following **growth strategies**. This is because there's **likely** to be a lot of the market that **isn't occupied** so it's a **race** to achieve the **majority**.

Strategies to reduce the effects of rivalry:

- Some businesses try to make it **easy** for customers to switch between goods. E.g. it can be a **hassle** to **switch bank accounts** so your new bank often handles the process of switching direct debits for you.

- Businesses could use **bigger promotional campaigns** to **attract more customers** to their business. However, this would require a **bigger promotional budget**, so it wouldn't be possible for all businesses.

The Competitive Environment is Dynamic

1) Porter's Five Forces model and PESTLE analysis (p.109) can be used to examine the **external influences** acting on a business. However, they only provide **information** for a **given point in time**.

2) Businesses need to be aware that these influences are **dynamic** and may **change over time**. This means that the competitive environment is always changing, so it's important that businesses **revisit** Porter's Five Forces and PESTLE analysis **regularly** to consider any changes.

3) For example, a change in the economy from a period of **prosperity** to a period of **recession** could affect the **number of rivals** within the industry. It could also affect how **likely** customers would be to **buy a substitute**, as they may become **less concerned** with buying good **quality** products and **focus** on buying **cheaper** products.

Warm-Up Question

Q1 What are the five forces in Porter's Five Forces model?

Exam Question

Q1 Amin is a manufacturer that is entering the pet food market, where it will supply pet food to pet shops. Within this market there are many other pet food suppliers and a high number of customers that visit pet shops to buy pet food. Assess how Porter's Five Forces model could help Amin to devise a strategy to maximise its profits. [12 marks]

Porter conveniently ignores the force of gravity...

... which isn't a luxury that most of us have, unfortunately. Darn pesky gravity, always making things fall down.

Organic and Inorganic Growth

A business might aim to grow so that it can reap the rewards that come with being a bigger business.

Businesses Want to Grow for **Different Reasons**

1) Business **size** is usually measured by **revenue**, **profit**, **market share**, **number of employees** or **assets**. When a business **grows** it means these measures are increasing.

2) One **objective** of growth can be to **increase profitability**, which in turn can **increase profits**. Any increase in profits could be **reinvested** back into the business to **stimulate more growth**.

See page 72 for more on profitability.

3) Another objective of growth might be to **increase market share**. Having a **bigger market share** means that a business has more **influence** over the market, which it can use to **control prices** for its customers and with its suppliers — the business has a **high market power**. This is an example of high **buyer** and **supplier power** (which you met on page 110). A high market power also means that a business's **brand** is likely to be **more recognisable**, which could **increase the number of sales**.

4) A business may **choose to grow** to take **advantage** of **economies of scale**, so the **cost** of producing **each item** (the unit cost) **decreases** — you met economies of scale on p.49. This can lead to **increased profit margins** — an increase in the **profitability** of the business. The business could also **lower the prices** of its products, which is **good news** for the **customers**.

5) **Economies of scale** can be **internal** or **external**.

6) **Internal** economies of scale increase efficiency **within** a business. This can be done in different ways:

- Large businesses can negotiate **bigger discounts** with **suppliers**, reducing the **costs** of **raw materials**.
- Large businesses are more able to **hire specialist managers** than smaller businesses. Managers can **oversee strategies** that result in work being done more **efficiently**, which can **reduce unit costs**.
- Large businesses can afford **new** or **better machinery** to **increase efficiency** and **reduce unit costs**.

Example:
A chocolate bar manufacturer currently pays £1000 per month to cover its costs, including rent and machine maintenance. The current output is 2000 chocolate bars a month. This means that the unit cost is 50p per chocolate bar. The owners want to add more machines to their warehouse, which will increase the monthly costs to £1500 and the output to 4000 bars per month.

Unit cost = total costs ÷ output = £1500 ÷ 4000 = £0.375 = 37.5p per chocolate bar
Decrease in unit cost = 50p – 37.5p = 12.5p decrease

7) **External economies of scale** happen when industries are concentrated in **small geographical areas**.

8) For example, having a large number of **suppliers** to choose from gives **economies of scale**. Locating near lots of suppliers means businesses can **easily negotiate** with a **range of suppliers**, which tends to **increase quality** and **reduce prices**.

Inorganic Growth Can Help **Businesses** to **Grow Quickly**

As soon as Zac masters inorganic growth, he'll have those cookies.

1) Growth can be **organic** (see next page) or **inorganic**.

2) **Inorganic growth** can take many forms including **mergers** and **takeovers**.

3) **Mergers** are when two businesses join together to form one business. They might **keep the name** of one of the original businesses, or come up with a **new name**. The **shares** of the merged business are **transferred** to the shareholders of the old businesses.

4) **Takeovers** (also called **acquisitions**) are when one business buys **enough shares** in another so that it has **more than 50%** of the total shares. This is called a **controlling interest**, and it means the buyer will **always win** in a vote of all shareholders. The **target business** is often **absorbed** into the **buyer's operations**.

5) The main motive for mergers and takeovers is **financial reward** — the business after the merger or takeover is **more profitable** than all the individual businesses. This is a result of the **new business** generating **more revenue** or **cost savings** (e.g. through economies of scale) than the **independent businesses** could.

6) Inorganic growth could also be part of a **strategic** or **tactical decision**. For example, a merger or takeover could be a **tactical decision** to **gain access to technologies** held by one of the businesses, or part of a **strategic decision** to **gain access to new markets**.

Organic and Inorganic Growth

Inorganic Growth Can Be Horizontal or Vertical

1) A **supply chain** includes all the **firms involved** in the **production and sale** of a product, taking it from its **source** of raw materials to the **customer**. For example, the diagram shows **two** supply chains for jewellery.

2) **Horizontal integration** happens when a business combines with another business in the **same industry** at the **same stage** of the production process. It's a very **common** type of takeover or merger. It **reduces** the **competition** in the market — for example, the Morrisons supermarket chain bought out Safeway to extend its branch network and reduce competition.

3) **Vertical integration** occurs when a business combines with another business in the **same industry** but at a **different stage** of the **production process**.

	Supply Chain A	Supply Chain B
primary sector, e.g. diamond mine	firm 1	firm 2
secondary sector, e.g. jewellery manufacturer	firm 3	firm 4
tertiary sector, e.g. jewellery retailer	firm 5	firm 6

> **Example:** If **firm 3** was to merge with or take over **firm 4** in the diagram above, this would be **horizontal integration**. And if **firm 4** took over or merged with **firm 6**, this would be **vertical integration**.

Organic Growth is When a Business Grows From Within

1) Expansion from within a business is known as **organic growth**, and **doesn't involve** any **other businesses** — a business can come up with **strategies** to sell or make new products, expand into new markets, open more stores etc. in order to **grow** organically.

A business can use Ansoff's matrix when deciding on a growth strategy (p.105).

2) Businesses that grow organically are often able to **finance** their growth (increased capacity, new premises, more staff, etc.) by **reinvesting** profits into the business.

3) Businesses find it easiest to grow organically when the **markets** they are in are **growing quickly** and when they are **outperforming** their competitors, enabling them to increase their **market share**.

4) Organic growth is **slower** and **more gradual** than **inorganic growth**, which means that it's easier for the business to **adapt** to growth.

Advantages of Organic Growth	Disadvantages of Organic Growth
• Can maintain current **management style**, **culture** and **ethics** of the business.	• It can take a **long time** to grow a business organically and it can take a while for the business to **adapt to big changes** in the market.
• **Less risk** as it's expanding what the business is good at and it's usually **financed using profits**.	• **Market size** isn't affected by organic growth. If the **market isn't growing**, the business is **restricted** to increasing its **market share** or finding a **new market** to sell products to.
• It's easy for the business to **manage** organic growth and **control** how much the business will grow.	• Businesses might miss out on **opportunities** for **ambitious growth** if they only grow organically.
• Less disruptive changes mean that workers' **efficiency**, **productivity** and **morale** remain high.	

Warm-Up Questions

Q1 What's the difference between a takeover and a merger?

Q2 Give two advantages and two disadvantages of organic growth.

Exam Questions

Q1 Explain the advantages of economies of scale for a manufacturing business. [4 marks]

Q2 Go! Nosh is a fast-food restaurant that is looking to grow in an attempt to increase its profitability. Assess the benefits and drawbacks to Go! Nosh of growing inorganically instead of organically. [12 marks]

Organic growth — much better for the environment...

There are a few different terms to learn on these pages — mergers, horizontal integration, vertical integration... Try not to get too bogged down — all the terms are quite descriptive, so you'll probably find they're not too hard to remember.

Problems With Growth

Personal growth is great and something we should all aspire to, but business growth can sometimes spell trouble...

Growing in Size Can Cause Problems for Businesses

You saw on page 112 the **objectives** a business might be **hoping** to **achieve** by growing, but becoming larger can lead to **problems** for a business too:

1) Large businesses can suffer from **diseconomies of scale** — this is when **unit costs increase** as the scale of production increases. They happen because large firms are **harder to manage** than small ones, which causes **financial costs** to a firm.

2) For example, it can be hard to **motivate** people in a large firm. In a **small firm**, managers are in **close contact** with staff, and it's easier for people to feel like they **belong** and that they're working towards the **same aims**. When people feel they don't belong, and there's no point to what they're doing, they get **demotivated**.

3) A **long-run average cost curve** shows how the **costs** of a business **change** with an increasing production output.

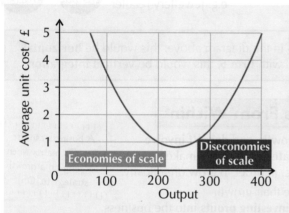

The graph on the left shows the sort of long-run average cost curve a business might have. The curve has an initially decreasing average unit cost for an increasing output — this is economies of scale (see p.112). The curve then turns and has an increasing average unit cost for an increasing output — this is diseconomies of scale.

In the graph on the left you can see that at an output of 100 units, the average unit cost is about £3.50. When output increases to 200, the unit cost goes down to £1 per unit — this is due to economies of scale. However, due to diseconomies of scale, when output reaches 400 units, the average unit cost increases to £5 per unit.

You can use long-run average cost curves to work out the average total cost at a certain output. You do this by multiplying the output by the average unit cost. For example, in the graph above, the average total cost for 200 units is 200 × £1 = £200. At 400 units, it's 400 × £5 = £2000.

4) **Internal communication** is harder in a big business. It can be **slow** and **difficult** to get **messages** to the **right people**, especially when there are **long chains of command**, which makes it **harder** to **coordinate activities** between **different departments**. This makes a business **less efficient**.

5) Growth also increases the risk of **overtrading** — increased **demand** means the business needs to buy more **raw materials** and employ more **people**. This **reduces** the amount of **working capital** available to pay **bills**, and the business runs the **risk** that it'll **go bust** before it has the chance to get **paid** by its customers.

6) Overtrading is **common** in **new businesses** — there are often **lots of start-up costs** for new businesses and it's **unlikely** that there'll be **many customers** initially, so the business has **high costs** but **low revenue** at first.

Nikhil really hated these team building days — he just couldn't understand how this activity would improve internal communication.

Quick Inorganic Growth Can Be a Risky Strategy

Inorganic growth lets businesses **grow rapidly** (see page 112), but it comes with **financial risks** too:

1) Businesses involved in mergers may have **different objectives** and **cultures**. This could lead to **clashes on important issues** and **inefficiency** which may result in **diseconomies of scale** (see above).

2) The staff of merged businesses will need **time** to **learn** new procedures, which may lead to **poor customer service**, which could lead to loss of sales.

3) Inorganic growth can lead to **duplicate roles**, so some parts of the new business may be **sold off**, **closed** or have staff made **redundant**. This could mean additional **redundancy costs**, which would **reduce profitability**.

4) During a takeover, the buyer business will take on any **liabilities** of the other business — these would be any **payments** that the other business **owed** (for example, payments for any **assets bought on credit**).

5) If a takeover is part of a **diversification strategy** (see p.104), the purchasing business will have **limited experience** in the new industry and it will take time to **learn** how it works. Mistakes would **reduce profitability**.

Problems With Growth

Not All Businesses Want to Grow as Much as Possible

Business owners may choose to **restrict** growth or **demerge** for the following reasons:

1) They may want to **maintain the culture** of a small business.

2) The business will become more **complicated** to manage as it gets bigger.

3) Growth may require the business to **secure additional financial resources**, which can be complicated and they may not want to put too much **strain** on their **cash-flow** position.

> A demerger is when a large business splits up into two or more smaller businesses.

Some Businesses May Choose to Stay Small

1) Not all businesses **choose to grow**, and it's often small established businesses that choose to stay small.

2) Businesses might choose to stay small in an attempt to survive in a competitive market. This can be done by **strengthening Kay's distinctive capabilities** (p.106):

Product Differentiation

1) A business that makes a **highly differentiated** product or that offers a **bespoke service** may be **unable to grow**. This could be because the **production process** for the product isn't suited to **mass production** and would result in a business losing its **USP**. For example, many products sold on **Etsy** are **handmade** and this is what **differentiates** them from **mass market** products.

2) This can help to maintain **Kay's distinctive capability** of **innovation** — by staying small a business can **invest more** in creating **new**, **innovative** products with a new **USP**, rather than investing in production.

Flexibility in Responding to Customer Needs

1) A small business is able to **respond** to **customer needs** more easily. Because the business is small, **communication** between **staff** and **customers** can be **quick** and **easy**. By keeping in **close contact** with its **customers** and **suppliers**, a small business can **quickly respond** to any changes in their needs.

2) This would help the business to create **good relationships** with **external people**, which could strengthen Kay's distinctive capability of **architecture**.

Customer Service

1) A small business is more likely to be **run** by the **original owner**, which may result in a more **personal** and **higher quality customer service experience**. If the business grew this may be lost as the original owner would not then have the time to, for example, **individually meet** with all of their customers. This helps to **build brand loyalty** and strengthen Kay's distinctive capability of **reputation**.

2) Remaining small can also mean that the original owner is in **close contact** with all of their **staff**, which helps them to **ensure** that the business is always **working towards** its **corporate aims** (p.102).

3) The growth of **e-commerce** and **online retailing** means it's **easier** for some small businesses to **survive**. It allows people to **operate** their business from **home** without the need for offices or warehouses (p.52).

Warm-Up Questions

Q1 What is meant by diseconomies of scale?

Q2 Describe one way that growth can cause problems for a business.

Q3 Explain how a smaller business is able to strengthen Kay's distinctive capability of architecture.

Q4 Explain how e-commerce has made it easier for small businesses to survive.

Exam Question

Q1 Bamber's is a successful small business that specialises in restoring old properties to their original grandeur using Victorian and Edwardian interior designs and colour schemes. It currently employs five people. The owner is considering a strategy of growth. Assess two benefits to the business of staying small. [8 marks]

"To grow or not to grow?" — that is the question...

Make sure you know the risks of becoming bigger and the reasons for staying small as well as the hairs on your knuckles.

Quantitative Sales Forecasting

You might remember from Section 7 that it's important for businesses to forecast sales in order to make strategic decisions. Well, now it's time to find out how firms use past data to predict future sales. Better find your calculator...

Moving Averages Can be Used to Smooth Fluctuations in Data

1) **Sales figures** can be collected at **consistent time intervals** (e.g. every month) and presented in **time order** — this is **time-series data**. **Time-series analysis** is used to reveal **underlying patterns** in time-series data.

2) Time-series data can be **difficult** to **interpret** if the data has **fluctuations**. To get around this, businesses can take **moving averages** of the data — this smooths out the **fluctuations** in the data, making it easier to identify **underlying trends**. Trends are the **long-term movement** of a variable.

3) You need to know how to calculate **three-period moving averages** and **four-quarter moving averages**:

Three-Period Moving Averages

A **three-period** moving average calculates the **average** of periods **1**, **2** and **3**, then periods **2**, **3** and **4**, and so on.

Example: The table shows the annual sales of a business over a 5-year period. The three-year moving averages have been calculated — so, for example, in the second row this has been calculated as the average of sales in year 1, year 2 and year 3.
You can see that there are no averages in the first and last rows. These would need the sales values for before year 1 and after year 5.

Year	Total Sales (£000)	3-Year Moving Average (£000)
1	65	
2	92	$\frac{65 + 92 + 71}{3} = 76$
3	71	$\frac{92 + 71 + 93}{3} = 85.33$
4	93	$\frac{71 + 93 + 98}{3} = 87.33$
5	98	

A period is any fixed amount of time, e.g. a week, a month, a decade, etc.

The moving average is always placed in the same row as the middle of the time period — this 76 is in the year 2 row as it's the average of years 1, 2 and 3.

Four-Quarter Moving Averages

1) The **four-quarter moving average** takes the averages over the **quarters** of a year. This can remove **seasonal variation** in the data.

A 'quarter' means a three-month time period.

2) The method is **basically the same** as described above for three-period moving averages, but this time you're finding the average of **four consecutive quarters**. However, because you're using **four** time periods now rather than **three**, there isn't a clear **middle point** — it'd lie **midway** between the **second** and **third values**.

3) To solve this problem, you can use a technique called **centring**. This is where you find the **average** of **two** four-quarter moving averages. You then place this against the **third quarter** of the **first** moving average.

Example: The table shows sales and quarterly centred moving averages for Sneezy Bees garden centre.

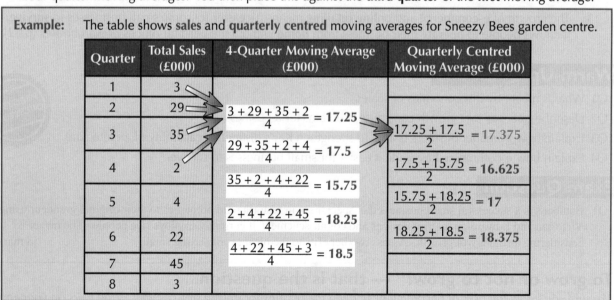

Quarter	Total Sales (£000)	4-Quarter Moving Average (£000)	Quarterly Centred Moving Average (£000)
1	3		
2	29	$\frac{3 + 29 + 35 + 2}{4} = 17.25$	
3	35	$\frac{29 + 35 + 2 + 4}{4} = 17.5$	$\frac{17.25 + 17.5}{2} = 17.375$
4	2	$\frac{35 + 2 + 4 + 22}{4} = 15.75$	$\frac{17.5 + 15.75}{2} = 16.625$
5	4	$\frac{2 + 4 + 22 + 45}{4} = 18.25$	$\frac{15.75 + 18.25}{2} = 17$
6	22	$\frac{4 + 22 + 45 + 3}{4} = 18.5$	$\frac{18.25 + 18.5}{2} = 18.375$
7	45		
8	3		

Quantitative Sales Forecasting

Scatter Graphs and Lines of Best Fit Show Trends in Data

1) Sales data over time can be **displayed** as a **scatter graph** to see if there are any **trends** — for example, in the sales of a particular product over a number of years.

2) You can draw a **line of best fit** through the data points — the line should be as **close** as possible to **all** the **points** on the graph. This shows the **overall trend** in the data.

Example: Each **quarterly centred moving average** for sales at **Sneezy Bees** garden centre has been plotted with a **green x**. A **line of best fit** has been drawn through the centred quarterly moving averages. It shows that there is an **upward trend** — **sales** are **increasing** over time.

This is the line of best fit.

3) You can also use a scatter graph to look for a **correlation** between two variables — this is a measure of how **closely** two variables are **related**, e.g. the value of monthly sales in relation to the amount spent on promotion. The **closer** the **line of best fit** is to the data points, the **stronger** the **correlation** is.

4) It's a **useful tool**, but correlation **doesn't** prove **cause and effect**. Other variables may be important — e.g. a **strong positive correlation** between monthly sales and the amount spent on promotion doesn't mean that one **causes** the other — they could both be affected by an **external factor**, e.g. what competitors are doing.

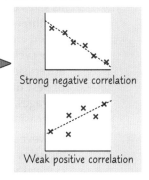

Strong negative correlation

Weak positive correlation

Extrapolation Can be Used to Predict Future Sales

1) **Trends** in past sales data can be continued into the future (**extrapolated**) to **forecast future sales**. This allows managers to set **sales targets**. Sales **performance** can then be measured against these targets.

Example: The four-quarter moving averages revealed that the sales for Sneezy Bees garden centre increased over quarters 1 to 6. You can use the line of best fit to extrapolate the data and predict future sales.

So in quarter 9 you might predict that the sales will be £19 250.

However, this prediction doesn't take into account that the real sales data varies around the moving averages (see next page).

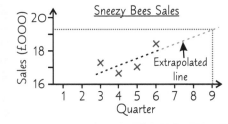

Extrapolated line

2) You can also **extrapolate** on a **graph** that doesn't have a line of best fit. If there is a **curved line** like in the graph on the right, you can **predict** how the trend will **continue** in the **future**. The most **recent trend** was a **decrease** in sales, so the line has been **extrapolated** to show this **trend continuing**.

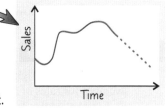

3) Unlike extrapolating a line of best fit, this method mainly focuses on the most **recent changes** in the data. However, it's **hard** to know **how long** a **short-term trend** will continue, or whether **long-term trends** are **more important**.

4) Extrapolation relies on the assumption that **past trends** will remain **true**. However, **past performance** is **no guarantee** of the future — a firm's **sales performance** can be heavily **influenced** by **external factors** (e.g. changes in technology, consumer preferences, competitor products) as well as **internal factors** (e.g. price changes, quality issues). So extrapolations from the past **don't** always **predict** the future very **accurately**.

5) Extrapolation is most useful in fairly **stable** environments, e.g. where the **size** of the **market** or the number of **competitors** is **unlikely** to **change** much.

6) In more **dynamic markets**, it's best to use extrapolation for predicting just a **few time steps** (e.g. 3 quarters) ahead because the **future** is more **uncertain**.

Theme 3: Section 13 — Making Business Decisions

Quantitative Sales Forecasting

Variations from Trends Can Provide Useful Information for Businesses

1) Some businesses will see their sales figures **fluctuate** in a **regular cycle**. For example, they might bring out a **new model** of a product **every five years** — sales could **rise quickly** in the **year after** the **launch** and then **fall steadily** for the **next four years** until the next model is released.

2) So although the **moving averages** might show the long-term trend, the **actual sales** can **differ** quite a lot from the **moving averages**, depending on **where** in its **cycle** the business is.

3) The **difference** between the **actual sales figure** and the **moving average** for a period is called the **cyclical variation**. Firms can calculate the **average cyclical variation** for each point in the cycle to help make more **accurate sales forecasts**. Here's an example:

Cyclical variation = actual sales figure − moving average.

Example: Sneezy Bees garden centre invests in an **advertising campaign** every **three years**. The graph on the right shows its **sales data** (blue line), along with the **three-period moving averages** (green crosses). Its sales go in a **three year cycle**, following each round of advertising. By **extrapolating** the **line** of **best fit** drawn through the moving averages, its **sales** for **2022** are **forecast** to be around **£158 000**.

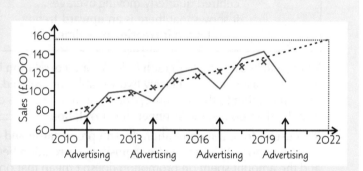

However, 2022 is **2 years after** the next **advertising campaign**, and at this point in the sales cycle the **sales** are usually **higher** than the moving average. To work out **how much** higher, the **average cyclical variation** that occurs 2 years after it has advertised needs to be calculated.

These years are all 2 years after an advertising campaign.

Year	Total Sales (£000)	3-Period Moving Average (£000)	Cyclical Variation (£000)
2013	102	97	102 − 97 = 5
2016	125	116.33	125 − 116.33 = 8.67
2019	142	129.33	142 − 129.33 = 12.67
		Average	$\frac{5 + 8.67 + 12.67}{3} = 8.78$

This figure shows that 2 years after each advertising campaign, actual sales are on average £8780 higher than the moving average.

So a **more accurate** sales forecast for **2022** is £158 000 + £8780 = **£166 780**.

4) Adjusting forecasts using average cyclical variations assumes that the **average cyclical variation** will stay **the same**, but this could **change** over time.

Warm-Up Questions

Q1 How do moving averages of sales data help determine if there is a trend in sales data?

Q2 Briefly describe how you would calculate a three-period moving average.

Exam Question

Answer on p.194.

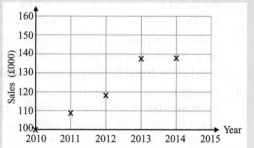

Q1 The graph on the right shows the three-year moving averages for sales of a children's computer tablet.
  a) Extrapolate the data on the graph and calculate the predicted percentage increase in sales between 2010 and 2015. You are advised to show your working. **[4 marks]**
  b) Assess two possible drawbacks to the firm of using extrapolation as a method of forecasting sales. **[8 marks]**

A surprise guest came to my dinner party — I didn't have an extra plate...

Businesses have a fair few tricks up their sleeves to try to make their predictions about the future more accurate. The methods on these pages can also be used to forecast the future values of variables other than sales, such as costs.

Investment Appraisal

Investment appraisal helps businesses decide what projects to invest in, so that they get the best, fastest, least risky return for their money. Probably a better method than picking investment projects out of a hat. Less fun though...

Investment Decisions Must Balance Risk and Return

Havier had a different understanding of balancing risks in business.

1) Businesses often need to **invest** in order to achieve their **objectives** — e.g. if a firm's objective is to **increase sales** by 25% over three years, it might need to invest in extra **staff** and **machinery** so that it can make the extra products it hopes to sell.

2) Any situation where you have to **spend** money in the hope of **making** money in the future is **risky**, because there's always the possibility that you **won't** make as much money as you expect. Businesses like the **risks** to be **low** and the **return** (the profit on the investment) to be **high**.

3) When firms are making strategic **decisions** about how to **invest** their money (whether to launch a new product, take on more staff, relocate their call centre, etc.) they gather as much **data** as possible so that they can work out the **risk** and **reward** involved.

4) There are **two** main **questions** that firms try to answer to enable them to make good investment decisions:
   - **How long** will it take to get back the money that they spend?
   - How much **profit** will they get from the investment?

5) There are **three** main **methods** that businesses can use to help them **answer** these questions and **decide** whether **investments** are a good idea: calculating the **payback period** (see below), calculating the **average rate of return** (p.120) and **discounted cash flows** (p.121).

6) These **investment appraisal methods** use **predicted** cash flows for **different projects** that a firm is **considering**. The predicted cash flows estimate **how much money** the project will **make** and **when**, as well as **how much** will need to be **spent** on the project and **when**. The business uses this data to predict **how much profit** a project might make, and **how fast** the money could come in. The **faster** money comes in, the **less** risk in the long run.

7) All of the investment appraisal methods are **useful**, but they're only as good as the **data** used to calculate them.

8) Because the appraisal methods use **predictions** about **how much money** the projects will make in the future, any **incorrect predictions** will mean that the **calculations** in the **investment appraisals** are wrong, which may result in the business **making** the **wrong choice**.

Payback Measures How Long it Takes to Get Your Money Back

1) The **payback period** is the time it takes for a project to make enough money to pay back the **initial investment**.

2) To calculate it, you need to know the **annual net cash flow** of the project — this is how much money the project will **generate** each year **minus** how much it will **cost** the business each year.

3) If the project will have a **consistent annual net cash flow** then the payback period is **easy** to calculate — you just use this **simple payback formula**:

$$\text{Payback period} = \frac{\text{Amount invested}}{\text{Annual net cash flow}}$$

4) However, when things aren't this straightforward, the business may need to look more closely at the **cash flow forecast** to work out the payback period:

   Numbers in brackets are negative.

   Example: A firm needs to make an initial investment of £4500 to fund a project. The predicted annual and cumulative net cash flows of the project are shown in the table:

   By the end of year 3 the project no longer has a negative cumulative net cash flow — it has generated enough money to pay for itself. The actual payback period lies somewhere between years 2 and 3. To work out where it lies within this time period, you need to find how much is left to be paid back at the end of year 2 (£1400) and work out what proportion this is of year 3's net cash flow (£2200): $\frac{1400}{2200} = 0.6$ (1 d.p.).

Years since investment	Annual net cash flow	Cumulative net cash flow
0	(£4500)	(£4500)
1	£2000	(£2500)
2	£1100	(£1400)
3	£2200	£800

   So the payback period for the project is approximately 2.6 years.

5) Managers **compare** the payback periods of different projects to **choose** which project to go ahead with — managers usually want to get their money back as soon as possible, so they prefer a **short payback period**.

Investment Appraisal

Average Rate of Return (ARR) Compares Net Return with Investment

1) **Average rate of return** (ARR — sometimes called accounting rate of return) compares the **net return** with the level of investment. The **net return** is the **income** of the project **minus costs**, including the **investment**.

2) The **higher the ARR**, the more **favourable** the project will appear.

3) ARR is expressed as a **percentage** and is calculated like this: $$ARR = \frac{Average\ Net\ Return}{Investment} \times 100$$

Example: A business is considering two **investment options**. The table shows the **investments** and the predicted **net cash flow** from **both projects** over five years.

	Investment	Year 1	Year 2	Year 3	Year 4	Year 5
Project A	(£10m)	£4m	£5m	£6m	£7m	£5m
Project B	(£8m)	£3m	£3m	£5m	£6m	£7m

- **Net return** (in £m) of **Project A** = −10 + 4 + 5 + 6 + 7 + 5 = **£17m**

  Average net return = £17m ÷ 5 years = **£3.4m**

  The investment was £10m, so **ARR** = $\frac{£3.4m}{£10m} \times 100$ = **34%**

- **Net return** (in £m) of **Project B** = −8 + 3 + 3 + 5 + 6 + 7 = **£16m**

  Average net return = £16m ÷ 5 years = **£3.2m**

  The investment was £8m, so **ARR** = $\frac{£3.2m}{£8m} \times 100$ = **40%**

So managers would probably **choose project B** because it has a **higher ARR**.

ARR!

Pirate accountants like the average rate of return.

There are Advantages and Disadvantages to Payback and ARR

1) Calculating the payback period and ARR can both be **helpful**, but they have **drawbacks** too.

2) One of the biggest drawbacks of **both methods** is that the **time value of money** is ignored.

3) The time value of money is the idea that a certain amount of **money** (let's say £100) is worth **more today** than it will be in the **future**. This is because:

- The money is likely to be **worth less** in the future due to **inflation** — you probably can't buy as much with £100 in a year as you can now.

- There's an **opportunity cost** — if you had the money now you could **invest it** in a **high interest bank account** and end up with **more than £100** in a year's time.

4) So the investment appraisal methods assume that, for example, **£5m** net cash flow in **Year 5** will have the **same value** as **£5m** in **Year 1**, but this **isn't true**.

Here's a summary of the **advantages** and **disadvantages** of using the payback period and ARR:

	Advantages	Disadvantages
Payback Period	- It's **easy** to **calculate** and **understand**. - It's very good for **high tech** projects (technology tends to become **obsolete** fairly quickly, so businesses need to be sure that they'll get their initial investment back before the products **stop** generating a return) or any project that might not provide **long-term** returns.	- It **ignores cash flow** after payback. E.g. two projects (project A and project B) might both have a payback period of three years. Project A will continue to provide a return of £20 000 a year after the payback period, while project B won't provide any more return after its payback period. Project A is clearly the **better investment**, but the payback period calculation **doesn't** take this into account. - It **ignores** the **time value** of money.
Average Rate of Return	- It's **easy** to **calculate** and **understand**. - It takes account of all the project's **cash flows** — i.e. it doesn't stop counting cash flow after a certain point, like the payback period does.	- It ignores the **timing** of the **cash flows** — e.g. a firm might put more value on money that they get **sooner** rather than later. - It **ignores** the **time value** of money.

Investment Appraisal

Discounted Cash Flows Consider the Present Value of Returns

1) **Discounted cash flow** (DCF) is an investment appraisal tool that takes into account the **time value** of **money** (see previous page). It **adjusts** the **value** of cash flows in the future to calculate their **present value**.

2) To calculate the **present value** of cash flows, the **net cash flow** in each year is multiplied by a **discount factor**. Discount factors **depend** on what the **interest rate** is predicted to be. **High interest rates** mean the future payments have to be **discounted a lot** to give the correct present values. This is so the **present value** reflects the **opportunity cost** of not investing the money in the **bank** where it could earn a **high interest rate**.

3) The **net present value** (NPV) is the **sum** of the **present values** of cash flows, **minus** the **cost** of the **initial investment** — so what the **returns** would be **worth** if you had them all **now**.

4) If you end up with a **negative NPV**, that means that the business could get a better return by putting their money into a **savings account** rather than going ahead with the project. Businesses will usually only go ahead with projects with a **positive NPV** — projects that are going to **make them money**.

5) The **downsides** of discounted cash flow are that it's a bit **hard to calculate**, and that it's difficult for businesses to work out what the **discount factor** ought to be, because they don't know what the bank interest rates are going to be in the future. The **longer** the project is set to last, the **harder** it is to predict the discount factor.

6) In the table below, **project A** has an initial investment of **£8m**, and **project B** has an initial investment of **£6m**. The **expected rate of interest** is **10%**. The discount factors are given in the table.

Project A	Net Cash Flow	Discount Factor (10%)	Present Value
Year 1	£4m	0.909	£4m × 0.909 = £3 636 000
Year 2	£5m	0.826	£5m × 0.826 = £4 130 000
Year 3	£6m	0.751	£6m × 0.751 = £4 506 000
Year 4	£7m	0.683	£7m × 0.683 = £4 781 000
Total Present Value of Net Cash Flows			£17 053 000
Net Present Value (Total minus Investment)			£17 053 000 − £8m = £9 053 000
Return ((Net Present Value ÷ Investment) × 100)			(£9 053 000 ÷ £8m) × 100 = 113.2%

Money is discounted more the further into the future you go — so £5m in 4 years is worth less today than £5m in 2 years.

Project B	Net Cash Flow	Discount Factor (10%)	Present Value
Year 1	£3m	0.909	£3m × 0.909 = £2 727 000
Year 2	£3m	0.826	£3m × 0.826 = £2 478 000
Year 3	£4m	0.751	£4m × 0.751 = £3 004 000
Year 4	£6m	0.683	£6m × 0.683 = £4 098 000
Total Present Value of Net Cash Flows			£12 307 000
Net Present Value (Total minus Investment)			£12 307 000 − £6m = £6 307 000
Return ((Net Present Value ÷ Investment) × 100)			(£6 307 000 ÷ £6m) × 100 = 105.1%

The return gives a percentage, so that two different projects can be compared more easily. If the projects had the same level of investment you could leave out this step — the project with the highest NPV would be the best option.

The **positive NPVs** show that **both** projects are **worthwhile**. The **return** on both projects is **more** than 100% — so they more than **double** the investment. **Project A** gives a **slightly better** return than **project B**.

Warm-Up Questions

Q1 How do you find an investment's payback period when the annual net cash flows are constant?

Q2 Give two advantages of using the average rate of return to compare investment options.

Q3 What does it mean if a project has a negative net present value?

PRACTICE QUESTIONS

Exam Question

Q1 Bea's Breads is a bakery that is considering two investment options. Project A is to open a second bakery and needs an investment of £60 000. Project B is to create an app so that customers can order products for delivery using their phones, and needs an investment of £35 000. The table on the right shows the results from different investment appraisal methods. Evaluate the two investment options for Bea's Breads and recommend which option it should choose. [20 marks]

	Project A	Project B
Payback Period	2.4 years	2.1 years
ARR	41.7%	47.6%
Net Present Value	£34 750	£28 200

Discounts? Brilliant — I love a bargain...

This is a tricky section to get your head around — if you're stumped, keep going over these pages until you understand.

Decision Trees

Unfortunately, decision trees aren't wise forest dwellers that tell businesses what to do. But they can help businesses compare different options, whilst taking into account how likely they are to succeed. Close enough I guess.

Decision Trees Combine **Probability** and **Expected Pay-Off**

1) When businesses make decisions (e.g. whether to open a new outlet, whether to develop a new product to add to their range), they **know** what the **cost** will be, but often the **outcome isn't certain**.

2) **Probability** is the **likelihood** of an event occurring. Managers often **don't know** how likely it is that an outcome will happen, so they make a **subjective estimate** based on **experience** or **past data**.

3) Probability is usually expressed as a **decimal** in decision trees — e.g. 0.6 for a 60% probability. The probability of an event **happening** and the probability of it **not happening** have to add up to **1** (certainty).

4) The **expected monetary value (EMV)** of an outcome is the **probability** of the outcome occurring, **multiplied** by the **pay-off** the business can expect to get. To work out the EMV of a **course of action**, you **add** the EMVs of the **different outcomes** together.

5) **Net gain** is the financial gain after **initial costs** have been **subtracted**. Net gain = EMV − initial costs.

Learn These **Features** of **Decision Trees**

1) A **square** represents a **decision node**. The **lines** coming from a square show the possible **courses of action** and the **costs** of each action.

2) A **circle** represents a **chance node**, which shows there are **alternative outcomes** for a course of action, which are shown by **lines** coming out of the circle.

3) The **decimals** on the lines are the **probabilities** of each outcome occurring.

4) The **values in £s** represent the **pay-off** for the business if that outcome happens.

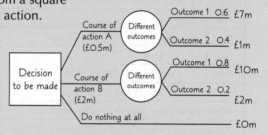

Decision Trees Show Which **Course of Action** is Probably **Best**

1) When creating a decision tree, managers first identify which **courses of action** are open to the business.

2) They outline the **possible outcomes** of each course of action and assign **probabilities** to them, estimating the probabilities they don't know.

3) The next step is to **calculate** the **EMV** and **net gain** of each course of action.

4) Managers should usually choose the course of action with the **highest net gain**.

Example — decision tree for launching a new chocolate bar

A confectionery business is about to launch a new chocolate bar.

1) With a **marketing** budget of **£15K** the chance of a **successful launch** is estimated at **0.75**. **Without** marketing, the chance is estimated at **0.5**. The basic launch costs are **£1K**.

2) A **successful** launch would earn a revenue of **£100K** — but if it **failed**, revenue would be **£20K** at best.

Calculate the **net gain** for each course of action. **Add** the EMVs for each outcome together, then **subtract** the initial costs (here, it's the **launch costs**):

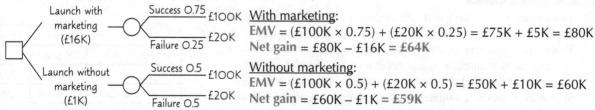

With marketing:
EMV = (£100K × 0.75) + (£20K × 0.25) = £75K + £5K = £80K
Net gain = £80K − £16K = **£64K**

Without marketing:
EMV = (£100K × 0.5) + (£20K × 0.5) = £50K + £10K = £60K
Net gain = £60K − £1K = **£59K**

Compare the net gain of launching **with** marketing (**£64K**) with the net gain of launching **without** marketing (**£59K**). This shows that spending £15K on marketing is **worthwhile**, so the best course of action is to launch the new chocolate bar with **marketing**.

Decision Trees

Decision Trees Have Advantages...

1) Decision trees make managers **work out** and **think about** the **probability** and the **potential pay-off** of each outcome of their chosen action. Managers have to come up with **real numerical values** for these — much better than **vague statements** like "this will increase sales".

2) Decision trees are a nice **visual representation** of the potential outcomes of a decision.

3) Decision trees allow managers to compare options **quantitatively** and **objectively**, rather than going for the fashionable option or the option they thought of first.

4) Decision trees are useful in **familiar situations** where the business has enough experience to make **accurate** estimates of **probabilities** and **benefits**.

Stay small. The expected benefit from growth is lower than you think.

...and Disadvantages

1) Decision trees are **quantitative** — i.e. they're based on numbers and ignore non-numerical **qualitative data**. **Qualitative data** includes things like the **employees' opinions** about business decisions, and businesses should take qualitative data into account before deciding on a course of action.

2) **Probabilities** are very hard to **predict accurately** so there can be a lot of **uncertainty** around the probabilities that are used. **Estimated pay-offs** are also assumed to be accurate — in real life things may work out differently. If either of these estimates are based on **dodgy** information, the decision is **flawed** too.

3) The **values** on a decision tree can **depend** on the **person** who makes it — **different people** might think the **probabilities** and **pay-offs** on the tree should be **different values**, depending on their **opinions** and **experience**. So the tree might be **biased** towards particular outcomes if the person making it is biased.

4) In reality there's a **wider range** of potential **outcomes** than the decision tree suggests. For example, a new marketing campaign might **increase sales** for a **shorter period** than predicted — the decision tree might only allow for success or failure, not for **short-term success** versus **long-term success**.

Warm-Up Questions

Q1 Explain the difference between the circles and the squares on a decision tree.
Q2 Outline the steps used in decision tree construction.
Q3 Give one disadvantage of using a decision tree to choose the best course of action to take.

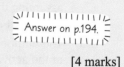

Exam Question

Q1 Chuse PLC is a multinational business that maintains electronic defence systems. It has won a contract to update the electronics on a submarine. Chuse does not currently have the capacity to complete this contract in the time available. To complete the work in time, Chuse has two options: increase its capacity, or subcontract two-thirds of the work. Expected outcomes are as follows:

Option (cost)	Outcomes	Probability	Profit (£m)
Increase existing capacity (£25 million)	Success Failure	0.6 0.4	500 −100
Subcontract (£50 million)	Success	1	400

Answer on p.194.

Construct a decision tree and calculate the expected monetary value to Chuse PLC of choosing to increase capacity. You are advised to show your working. [4 marks]

I tried to branch out into tree jokes — I was asked to leave...

You've probably twigged that a decision tree is a nifty way for a manager to work out the best option when faced with an important decision. It's based on the potential benefit if things work out well, and how likely it is that things will work out well or badly. Work your way through a few decision trees to make sure it's taken root in your head.

Critical Path Analysis

Critical path analysis is used to find the most time-efficient way of doing a complex project. It's a really handy tool for working out how best to organise resources and activities when implementing a strategy.

Critical Path Analysis Works Out the **Quickest Way** to Finish a **Set of Tasks**

Critical path analysis identifies the most **efficient** and **cost-effective** way of completing a complex project — i.e. a project made up of a series of **activities**. Critical path analysis is sometimes called 'network analysis'.

1) The various activities which make up the project are **identified**, and the **order** or **sequence** that these activities must be performed in is worked out.

2) The **duration** (how long each activity will take) is **estimated**.

3) These **activities** are then arranged as a **network** or graph, showing the **whole project** from start to finish, and showing which tasks can be **performed** at the **same time**. For large, **complicated** projects made up of lots of activities, **computer programs** are used to construct the network.

4) The **shortest time** required to get from start to finish can then be identified. The sequence of tasks which have to be done one after another with **no gaps in between**, to get the project done as fast as possible, is called the **critical path**. Activities on the critical path are called **critical activities** — if they're delayed, the **whole project** is delayed.

Example:

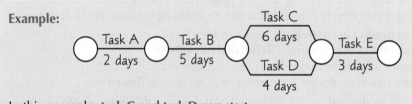

In this example, **task C** and **task D** can start at the **same time** (once task B is completed).

The **critical path** here is tasks **A, B, C** and **E** — task D **isn't** on the critical path because task D could be **delayed** by 2 days and it **wouldn't** delay the overall project.

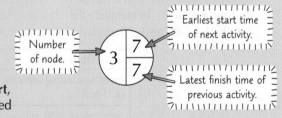

"Dearest, we really must get back to the path before we ruin our skirts. It's absolutely critical."

Nodes Show When One Task **Must Finish** and When the Next Task **Can Start**

1) The **circles** on the network are called **nodes** — they show where one activity **stops** and another activity **begins**.

2) Each node is split into **three** parts. The numbers inside each node show the **number** of the **node**, the **latest** time that the **previous** task can **finish**, and the **earliest** time that the **next** task can **start**:

1) The **left** part of the node shows you which **number** node it is.

2) The number in the **top right** is the **earliest start time** (EST — see next page) of the activity **following** the node. That's the **earliest** time from the beginning of the project that the activity can **start**, assuming that all the activities before it are completed in as short a time as possible.

3) The number in the **bottom right** of the node is the **latest finishing time** (LFT — see next page) of the activity immediately **before** the node. That's the **latest** time that the activity can **finish** without having the knock-on effect of making the whole project **late**.

4) If the **EST** and the **LFT** are the **same**, then the node is on the **critical path**.

Critical Path Analysis

Networks Include Start Times, Finishing Times and Float Time

It's really important to know the **earliest** and **latest start** and **finishing times** for each activity so that you can make sure the whole project can be completed **on time** — if you **miss** the **latest start time** of an activity, there's **no way** you can **finish** the project **on time** (unless you can do individual activities **more quickly** than you predicted).

Earliest start time

1) **EST = earliest start time** (in number of e.g. days, weeks, months) since the start of the project. An activity can't start until the activity before it has been completed — e.g. you can't ice a cake before it's baked.

2) EST is worked out by **adding** the **duration** of the **previous activity** to its **EST**. The EST of the first activity is always 0.

3) For example, a business wants to trade internationally. Their strategy involves **opening** a new office (**1 month**), then **hiring** new staff (**3 months**), then **producing** the product (**6 months**) and then **launching** the product in the new market (**2 months**). So, the **EST** (in months) of **producing** is: 0 + 1 + 3 = 4.

Earliest finishing time

1) **EFT = earliest finishing time**. It's the time that an activity will **finish** if it's **started** at the **earliest start time**.

2) You can work out the EFT for an activity by **adding** its **duration** (in months here) to its **EST**.

3) Using the same example, the **EFT** of **producing** is: 4 + 6 = 10.

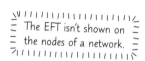
The EFT isn't shown on the nodes of a network.

Latest finishing time

1) **LFT = latest finishing time**. This is the **latest** time by which the activity can be completed without **holding up** the **completion** of the project.

2) It's **calculated** by working **backwards** from the **final** node. The LFT of the final node is **equal** to the EST of the final node. To work out the LFT of the node before, you subtract the duration of the next activity from its LFT.

3) If the business needs the product launched by the end of **month 12**, the **LFT** of **hiring** is: 12 – 2 – 6 = 4.

Latest start time

1) **LST = latest start time**. It's the **latest time** an activity can be **started** and still be **finished** by its **LFT**.

2) To calculate LST, **subtract** the **duration** of the activity from its **LFT**.

3) The **LST** of **hiring** in the example above is: 4 – 3 = 1.

The LST isn't shown on the nodes of a network.

Float time

1) **Float time** (also called **total float**) is the length of **time** you can **delay** an activity without delaying the **completion** of the **project**. You can work it out by:

Total float = LFT – duration – EST

2) Only **non-critical** activities have **float time**.

3) For example, the business in the example above is making a **TV advert** at the **same time** as **production**, with a **duration** of **4 months**. It has the same **LFT** and **EST** as production. So its total float time is 10 – 4 – 4 = 2.

Nathan loved having float time.

Critical Path Analysis

Here's an **Example** of **Critical Path Analysis**

A project is made up of **nine separate tasks** — A to I:

- **Task A** takes **4 days** to complete and can be done at the same time as **task G** (5 days).
- **Task B** (7 days) and **task C** (9 days) can be done at the **same time** once **task A** is finished.
- **Task D** (6 days) can start once **task B** is completed.
- **Task E** (5 days) can start once **task B** and **task C** have **both** finished.
  Task E can be done at the **same time** as **task D**.
- **Task F** (3 days) can start once **task D** and **task E** have both finished.
- **Task H** (7 days) can start once **task G** has finished.
- **Task I** (4 days) can start once **task F** and **task H** have both finished.

You can work out the **ESTs** of all the tasks by working **forwards** from the start of the project, and then work out the **LFTs** of the tasks by working **backwards** from the end of the project. The network looks like this:

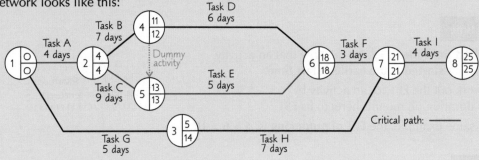

The critical path can also be shown using marks on the path, like this:

1) The **critical path** (in pink) is task **A**, then task **C**, task **E**, task **F** and finally task **I**.
   If you add up the time taken to do each task, it shows that the project can be completed in 4 + 9 + 5 + 3 + 4 = **25 days** in total. The LFT of task I in the final node is 25 days.

2) In each node on the **critical path**, the **EST** equals the **LFT**.
   For nodes that aren't on the critical path, the **EST** and **LFT** are **different**.

3) **Task B** and **task D** both have a **total float time** of 1 day, and **task G** and **task H** have a total float time of 9 days. These tasks are **non-critical activities** — if there is a **delay** in starting them, it's still possible to complete the project **on time**. E.g. if task G starts on day 5 instead of day 0, it will still be completed before its latest finishing time. If **critical tasks** start **late** or take **longer** than they're expected to, the project **can't** be completed on time.

> There is a **dummy activity** between node 4 and node 5. A **dummy activity** is an **imaginary activity** — it just shows that one activity is **dependent** on another. In the example, the dummy activity shows that **task E can't start** until **task B** and **task C** have **both** finished. **Without** the dummy activity it would look as though **task E** was only dependent on **task C**, but having only **one node** between tasks B and C and tasks D and E would imply that **task D** was dependent on **both task B** and **task C**, instead of just **task B**.

Critical Path Analysis Can be Used for **Time Management** of **Strategies**

1) Critical path analysis is used when **implementing** a **strategy** or **planning** a **complicated project**, such as the launch of a new product, delivering a marketing campaign or building a new office block.

2) It allows businesses to work out when they'll need **resources** to be **available**, e.g. that a certain **machine** will need to be **free** on Friday or that a **new office** will need to be open and ready to use 15 months into a project.

3) In many cases, it's possible to **shorten** the **critical path** by allocating **additional resources** to an activity. For example, sewing buttons onto a batch of jumpers might be expected to take 5 days, but if the business hired extra machinists, it might be possible to reduce that to 3 days.

4) Some **resources** can be **switched** between activities — e.g. recruiters can be moved from hiring manual labour to hiring managers.

5) Critical path analysis also helps managers with **decision-making**. Knowing the **latest finish time** of a project makes it easier to decide when to launch an **ad campaign** or when to become a **public company**.

Critical Path Analysis

Critical Path Analysis Has Several Advantages

1) Critical path analysis identifies the **critical activities** (activities on the critical path), which need to be supervised closely, to make sure they meet their deadlines.

2) Resources can be transferred from activities with **float time** to **critical activities**, if needed. For example, **people** packing items could **change roles** to making them.

3) If different **functions** such as finance, operations, marketing and human resources can start work at the **earliest start time**, then this will make the implementation of **strategy** as speedy as possible. This saves on many **costs**, including the opportunity costs of not working on other projects.

4) Critical path analysis helps firms forecast their **cash flow** — it gives definite earliest start times when cash will need to be spent by different functions, which allows the firm to budget accurately.

5) Critical path analysis finds the **shortest time possible** for completing a complex project. This can give a **competitive advantage**, e.g. it could mean that a firm is the **first** to get a **product** to market.

6) It's an excellent **visual aid** to communications, because it shows at a glance which steps take place at the **same time**, and which have any **float time**.

7) Critical path analysis forces managers to think about the **activities** involved in a strategy. Without the **systematic approach** of critical path analysis, something might be forgotten.

8) Critical path analysis can be used to review progress on **individual tasks**, e.g. if a task overruns its total float time you can see how it will affect the overall project.

9) If there are changes and modifications to the progress of the project, the network can be **amended** as the project goes on.

Critical Path Analysis Has Disadvantages As Well

1) Critical path analysis relies on **estimates** of how long each task will take. If these aren't accurate, the whole analysis will be wrong.

2) **Constructing** and **amending** the network could require a significant amount of **planning** and **time**.

3) Critical path analysis sets **tight deadlines**, especially for critical activities. It's tempting for employees to **cut corners** in the rush to meet deadlines, which means that **quality** can suffer.

4) Critical path analysis can't tell you anything about **costs** — or anything about **how good** the project is.

5) Critical path analysis doesn't take into **account** some **factors** that could **delay** the project, such as the **weather** or **staff illness**.

Warm-Up Questions

Q1 What is meant by the "critical path"?
Q2 How do you calculate the latest finishing time of an activity?
Q3 Explain the term "total float".

Exam Question

Q1 Nica Ltd makes luxury beds. It is refurbishing a building that will become its call centre. The call centre needs to be operational 30 days after the start of the refurbishment to make sure it is available before new products are launched. The network below shows the critical path analysis for the refurbishment project:

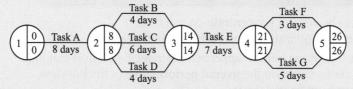

Tasks C and D involve external work, which can only be carried out in dry weather.
Ten days after the start of the project, there were 3 days of wet weather.
Assess the importance to Nica Ltd of critcal path analysis during the period of wet weather. [10 marks]

The lane outside my house judges what I wear — it's a critical path...

Critical path analysis can seem a bit tricky, but don't be put off by a scary-looking network — just break it down and it'll seem a whole lot simpler. Make sure you know its limitations too — that could easily come up in the exam.

Corporate Influences

There are a lot of influences on the decisions businesses make — they don't just flip a coin. Firms consider when they want to get returns on investments, and whether they use data or personal opinions to make their decisions.

Firms Can Have Different Timescales for When They Expect Returns

1) **Corporate timescales** refer to **when** a business expects to gain **returns on investments** (e.g. in two months or two years), as well as how far into the **future** they set **strategies** for.

2) The corporate timescales used by a business affect the **relative importance** that managers place on **short-term** and **long-term strategic decisions**.

3) A business can either take a '**short-termism**' or a '**long-termism**' approach.

Short-Termism Focuses on Quick Rewards

1) **Short-termism** is where firms make decisions to **increase financial performance** over **short time periods** (e.g. maximising **quarterly profit** or increasing **monthly sales**), often at the **expense** of **long-term** performance.

2) In **limited companies**, short-termism is often used to keep **shareholders happy**. Many shareholders look at the **short-term performance** of a business — if it looks like **profits** are **falling** they might worry they're not going to get very high **dividends** and decide to **sell their shares**. If lots of shareholders **sell** their **shares** the **share price** will **fall**, which **reflects badly** on the business and means they may find it **harder** to get **new investors**.

3) Short-termism is often attractive to **managers** as their **bonuses** are often based on **short-term performance**, such as short-term **increases** in **share prices**.

4) Short-termism may also be used by **very new businesses** — they're unlikely to focus on **long-term goals** until they're making a **profit** and are **financially stable**.

5) Short-termism tends to mean that a business has little or no investment in **technology**, **training**, **research** and **development**, **maintenance**, and **increasing efficiency**. Although this **reduces costs** and **increases profits** in the short term, it could mean a firm is **unprepared** for **changes** that might happen in the long term, which could reduce its **competitiveness** and potential **future profit**. For example, a firm might increase its **short-term profit** by **spending** very **little** on research and development, but if **competitors** bring out **new**, **innovative products** the firm might struggle to **maintain** its **market share**.

6) As well as a **lack of investment**, short-termism can also lead to the following **behaviours** by businesses:

- Adjusting the **financial accounts** to show increased profits for a particular time period, which can attract **additional investment** in the short term. E.g. **large costs** for **2019** could be added to the accounts for **2020** — this would **increase** 2019's **profit** figure, making the firm appear **more appealing** to investors.

- Choosing **short-term contracts** with **customers**, **suppliers** and **staff** instead of fostering long-term relationships — this allows the firm to **change direction quickly** to maximise **short-term returns** and to take advantage of **new opportunities** as soon as they appear.

- **Cutting staff** numbers to **reduce costs**, often losing **skilled** and **experienced** staff.

- Paying extra **dividends** to **shareholders**, rather than **investing** extra money into the **business**.

- Using **inorganic** rather than organic **growth methods** (see p.112-113) in order to **grow more quickly**.

Long-Termism Sets Goals for Longer Periods of Time

1) **Long-termism** is where businesses **concentrate** on reaching **long-term goals** rather than prioritising **short-term** financial gains.

2) **Long-termism** allows for a more **holistic approach** to strategic decision-making — this means a firm concentrates on the **overall performance** of the business, rather than just its short-term financial state.

3) Long-termism means that firms are more willing to **invest** in things such as **research** and **development**, **staff training**, and **long-term projects** that might not generate returns for **several years**. Investing in these things helps to make the business prepared for the future, and more **competitive** and **profitable** in the **long term**.

4) Firms that use long-termism might still **use short-termism** at times. For example, a **new competitor** entering the market could mean that **demand** for a firm's product **falls drastically**. In order to survive, it might need to **focus less** on its **long-term** strategies and more on **maximising sales** in the short term.

Saffia was a long-termism kinda kid.

Corporate Influences

Firms Can Use Different Approaches to Making Decisions

1) Firms make **tactical** (short-term) and **strategic** (long-term) decisions (see p.104). These decisions have to be made so that a firm can **meet** its **objectives** and overall **aims**.

2) Decisions can be made using an **evidence-based approach** or a **subjective approach**.

3) An **evidence-based** approach is a **structured** approach to decision-making — it's where managers use **data** that's been **gathered** and **analysed** to help them make their decisions. The decision-making **methods** covered in **Section 13** (quantitative sales forecasts, investment appraisals, decision trees and critical path analysis) are examples of the **techniques** a firm might use as part of an **evidence-based** approach to decision-making.

Firms might also use the calculations in Section 15 in evidence-based decision-making.

4) A **subjective** approach to decision-making is much **less structured** — it's where decisions are based on the **opinions**, **experience**, and the **'gut' instinct** of the **main individuals** within the firm.

	Advantages	Disadvantages
Evidence-based decision-making	• It is based on facts that can be verified, making it easier to justify a decision to others. • It uses validated decision-making tools, such as critical path analysis. • The decision is well structured and there is a record of how the decision was reached.	• It can take a long time to reach a decision — circumstances related to the decision might change in the meantime. • Different interpretations are possible from the evidence, so the best decision may not be clear. • Focusing too heavily on evidence might lead a firm to overlook other aspects of the decision, such as how ethical it is.
Subjective decision-making	• Decisions can be made quickly, which can let a firm take advantage of a short-lived opportunity. • It can be used when there's a lack of data to base the decision on or when an opinion is needed, e.g. when deciding if something looks right.	• People's instincts might be wrong or biased, leading to poor decisions being made. • It can be difficult to justify the decision. • It can lead to managers making snap decisions, without fully considering the long-term consequences of the decision.

Different Approaches are Appropriate for Different Situations

1) The **decision-making** approach that's usually chosen will **vary** between businesses. For example, a **start-up** might be more likely to frequently use **subjective** decision-making as the owners have **little data** to **inform** evidence-based decisions, and might **lack** the **expertise** or **time** needed to gather and analyse data. Also, at an **early stage**, business owners might make **decisions** based on the **overall vision** they have for the business and the **direction** they want it to go in, rather than focusing too heavily on which options are **best financially**.

2) The **approach** used can depend on the **nature** of the decision. For example, a firm might use **evidence-based** decision-making for **big decisions** that are **expensive** and **hard to reverse**, such as stopping the production of a product. However, it might use **subjective** decision-making for **smaller decisions** that are **less costly** and **easily reversed**, such as whether to offer customers **free refreshments** when looking around a showroom.

Warm-Up Questions

Q1 Give one reason why a business might choose short-termism over long-termism.
Q2 What is an evidence-based approach to decision-making?
Q3 Give two disadvantages of using a subjective approach to decision-making.

Exam Question

Q1 Stevens and Judd PLC is a world-renowned producer of medical imaging products. The company invests in employees by sending them on training courses. It is also a leading investor in research and development. Explain how the use of long-termism could benefit Stevens and Judd PLC. [4 marks]

My school cut the summer holiday to two weeks — it had long-termism...

There is no one-size-fits-all approach for making decisions in business — the choice between long- and short-termism, and evidence-based and subjective decision-making depends on the business and the decisions that are being made.

Corporate Culture

A business's corporate culture (or organisational culture) is based on the business's values and objectives.

Corporate Culture is the Way Things are Done in a Business

1) **Corporate culture** is the way that people do things in a firm, and the way that they **expect** things to be done. It reflects the firm's **values** and is an important way to shape the **expectations** and **attitudes** of staff and managers.

2) Because corporate culture **affects staff behaviour** and how they make **decisions**, it has an effect on **planning**, **objective setting** and **strategy**. It also affects staff **motivation** and **productivity**.

3) Corporate culture is **created** and **reinforced** by business **rules**, **managerial attitudes**, **managerial behaviour** and **recruitment** policies that recruit people who "fit in". The **induction** and **training** of new staff should reflect the firm's corporate culture.

4) A business's culture can be **identified** by looking at its **founders** (the people who **developed** the business and its values), the **history** of the business, **symbols** that represent the business's values (like staff mottos and sayings), and the **ceremonies** that the business holds (such as office parties).

5) The **more** that a business's **core values** are reflected in **everything** it **does**, the **stronger** the **culture** will become (see below).

Corporate Culture Can be Strong or Weak

1) Corporate culture is **strong** when employees **agree** with the **corporate values** of the business.

2) Having a **strong** corporate culture has the advantage that employees need **less supervision**, because their behaviour will naturally tend to fit in with the business's values. Staff also tend to be more **loyal** to the business, so **staff turnover** is lower, and it increases employees' **motivation**, so they work more **productively**.

3) **Weak** culture is where the employees of a firm **don't** share the firm's values, and have to be **forced** to comply with them (e.g. through **business policies**).

Mike was determined to show his enthusiasm for a strong culture.

There are Four Main Types of Corporate Culture

1) **Corporate culture** has a big impact on how businesses handle change, and whether staff are **open** to change or **resistant** to it. In 1993, Charles Handy identified the following **four main types** of corporate culture:

1) Power Culture

1) Power cultures have a centralised structure where decision-making authority is limited to a small number of people — perhaps just one person in the centre (possibly the owner).

2) Power cultures may begin to struggle if the business grows and cannot be run from the centre.

3) Employees are likely to be more resistant to change, because they don't have the opportunity to give their opinions on what changes should and shouldn't be made.

4) They might also be resistant to changes because they don't have enough faith in senior managers who they feel are out of touch with the day-to-day activities of the business.

2) Role Culture

1) **Role cultures** are common in **bureaucratic firms** where authority is defined by job title. **Decisions** come from **senior managers**, so employees don't have the **opportunity** to get involved in the **decision-making process**.

2) Organisations with role cultures tend to have **poor communication** between departments so they **respond slowly** to change — this could result in them **losing out** to **competitors** in **new** or **expanding** markets where strategies need to be developed and implemented quickly.

3) These organisations also tend to **avoid risk** for fear of failure, which means that **change is quite rare**.

4) Any changes that are brought in will meet **resistance** as staff are **not used** to doing things differently.

Corporate Culture

3) Person Culture

1) **Person culture** is common in loose organisations of **individual workers**, usually **professional partnerships** such as solicitors, accountants, doctors, etc.

2) The **objectives** of these firms will be defined by the **personal ambitions** of the individuals involved. The firms have to ensure that the individuals actually have **common goals**.

3) **Decisions** are made **jointly**, so all employees are likely to be **comfortable** and **accepting** of any changes that are made because they have agreed to them.

4) However, decisions on **change** can be **difficult** to make — individuals will often think about what is **best** for **themselves** rather than thinking about what is **best** for the **organisation**.

4) Task Culture

1) Organisations with a **task culture** place an emphasis on getting specific **tasks** done.

2) Task culture gets **small teams** together to work on a project, then disbands them. There may be **conflict** between teams for **resources** and **budgets**. It can be confusing if a firm has too many **products** or **projects**.

3) This culture supports **objectives** which are based around **products** (e.g. make Product X the market leader).

4) Task cultures respond well to **management by objectives**, which translates corporate objectives into **specific targets** for each **department** and for each **individual employee**.

5) Staff working in a business with a task culture are likely to think that change is normal because they are used to **changing teams** often and working with a variety of people. This means that they are likely to be **less resistant** to change in general.

2) There are many other types of corporate culture, including **customer-focused** culture (which bases its values on customer **feedback** and **satisfaction**), **clan** culture (where the organisation acts more like a **family** with managers as **parent-figures**), **market** culture (where the focus is on **competition** with **other firms** and **between employees**), and **entrepreneurial culture** (which focuses on **employees thinking** of ways to **improve** the firm).

3) Large organisations can have **sub-cultures** in **different areas** of the business. For example, a **research** and **development** department might use **task culture**, whereas the **finances department** might use **role culture**.

Lots of **Factors Affect** How a **Corporate Culture** is **Formed**

The **type** and **strength** of **corporate culture** that a business develops can be **influenced** by **many factors**. E.g.:

- A business's founders — the founders 'set the tone' for their firm's culture. If they are still heavily involved in the running of the business then it's more likely that their values and vision of the business will be passed on to employees, creating a strong culture. The personality of founders could also influence the business's culture — for example, a strong-minded founder might establish a power culture. This culture could continue even if the founders are no longer involved in the business.

- The history of the business — for example, a firm that started small and had a lot of success as it grew could have a stronger culture than one which has had a lot of problems and several different owners.

- The nature of the business and its products — for example, a hair salon might have a person culture as each hairdresser has their own customers and aims. However, a firm that makes hair products might have a power culture, as the focus is on making the products, so employees have less say.

- The business environment in which the business was formed — this can include any external influences on a business's strategy that are identified in a PESTLE analysis (p.109). For example, if the firm had little competition for a long time, it's unlikely to have developed a customer-focused culture.

- The recruitment and promotion of staff — the attitudes of staff that a business chooses to hire and promote can affect the culture that develops within the business. For example, a business that hires lots of forward-thinking, creative people may develop an entrepreneurial culture.

- Working conditions and rewards — these can affect employees' motivation and attitudes towards the business. When staff feel more valued the culture of the business is likely to be stronger.

- Attitude to customer service — businesses that value their customers and offer high levels of customer service are more likely to develop a customer-focused culture.

Corporate Culture

Managers Might Want to Change the Corporate Culture

There are **two** main reasons why the managers of a business might want to **change** the corporate culture:

1) The corporate culture of a business depends on the **preferences** of its **leaders**. When a new manager joins a business, they might change it to make it more **similar** to businesses they have worked in **before**. E.g. if a manager who is used to working in a business with a **role culture** starts working in a business with a **task culture**, they might **force** the business to adopt a role culture because that is what they are used to.

2) A business might change its culture in order to be more **competitive**. E.g. businesses with a **power culture** can be **slow** to spot ways to **save money**, or more **efficient** ways of working, and staff may be **resistant** to any **changes** in their ways of working. Adopting a **task culture** where all the staff are **frequently changing** roles means that they will be **less resistant** to changes that make the business more **competitive**.

Changing the Corporate Culture Can be Difficult

1) Employees usually **resist** any kind of change, including changes in **corporate culture**. Employees who have worked for the business for a **long time** are **especially likely** to resist changes to the **corporate culture**, because they'll think the way they've **always done** things is better. Telling employees **why** a **change** to culture is **necessary** can help to **minimise** their reluctance to change.

"They can take away our corporate culture, but they can never take away our free tea and biscuits."

2) Changing corporate culture means changing the **attitudes** and **behaviour** of staff, so it's much more **complicated** than changing things like pricing structure. E.g. the managers of a firm might want to change from a **person culture** to a **task culture**, but splitting people up into **small teams** and giving them **a project** won't achieve anything if employees just want to work **individually** and in their own **interests**.

3) It can be **more difficult** to make changes if the business already has a **strong culture**. The culture can be **woven into** all aspects of the business, such as its **objectives**, **values** and **communication** practices. These could **reinforce** one another, making it very hard to **change** the **culture** in **one part** of the business, as other parts of the business might cause it to **change back**.

4) Changing the corporate culture can also be very **expensive**. It might involve changing the **office layout**, giving **extra training** to staff, devising **new processes**, changing the **business motto** on marketing material, etc. This means that businesses can't always **afford** to **change their culture** as much as they would like to.

5) The **HR department** plays a **big role** in changing the corporate culture of a business — for example, they might need to change their **recruitment** and **induction procedures**, or their **payment** and **reward system**.

Warm-Up Questions

Q1 What is corporate culture?

Q2 Give three benefits of a business having a strong culture.

Q3 Describe a role culture.

Q4 Why is changing corporate culture difficult?

Exam Question

Q1 MindGadgitz is a 20-year-old business that develops new gadgets for sale to the public. It currently has a strong power culture, but in order to improve efficiency, new managers are planning to change the culture to a task culture. Assess how the change may affect employee motivation within the business. [10 marks]

One day I'm going to open my own bakery — it will have a roll culture...

This stuff on corporate culture's pretty interesting, or at least I think so. Remember that the corporate culture of a business affects all sorts of things — from whether it takes financial risks, to whether it has office parties.

Stakeholders

Businesses have to take into account their stakeholders when making decisions. Decisions will affect different stakeholders in different ways — so businesses may prioritise certain groups of stakeholders (like their shareholders), or they may try to satisfy all their stakeholders at once. It would be so much simpler if they could all just agree...

Businesses Have to Meet the Needs of Stakeholders

1) Everyone who is **affected by a business** is called a **stakeholder**.
2) Each **group** of **stakeholders** has their **own objectives** — things that they **want to achieve**.
3) Sometimes these **complement** the **business's objectives** (e.g. when the firm wants to maximise profits and stakeholders want this too) and sometimes they **conflict** with them (e.g. when the firm wants to move production abroad but stakeholders don't want this).
4) Businesses consider **stakeholder objectives** when **making decisions** and setting **business objectives**.
5) Stakeholders can be **internal** or **external**.

Internal Stakeholders

1) **Internal stakeholders** are the **people inside** a business.
2) The **owners** are the **most important** stakeholders. They make a **profit** if the business is **successful** and **decide** what happens to the business. Making **profit** might be the owners' **main objective**, but it probably isn't their only one. For example, they might also be interested in making sure the business is **acting ethically**.

- In limited companies, shareholders are the owners of the business — a shareholder is anyone who owns at least one share in a limited company (see page 51). In a private limited company, shares are usually bought by friends and family of the original owners, whereas they can be bought by anyone in a public limited company.
- Shareholders have the right to receive a dividend, if the profit is being used in this way, so shareholders usually want the business to have high dividends and a high share price.
- Shareholders have the right to vote on key decisions and the performance of the company. If a shareholder owns more than 50% of the shares, they're called the majority shareholder. The majority shareholder has the most power in decision-making.

Bert isn't a big fan of stakeholders.

3) **Employees** are also internal stakeholders. Their **main objectives** are to earn a **decent wage** and have **pleasant working conditions**. They're also interested in **job security** and **promotion prospects**. Managers have **extra concerns** — they'll probably get some of the **blame** if the firm does **badly**, and some of the **credit** if things **go well**.

External Stakeholders

1) **External stakeholders** are the people **outside** of a **business** who are **affected** by it.
2) **Customers'** main objectives are usually to get **high quality** products at **low prices**. They probably also want good **customer service** and **communication** from the business.
3) **Suppliers** are the people and businesses who **sell products** to the business. The business provides them with their **income** — if it can't pay quickly enough, the suppliers can have **cash flow** problems. **Suppliers'** objectives are to be paid a **fair price**, and to be paid **on time**.
4) **Members** of the **local community** are stakeholders — their objectives are for the business to **maintain** or **improve** the **standard of living** in the community. The **local community** will **gain** if the business provides **local employment** and **sponsors** local activities. The community will **suffer** if the business causes noise and pollution, or if the business has to **cut jobs**.
5) One of the **government's** objectives is to **get money** from the business — the government gets more in **taxes** when the business makes **more profit**. The government could also have an objective for **business growth** — this will **create jobs**, meaning the government will get **even more** in taxes (from workers) and will have to **pay out less** to support unemployed people. The government also wants firms to **act lawfully**.
6) **Pressure groups** and **campaigners** fight for a **certain cause**, such as protecting the environment or employee rights. Their objectives are to make sure the business's **behaviours** are in line with what they fight for.

Stakeholders

Different Stakeholders' Objectives Can Conflict with Each Other

1) As you saw on the previous page, stakeholders all have their own **objectives** — it's usual for the objectives of **different stakeholders** to **conflict** with each other.

2) In particular, the objectives of **shareholders** can conflict with those of **other stakeholders**.

> **Example:** **Shareholders** might be happy if a firm **cut costs** in order to **increase its profit**. But if this reduces the **quality** of the products, **customers** won't be happy and could **stop buying** the firm's products. If the firm reduces its costs by **paying employees less**, **refusing** to give **pay rises** and **promotions**, or **reducing training**, staff may become **demotivated** and may be more likely to **leave** the firm. **Suppliers** might also be unhappy if the firm changes to a **cheaper source** of raw materials.

3) Businesses can have **different approaches** to the way stakeholders **influence** their **decision-making**. Some may focus particularly on **shareholders**, whereas others may **consider all** of their stakeholders.

4) A business that **prioritises** the **objectives** of its **shareholders** over those of other stakeholders will tend to focus on **profit-based** objectives. This helps to ensure that shareholders get good returns by increasing the **share price** and the **dividend payments**. A business with **profit-based** objectives might be more likely to use a **short-termism** approach to decision-making (p.128).

Remember, shareholders might not only be interested in profit — they're often interested in the business's other objectives too.

5) A business that takes a **stakeholder approach** and considers the objectives of **all** of its **stakeholders** in its business decisions is likely to focus less heavily on maximising profit. Its corporate objectives are likely to be **wider-ranging** and put more focus on **acting ethically** and being **socially responsible** (see p.136-137). A business with a **stakeholder approach** is more likely to use a **long-termism** approach to decision-making (p.128).

> **Example:** Lush is a private limited company that makes cosmetics. It has business objectives that are influenced by a wide range of stakeholders. This includes paying staff above the minimum wage, sourcing ingredients ethically, and giving money to charities. These actions mean that shareholders might get fewer returns than they would do if Lush prioritised maximising profit.

Vrinda felt like her stakeholders always had conflicting objectives.

6) Businesses that aim to consider the interests of all their stakeholders must try to satisfy as **many** groups as possible and **still survive financially**. This might **not** always be **possible**, so the business might need to **decide** which group to **prioritise**. This might be done using **stakeholder mapping** (see next page).

7) Stakeholders **don't always disagree** though — sometimes their interests **overlap**. For example, making workers **happy** can actually help **productivity** and **raise profits**.

Relationships with Stakeholders are Important

1) Firms need to **manage** their relationships with stakeholders. If they focus on satisfying **one** stakeholder (e.g. the shareholders) at the **expense** of another (e.g. the employees), it could result in problems (e.g. staff **leaving** or **going on strike**), which will **damage** the firm. Managing these relationships can **prevent** this from happening.

2) One way of managing relationships is by **consulting** key stakeholders before making any major decisions. Stakeholders are more likely to feel **valued** if their **opinions** are considered. If the stakeholders have **specialist knowledge**, this will benefit the business as well.

3) Good **communication** is vital in managing relationships with stakeholders. For example, keeping **employees** informed about any changes to the business will make them feel included. Businesses can use **social media** and their **website** to communicate with **customers**.

Stakeholders

Stakeholder Mapping Considers Power and Interest

Managers consider which stakeholders are **most important** to them when setting objectives. **Stakeholder mapping** helps identify how much **interest in** and **power** (or **influence**) **over** the business different stakeholders have.

1) A stakeholder map helps a business decide how to best manage its stakeholders. Each group is mapped to one of four quadrants, which determines how much communication is needed and how much attention is paid to their views when making decisions.

2) Stakeholders with high levels of power and high levels of interest in the business need to be managed most closely, as their satisfaction is vital to the business. This group requires the most effort.

3) Stakeholders with little power and little interest in the business require monitoring but are less important to the business.

Stakeholder Mapping for a Small Italian Restaurant

If you were thinking this whole **stakeholder mapping** thing would make more sense with a **real-life example**, you're in luck. Here's a stakeholder map for a **small Italian restaurant** (i.e. not a chain).

The **local council's environmental health department** has a **lot of power**, but **less** interest in the restaurant. **Local media** can have a **big influence** — if the restaurant is **reviewed** in the local press, it needs to make a **good impression**. These groups mustn't be allowed to become dissatisfied.

The **shareholders** need to be kept **informed** about new developments (e.g. plans for an outside eating area) and their **opinions** taken into account. They are a **key group** as their investment is **vital** to the restaurant's **future**.

Local residents need to be **monitored** to make sure that they are not experiencing any **disturbance** (e.g. from any late night events). This stakeholder group should require the **least communication effort**.

The **employees**, **suppliers** and **customers** all have a **strong interest** in the business, but not as much **power** as the **shareholders**. They need to be **informed** about **small changes** and **consulted** on **bigger** ones (e.g. customers should be informed about a new menu and employees should be consulted about changes to opening hours).

Warm-Up Questions

Q1 State whether the following groups are internal or external stakeholders:
a) part-time staff, b) suppliers, c) the government.

Q2 Give one example where shareholders' interests are in conflict with another stakeholder group.

Q3 Which area has the least important stakeholders in a stakeholder map?

Exam Question

Q1 Oxforth Ltd makes fertilisers and pesticides. Managers are given a large amount of responsibility and are paid bonuses depending on the business's profits. Demand for its products is higher at some times of the year than others, so it takes on temporary production staff to meet demand. Environmental campaigners have been targeting the firm due to concerns about the pollution created in the manufacturing process. The company's directors have decided that its main objectives will be centred around maximising profit.
Assess whether Oxforth Ltd's objectives might create conflict between its stakeholders. [12 marks]

My dad loves eating beef — he's a big steak holder for the local butcher...

Don't get confused between stakeholders and shareholders. Shareholders are stakeholders, but not all stakeholders are shareholders, which is a little bit befuddling. Anyway, you have to think about how important each group of stakeholders are and how to keep the most important ones happy (you could write them a poem, that would be nice).

Ethics in Business

As well as all the other things they have to think about, firms have to think about the ethics of their decisions. Even if they have the most amazing products ever, acting unethically could mean that customers won't buy them.

Firms Make Decisions About Whether to Behave Ethically

1) **Ethics** are principles that govern which **behaviours** are **morally acceptable** to **society**, **individuals** or **groups**.

2) A firm might have a strong **ethical stance** that is clear from its **mission statement** and its **corporate culture**. For example, it might strive to **reduce** the **impact** that all of its **business activities** have on the **environment**.

3) Even firms **without** a **strong ethical stance** are likely to have an **ethical code** to guide the **decisions** and **behaviours** of its employees according to the firm's values. Managers will **consider** the **ethics** of the **strategic decisions** that they make — they'll consider whether their decision might be **viewed** as being **morally wrong** by some people, and how this could **affect** the **business** as a whole.

4) Some **ethical issues** a business may have to think about **include**:

The ethical issues faced by firms that operate overseas are covered in more detail on pages 180-181.

- **Location** — e.g. **labour costs** might be **cheaper overseas**, but this can be because there are **fewer laws** about **workers' welfare** in some countries, e.g. workers might be forced to work in **unsafe conditions**.
- **Suppliers** — businesses might need to think about the **ethical stance** of their **suppliers**. For example, suppliers might be **exploiting** their **workers** to keep their **prices low**. So businesses need to **decide** whether they are willing to buy from these suppliers to **reduce costs**, or whether they should buy from a **more expensive** supplier that **treats workers** more **fairly**.
- **Bribery and corruption** — in some markets, it might not be uncommon for firms to **bribe people**, or use other **corrupt behaviours**, in order to get their business **activities approved**. Adopting these behaviours **benefits** the business, but puts them at an **unfair advantage** over other firms in the market.
- **Selling tactics** — e.g. staff might persuade customers into signing up for contracts (e.g. for **broadband**) by promoting their **low price**, but fail to inform customers **clearly** of any **hidden costs**. The firm might also make it very **hard** for customers to **leave** the contract, such as by charging very **high exit fees**.

There Can be a Trade-Off Between Ethics and Profit

1) **Acting ethically** usually means a business **isn't as profitable** as it could be. This is often because being ethical **increases** a firm's **costs**. For example, a business might choose to **ethically source** its **raw materials**, which are unlikely to be the cheapest available. It might also **pay more** than the lowest possible **wages**.

2) This means the firm makes **less profit** on each item sold, or it will have to charge **higher prices** to earn the same amount of profit, but this could lead to a **loss of sales** if a **competitor's products** are cheaper.

3) So there is a **trade-off** between ethics and profit — being **more ethical** means having to **sacrifice profit**. Firms have to decide **how much** profit they're prepared to **sacrifice** in order to **act ethically** — if they sacrifice too much profit it could **damage the business**, such as by **limiting** its **growth** and making people **less likely** to **invest**. Often a firm can't be as ethical as it would like to be, to ensure it's still making **acceptable levels** of **profit**.

4) However, there isn't always a **trade-off** between **acting ethically** and making **profit**. **Customers** who are **concerned** about **ethical issues** might be **willing** to **pay higher prices** for ethical products. **Employees** might also **prefer** to **work** for ethical businesses, which will **reduce recruitment costs** and **staff turnover**.

How Businesses Reward Their Employees is an Ethical Issue

1) There's **growing concern** in **business ethics** about the **relative** levels of **pay** between different levels of **staff**. Often, **senior managers** get paid **huge sums** of money while many other employees get the **minimum wage**.

2) The **ethical issue** is whether the **additional skills** and **experience** of senior **executives**, as well as the **importance** of the **work** they do, is **worth** the **additional pay** they receive.

3) **Firms** employing executives with high salaries **argue** that the pay levels are **necessary** to **attract** the **best candidates** for the job in an **international labour market**.

4) Some people might object to businesses **rewarding** senior members of staff with **big performance-related bonuses** — this could be viewed as **unethical** if the business has **let customers down**. For example, the owners of some **train businesses** are paid **large bonuses**, despite frequent **delays** and **cancellations** of trains.

Ethics in Business

CSR — Making the World a Better Place

1) **Ethics** are such a big thing in business that firms (especially larger ones) often have a **Corporate Social Responsibility** (CSR) policy.

2) **CSR** is **more** than just **acting ethically** when making strategic **decisions** — it's the idea that a business should go **above and beyond** what is required by law to help **society** as a **whole**.

3) Businesses' CSR policies often include **reducing** their **negative impact** on the **environment**, supporting **charities** and **community projects**, and **treating** their **workforce ethically**.

4) The public are **more aware** of what businesses do now than they were in the past, so many businesses now **publicise** how they meet their **social responsibilities**.

> **Examples of CSR initiatives**
>
> - Barclays have a partnership with Teach First (a charity aiming to recruit and train high quality teachers to teach in low income areas).
> - Marks and Spencer work to ensure their suppliers' employees have good working conditions. They agree standards with suppliers, visit them regularly and work with them to improve conditions.
> - McDonald's Planet Champion Programme trains employees to find ways of reducing the environmental impact of the company. McDonald's also runs daily litter picking patrols, as well as employing full-time 'litter champions' in some city centres.

CSR Costs Money but has Advantages

1) Businesses implementing CSR can gain a **competitive advantage**:

> - It improves **brand loyalty** and attracts **new customers** through **positive publicity** — although the public may be **sceptical** and think it's just a **PR stunt**.
> - People will choose to work for firms with **good CSR records** over firms with bad ones — this means that the business will attract more **talented** applicants.
> - **Staff morale** will **improve** and they will be **more motivated** to work for and stay with the firm.

2) However, CSR can have its **downsides**:

> - CSR has **costs**, which **shareholders** may see as a **misuse of funds**. This can lead to them **withdrawing their investment**, or **pressuring firms** to stop their CSR activities.
> - The costs may be **passed on to customers**. Many customers are prepared to pay **more** for 'socially responsible' products — but if the market is **price-sensitive** (e.g. during a recession), sales will fall.
> - The expectation of CSR puts **small businesses** at a disadvantage. They are less likely to have **funds** to spare for CSR projects, or to be able to **employ** someone to organise their CSR activities.

Warm-Up Questions

Q1 Give one reason why it might be considered unethical to pay large bonuses to senior managers.

Q2 What is meant by corporate social responsibility?

PRACTICE QUESTIONS

Exam Question

Q1 GBB PLC is a UK-based furniture manufacturer. It has an extensive CSR policy, which includes paying all workers at least 15% more than the minimum wage. It also donates money to charities, and often has volunteer days, where its employees help on local projects. One of the firm's long-term aims is to eliminate the use of all unnecessary plastic in its manufacturing and packaging.
Assess two drawbacks that GBB PLC's CSR policy could have to the firm. [8 marks]

CSR — not just a new TV crime series...

Consumers are taking more and more notice of what firms do — time to pull their (ethically-sourced) socks up.

Interpretation of Financial Statements

You covered financial statements on pages 71 and 74-75 — the next two pages look at stakeholders' interests in them.

Stakeholders are Interested in a Firm's Statement of Comprehensive Income

1) The **statement** of **comprehensive income** (also called a profit and loss account, see p.71) shows a firm's **revenue**, **costs** and **profit**. It indicates if a firm is **profitable** — a **profitable firm** has a positive **net profit**.

2) Different **stakeholders** have **different interests** in a firm (p.133), so they'll be interested in different parts of the **statement of comprehensive income**. **Comparing** statements across **several years** lets them look for **trends**.

> *Remember, when reading a statement of comprehensive income, you start from the top and work your way down through the different measures of profit.*

Shareholders

- **Shareholders** will look at a firm's statement of comprehensive income to see how **profitable** it is (p.72). The higher the profitability, the higher the **dividends** can be.

- **Trends** in net profit **over time** can show shareholders **how risky** investments are — a firm with a **fluctuating profit** is probably a **more risky investment** than one with a **steadily increasing** profit.

- Shareholders might also look at **trends** in **how much** of a business's **profit** is spent on **dividends** — if it **fluctuates** a lot, or is **decreasing**, then shareholders might not think it's **worth investing**.

- A good firm to invest in is one that can **increase its revenue** without increasing its **costs** too much. So shareholders might look at the **relative changes** in a firm's **revenue** and **costs** over time.

> *Shareholders will be interested in a firm's net profit after tax, as this determines their dividend payments.*

> *An owner can have the same interests in the statement of comprehensive income as shareholders and managers, depending on the owner's role within the business.*

Managers

- Managers will be interested in the revenue and expenses of the firm over time to see if they're changing — if revenues are decreasing or expenses are increasing they might then need to figure out why and make any necessary changes to the business.

- Statements of comprehensive income might be made for each department, so managers can compare between departments to help identify where costs could be reduced.

- Managers could compare their firm's statement of comprehensive income with competitors' to see how it's performing. From this, managers can make decisions about strategies and tactics and whether they need to make any changes. For example, if a firm's revenue is decreasing but a competitor's is increasing, then the competitor might be taking some of the firm's market share. Managers might then decide to create new advertisements to attract more customers.

- Comparing statements of comprehensive income with competitors' can also indicate if a firm's costs are too high. If this is the case, managers might look at ways to reduce costs.

Loan providers

- **Loan providers** (e.g. banks) that have **loaned money** to a firm might be interested in its **operating profit**, as this is where the **interest** on **loans** is paid from.

- A **loan provider** might be **unwilling** to lend money to a business with a **low operating profit**, as there is a **risk** that the business won't be able to **pay** the **interest**.

> *There are several other sources of finance for businesses* — see pages 54-55.

Suppliers

- Suppliers might check if a firm's revenue in the past has been enough to pay its suppliers — a new supplier won't start selling to a firm if it's unlikely to get paid.

Employees

- **Employees** might be interested in the **profitability** of the business — a profitable business is more likely to **continue trading** and **maintain employment**.

- Workers might also look at **net profit** — depending on the firm, this could indicate whether employees will get a **pay rise** or **bonus**, and **how much** they might get.

Geoffrey was pretty sure his firm had enough profit to buy 20% more treats per month.

Interpretation of Financial Statements

Statements of Financial Position Give Information to Stakeholders

1) The statement of financial position (also called a balance sheet, p.74) shows the **assets** and **liabilities** of a firm at a particular **point in time**. This shows how much a firm is **worth**, which is useful for **stakeholders**.

2) **Comparing** the statement of financial position from the **same date** in **different years** allows stakeholders to pick out **trends** in a firm's finances and evaluate its **financial performance**.

3) **Shareholders** can use the statement of financial position as an **indicator** of whether a firm's **profit** is likely to increase or decrease. For example, a **quick increase** in **non-current assets** shows that a firm has invested in property or machinery. This means that the firm is investing in a **growth strategy**, which may increase its profit over the medium term — this is useful information for shareholders and potential shareholders, who want to see **more profit**.

4) An increase in **reserves** also suggests an increase in **profits** — this is good news for shareholders if the business has also had an increase in **cash**, as they could receive **higher dividends**.

5) **Shareholders** might also be interested in the firm's sources of capital — a firm with a lot of loans has to **pay** them **back** with interest, so there is a risk that the business might make **little profit** after these have been paid.

6) Managers might look at whether the business has the **financial flexibility** to **acquire capital** if it needs to. So they might consider if the business can **cope** with **borrowing** more money to raise capital, rather than **selling off** non-current **assets** — it can cope with more **debt** from **long-term loans** if its net current and non-current **assets** are larger than the **non-current liabilities** it will have when it takes out the loan.

Stakeholders are Interested in Solvency and Liquidity

1) Statements of financial position show a business's **liquidity** and **solvency**.

2) **Liquidity** is the ability of a business to turn assets into cash (p.76) — **current assets** are more liquid than **non-current assets**, so a business with a **low value** of **current assets** will have **low liquidity**.

3) **Solvency** is a business's ability to pay its debts (p.76). If a business's **current assets** are **larger** than its **current liabilities** it is **solvent**, but if its **liabilities exceed** its **assets** it is unable to pay its debts and is **insolvent**.

4) Different **stakeholder groups** are affected by a business's solvency and liquidity:

- Managers and owners can look at a firm's solvency and liquidity to assess if it's about to go bankrupt. They can then make changes to prevent this, for example by selling some of their non-current assets.

- Suppliers can look at the statement of financial position to see how liquid a firm's assets are, as well as its solvency. A solvent firm with more liquid assets will be better at paying bills on time. This helps suppliers to decide whether to offer the firm supplies on credit, and how much credit to offer.

- Loan providers will want to know a firm's ability to pay back loans and interest. A firm with assets that are much larger than its liabilities is less of a risk to lend to than one that is close to insolvency.

Warm-Up Questions

Q1 Explain what shareholders might be interested in from a firm's statement of comprehensive income.

Q2 Explain why a bank might be interested in a business's solvency.

Exam Question

Q1 HB Ltd is a chain of stationery shops. Extracts from the firm's statements of financial position in 2016 and 2017 are on the right.
   a) Explain whether a supplier was more likely to offer credit to HB Ltd in 2016 or 2017, based on the values in the table. [4 marks]
   b) Using the information in the table, assess how the changes in the firm's finances might have affected managers' decisions about how to raise capital in 2018. [10 marks]

	1.4.16 £000	1.4.17 £000
Total non-current assets	4.9	11.2
Total current assets	16.5	6.2
Total current liabilities	(5.4)	(11.2)
Net current assets	11.1	(5)
Non-current liabilities	5	5
Net assets	11	1.2
Share capital	2	(0.8)
Retained profit	9	2.4

Water firms make for great investments — they have high liquidity...

Make sure you understand which stakeholders will be interested in which parts of a financial statement, and why.

Gearing, ROCE and Analysing Ratios

Just in case you were really missing accounting ratios, here are some more to float your boat. Make sure you have a look back at the ratios on pages 72 and 76 first to prepare for the thrills of gearing and return on capital employed.

Gearing Shows **Where** a Business gets its **Capital** From

1) The **gearing ratio** is an important accounting ratio. It shows the proportion of a firm's finance that's from **non-current liabilities** (long-term debt), rather than **share capital** or **reserves** (equity).

2) The **gearing ratio** is calculated using information from the lower part of a **statement** of **financial position** (see p.74) — the part that shows where the money comes from. To work out the gearing ratio, you first have to calculate the **capital employed**:

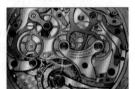

Capital employed shows the total amount of finance in the business (from loans, reserves and shares).

Capital employed = non-current liabilities + total equity

3) You can then work out the gearing ratio by dividing the amount of finance that comes from **non-current liabilities** by the **capital employed**.

$$\text{Gearing ratio (\%)} = \frac{\text{non-current liabilities}}{\text{capital employed}} \times 100$$

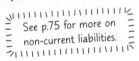

See p.75 for more on non-current liabilities.

4) A gearing **above 50%** shows that **over half** of a firm's finance is from **long-term debt** — the business is **high geared**. A gearing **below 50%** shows that a business is **low geared**, because **less than half** of the finance comes from long-term debt.

5) Gearing shows how **vulnerable** a business is to changes in **interest rates**. When a business **borrows money** from **banks** and other loan providers, it has to **pay interest back** to the lender, on top of the money it borrowed. The amount of interest it has to **pay back** is determined by **interest rates** and any changes in them (p.90).

Looks pretty high geared to me.

6) The **amount** a firm can **borrow** depends on its profitability and the value of its **assets** — the more assets a firm can offer as **security**, the more money it will be able to borrow.

> **Example:** A firm has a gearing of 11% — it's low geared.
> - This tells you that most long-term funds come from shareholders or reserves, not borrowing.
> - This could be a sign that the firm is risk averse — it doesn't want to run the risk of spending too much money on interest payments.
> - Because the firm doesn't have to spend its profits on interest payments, it can withstand a fall in profits more easily than a highly geared firm — the firm can reduce dividend payments to shareholders, unlike loan repayments which have to be made.

> **Example:** Another firm has a gearing of 72% — it's high geared.
> - This tells you that most long-term funds come from borrowing.
> - It's obvious that the firm is willing to take risks — if profits fall, or interest rates rise, the business still has to keep up with the loan repayments or it could lose the assets the loans are secured on (e.g. business premises).
> - The business might be high geared in order to fund growth (see below), or because its directors don't want outside shareholders to own a large part of the business, and so they prefer to borrow money rather than sell shares.

High Gearing has Rewards for Businesses

High gearing can be **risky**, but some businesses are willing to take these risks because of the **potential rewards**:

1) One benefit of **borrowing** money for a business is extra **funds** for expansion. Ideally, a loan is invested in projects or technology that **increase profits** by more than enough to pay off the loan repayments.

2) **High gearing** can be attractive during a **growth phase**. A firm that's trying to become the market leader, and has growing profits along with a strong product portfolio, may decide to borrow heavily in order to **fund expansion** and gain a **competitive advantage**. This will **increase** the firm's **gearing**.

3) During times of **growth**, there is plenty of **profit** even after they've paid the loan interest and repayments, so high gearing can be good for the business.

Gearing, ROCE and Analysing Ratios

High Gearing also has Risks for Businesses

1) The **risk** to the business of borrowing money is that it might not be able to afford the **repayments** — it might not make enough profit to pay back the **loan** and **interest**.

2) Taking out loans can be **risky** even when interest rates are low, because they might **go up** later and the business will still be committed to making the **repayments**.

3) The more the firm is **borrowing**, the harder they'll be hit by a **rise** in **interest rates**. So a firm with a **high gearing ratio** is more likely to be **affected** by a **change** in interest rates than one with a **low gearing ratio**. Remember, interest rates are affected by the **Bank of England base rate** (p.90).

When interest rates are very low, high gearing is less risky because interest payments are lower.

Businesses Borrow Money for Different Reasons

The **risks** of being a **high geared** business can be **different** for different businesses — it can depend on **why** the business has **borrowed money** in the first place. For example:

Example: Business A has a gearing ratio of 70%. It's borrowed money to buy new machinery, so that it can lower its unit costs. This is forecast to increase its gross profit in the long-term — this should mean that the firm can cover the costs of loan repayments and interest.

Business B also has a gearing ratio of 70%, but it's borrowed money to pay its staff and creditors after a surprise fall in sales that has left it struggling to cover costs. The fall in sales means it might struggle to make enough revenue to repay the loan and its interest.

High Gearing has Risks and Rewards for Investors too

1) A lender's **reward** for investing money in a business is getting **paid interest** on the money they loaned. The reward to a **shareholder** for their investment is a share **dividend** (often paid out twice a year). Shareholders can also sell their shares at a **profit** if the share price goes up.

2) Gearing is a crude **risk assessment** that investors can use to help decide whether to invest in a firm. The more the firm borrows, the **more interest** it has to pay — this may affect **profit** and the **return** on **investment**.

3) Since **high gearing** can lead to high profits for firms, shareholders might expect to see **large dividends** and a **big increase** in the share price. So they might be **more likely** to **invest** in a **high geared business**.

4) The **risk** to the **shareholder** of high gearing is that the business may **fail** if it can't afford to keep up with loan repayments. When a business goes into **liquidation**, lenders will probably get the money they're owed, but the shareholders could **lose** most or all of the **money** they've **invested** in the business.

5) Investors might look at **why** a business has **borrowed money**, e.g. to **fund growth** or to **cover financial problems**, to decide whether it's **worth investing** in a **high geared** business.

Return on Capital Employed (ROCE) is a Profitability Ratio

1) Another important accounting ratio is the **return on capital employed** (**ROCE**). It's a profitability ratio that's considered to be the best way of analysing **profitability**. It's expressed as a **percentage**, calculated by:

There are other profitability ratios on p.72.

$$\text{Return on Capital Employed (\%)} = \frac{\text{operating profit}}{\text{capital employed}} \times 100$$

The operating profit is on the statement of comprehensive income (p.71).

2) The **ROCE** tells you how much money is **made** by the firm, compared to the amount **put into** the business. For example, a firm with a ROCE of **10%** is making **10p** in **operating profit** for every **£1** that's been put in. The **higher** the ROCE, the **better**.

3) It's important to **compare** the ROCE with the Bank of England **base rate** (see p.90) — this helps investors decide if they'd be better off putting their money in the **bank**.

4) ROCE can be **improved** by **paying off debt** to reduce non-current liabilities, or by making the business more **efficient** to **increase operating profit**.

5) ROCE is just one measure of **return** on **investment** — another important one is the **average rate of return** (see p.120).

No Danny. I said you had to convince investors with a good ROCE.

Theme 3: Section 15 — Assessing Competitiveness

Gearing, ROCE and Analysing Ratios

Ratio Analysis can be Very Useful...

1) **Accounting ratios** are a really good way of looking at a business's **performance** over a period of time. By interpreting the ratios, stakeholders can spot **trends**, and identify the **financial strengths** and **weaknesses** of the business.

2) However, these trends need to take account of **variable factors** — things which change over time, such as **inflation**, **accounting procedures**, the **business activities** of the firm and the market **environment**.

3) Ratio analysis can be used to make **business decisions**. For example:

- Managers can use gearing ratios to decide how to **finance growth**. If the firm is already **high geared**, it might be better to **raise capital** through **issuing shares**, to avoid increasing gearing with more loans.

- **Potential lenders** can use accounting ratios to help them decide if they want to **lend** to a firm — for example, they might use the **current ratio** and the **acid test ratio** (page 76) to look at a firm's liquidity.

- **Potential shareholders** might compare the accounting ratios between firms to decide where to **buy shares**. This could include **net profit margins** (p.72) — a higher net profit margin could indicate higher **dividends**.

4) It's also useful to **compare** ratios with **other firms**, either in the same or different industries. Ratios provide a more **meaningful** comparison when looking at **different-sized** firms (which may have different **finances**).

... but it has its Limitations

All accounting **ratios** compare figures from the **statement of financial position** or **statement of comprehensive income** and give you a raw **number** as an answer. However, they ignore any **non-numerical factors**, so they don't provide an absolute means of assessing a firm's financial health. Analysing ratios has several **limitations**:

1) The ratios are only as good as the **data** they're **based on**. For example, the **statement of financial position** is a **snapshot** of the firm's finances on a **given day** — on a **different day** they could easily be **different**, which will change the ratios. This might not be a problem if the ratios are available over a **long period** of **time**, as it allows **trends** to be seen.

2) **Internal strengths**, such as the quality of staff, don't appear in the figures, so they won't be in **ratios**.

3) **External factors**, such as the **economic** climate, aren't reflected in the figures, so a firm might need to compare its accounting ratios with **competitors'** to understand them. For example, if a firm's **ROCE** **decreases**, it could look at trends in **competitors'** ROCE values — if competitors' have also worsened, this could indicate that an **economic downturn** has **caused** the **changes**.

4) **Future changes** such as technological advances or changes in interest rates can't be predicted by the figures, so they won't show up in the ratios.

5) Ratios only contain information about the **past** and **present**. A firm which has **started** investing for growth will have poor ratios until the investment **pays off** — it doesn't mean it's not worth investing in.

Warm-Up Questions

Q1 What is meant by "high gearing"?
Q2 How does the gearing of a business affect its vulnerability to changes in interest rates?
Q3 What does ROCE show?
Q4 A business has an operating profit of £50 000, total equity of £85 000 and non-current liabilities of £40 000. Calculate its return on capital employed.

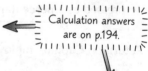
Calculation answers are on p.194.

Q5 Give three limitations of using accounting ratios to assess a business.

Exam Question

Q1 Doodads Ltd is a business that sells decorative homeware in its 3 shops. It is planning to open 2 new shops next year, for which it will need to raise capital. At the end of the previous year, its total equity was £1 300 000, its non-current liabilities were £300 000 and its operating profit was £850 000. The Bank of England base rate was 0.25%. Calculate the gearing ratio and ROCE for Doodads Ltd and evaluate the two options of financing its expansion using long-term loans or reserves. Recommend which option is most suitable for Doodads Ltd. You are advised to show your working. [20 marks]

I get ir-ratio-nally excited about all this gearing...

Gearing and ROCE use similar numbers from financial statements, so make sure you know how each is calculated.

Interpreting Human Resource Data

A firm needs to measure the effectiveness of all the resources it uses, including employees, and then improve them.

Human Resource Data is Analysed Before Making Decisions

1) There are many **figures** that **human resources** (HR) consider when making decisions about recruitment and how they treat the firm's employees — these include **labour productivity**, **labour turnover**, **labour retention** and **absenteeism**.

2) These figures are often calculated using a **performance management system** and are used to check that the business's human resources are always being used to **maximum efficiency**.

3) HR will also compare these figures to their **competitors'** to see who is utilising their **human resources** better and if they need to **improve** in certain areas. E.g. if **labour retention** rates are **higher** in a competitor's business, HR need to look at why employees **don't want to stay** in their business.

Labour Productivity Tells You the Output Per Employee

HR should look at **labour productivity trends** before making decisions on **training**, **recruitment** and **pay**.

$$\text{Labour Productivity} = \frac{\text{Output per period}}{\text{Number of employees}}$$

1) HR can have a **positive impact** on labour productivity by making sure that all employees feel **engaged** and **motivated**. They can also make sure the right people are in the **right roles**.

2) If labour productivity is **increasing** (e.g. after **changing production** methods), HR might reward employees with **bonuses** and **pay rises**. This will keep **motivation levels** high as workers know their hard work is **valued**.

3) If labour productivity is **decreasing** (e.g. if **morale** has fallen) then HR might choose to **retrain** staff, offer bigger **incentives** or even offer **redundancies** and **replace** employees with more skilled labour.

4) HR should **consult** with **staff** to see **why** productivity has fallen **before** they make a decision, as a fall in **productivity** might **not** be because staff aren't **working** as **hard**. For example, if a firm starts making a **new product** that **takes longer** to make than previous products, its productivity will **fall**. HR might not know what caused this until **discussing** the issue with staff.

5) HR could also **compare** their labour productivity data to **competitors'** to see if they need to **improve**, or if they're already ahead of the game.

Labour Turnover Measures the Proportion of Staff Who Leave

$$\text{Labour Turnover (\%)} = \frac{\text{Number of staff leaving}}{\text{Average number of staff employed}} \times 100$$

Average number of staff employed = (staff at the beginning of the time period + staff at the end of the time period) ÷ 2.

1) The **higher** the labour turnover, the **larger** the proportion of workers **leaving** the firm. **High turnover** increases a firm's **costs**, as they will have to pay more to **recruit** and **train** **new staff**. It can also mean that they **lose experienced staff** who know the business.

2) **External causes** of high labour turnover include the growth of other local firms using staff with **similar skills**.

3) **Internal causes** of high labour turnover include **poor motivation** of staff, **low wages**, and a lack of opportunities for **promotion**. Staff will **join other firms** to increase their pay and job responsibilities.

4) A **poor recruitment** process that selects **unsuitable candidates** will also increase labour turnover.

5) Increased **delegation**, **job enrichment**, higher **wages** and better **training** can reduce labour turnover. However, HR should **consult staff** before deciding how to reduce turnover, to find out **why** employees are leaving. For example, **increasing wages** might not reduce labour turnover if staff are leaving because they don't think there's any chance of **career progression**.

6) Some firms **might not** want to **reduce turnover**. For example, **creative firms** might encourage a high turnover to bring in **new ideas**.

Harriet felt like she'd mastered labour turnover now.

Interpreting Human Resource Data

Labour Retention Measures a Business's Ability to Keep its Employees

$$\text{Labour Retention (\%)} = \frac{\text{Number of staff employed at start of period} - \text{number of leavers}}{\text{Number of staff employed at start of period}} \times 100$$

1) **Labour retention** is closely related to **labour turnover**. The **higher** the turnover, the **lower** the retention rate.

2) A **low retention rate** means that the business only keeps a **small proportion** of its employees.

3) HR could deal with a **low retention rate** by improving the **induction** process. They could highlight the **opportunities** available to all employees and reinforce the **values** and **goals** of the business so that employees feel **included** and **valued**.

4) Not all businesses will **interpret** their rates of **labour retention** and **turnover** the same way. For example, a **high** rate of labour **turnover** and **low** labour **retention** could be **bad news** for an **accountancy** firm. However, it might **not** be seen as **a problem** for a firm that has intentionally hired staff for a short time period, like a shop that hires a lot of **temporary staff** close to Christmas.

Absenteeism is the Proportion of Days Missed by Employees

1) Absenteeism shows HR what **percentage** of the labour force is **absent** over a **particular time period**.

$$\text{Absenteeism (\%)} = \frac{\text{Number of days of staff absence in a time period}}{\text{Number of staff employed} \times \text{time period}} \times 100$$

Example: A business has **9** of its **45** staff absent on a given day,

so its absenteeism that day is: $\frac{9}{45} \times 100 = \textbf{20\%}$

Over the **entire year**, all 45 staff should each work 220 days. In 2017, there were 180 days of staff absence.

So the absenteeism for the year is: $\frac{180}{45 \times 220} \times 100 = \textbf{1.82\%}$

Levi was somewhat disappointed with the turnout for the meeting about absenteeism.

2) Absenteeism doesn't distinguish between different **causes of absence**. For example, a **high rate** of absenteeism might be **caused by**:

- A genuine **physical** or **mental illness**.
- **High** levels of **stress**, which can lead to staff **avoiding work**, or **becoming ill**.
- Low staff **morale** or **motivation**, meaning staff don't feel inclined to work.
- **Bullying** or **harassment**, so staff might miss work to **avoid the situation**.
- **Dangerous work**, which could lead to **injuries**, so staff are **unable** to **work**.
- A **culture** of using absenteeism to **increase holidays**.

3) **Absenteeism** can be costly for a business, as it might have to pay **sick pay** or hire **temporary staff**. If the **absenteeism** of a business is high or increasing, HR could consider how it could be **reduced** in order to **reduce costs**. For example, a firm with a **bullying manager** who puts employees under a lot of **pressure** might have a high absenteeism due to **stress** and **exhaustion**. HR could reduce absenteeism by **retraining** the **manager** and **reducing workloads**.

4) HR should **consult** with **staff** before they make any decisions to make sure their strategies are **effective**. For example, HR might give employees **more responsibilities** to **motivate** them, but that won't work if **staff absences** are due to high levels of **stress** from being **overworked**.

5) HR can **compare** their **absenteeism** to that of **competitors** and the **industry average** to determine whether their own rates are **high or not**. If the firm has higher absenteeism than its **competitors** the business should look at the reasons it has higher absenteeism and find ways to **reduce it**.

6) In some cases of high absenteeism, HR might **not take action** — for example, if a lot of staff are absent due to **catching** the **flu**. In this case the **high absenteeism** would probably only be **temporary**.

Interpreting Human Resource Data

Firms Adopt Strategies to Improve Human Resource Figures

Firms can use various **strategies** to **increase** labour **productivity** and **retention**, and **reduce turnover** and **absenteeism**.

Financial Rewards

1) You covered **financial rewards** on pages 40-41. These might motivate employees to **work harder** and **increase** their **productivity**, and can **increase staff retention** if staff aren't likely to get **better** financial rewards elsewhere.

2) Some firms pay bonuses for **long-service** or for a **lack of absenteeism**. However, if staff have **genuine reasons** to be absent (e.g. a **long-term illness**) they might find the system **unfair** and **demotivating**.

Employee Share Ownership

1) Firms may **reward** staff with **company shares**. This can include Save As You Earn (SAYE) schemes, where employees **save** some of their **salary** each month for a **fixed period** (e.g. 3 years), and then use those savings to **buy** company **shares**, often **below market value**.

2) These schemes can **reduce staff turnover** because staff leaving will lose their right to obtain shares. It can also **increase staff productivity** and reduce absenteeism, as staff are **motivated** to make the firm more **profitable** and increase the **dividends** they receive. However, it can be **difficult** for employees to **see** the **connection** between their own **efforts** and the firm's **profit levels** and **dividends**.

Consultation Strategies

1) Some firms use **consultation strategies**, which is where they involve employees in **decision-making**. This should improve **morale** because staff will feel more **valued**. This could then help to **reduce absenteeism** and **increase labour retention** and **productivity**.

2) However, consultation can make the decision-making process much **longer** and **costly**, particularly in very big firms.

Empowerment Strategies

1) Firms can empower employees by giving them more **control** and **responsibility** over their work. This aims to increase **motivation** and **productivity**, which should **reduce absenteeism** and **turnover**.

2) Firms can empower staff by giving them the power to **make decisions** and **suggest improvements** (e.g. in quality circles p.89), as well as giving them the **resources** and **training** to do their job well.

3) Management who **distrust** their employees or **dislike delegation** will **struggle** with empowerment.

Warm-Up Questions

Q1 A firm has 25 employees. They make 24 000 bath bombs per week. Calculate the firm's labour productivity over a week.

Q2 What is meant by a high labour turnover? Suggest one cause of this.

Q3 Explain one strategy that HR could use to reduce absenteeism.

Calculation answers are on p.194.

Exam Question

Q1 Slapdash PLC is a paint manufacturer, with 24 staff in production, who each work 225 days per year. There were 120 days of staff absence in 2016, and 360 in 2017. At the start of 2017 there was a change in management, which led to a reduction in the responsibilities of production staff. Calculate Slapdash PLC's absenteeism for 2016 and 2017 and assess what changes HR could make to reduce absenteeism in the future. You are advised to show your working. [12 marks]

My productivity is one terrible joke per day...

HR shouldn't just look at data before making decisions — they should consult staff to work out what's causing issues.

Causes and Effects of Change

The next four pages draw together ideas from the previous sections. Well, put me in a toaster and call me a crumpet.

There Can Be **Internal Causes of Change** for a Business

There are **several internal factors** that can **lead to change** in a business, for example:

1) a change in the organisational size (the size of the business)
2) **new ownership**
3) **poor business performance**
4) **transformational leadership**

Jessica's plan to boost her level of internal change was going well.

You need to be able to **understand how** the **internal factors** above can cause **changes to a business** and how any **negative changes** could be **managed**.

1) A **Change** in **Organisational Size** Can Affect a Business

1) An **increase** in a business's **organisational size**, for example if it **expands abroad**, could mean that there's an **increase** in the **number of workers** (this expansion could be through organic or inorganic growth).

The advantages and disadvantages of organic and inorganic growth can be found on pages 112-115.

2) An increase in the number of workers can lead to **reduced production time** and **economies of scale**, which will **reduce unit costs** for the business. These reduced costs can be passed on to customers in the form of **cheaper prices**, making the business more **competitive**.

3) If the business is **unable** to **manage** an increase in the number of new workers effectively, then **productivity** can **decrease**. This can occur if, for example, there's **not enough machinery** or **resources** for the new workers. This can result in **increased production time** and **diseconomies of scale**, which can lead to reduced competitiveness.

'Economies of scale' is covered on page 112 and 'diseconomies of scale' is covered on page 114.

4) Having **more workers** also means it's **harder** to **communicate quickly** and **effectively**. **Slow communication** can lead to **appropriate action not being taken** as staff are **not informed of decisions** in time, which can **reduce productivity**. So changes to the **communication chains**, such as **reducing** the number of **layers** in an **organisational hierarchy** (see p.36), may be needed as a business grows.

5) Growth could also affect **external stakeholders**, such as **shareholders** or other **investors**. If the business is growing and **increasing** its **profits** then the shareholders might receive **larger dividends**. However, if the growth is reducing the business's competitiveness then **potential investors** may choose **not to invest**, or **current shareholders** may choose to **sell their shares**, because they **lose confidence** in the business.

6) There may need to be **changes** made to the business's **production methods**, such as switching to **newer technology** or hiring a new **supervisor**, to ensure that there **isn't a fall** in **productivity** as the business grows. This will help the business to **maintain** or **increase** its **competitiveness**, which will also give **investors** more **confidence** in the business.

7) **Cash flow** is usually affected during periods of growth. Cash flow needs to be **managed** as the business grows otherwise, for example, the business might **overtrade** (see page 114). Overtrading could lead to the business **not having enough cash** to pay its **day-to-day costs** and its **financial performance** being **poor**.

A Decreased Organisational Size Can Affect a Business

1) A **reduction in size** could arise, for example, when a **business** undertakes a **demerger** (see page 115).

2) Any advantages from having **economies of scale** may be **lost** as the business reduces in size. This may cause **competitiveness to reduce** because **production costs per unit**, and therefore **prices, increase**.

3) A reduction in profits would mean that **shareholders** get **less** in the form of **dividends**.

4) The business may **sell assets**, such as machinery, or make staff **redundant** to reduce costs and increase profits, which would mean the business **remains competitive** and can give shareholders **larger dividends**.

5) Redundancies may cause the **motivation** of the **remaining staff** to fall, as they become **concerned** that they may **lose their jobs** as well. **Reduced staff motivation** can cause **productivity to fall** (see p.38), which can lead to **higher prices** and a **fall in sales and profits**. Motivation could be **increased** through various **incentives**, such as **delegation** of work or using **piecework pay** (see p.40-41 for more).

Causes and Effects of Change

2) A **Change in Ownership** Can Affect a Business

1) There are **several reasons** why a business might experience a **change in ownership**. For example:

   - The firm could transition from being a sole trader to a partnership, or from a sole trader or partnership to a limited company (see page 51). This could lead to there being additional owners of the business.

     A firm's owner(s) can be shareholders, sole traders or partners — see pages 50-51.

   - A private limited company (Ltd) could become a public limited company (PLC).
   - The owner(s) could retire and sell or gift the business to new owners.
   - Ownership can also change following a takeover or a merger with another business (see page 112).
   - Management buyouts are when the management of a business purchases a majority of the shares in the business, and therefore takes over control of the business from the owners.

2) **New owners** will often have their **own** beliefs about the **direction** the firm should take and the **way it should be managed**. This **change in vision** may result in **changes** to the firm's **aims and objectives**, **staffing structure**, **production**, **policies** and **culture**.

3) Any **changes** made by new owners will **affect** the firm's **stakeholders**, for example:

   - **Managers** might see a change in their **responsibilities** or the business's **aims**.
   - **Customers** might find that there are **changes** to the **quality of customer service** offered by the firm.
   - **Local residents** of a factory might experience **changes** in things like the **level of pollution or noise** produced by the factory.

4) **Stakeholders** that are **negatively affected** by a change in ownership might **resist the change**.

5) One way to combat resistance to change is for the business to ensure that it **communicates** with its **stakeholders** so that they're **all aware** of any **changes to the organisation**, its **goals** or its **objectives** as a result of the new ownership. This will help to make the stakeholders feel **valued** and **supported**, and so **less likely to resist** any changes.

   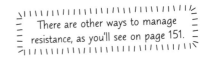

   There are other ways to manage resistance, as you'll see on page 151.

6) A change in ownership can cause **economies of scale** to occur. For example, the **new owners** of the firm could grow the business by **increasing investment** in machinery (see page 81) or in the recruitment of staff — this would increase the **production levels** of the firm and could lead to economies of scale (see previous page).

7) However, if this growth isn't **managed** then **diseconomies of scale** can occur (see previous page). Diseconomies of scale can **reduce** the **competitiveness** of a business as its unit costs are higher and these may be passed on to customers in the form of **increased prices**.

   Mr. Flufflesnug felt like it was time for a change in ownership.

8) Diseconomies of scale could also occur following a merger or takeover due to a culture clash between the **owners** and the **employees** of the two businesses.

- Any change resulting from a **change in ownership** can affect the **financial performance** of the business. Whether the financial performance of a business improves or worsens depends on whether the change was **positive or negative**. For example, if a **change in ownership** leads to **economies of scale**, the **financial performance** of the business would most likely **improve**.

- An improved financial performance could affect **shareholders** because it will lead to them receiving higher dividends. An improved financial performance could also cause the **price of shares** in the business to **go up**. This means that **shareholders** could see an **increase** in the **value of their investments**.

  See p.51 for how and why share prices might change.

Causes and Effects of Change

3) Poor Business Performance Can Affect a Business

1) There are **several reasons** why a business could be considered to be **performing badly**. For example, if it has **lower sales** or **profits** than expected, if the **operating expenses** (see pages 70-71) are **rising faster than revenue** or if the business is **growing slower** than expected.

2) Poor business performance can **reduce competitiveness**. For example, **lower sales** than expected might mean that the business has to **increase its prices** to customers to make up for the **lower sales volume**. **High prices** can reduce **competitiveness**. A **lack of competitiveness** can result in **poor financial performance** due to a **loss of sales** and a **decrease** in **cash flow** and **profits**.

3) Poor business performance can also **negatively affect** the **productivity** and **efficiency** of the business. For example, if a firm had experienced a **period of low sales** it might decide to **reduce its output**. This would **reduce productivity** and **efficiency** as the firm would have the **same number** of **workers and machines**, but they would each be **producing less**. To avoid a fall in **productivity** or **efficiency**, the business might **sell off machinery** or make some members of staff **redundant**.

4) **Stakeholders** can be affected by poor business performance. For example, if staff are **made redundant** in an effort to increase productivity then this could lead to **uncertainty** and **reduced morale** for remaining employees, which could **reduce business performance** further.

5) The **value of shares** in a business could **decrease** due to its **poor business performance**, so shareholders could find that the value of their **investments fall**.

Managers Will Need to Make Changes to Poorly Performing Firms

1) Managers at the top of a firm will often try to **make changes** to **correct poor business performance** — this may lead to **new senior managers** being recruited to **direct the firm** in a more **successful direction**.

2) The **changes** introduced may need to be **quick and extensive** (covering most of the organisation). These might include **reducing costs**, **improving product quality**, **improving marketing** or **increasing investment** in the firm.

3) It may be necessary for the managers to **make changes** to the business's **corporate objectives** or **corporate strategy** (see p.103 and p.104) to allow the business to **improve performance** while continuing to work towards its **business aims**.

4) A Transformational Leader Can Affect a Business

1) A **transformational leader** is an owner or manager who makes **large, innovative changes** to a firm (see page 42). A transformational leader can also **change the business's ethos**.

A business's ethos is its values, operating principles or the way it aspires to behave.

2) They'll **identify a need** and **have a vision** for change, and will **motivate employees** to make changes. These could include **new strategies and objectives** with the aim of **improving business performance**.

3) Transformational leaders are **often recruited** when a firm has had a **period of poor performance**. The business often hopes that the leader will **improve the competitiveness**, **productivity** and **financial performance** of the business — but how well these factors are improved will **depend** on the **leader**, the **business** and its **circumstances**.

4) The recruitment of a transformational leader could affect stakeholders — the leader may **make changes** to **employee roles**, to the **products sold** and to the **quality of customer service**.

5) The firm's employees may be **resistant to change**, and **methods of overcoming** this resistance will need to be found (see page 151).

6) Sometimes **shareholders push** for a **change** of leader if the **firm isn't meeting its objectives**.

Example:	Zumo is a business that sells second-hand cars. Over the last few years its **financial performance** has been **poor** — its **profits** have **decreased** by 72% over the last three years. The managers decide to recruit a **transformational leader** to help turn the business around. The new leader decides that the **quality of customer service** needs to improve in order to increase profits, so she sends **all** the employees on **training courses** to **improve** their customer service skills. However, she faces **resistance** from the workforce, as most of the employees are **concerned** that they won't be able to **learn the new skills** and are happy with how they already do things. She decides to **overcome** this **resistance** by offering the employees **cash bonuses** for successfully completing the training courses.

Causes and Effects of Change

The **External Environment** Can Create a **Lot of Change** for a Business

A **manager** can use a **PESTLE analysis** to **look at** the **external factors** that may cause change for a business — you met PESTLE analysis on page 109. Here are some **examples** of how these **changes** can **affect businesses**:

Political: A change in government policy can affect how a firm behaves — for example, after government legislation introduced a 5p charge on single-use plastic carrier bags, TESCO decided to remove these bags from its stores.

Economic: If the economy enters a recession, the amount of disposable income people have reduces and firms may need to reduce prices to maintain sales levels.

Social: Changing social trends can lead to a business needing to alter its product range to fit in with changing demand. For example, food producers might reduce the fat content of their products to meet the growing demand for healthier food.

Technological: Firms may change their production processes if new technology allows production to be faster or cheaper — this could lead to increased productivity and efficiency, so the business could charge lower prices to its customers. This could help to improve the financial performance of the business.

Legal: Changes in legislation can affect businesses — for example, the release in 2018 of the General Data Protection Regulation (GDPR) meant that some businesses needed to alter the way they collected and stored customer data.

Environmental: Some firms may have to alter production processes to reduce their emissions due to an increased concern for the environment. This would help to prevent customers refusing to do business with the firm due to their ethical concerns over the environment.

The **Market** is Another Key **External Factor** that Can Affect a Business

1) The **market** and the **competitive forces** surrounding it are a **major cause of change** within firms — you'll have met these in **Porter's Five Forces** model on pages 110-111.

2) A business may need to, for example, **change** its **objectives**, decide on a new **strategy**, **invest** in **research and development**, or **look at its branding** strategy to deal with changes in the external market.

3) **New entrants** to the market can **cause a loss of market share** for a business already in the market, and **reduce its competitiveness**. Managers of the business already in the market may need to **adapt** to the presence of new competitors by **developing new strategies**. For example, they may choose to use a **differentiation strategy** (see **Porter's generic strategies** on page 105).

4) The **removal of a competitor** from the market can **improve** a firm's **financial performance** in the **long term** as it's likely to mean that the firm will have a **larger market share**. The removal of a competitor could also **affect stakeholders**. For example, the **loss of a competitor** could **increase job security** for **employees**. However, it could also **reduce choice** for **customers** and lead to **higher prices**.

5) It's often **advantageous** for firms to **react quickly** to external changes. For example, the **first firm to supply new products** or **adopt new ways of working** often obtains a **competitive advantage**. Or if a firm **reacts quickly** to an **increase in demand** or a **competitor leaving** the market, it may be able to **increase its market share** and **profit level**.

Warm-Up Questions

Q1 Give one way that a decrease in a business's organisational size could affect its customers.

Q2 Give one example of a change that a manager might make following a fall in business performance.

Q3 Explain how the removal of a competitor from a market could benefit another business in that market.

Exam Question

Q1 Swaite's Ltd is a producer of unhealthy, convenience food, shrink-wrapped in plastic. Its biggest competitor is a company called BrigFax PLC, that is diversifying into healthy convenience food in eco-friendly packaging. The two businesses agree to undertake a merger to form a new business called SwaiteFax PLC. Assess how this change could impact the current stakeholders of Swaite's Ltd. [10 marks]

I'm lactose intolerant, so dairy is a big internal cause of change for me...

Firms often face, and have to manage, several changes at once. Gosh — and I can't even eat my lunch while wri...

Key Factors in Change

OK, so you've seen a load of causes and effects of changes in a firm. Now it's time to look at some of the key factors that affect, and are part of, these changes. Who could have predicted it was going to get any more exciting? I didn't.

The **Success** of Change Depends on **Key Factors**

1) You've **already seen** some of the **factors** that can **cause change**, on pages 146-149.

2) For change to be **successful**, there needs to be good change management. **Change management** is the processes and procedures performed by **managers** to **plan** and **prepare** for changes, **carry out** the changes and **assess** the possible effects of the changes on the business and its stakeholders.

3) When a manager is planning and carrying out a change they need to consider different **key factors** that can **affect** the outcome of the change. These factors include the business's **culture** and **size**, the **speed** at which the change can happen, and the potential **resistance** of stakeholders to change.

Organisational Culture Impacts on a Business's **Reaction to Change**

1) An **organisation's culture** is a **key factor** as to how it manages change.

2) A firm's culture can either be **open** or **resistant** to change. A culture that's **open to change** sees it as a way to **improve** the firm and its **ability** to **achieve its objectives**.

You met organisational culture (also called corporate culture) on p.130.

3) **Resistance to change** (see next page) can be displayed either **passively** (e.g. employees deliberately sticking to the old ways of working) or **actively** (direct confrontations about the changes). Change management can be **harder** in a **resistant firm** than it is in an **open** firm.

4) A **rapidly changing market** will need firms to **react quickly** to remain **competitive** — this is better done by firms with an **open culture**.

5) **Large firms** may have **sub-cultures** in different parts of the business. This can make change management even **more difficult** because the **different sub-groups** may **react differently** to the proposed changes.

6) A business may need to **change** its **culture** following a change, in order to **remain competitive**. For example, a small business that has **one person** making all the **decisions** and **managing** all the workers (power culture) expands into a **larger market**, so it needs to **increase** its **production output**. This means that it may need to **change its culture** so decisions are split between **more people** and workers are split into **teams** (task culture).

7) **Changing** a firm's **culture** can be **difficult** because it involves **changing staff attitudes and behaviour**. It may need **new procedures** or extra **staff training**, which can create extra **expenses** for the business.

The **Success** of **Mergers** and **Takeovers** is Determined by **Compatibility**

1) **Mergers** and **takeovers** are often more **successful** when the businesses' **cultures** are **compatible**.

2) If the cultures **aren't** compatible, one of them might need to **change**.

> **Example:** In 2001, **HP** and **Compaq**, two businesses in the **computing industry**, announced they were undertaking a **merger**. The two businesses had two very different cultures — HP's culture focused on **engineering** and Compaq's on **sales**. HP's **culture changed** following the merger, becoming more like Compaq's, which meant the merger was **successful**.

CGP Party Tip #167 — pico de gallo is perfectly compatible with tortilla chips.

The **Size of an Organisation** Affects How Well it **Reacts to Change**

1) **Communication** can be **slow and difficult** in **large firms** (see page 114). If a change is required in a large business with poor communication, it can be **hard for managers** to make sure that employees have a full **understanding** of the change — **details** of the change and its requirements can be **distorted**.

2) Also, if employees don't have a full understanding of the change, it can be difficult to **motivate employees** to take the **necessary steps** for changes to be implemented.

3) Change management can also be **difficult** in **small firms**, but for **different reasons**.

4) **Small businesses** may have **one dominant leader** and it might be **difficult** for others involved in the business to get them to consider the **need for change** and to **consider alternative** ways of implementing change.

5) It may also be that small firms **lack** the **finance**, **skills** and **spare resources** needed for effective change.

Key Factors in Change

Change Can Happen at **Different Speeds** Within **Different Businesses**

1) Change can be **incremental**, **disruptive** or somewhere **between** the two.

2) **Incremental change** is **gradual** and involves lots of **small changes over time** to **minimise disruption**.

3) **Disruptive change** is **sudden** and **forces** a **quick response**. It can be **negative** — for example, businesses can be **forced to change** and **cut their prices** to avoid a **fall in demand**. Disruptive changes can also be **positive** — for example, an **increase in demand** could force a firm to **quickly expand**.

Resistance to Change is **Common**

1) **Stakeholders** may be **resistant to change** because of a **lack of understanding** as to **what** the change is and **why** it's needed, and because they're **happy** with the **current situation**.

2) **Staff** may be resistant to change because they **fear** that they'll be **unable to develop** any **new skills** required. They may also resist a change if they're **unable to see any benefits** for themselves, or if they **misunderstand** the change. Staff members' resistance to change may even mean they choose to **leave their jobs**.

3) **Suppliers** may be resistant to a change the firm is planning, especially if they're **required** to **alter** their **behaviour**. For example, a **supplier** may be **reluctant** to alter its **production schedules** to meet a **new pattern of demand** from a firm.

4) **Customers** might **resist change** if, for example, the business is trying to **alter** its **product line**, because they **like** the **current products** that the business sells.

5) **Shareholders** might resist change because of **costs** or a **fear** that the **change** might lead to **business failure**.

6) There are **several methods** that managers can use to **overcome resistance**:

- **Raise awareness** of the **reasons** for the change and **how it'll be carried out**, as well as the **benefits** of it.

- **Involve** key stakeholders in the **design and implementation** of the change. If they **participate** in the **decision-making** process then they'll **feel more engaged** with the change and be less likely to **resist** it. This also gives stakeholders **opportunities** to **negotiate** and **compromise** over key sticking points, which can lead to **agreement** over the proposed change.

- **Listen** to employees' **concerns** and **provide training** to the workforce. This can help the workers to feel **supported** and to **overcome** their **anxiety** about the changes.

- **Bargain**, by offering **financial** or **non-financial incentives** in order to obtain **acceptance** of the change.

- **Manipulate** the **information** regarding the change, e.g. **exaggerate** the extent of a **financial crisis** and state there's **no alternative**. However, if the firm's **found out**, they could **lose their** stakeholders' **trust**.

- **Threaten** (either **directly** or in an **implied way**) stakeholders who are attempting to block the changes. For example, **threaten employees** with **redundancy**. This action is often taken as a **last resort**.

Warm-Up Questions

Q1 Why might a business need to change its culture following a change in the business?

Q2 Give two difficulties faced when managing change in a large business.

Exam Question

Q1 Bridget runs a successful hair salon and has a loyal customer base, mainly of retired women. Bridget has taken on a new manager, Di, who wishes to introduce a number of changes. Di wants the salon to begin offering beauty treatments, introduce a mobile service, and to make changes to the salon's marketing materials and staff uniforms. These changes will increase costs. Di has faced resistance from members of staff as well as from some customers. The staff have been happy with the way things already work and resent being given more work and responsibility.

a) Explain the resistance Di could face from the customers of the hair salon. [4 marks]

b) Assess the ways that Di could overcome the resistance from the staff members of the hair salon. [12 marks]

The Borg won't be too happy to hear about all this resistance...

Not only do you need to know the causes and effects of change from the previous few pages, you also need to know how businesses might react based on their culture, size, resistance and how fast change is happening.

Anticipating Change

Ah, smell that change. Earth. Eggs? Yesterday's dinner? Oh, that's not the smell of change — the dog's just come in.

Scenario Planning Involves Planning for Events that Might Occur

1) **Scenario planning** is where businesses consider **specific events** that may happen in the **future** and **plan** how they would **operate** should one of the events occur. An event could be, for example, a specific **natural disaster**, the **loss of a particular member of staff**, or the **failure of an IT system**. Scenario planning also includes how to **mitigate** (reduce) the effects of any **negative changes** the events might cause.

2) Scenario planning can be **expensive** and **time-consuming**. It can also require **specialist knowledge**, so a firm might need to **hire an expert** with this knowledge. These drawbacks, and the fact that the events considered **might not happen**, mean that firms **don't carry out** scenario planning for all possible events. A firm might carry out **risk assessment** as the **first step** in **scenario planning**.

3) Risk assessment **identifies** the **risks** associated with an **event** and any **expected consequences** of the event. A business then looks at the **probability** of specific events occurring and develops **plans** for those with the **highest probabilities or most detrimental effects**. For example:

   1) A business might consider making a **scenario plan** for a **natural disaster**, but it could carry out a **risk assessment first**. For example, locating an office **near a river** means it has a **high probability** of being **flooded**, but if the office is **raised up** on stilts the **effect** of flooding to the business is **quite low** so it may choose to **not create** a **plan** for this.

   2) A **natural disaster** can **impact** a business even if it **doesn't affect** the business **directly** — for example, a **storm** could **close an airport** meaning a business **can't get raw materials** from its **suppliers**. This could cause **both** the business and its suppliers to **lose money** due to **lost trade**. A business that's located, or has a supplier that's located, somewhere where there is a **high probability** of a natural disaster occurring would therefore **invest** in creating a **plan** for it. Natural disasters can have financial **costs** beyond the **loss of trade**, for example, **clean-up costs**.

   3) A business might make a scenario plan for a **hacking attempt** or the **failure** of an **IT system**, as it could have a **major impact** on a firm's **operations**, **stakeholders** and **reputation**. Many firms, especially larger ones, now **rely on IT systems** in nearly **all areas**, so **IT issues** can cause work to **cease** for a long time. This could mean that IT failure could cause a business to lose a lot of money, so businesses may **invest** a lot in **planning** to prepare for this, even if they decide the **probability** of it occurring is **low**.

   4) A scenario plan might be made for **losing** a staff member. Some **staff members** are **vital** to the running of a firm. The **loss** of a **key staff member** can create **problems** for a firm when **other staff** members are **unable to take on** their **work**. Businesses need to assess the **probability** that a **worker will leave**. For example, someone approaching **retirement age** is **likely** to leave soon, so the business may decide to create a plan for it.

   Planning for what to do if key employees leave a business is known as succession planning (see the next page).

Businesses can Mitigate Risks

1) **Risk mitigation** is part of planning (see above and the next page) and it looks at **reducing the probability** of a risk to a business occurring, or **reducing the negative effects** once a risk has been realised.

2) The most **common forms** of **risk mitigation** are **acceptance**, **avoidance**, **limitation** and **transference**:

   • **Risk acceptance** is when the business decides to accept the risk, without creating a plan. It's used when the **likely cost** of **planning** for and **dealing** with the risk are **greater** than the cost that might occur from **letting it happen** — this is common for small businesses. Risk acceptance is usually used when the risk has only a **small probability**.

   • **Risk avoidance** simply means **avoiding the risk** altogether — for example, **not locating near to a river** to avoid the risk of **flooding**.

   • **Risk limitation reduces the impact** of the risk — for example, if a firm **relies heavily** on having **regular access to power**, then it may ensure it has a **back-up generator** on-site.

   • **Risk transference** is when the **risk is transferred** to a **third party** — for example, a business may **insure against theft** through an **external firm**. This means that the **negative effects** of theft (e.g. a loss of capital) would be **faced by the external firm** rather than the business.

Anticipating Change

Continuity Planning is Planning How to Keep Going After a Major Incident

1) Business **continuity planning** is similar to scenario planning but is **much more general**. Scenario planning is for **specific** events — see previous page.

2) Continuity planning aims to **mitigate the risks** and **keep the firm working** by providing a **recovery plan** should **any number** of **unspecified incidents** occur. For example, a firm may have **identified a location** to move its operations to in case the office is **no longer suitable for use**, for example if there was a fire or a long-term power cut. This allows the firm to **resume normal business** as **quickly as possible** following a major incident.

3) A business should determine what is a **minimum acceptable level** of operations to keep the business running and what **resources** would be required to achieve this. The business could then **plan ways** to **achieve this minimum** level of operations and resources in the event of a major incident.

4) Plans would need to be **reviewed regularly** and staff would need to have **training** on how to enact the plans.

> **Example:** Print Inc. is a business that prints books using automated IT systems. Usually, it prints books in excess of the current demand, which helps it to respond to future orders quickly. If its IT systems fail, Print Inc. has planned to only print enough books to meet current customers' orders. It can do this using a team of five workers to operate the printers manually. So Print Inc. will need to provide appropriate training to at least five members of its staff.

Succession Planning is Planning for the Loss of a Key Member of Staff

1) **Succession** is when **one person takes over** the **role or responsibility** of another person. This happens when the previous person has **left the role** or **given up the responsibility** (e.g. due to retirement, change of job or illness).

2) **Succession planning** involves the **identification** and **development** of staff members that would be able to **fill key roles** to allow the business to **mitigate the risks** from the **loss of a key member of staff**.

It wouldn't be long before Diane's colleagues realised they'd lost her again.

3) When creating succession plans, **managers** need to consider the **qualifications**, **experience** and **characteristics** the staff member should have. They'll then need to assess available candidates and **provide** any **training** necessary to **prepare candidates** to fill the role.

4) Training can involve such techniques as **job rotation** (moving staff between roles to increase their experience) and **shadowing** (observing the member of staff carrying out their job).

5) If succession planning is **done well** then it should make the **transition** from one member of staff to another as **smooth as possible** for the business, and should **reduce the risks** and **expense** of recruiting someone who does a **poor job**.

Warm-Up Questions

Q1 What is scenario planning?

Q2 Give two types of risk mitigation.

Q3 What is business continuity planning?

Q4 What is succession planning?

Exam Question

Q1 Mosh is a French business that generates electricity from imported gas and various renewable sources. It supplies electricity to several countries. Mosh has recently identified a number of potential changes to its environment, including a prediction that there will be a shortage of its imported gas in the short-term, as well as an expected rapid increase in the population sizes of the countries it supplies to.

    a) Explain how Mosh could use continuity planning to ensure that it can continue to supply its customers during a gas shortage. [4 marks]

    b) Assess two ways that Mosh could mitigate the risks associated with the increasing population sizes in the countries it supplies to. [8 marks]

Risk® assessment: great board game, 10 out of 10, will ruin friendships...

Creating plans allows a firm to mitigate risks. These plans can be made for specific events (scenario plans) or they can be broader (continuity plans). My continuity plan when I need to do some washing is to buy more underwear.

Growing Economies

Many firms don't just operate in one country — a connected world means they can trade with people all over. Firms often look at the size of a country's economy and how quickly it's growing when deciding where to do business...

Globalisation is the Increase in How Interconnected the World is

1) **Globalisation** has resulted in businesses operating in **lots of countries** across the world. They can be **based** anywhere, and can **buy** from and **sell** to any country.

2) Globalisation allows businesses to make **strategic decisions** about where to get **raw materials** from, as well as where to **manufacture products** (e.g. in countries with cheaper labour).

3) **Global trade** means that firms and consumers in one country can **affect** the **economies** of other countries. This is leading to the growth of some **Less Economically Developed Countries (LEDCs)** — these are countries with **smaller economies** and generally a **lower standard of living** than (wait for it...) **More Economically Developed Countries (MEDCs)**.

E.g. Ethiopia, Uganda and Chad are LEDCs, and the UK, Japan and Spain are MEDCs.

GDP Indicates the Size of a Nation's Economy

1) **GDP (gross domestic product)** is the **total market value** of **goods** and **services** produced **within** a nation over a period of time (usually a year). It is used to measure the **economic performance** of a country, an area (such as the EU), or the whole world. It is calculated in **real terms**, i.e. it is adjusted so that **inflation** is ignored.

2) A country's GDP is often expressed **per capita** — this means the GDP is **divided by the number of people** in the country. This can lead to **fairer comparisons** of the economic performance of different countries.

3) Calculating the **percentage difference** in GDP or GDP per capita of a country from one year to the next lets you see how **quickly the economy is growing**.

4) Some **emerging economies** (see next page) are growing **very quickly** — much faster than the **UK economy**. For example, in 2017 the **UK economy** had a growth rate of **1.7%**, but **Panama** had a growth rate of **5.4%** and **Turkey** had a growth rate of **7.4%**.

Be aware that the growth rate doesn't tell you about the actual size of an economy. E.g. in 2017, the UK's GDP was $2.93 trillion, whilst Panama's was only $104.1 billion.

5) You need to be careful when interpreting figures about GDP, as there are **limitations** to what they can tell you. For example, in 2017, **China's total GDP** was over $23 trillion, whereas Japan's was only $5.4 trillion. This might suggest that there is a **higher standard of living** in China, but the GDP **per capita** shows that this isn't true — China's **GDP per capita** was $16,700 compared to $42,900 in Japan. **Fewer people** live in Japan than in China, so a typical person in Japan is likely to be wealthier than a typical person in China.

6) GDP also doesn't show the **distribution of wealth** in a country, **levels of disposable income** or **costs of living**.

GDP is Not the Only Indicator of Economic Growth

Literacy Rate

1) The **adult literacy rate** of a country is the **percentage** of the **population** aged **15** and **above** who can **read** and **write**.

2) Rates vary around the world — for example, in 2015, the literacy rate in Colombia was **94.2%**, whereas the rate in Mali was **33.1%**.

3) An **increasing** literacy rate indicates **economic growth**, as it suggests that **more** of the population are **educated** and able to work in **skilled** jobs.

A rather different type of gross domestic product.

Health

1) The **World Health Organisation** (WHO) considers a number of **indicators** when **assessing** the **level** of a country's **health**. This includes **life expectancy**, **mortality** (death) **rates** from a range of **causes**, and **morbidity** (sickness) rates for several diseases. They also consider **risk factors** for health, such as a lack of safe **sanitation**.

2) An increasing level of **health** suggests that an economy is growing — it suggests that the **government** is **spending** more on **healthcare** and that more of the population is **fit** to work.

The Human Development Index

1) The **Human Development Index** (HDI) is a statistic that measures how 'developed' people in a country are. It's based on **life expectancy**, **average** number of years of **schooling** and the average **income** of each person.

2) The **higher** a country's HDI score, the **higher** its **development level** is considered to be — for example, in 2017, the HDI was **0.452** for **Yemen** and **0.924** for the **USA**, so the USA is considered more developed.

Growing Economies

Economic Growth is Important for Individuals and Businesses

1) When an economy is **growing**, it means that there is **increasing demand** in the economy and **increasing output** to meet that demand. This is **beneficial** to **individuals and businesses** within the economy.

2) A greater level of **output** leads to increased **employment opportunities** for people living in that country. This means that **more people** are **earning money** and the **amount** that they are earning often **increases** too. People **move out of poverty** and into the **middle class**.

3) As people start earning more money, the demand for products that have a **positive income elasticity** of **demand** will **increase**. Having more demand for products can create more **opportunities** for businesses within the **economy**, leading to increased **sales** and **profits**.

4) Businesses from foreign economies can respond to **increased demand** in the growing economy and start to **sell their goods** there. This will **increase sales** of the foreign firms, and could create **more work** for foreign workers.

5) Economic growth can increase the demand for **recognisable Western brands**, which are seen as **luxury items** and **indicators of wealth** in some countries. This creates opportunities for Western businesses to expand to **new markets**.

6) Foreign businesses may also start **operating** parts of their businesses in countries with **growing economies**. This can be done to **reduce costs** if there is **cheaper labour** available in the growing economy, or to save on **transportation costs** to sell goods there. This can help **boost the growing economy** even more by providing **local jobs** and increasing incomes.

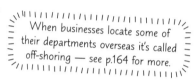
When businesses locate some of their departments overseas it's called off-shoring — see p.164 for more.

7) However, operating parts of a business **overseas** can have **negative effects** on individuals in the business's **home country**, as it may mean **cutting jobs** there.

Some Economies are Growing Very Quickly

1) An **emerging economy** is one that is **fast-growing**, but is **not yet** fully developed.

2) Some of the most significant emerging economies are the **BRICS** economies (**Brazil, Russia, India, China** and **South Africa**) and the **MINT** economies (**Mexico, Indonesia, Nigeria** and **Turkey**).

3) The **BRICS** economies contain over **40% of the world's population**, and have **cheap labour costs**, so many businesses have **located manufacturing** in these countries. China has also **removed** many of its **barriers** to international trade, meaning that it now **trades more** with other countries, which is causing its economy to grow.

4) The **MINT** economies are considered to be important **emerging economies** due in part to their **growing population sizes**, with a lot of **young people** who are entering the workforce. They are also **close to large markets** (such as the USA and Europe) that they can **export to**, meaning that **demand** for their products may be **high**, which contributes to **economic growth**.

Warm-Up Questions

Q1 How can a country's literacy rate be used as an indicator of economic growth?
Q2 What is the Human Development Index?
Q3 Give two reasons why the economic growth of a country might benefit individuals living there.

Exam Question

Q1 TokTik Ltd is a UK watchmaker that wants to expand by selling in new countries.
Explain why TokTik Ltd might consider a country's GDP per capita when deciding which country to start selling to.
[4 marks]

Doctor, Doctor, I feel like an emerging economy (I've got an economic growth)...

It might not be a barrel of laughs to learn about economic growth, but you've got to know about it all the same. Make sure you know how economic growth can be measured, as well as its effects on businesses and individuals.

International Trade

International trade is all about, well... trading between nations. There are several ways businesses can do this — for example, they can export to foreign markets, import raw materials or invest directly in businesses abroad.

International Trade is Importing and Exporting

Businesses involved in **international markets import** and/or **export** products:

Imports

- **Imports** are products **bought** from **overseas**.
- When someone buys an imported product, the money goes back to the foreign country where the product came from. So imports cause **money** to **flow out of** an economy.
- Imports increase the **variety of goods** and **services** available to firms and consumers in a particular country.
- Imported products can often be **cheaper** than **domestically produced** ones.

Exports

- **Exports** are products **sold overseas**.
- When a business sells an exported product, they get money from the person or business that they sold it to in another country. So exports result in **money flowing into** an economy.
- Businesses use exporting as a way to **expand** — benefiting from an **increased market size**.
- Exporting can be the **simplest** and **least risky** way to access overseas markets.

Kevin realised that importing all that sun cream might have been a mistake.

Specialisation May Help a Firm to Trade Internationally

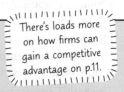

There's loads more on how firms can gain a competitive advantage on p.11.

1) A **competitive advantage** is something that allows a business to generate **more sales** or be **more profitable** than its rivals. For example, a business could gain a competitive advantage by producing **higher quality products**, having **lower costs** or **specialist staff**.

2) Having a **competitive advantage** can be especially important for firms operating in an **international market**, as they often face **more competition** than firms only operating in a domestic market.

3) A business can **gain** a **competitive advantage** through **specialisation** — this is when a **firm** focuses on **producing just one** product (or a very **narrow range** of products). E.g. a firm in the **food industry** could produce different types of cakes, pies and biscuits, or it could **specialise** and **only produce cakes**.

4) Occasionally, a **whole country** will specialise in a particular product. For example, **Norway** specialises in **oil production**. (There's more about countries that specialise in particular products on p.164.)

5) Specialisation improves the **efficiency** of a business. This is largely because **workers** become **highly skilled** at making a particular product — this means that the **speed** at which they work is likely to **increase** along with the **quality** of what they produce.

6) Increasing efficiency **reduces** the **cost per unit** — this allows the **price** to be reduced (which may generate greater sales), or the **profit margin** to be increased. Producing **higher quality** products may also generate **more sales** and allow a **higher price** to be charged. All of these factors can result in the business generating **higher profits**.

7) Specialisation also has **disadvantages**. Specialised businesses will risk **losing sales** if there's a **decrease** in the **demand** for their product, and won't have other sources of revenue to make up for the loss.

8) Specialisation can also increase the **cost** of **training staff** — if new staff are not experts, they may need **extensive training** to gain the **skills** they need to become **specialised** in making their products.

International Trade

Foreign Direct Investment is One Form of Foreign Expansion for Firms

1) As well as exporting, another way that firms can take advantage of opportunities in foreign markets is to undertake **foreign direct investment** (**FDI**).

2) FDI is when a **firm** in one **country invests** in **business** in **another country** — this can be by merging with or taking over an **existing foreign business**, opening an **office** or **branch** overseas, or starting up a **new enterprise** in another country.

3) To be **classed as FDI**, the investing firm has to have some **managerial control** of a business in a foreign country — it **doesn't count** as FDI if a firm just buys some shares in a foreign business.

4) For example, **Skoolbo**, a Singaporean educational company, has **invested** in the **UK**. To do so, it has **recruited** British staff to **market** and **support its product** in the UK.

5) Most FDI is **horizontal** — this is where a firm **invests** in a foreign business that is at the **same stage** of the **production process** as the business in their home country. For example, **Toyota™** (a Japanese car manufacturer) built a **car production** plant in the UK in the 1990s.

6) FDI can also be **vertical** — this is where a firm invests in a **foreign business** that is in a **different place** in the **supply chain** to its original business. For example, a manufacturer might invest in the foreign firm that supplies it with **raw materials**.

7) FDI can help businesses to **grow** and **increase sales**:

> - FDI gives a firm access to **new markets** — this can **increase sales** as there are more people to sell to. It may also **reduce a firm's costs**, e.g. production and labour costs may be cheaper in a foreign country. This can make the firm **more profitable**.
> - FDI can allow a business to take advantage of **skilled local labour** in the foreign country, which can increase **productivity**.
> - Operating in a foreign country will allow a firm to obtain **first-hand knowledge** about a nation's **legal system**, **consumer tastes** and **markets**. This may allow the firm to generate **more sales** in the foreign country than they would by **simply exporting** their goods.
> - Investing in a foreign business can help a business to overcome **international trade barriers**, such as **tariffs** or **quotas**, which can **prevent access** to a market (see p.160).

8) The level of FDI in, or by, a country can have a **significant impact** on its **economy**.

9) In **developing** and **emerging economies**, inward investment can improve the local **standard of living**, and cause **economic growth**. The additional spending by foreign businesses and investors can **increase GDP**, and any **taxes** paid will increase **government income**, which might then be spent on things such as **schools** and **healthcare**.

Warm-Up Questions

Q1 Does money flow into or out of an economy with imports?
Q2 Explain how exporting goods can affect a country's economy.
Q3 Give two disadvantages of a firm being specialised.

Exam Question

Q1 Kiri Ltd is an Australian firm that specialises in producing clothing for disabled athletes. The company imports 70% of its raw materials from China and Thailand. As part of Kiri Ltd's growth strategy, it is considering FDI into a clothes manufacturer in China.
a) Explain how specialisation could give Kiri Ltd a competitive advantage. [4 marks]
b) Assess the likely impact on Kiri Ltd of FDI in China. [12 marks]

Postcards — an under-appreciated export...

Imports and exports are pretty tightly linked — after all, something exported from the UK has to be imported into another country somewhere else. Just make sure you know which one's which, and where the money is going. I tell you what, all this talk of international trade is making me want to import some Swiss chocolate into my belly...

Causes of Increased Globalisation

There's been trade across the world for donkey's years, but globalisation has really skyrocketed in the last century. There are eight reasons for this increase in globalisation that you need to know about. Time to get learning...

1) Trade Liberalisation Removes Restrictions to International Trade

1) International trade can be restricted by **international trade barriers** — these are things that make trade between different countries **more difficult** or **expensive**. For example, there may be complicated **procedures** and **regulations**, **tariffs** and **quotas** (see p.160).

2) The **reduction** and **removal** of these restrictions to trade is known as **trade liberalisation**. Increased liberalisation has led to an increase in **international trade** and **globalisation**.

3) The **World Trade Organisation** (**WTO**) is often used to help **negotiate** trade agreements, and promotes trade liberalisation.

4) There are **advantages** and **disadvantages** of trade liberalisation — here are some examples:

Advantages

1) Any **raw materials** that a firm **imports** will become **cheaper** — this will **lower** the firm's **costs**, which could make it more **competitive** as it could reduce its prices.

2) **Exporting** goods becomes **easier** and **cheaper**, so there are **more markets** for firms to expand into.

3) Consumer **choice** is increased to include **products** from all over the **world**.

4) **Increased competition** between firms in different countries will mean that products are **cheaper** for consumers as firms compete for sales.

Disadvantages

1) Removal of trade barriers will reduce the cost of imports. Domestic businesses can be forced out by the increased imports if they are not competitive, which can increase unemployment.

2) Some feel that trade liberalisation is leading to a removal of national cultures.

2) Political Change can Make Countries More Open to Trade

1) Restrictions to international trade put in place by one government might be **removed** if the **political system** changes to one that supports **trade liberalisation**. This leads to more trade with that country, and so **increases globalisation**.

2) For example, there was **political** and **economic reform** in India in the 1990s, which included a reduction in **import tariffs** (see p.160) and an increase in **foreign investment**.

3) **China** has also undergone a period of economic and trade reform since the 1970s, which has included **opening** its economy to **trade**.

4) Political agreements between countries have led to a growth in **trading blocs** — these **reduce trade barriers** between **certain countries** (see pages 160-161 for more).

3) Economic Development Leads to Structural Change

1) The **structure** of a country's economy can be thought of as the **different industries** it contains:

- **Primary** industries are concerned with obtaining raw materials, such as agriculture and mining.
- **Secondary** industries manufacture goods from those raw materials.
- **Tertiary** industries are services, such as financial and health services.
- **Quarternary** industries are knowledge-based services, such as IT and scientific research.

2) As a country develops, its reliance on **primary** and **secondary** industries falls, whilst the **tertiary** and **quaternary** industries grow. This creates **growth** and more **demand** for goods and services.

3) This structural change is often matched by a growth in **national income**, as tertiary and quaternary industries often provide **higher rates of return** for investors.

4) Firms operating in **tertiary** and **quarternary** industries are likely to be **specialised** and have highly **skilled staff**. These firms often find that they need to **trade internationally** to obtain the **market share** required to maximise **economies of scale**. This leads to the businesses being global, with **global recruitment**.

Causes of Increased Globalisation

4) More People in the World are Able to Work

1) The **world population** is increasing, with people **living** and **working longer**, and with more **women** in work. This means that the **global labour force** (the number of people willing and able to work) is rising.

2) With **more people** able to work, firms have more **freedom** to set up business **operations** wherever they want (e.g. near to **raw materials** or **export** markets) and are **less likely** to be **restricted** by a **lack** of **labour** in their chosen area.

Cliff wasn't particularly thrilled about being part of the labour force.

5) People are More Likely to Migrate

1) **People move** about a lot more than they used to — people may **move** to a **different part** of the **same country**, or move to a **new country**. **Migration** increases **globalisation** because people might create a **new demand** for certain **products** in the place they **move to**, which creates **opportunities** for firms to **sell** in new **locations**.

2) As well as this, businesses can find it easier to **set up operations abroad** when **skilled staff** are **willing to migrate** to new countries for work. This allows businesses to become **global** more easily.

6) Firms are Investing More in Foreign Countries

1) **Governments** that want to **obtain** the **benefits** of increased trade often try to **encourage foreign direct investment** (FDI, see p.157) by offering firms **financial incentives**, such as **reduced tax rates** on profits.

2) This makes it more **cost-effective** for firms to **invest overseas**, which increases the **investment flow** into the country and therefore **increases globalisation**.

7) There's Been an Increase in Global Companies

1) **Multinational corporations** (MNCs) or **transnational companies** (TNCs) function in several countries, and the number of these businesses is growing.

2) **MNCs** and **TNCs** encourage globalisation as they can **boost the economies** of the countries that they locate in by **increasing employment**. This can lead to **more demand** for products, and encourage **other businesses to expand** into those countries.

There's lots more on MNCs and their effects on economies on p.178-179.

8) Transport and Communication Have Become Cheaper

1) A main cause of globalisation is a reduction in the **cost** and **time needed** for **transportation**, making goods **cheaper** to **export and import**. This is partly due to the development of **larger cargo ships** and **containerisation** — containerisation is where goods are shipped in **standard-sized** cargo containers, which makes cargo loading and unloading **quicker**.

2) **Improvements** in **technology** have also had a huge effect on globalisation. The growth of the **internet** across the world means that **information** can be **sent between countries** more easily and cheaply. So **communicating** with overseas **customers**, **suppliers** and **business partners** has become **more convenient** and **less expensive**, which has led to a growth in international trade.

Warm-Up Question

Q1 Explain how each of the following increases globalisation:
a) Political change.   b) Migration.   c) Cheaper transport.

PRACTICE QUESTIONS

Exam Question

Q1 HBags Ltd makes and sells handbags in the USA. China and America currently impose trade barriers on each other. Explain two benefits to HBags Ltd of trade liberalisation between these two countries.   [8 marks]

Globalisation was big in the 1500s — before then the Earth was flat...

As you've probably figured out by now, there are a lot of causes of globalisation, and lucky you — you get to learn all of them. Make sure you can explain how each one can increase globalisation — it might come up in your exam.

Protectionism and Trading Blocs

Not everyone wants to go global — governments can act to protect businesses in their own country from foreign imports and businesses. They can also negotiate trading blocs and open up trade to certain other countries.

Protectionism can Help to Boost an Economy

Protectionism is when a government protects **domestic businesses** and **jobs** from foreign competition. There are several ways it can do this:

1) Tariffs and Quotas

1) A **tariff** is a **tax** that has to be **paid** when certain products are **imported** into a country.
2) **Import quotas** are trade restrictions set by governments that put **limits** on the **volume** of particular products that can be **imported into** a country in a certain **time period**.
3) Tariffs and quotas **discourage** international trade by making **imported** products more **expensive** than domestic products or limiting **how much** can be brought into a country.
4) This can **help domestic firms** to grow as they face less **competition** from **foreign firms**.
5) However, this can **restrict consumer choice** and means that consumers might have to **pay more** for products than they would do otherwise.
6) The **lack** of **competition** also removes the **incentive** for domestic firms to **improve efficiency** and **quality**.

Bruiser took his job checking imports very seriously.

2) Government Legislation

1) **Government legislation** can restrict international trade. For example, **trade sanctions** **strongly restrict** trade with a certain country, and **trade embargoes** can **ban** trade with a country altogether. E.g. the USA has had an embargo against Cuba since 1962.
2) Sanctions and embargoes can make trade extremely **difficult** and **expensive**. They can also cause **retaliation** — another country might **respond** by **restricting trade** with your country.
3) This can **restrict a country's development**, as they cannot make money by **exporting goods**.

3) Domestic Subsidies

1) **Domestic subsidies** are **sums of money** provided by the government to domestic firms in a certain industry (e.g. steel).
2) These **reduce production costs**, allowing domestic products to have **lower prices** than imports. For example, the **EU's Common Agricultural Policy** gives subsidies to EU farmers to ensure that they have a **guaranteed income** without having to increase prices.
3) However, **subsidies cost** the government **money**, which might mean that **people** living in the country face **higher taxes** to **fund** the subsidies.

Trading Blocs Encourage Trade Between Certain Countries

1) Trading blocs are **associations** between different **governments** to **promote** and **manage trade** for a particular region. Members **sign agreements** to remove or reduce protectionist barriers between them. The **growth** in the number of trading blocs has helped **trade liberalisation** by the removal of trade restrictions.
2) You need to be aware of the following **trading blocs**:

- The **North American Free Trade Agreement (NAFTA)** is made up of **Canada, Mexico** and the **United States**. It is a free trade area, which means that **barriers** to **trade** have been **reduced** between the **member countries**, but individual countries can still **impose them** on **outside countries**.
- The **Association of Southeast Asian Nations (ASEAN)** is made up of **10 countries**, including Thailand, Malaysia and Indonesia. As well as being a **free trade area**, it also allows some **free movement** of **labour** and **capital** (money) between the member countries.
- The **European Union (the EU)** is made up of 28 European countries (in 2018). It is a **single market** — this means that there are **no borders** between member states for the movement of **labour, products** and **capital**. There is also a **harmonisation** of **standards** — this means that all countries have the **same regulations** about products, such as regulations regarding **quality** or **energy** use. Many EU member countries are also within a **monetary union** where all the countries use a **single currency**, the euro.

Protectionism and Trading Blocs

Trading Blocs Affect the Businesses in Them

There are **advantages and disadvantages** for a business operating inside a **trading bloc**:

Advantages:

1) When a country **becomes** a **member** of a trading bloc, the **removal** of **trade barriers** might mean that a **business** within that country becomes the **cheapest supplier** for other countries in the bloc. This can lead to a **surge in demand** for that business's products. It can also mean that businesses are able to **obtain their supplies** more cheaply than before, which **lowers their costs** and could **increase profitability**.

2) Fewer **regulations** between members of trading blocs can mean it's **easier** for businesses within the bloc to obtain materials, labour and capital. They may also have access to more **skilled workers**, which can improve the **efficiency** and **quality** of production.

3) As a trading bloc expands, firms in member states have an **expanding market** for their products. Selling to **larger markets** can increase **sales volume** and therefore **lower costs** because of economies of scale. Firms can also obtain economies of scale if **business regulations** and **laws** are **harmonised** throughout the trading bloc. For example, the EU has **common policies** on **product regulation**, such as how much **energy** appliances can consume, so businesses can make the **same product** to sell across the EU.

4) **Greater competition** from within the bloc can result in firms being **more efficient** — this is because firms will try to **reduce** their **costs** as much as possible so they can offer customers more **competitive prices**.

5) External tariffs help to **protect firms** in member countries from **international competition**.

Disadvantages:

1) When a **country** becomes part of a **trading bloc**, it can become **more expensive** to **import** products from countries not in the bloc. This may mean a business's **costs increase** (if it **needs** to **import** products from outside the bloc) or it needs to **spend time** finding **new suppliers**.

2) **Small firms** in a country that has just **joined** a trading bloc may be **forced out** of business because of **competition** from larger firms elsewhere in the bloc. This can **increase unemployment** levels in the country.

3) A business may find that it needs to **adjust** some of its **operations** in order to **comply** with **rules** and **regulations** set by the trading bloc. This is likely to **increase** the firm's **costs** in the **short term**.

Trading Blocs also Affect Businesses from Outside the Bloc

1) When a country **becomes part** of a trading bloc, it can have **disadvantages** for **firms** that **trade** with that country, if they are **based** in countries that are **not** part of the **bloc**. For example, the **cost** of **exporting products** to that country may rise (e.g. if there are **tariffs** on imports from **outside** the bloc), meaning that **demand** for a firm's products in that country might **fall**.

2) However, it can also be **advantageous** if a country that a firm **exports** to (or has **business operations** in) **becomes part** of a trading bloc. Initially the firm may need to **alter** its **products** so that it **meets** the **regulations** of the trading bloc, but if the bloc regulations are **harmonised** the product can then be **sold throughout** the **bloc**. This can allow the firm to benefit from economies of scale and become more **competitive**.

Alice was very proud of her new business — she was going to trade in blocks.

Warm-Up Questions

Q1 What is a trading bloc?

Q2 Give three disadvantages of trading blocs for domestic businesses.

Exam Question

Q1 Barkbytes PLC is a company based in Estonia that writes specialist software, which is exported to customers in Sweden. The business was set up in 1999. Sweden has been a member of the EU since 1995, and Estonia joined in 2004. Assess the likely impacts on Barkbytes PLC of Estonia joining the EU. [12 marks]

Someone ought to put a quota on my tea drinking...

Much as businesses might like to buy and sell goods in all countries, governments have other ideas. The government has to find the right balance between protecting domestic businesses and making money from international trade.

Causes of International Trade

Businesses don't always stay in the same country — expanding a business to trade abroad may be crucial for a firm's survival or growth. So pack a suitcase and grab your sunglasses and spare underwear, it's time to go abroad.

International Trade can be Done in Different Ways

1) Many firms want to **trade internationally**.

2) There can be many **opportunities** for a firm to **trade internationally**, including:

> * **Selling** products in **overseas markets**.
> * Obtaining **raw materials** from overseas.
> * Setting up an overseas **presence**, for example a **branch** in a foreign country.
> * Moving **production** abroad.
> * **Relocating** to another country.

There's more on this on p.166-167.

See pages 168-169.

3) There are several **circumstances** and **environments** which promote international trade, and these can be split into **push factors** (see below) and **pull factors** (see the next page).

4) Not all businesses will be affected by these factors in the same way. The **effects** of any **push** and **pull factors**, and a **business's response** to them, will depend on the **nature** of the business, its **market** and its **products**.

5) Any push and pull factors should be **considered** by a business when **assessing** whether it should **trade abroad** or not.

6) If a business does decide to **trade internationally**, there's a **potential** that the business could **grow**. It also increases a business's **chance** of **survival**.

7) However, trading internationally can be a **high risk strategy** if the firm doesn't fully **research** the new market.

Push Factors are Negative Factors in the Domestic Market

1) **Push factors** motivate a firm to look at **business opportunities** in other countries.

2) Push factors are often **threats** to a firm's **profitability** and **survival** in their current market.

3) Push factors include **saturation** and **competition** in the domestic market:

Push factors 'push' a business away from domestic markets.

Saturated Markets

1) A saturated market is one in which all consumer demand has been, or is being, met.

2) Saturated markets are crowded, so they have few opportunities for sales growth.

3) When domestic markets are saturated, firms may move into emerging markets. Moving to an unsaturated overseas market can increase sales.

4) For example, the market for coffee shops is becoming more and more saturated in the USA, so Starbucks® have moved into other countries' markets, including Columbia, Cambodia and Italy.

The push to move abroad wasn't going to plan.

Competition

1) High levels of competition can reduce sales and profitability to a point where firms are forced to go abroad.

2) For example, there are high levels of competition in the market for black tea bags in the UK. A manufacturer that is struggling to make a profit in the UK market might start selling in countries with less competition for black tea bags instead.

Businesses can deal with competition in many different ways (see p.4) — moving abroad is just one option.

4) Changes in the domestic **government's policies** can also push a business to trade abroad. For example, if **taxes rise** this will increase a firm's costs.

5) Businesses can also be pushed to move abroad by changes in **local tastes** and a decrease in **demand** for their product in the **domestic market**.

Causes of International Trade

Pull Factors are Positive Factors in Overseas Markets

1) A **pull factor** is something which makes it **attractive** for a business to **trade abroad**.

2) Pull factors are likely to be **opportunities**.

3) The **spreading of risk** and **economies of scale** are two common pull factors:

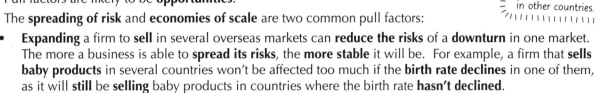

Pull factors 'pull' a business to markets in other countries.

- **Expanding** a firm to **sell** in several overseas markets can **reduce the risks** of a **downturn** in one market. The more a business is able to **spread its risks**, the **more stable** it will be. For example, a firm that **sells baby products** in several countries won't be affected too much if the **birth rate declines** in one of them, as it will **still** be **selling** baby products in countries where the birth rate **hasn't declined**.

- Businesses might expand abroad to achieve **global economies of scale**, which will **reduce** their **unit costs**. This is a strong **pull factor** for firms that need global economies of scale in order to **grow** and **survive**. For example, a **research facility** might need global economies of scale in order to afford **innovation** and **research and development**.

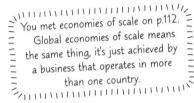

You met economies of scale on p.112. Global economies of scale means the same thing, it's just achieved by a business that operates in more than one country.

4) Firms might also be attracted by **other pull factors** in foreign countries:

- **New** and **untapped markets**.
- More **profitable** markets.
- Certain **education** and **training** in a country, giving **residents** (and therefore potential **staff**) specific **skills** and **knowledge**.

- Lower **production costs**.
- Lower **material costs**.
- Higher **availability** of **resources**.
- The ability to obtain **overseas trading licences**.

A trading licence is a document giving permission to buy or sell particular products in a particular country. Firms working without one could be fined.

Moving Abroad can Extend a Product's Life Cycle

1) Some businesses sell the **same product** in **more** than one **country**. The product might be at a **different stage** of its **life cycle** in each country's market.

2) So the product might be in the **mature** or **declining stage** in the **domestic market**, but in the **introductory** or **growth** stage in an **emerging market**.

3) This could be as a result of an **extension strategy** used by the business, where it has **extended** the product **life cycle**.

4) For example, if the sales of a **book** start to **decline** in the UK (its **domestic market**), its publisher might decide to **translate** it into more languages so that they can **sell** it in **other countries**. The book would be in the **introductory** or **growth** phases in new markets, so its **life cycle** would be **extended**.

See pages 26-27 for more on the product life cycle and extension strategies.

Warm-Up Questions

Q1 Give two push factors that could lead to a business choosing to trade internationally.

Q2 What is meant by a saturated market?

Q3 Give two pull factors that could lead to a business choosing to trade internationally.

Exam Question

Q1 Oak Ltd's market research shows that one of its key products, a smart-speaker called The Hub, is entering the decline stage of its life cycle in its domestic market in the USA. The domestic market for smart-speakers has become saturated and is highly competitive. Oak Ltd has decided to expand to sell The Hub in Brazil, which has a large market for IT and technology products. Assess the push and pull factors affecting Oak Ltd's decision to sell The Hub in Brazil. [10 marks]

There was a flood in the city centre last week — it saturated the market...

This selling-in-lots-of-different-countries lark sounds like a pretty decent deal to me. Potentially higher sales? Check. Spreading risk? Check. Free holidays, also known as "business trips"? Check. No wonder so many firms are doing it.

Offshoring and Outsourcing

Businesses can move some of their work to other countries (offshoring). They might also ask other businesses to do occasional work for them (outsourcing). Now if I can just find someone to outsource writing this page to...

Offshoring Means Moving Parts of a Business to Cheaper Countries

1) Many businesses locate some of their **departments overseas** — this is called **offshoring**.

2) **Offshoring** is often used for **customer service** and **manufacturing** departments.

3) The countries that firms move to most often are **China**, **India**, **Malaysia**, **Mexico** and **Indonesia** — these countries all have **emerging economies** and offer much **cheaper labour** than the UK.

4) Although offshoring is a good way to **cut costs**, it's not always good for a business's **image**. The **media** and **trade unions** often criticise businesses for **UK job losses** caused by offshoring.

Staff loved the new offshore department.

Reshoring

- Reshoring is when a business moves departments back to its country of origin.
- Changing consumer attitudes mean that some firms are moving their departments back to the UK.
- Consumers are becoming more aware of firms' overseas activities. Businesses that are seen to treat overseas staff poorly might get a bad reputation and face a backlash from consumers.
- Reshoring can allow a business to improve the quality of its products and processes as manufacturing is easier to monitor and control if everything is made in the same country.
- Reshoring also means that distribution to the home market is cheaper and more efficient as products don't have to be shipped all over the world. This means that businesses can offer a better delivery service to their customers.
- Sometimes the low wages of overseas labour are still too appealing for firms. However, many emerging economies have rising wages, and as the wage gap between UK workers and overseas workers decreases, more and more firms might begin to reshore.

Certain Countries can Offer Specific Skills to Businesses

1) As a result of offshoring, some countries have become **specialised** in providing certain skills or services.

2) Countries that **specialise** in particular areas will attract lots of business from **overseas firms**. This creates a **competitive environment** in that country, which can lead to even **cheaper prices** and **better services** being offered.

- **India** specialises in **communications** (e.g. call centres) and **IT services**, so they can offer competitive **prices** and a pool of suitably **trained workers**. Businesses might choose to take advantage of this by moving their **customer service department** to India.
- **China** and **Brazil** have lots of **cheap** and **skilled labour** — some businesses have moved their **manufacturing departments** to these countries to take advantage of this. Their products are made for **low labour costs** but often to quite a **low standard** as they focus on volume rather than quality.
- **China** also attracts lots of **Research & Development** departments as they relocate to be closer to the manufacturing department and to take advantage of the **skilled low-cost labour** and **infrastructure**.
- The **Philippines** has a lot of **young university graduates** with very **strong work ethics** and a very good **digital communication infrastructure**. Some businesses have begun moving their **IT departments** to the Philippines to benefit from the **people** and **technology** that they already have in place.

3) Countries that offer specialised services do run into **problems**. Workers may lose **motivation** as the majority of **available jobs** are in the **same industry**, or the size of the industry may lead to **diseconomies of scale**. There's also a risk that **another country** will find a way of providing the skills or service even **more efficiently**.

Offshoring and Outsourcing

Firms Locating Abroad have Non-Financial Benefits and Costs to a Country

1) **Non-financial benefits** and **costs** are the **positive** and **negative impacts** a business has on the **outside world**. These benefits and costs don't have a **direct impact** on the business's **profits** but they can affect its **reputation**.

2) Before making any **decisions** about locating abroad, a business needs to consider the **impact** that it's going to have on the country it's **moving into**.

3) The **non-financial benefits** of locating abroad are that the business will create **new jobs** in that country, which can increase people's **income** and **standard of living**. Businesses also **invest** in the host country by paying for things like factories and roads to be built, and by paying **taxes** to the local government.

4) However there are **non-financial costs** of locating abroad too — it will lead to a **loss of jobs** and **investment** in the original country. It can also have negative impacts on the country they're moving into — **overseas workers** can be **exploited** if they aren't protected by **employment laws** and there may be a **rise in pollution**.

5) These **costs** and **benefits** could affect a business's **reputation**, which could lead to changes in its **sales** and **profits**. It's difficult to know exactly how a business's **finances** would be **affected**, but a business should still **weigh up** the impact on its **reputation** before making any decisions.

Outsourcing can Help a Business to Meet Demand

1) **Outsourcing** (or **subcontracting**) is when businesses **contract out** some activities to other businesses rather than doing them **in-house**.

2) Businesses can outsource some or all of the **product manufacturing** to deal with **increased demand**. They might also outsource things like **finance**, **recruitment**, **advertising** and **IT** — things that the business doesn't **specialise** in but sometimes needs.

3) Outsourcing can be within the **same country** as the business, such as a music venue using an external security firm. However, businesses can also use **offshore outsourcing**, where work is outsourced to a **different country**. For example, a UK business setting up trading with Germany might outsource legal work to a German law firm.

4) Outsourcing can **benefit** businesses because they might be able to **accept contracts** that they would otherwise have turned down. They can also benefit from the **specialised knowledge** of the businesses they outsource to. Outsourcing also means that the business doesn't have to pay for permanent staff when they're only needed occasionally, so it **reduces costs**.

5) The main **disadvantage** of outsourcing is that the business doesn't have **control** over the **quality** of the outsourced work — if the work is bad, it can have a **negative effect** on the business's reputation.

Warm-Up Questions

Q1 What is meant by offshoring?

Q2 Give one benefit to a business of offshoring one of its departments.

Q3 Outline the non-financial costs of relocating a business abroad on the country you're leaving.

Q4 What is meant by outsourcing?

Exam Questions

Q1 Web Weaver Ltd creates custom websites for clients. It has started outsourcing to a graphic designer to create graphics for the websites. Explain how outsourcing may impact Web Weaver Ltd's profits. [4 marks]

Q2 Zaps & Sparks is a gas and electricity provider, with customers across the UK. Its UK call centre was unable to keep up with customer demand, so the decision was made to move the call centre to India. Assess the impact that this decision may have had on Zaps & Sparks. [12 marks]

I spent my weekend putting ketchup on food — I was out saucing...

Outsourcing and offshoring are similar ideas, so you need to make sure you understand how they're different.

Assessing a Country as a Market

Choosing which country to expand your business into isn't as simple as throwing a dart at a world map. If a firm wants to expand into another country, they first need to assess the country as a market. There are five factors you need to know that make some markets more attractive than others. So get reading, and I'll see you on the other side.

Firms Look at **How Much Money People** have to **Spend**

1) The **wealth** of the population will affect the size of a business's **potential market**. Businesses might want to move to a country with **high levels** of **disposable income** so that they have more customers.

> **Example:** A designer clothing business is more likely to open outlets in Switzerland where disposable income is **generally high** than in Bangladesh where disposable income it **generally low**.

2) Businesses might want to expand into **emerging economies**, where **incomes are rising** and there's a growing **middle class**. This gives a business a **growing market** to **sell in**.

Some Countries Will be **Easier** to **Sell** in than **Others**

1) A firm will look at the **ease of doing business** in **different countries** that it's **considering expanding** into.

2) Businesses will find it **easier** to trade with countries with **similar cultures** and **languages** to the one that they already operate in. For example, a business in the **UK** might expand to sell products in **Australia**, which avoids many **language** and **cultural barriers**.

3) Businesses entering **international markets** need to take into account the **laws** in the country they're entering, and any **political controls on trade** through **tariffs** and **quotas** (see p.160). Large amounts of control and regulation could make trading more **complicated**, and the business might need to spend more time and money on **paperwork**.

Betty was unwilling to admit that this wasn't an easy way to do business.

4) Countries that have **fewer restrictions** on the buying and selling of **certain products** can be appealing to some businesses.

> **Example:** There are many **restrictions** on selling **guns** in the UK, but not as many in the USA. So a **gun manufacturer** may have **easier access** and a **larger market** in the USA.

Firms Will Find it **Easier** to **Sell** in a Country with **Good Infrastructure**

1) **Infrastructure** is the **physical systems** and **services** a country has that allow society and businesses to **work effectively**, such as good **roads**, an **electricity supply**, **communications** and **law enforcement**.

2) A country with **poor infrastructure** would be a **difficult market** for a business to operate in. For example, a business selling **ice cream** might not wish to expand to a country with **unreliable electricity** supplies, as it might be hard to keep everything **frozen**.

3) The availability of **technology** can also affect the size of the market. For example, businesses making **electric cars** might not sell in countries without many **charging points** available.

4) If a business needs to **buy** or **sell** in a country with **poor infrastructure**, it might need to **pay** to improve it. This could be **expensive**, so a business should take this into account when making a **decision**.

Assessing a Country as a Market

A Country With **Political Instability** Might be **Difficult** to **Operate** in

1) **Political instability** can mean that a business in that country is at **risk** from unpredictable **changes** in **policies**.

2) These changes could affect people's **employment**, which would affect how much **disposable income** people have.

3) **Political changes** can also affect businesses directly, for example through changes in **business regulations** such as **tariffs**.

4) So if there's **political instability** in a country, a business might **wait** until the problem is **resolved** before entering the country.

After the election, there was some concern about the stability of the new president.

Exchange Rates can Also Affect the **Attractiveness** of a **Market**

1) You met exchange rates on p.92-93. Businesses have to consider exchange rates when making decisions about which countries to sell to or buy from.

2) The attractiveness of a country's market to a business will depend on whether the business imports or exports products, and whether the exchange rate is high or low.

3) For example, a UK business that exports goods to sell in other countries might decide not to sell to a country with a high exchange rate, because its exports would be expensive for the customers.

4) A UK business that imports products from other countries will find a country with a high exchange rate more attractive than one with a low exchange rate, as a high exchange rate means cheaper imports compared to other countries.

Warm-Up Questions

Q1 Give three factors that make some countries more attractive as a market than others for a business to expand into.

Q2 Is a high exchange rate from the pound to the US dollar good or bad for businesses that import from the USA to the UK? Why is this?

Exam Questions

Q1 Foto Flyer PLC is a UK business that makes camera drones. In 2017, it decided to sell to other European countries from within the UK. The pound to euro exchange rate was relatively low in 2017. Explain why a low exchange rate was an advantage to Foto Flyer PLC. [4 marks]

Q2 Brinda's Bling Ltd makes and sells high-end jewellery in the UK, France and Italy. In 2016, the owners were considering expanding into Turkey, which had good infrastructure, low average incomes and high unemployment. In 2016, there was conflict in several major Turkish cities when the military attempted to overthrow the government.
Assess the attractiveness of Turkey as a market for Brinda's Bling Ltd in 2016. [12 marks]

I like my markets like I like my bank account — full of disposable income...

There are a fair few factors that affect how good a country looks to a business as a market. Some countries might look good in some ways and poor in others, so a business should consider all the different factors and weigh up all the pros and cons. Then they can make an informed decision rather than just picking a country willy-nilly. How very sensible.

Assessing a Country as a Production Location

Firms have a lot to think about when choosing a country to locate their production in. Read on my friends, read on...

Businesses Have to **Decide Where** to **Locate Production**

1) Many firms **locate** their **production facilities abroad**, which is a type of **Foreign Direct Investment** (FDI, p.157).

2) When deciding **where** to locate production, firms have to **assess several factors**.

3) Different businesses will find **different factors** more important than others, and this depends on the **nature** of the business and its **aims**.

Businesses can use methods like SWOT analysis (p.108) to help them decide where they should locate production.

Costs of Production

1) One of the **main reasons** why businesses choose to **move production** overseas is that they can often pay **foreign workers** much **lower wages** than they would have to pay UK employees. This is **particularly useful** for businesses that don't need **skilled labour**.

2) For example, a large firm that makes **low cost clothing** might relocate production to a country with cheaper labour. Although the initial **cost** of **moving** may be high, cheaper labour will **lower** its overall **costs**.

3) The cost of **land** and **office space** also tends to be **cheaper** overseas, especially in emerging economies. **Utilities** like water and electricity might also be cheaper abroad.

Some businesses have been accused of not paying foreign workers enough to live on — this is unethical.

Skills and Availability of the Labour Force

1) Some businesses **need skilled labour**. So a business might choose to **relocate production** to a country with a **supply** of labour with the **right skills**. For example, India has a lot of trained engineers so some **high-tech** engineering firms have relocated production there.

2) Businesses might also look at the size of the **available labour force** in a country. For example, it might be easier to find workers in a country with a high **unemployment rate**.

Infrastructure

1) A business needs to see if a country's **infrastructure** is suited to its needs. For example, it might consider:

- If the transport links, like roads, railways and ports, could cope with the firm's imports and exports.
- The availability and quality of service and support industries, such as IT support, banks and interpreters. These would make it easier and quicker to set up production in the country.
- The availability of utilities, like waste disposal and energy supplies, which make production possible.
- The standard and effectiveness of security and law enforcement. For example, a firm might decide not to invest in a country that is seen to have high crime rates.

2) Different businesses will care about **different parts** of infrastructure. For example, a firm that creates **software** won't care too much about road and railways if it doesn't have **physical imports** and **exports**.

Trading Blocs

1) The governments of countries in a **trading bloc** can agree to reduce or remove **import duties** on **products** made and sold **within** the **bloc**. So a firm might **relocate production** to within a trade bloc to **reduce tariff payments** on imports or exports.

2) For example, a Japanese cosmetics company may decide to have a production facility within the **EU**, so that it can **sell** its products made there throughout the EU trade bloc **without paying tariffs**.

Ease of Doing Business

1) Businesses should consider a country's **regulations**, such as **environmental protection laws** that say how much **pollution** firms can **release** during production. **Sticking** to these laws could be **difficult** and **expensive**.

2) A business might also consider the **reaction** of people living in the country it wants to move its production to. For example, residents might **protest** if a production facility creates a lot of **pollution** — these protests could **slow down** production if they **create** a lot of **disruption**.

3) Businesses might consider moving production to countries that are **close** to the **markets** that they want to sell to — being close to the **market** will make the **distribution** of products to the market **easier** and cheaper.

Theme 4: Section 18 — Global Markets and Business Expansion

Assessing a Country as a Production Location

Government Incentives

1) Businesses might want to **locate production** in countries that have **government incentives**, such as:

- The availability of **specialist advice**, such as guidance on how to follow local **regulations** and **laws**.
- Lower **corporate tax rates** than other countries, and **tax relief** for firms moving production there.
- Offering **loans** with **low interest rates** to businesses that need more capital to move their production.
- **Grants** for **training staff** from the country they're moving production to.

2) For example, a business that makes computer components needs **skilled staff** and wants to move its production abroad, but it's struggling to raise enough **capital** to build a **new factory** and **train staff**. So it might move its production to a country with **incentives**, like low interest rates on **loans** and **grants** for training staff.

3) Governments provide these incentives to overseas businesses because they want to **attract** FDI, which brings **money** into the country through increased **employment** and **tax revenue**.

Political Stability

1) A firm might **avoid** locating in countries which are **politically unstable**, as it might be at risk of the government **seizing its assets**, like factories and stock. It also makes planning for the **future** more difficult.

2) Businesses may also avoid certain locations because of **corruption**. For example, businesses may wish to **avoid locating** production in a country where officials demand **bribes** to grant licences and permissions, as it would **increase costs** and could create **bad publicity** for the business.

Natural Resources

1) Firms might locate their production in a country that has the **raw materials** they need. For example, a **jewellery** maker might locate production in a country with **diamond mines**, such as South Africa.

2) Locating production close to raw materials **reduces delays** and the **costs** of **transporting** materials.

3) Firms that rely on **agriculture** are often located in areas with the **best climate** and **environment** for their crops. For example, many tea firms have located in **Kenya**, as it has the ideal climate for **growing tea**.

Likely **Return** on **Investment**

1) Businesses will look at the **long-term return** on investment when deciding where to locate production. This is how much **money** they're likely to **save** or **get back** from moving production abroad, compared to how much money they'll have to **spend** on moving.

2) Firms might use **investment appraisals** (p.119-121) to compare the **return on investments** of different **potential locations** for **production**.

Warm-Up Questions

Q1 Give one way that locating production abroad could reduce costs.
Q2 Why might a firm choose to locate its production facilities within a trade bloc?
Q3 Why might a government offer incentives to businesses to relocate production into its country?

Exam Question

Q1 Pip's Machines makes high specification aeroplane equipment in the UK, with many raw materials imported from China. Its products are sold throughout Europe and it's expanding to sell in Asian countries too. It wants to expand its production to Country A (in Asia) or Country B (in Europe). Country A has a minimum wage of $150 per month, a low rate of university education, and is in the ASEAN trading bloc. In Country B, over 30% of people aged 25-64 have a university degree and the minimum wage is $1500 per month. Evaluate the two countries as production locations for Pip's Machines, and recommend which country it should choose. [20 marks]

I'd be much better at producing these jokes if I relocated to a beach...

There's a boatload of reasons a business might relocate production abroad — they might want lower costs, skilled workers or to be close to raw materials. Not to mention the chance of going somewhere lovely and warm to work.

Global Mergers and Joint Ventures

For some firms, joining forces with another firm in another country can be a great idea. Read on to see why...

Mergers and Joint Ventures can be Between Firms in Different Countries

1) It can be easier for a firm to enter a country by **investing** in a **foreign business** rather developing an overseas business from scratch, especially if a business **lacks local knowledge** of the area. The most popular methods of doing this are **joint ventures** or **mergers** with foreign businesses.

2) A **joint venture** is a legal agreement between two or more firms to work together on a **joint project**. These can be for a **set length of time** and the joint venture exists as a **separate entity** from the businesses that created it. The businesses **share the equity** and **profits** in the venture.

3) You met **mergers** on page 112. A **global merger** is when two or more firms in **different countries** agree to **become a single business**, which usually create **multinational corporations** (**MNCs**). (There's more on MNCs on p.178-183.)

4) **Global joint ventures** and **mergers** can be done for different **reasons**:

Businesses can also use takeovers to expand abroad (which you met on p.112) — this is when one business takes control of the other by buying most or all of the other's shares.

Spreading risk

1) A business might enter into a joint venture or merger to spread risk across different countries or regions.

A region can include several different countries.

2) If a firm was to start trading internationally, there's a risk it could make costly mistakes from a lack of knowledge of the new country. However, a foreign firm in a joint venture or merger should bring good knowledge of the local market, customs and legal requirements, which will reduce these risks.

3) Also, if a business is in several countries, the effects of a downturn in one country's market are likely to have a smaller impact, as sales in the firm's other markets may not fall as much, or may even rise.

4) In a joint venture, any risk is shared between partners, which reduces its impact on each firm.

Access to different markets

1) The **firms involved** in an international merger or joint venture will have **access** to **different markets**.

2) If one of the firms in the merger or joint venture is in a **trading bloc**, this could allow the other firm to **access** that bloc without paying **tariffs**.

3) Firms may enter into joint ventures to **avoid government restrictions** on businesses. For example, there are restrictions in **China** that mean access to some markets is only allowed through **joint ventures** with **Chinese firms**. In 2014, **SONY®** (a Japanese firm) entered into a **joint venture** with the **Chinese firm** Shanghai Oriental Pearl Group — this allowed them to **make** and **sell** PlayStation consoles **in China**.

4) A business within a **More Economically Developed Country (MEDC)** with a **slow growing** market might **invest** in a business in a **Less Economically Developed Country (LEDC)** with an **emerging economy**, as this could allow it to **grow more** than it could have done in its **domestic country**.

5) Firms from **LEDCs** sometimes also enter into mergers or joint ventures with businesses in **MEDCs**, as this can give them **access** to more **established markets** and businesses. For example, the **Indian** company **Tata** merged with the **German steel firm**, Thyssenkrupp, which expanded its European operations.

Securing resources and supplies

1) Global joint ventures and mergers can give a firm **access** to, or help it **secure**, **supplies** of **raw materials** and other **resources** (such as land and labour).

Securing supplies is particularly important if the resource is scarce.

2) **One** of the **firms** involved in the joint venture or merger might have a good business **relationship** with a particular **supplier**, which the other firm might **want**.

3) A business might enter into a merger or joint venture with its supplier of raw materials, which will give the firm greater control over the **quantity**, **quality**, **reliability** and **price** of its supplies. The advantage to the supplier is that this **ensures** it has a **customer** for its products.

Global Mergers and Joint Ventures

Firms can Obtain Intellectual Property

1) Mergers and joint ventures can also be used to obtain **intellectual property**. This includes **copyrights** and **patents** for **creations**, **ideas** or **inventions**. These copyrights and patents can be **national**, where they cover a single country, or **international**, where they **cover more** than one country.

2) A **patent** held by one firm **prevents** others from **copying** its work for a certain period of time. A firm that wants to make a patented product might form a joint venture or merger with **the firm** that **owns the patent**.

3) Obtaining a **patent** can allow the business to **produce** the **good worldwide**, both in the countries **covered** by the patent and those **that aren't**.

4) **MNCs** have **better resources** than smaller businesses, such as **marketing expertise** and **distribution channels**, which means that they can make better **use** of **patents**, such as **selling** across **multiple countries**.

5) Firms can also enter into mergers or joint ventures to obtain a **well-known** national or international **brand name**. This means that the firm is likely to **gain customers** who are already **loyal** to the **existing brand**. If the firm also **adds** their own brand name to **established products**, they can increase their own **brand recognition** in a new market too.

Amani couldn't decide if it was worth patenting her blueberry and eel ice cream or not.

Mergers and Joint Ventures can Help a Firm Beat the Competition

Mergers and joint ventures can help maintain or increase a firm's **global competitiveness**. This can be achieved in **several** ways:

1) If a merger increases the size of a firm's global market, it can take advantage of economies of scale, which will reduce unit costs and allow the firm to reduce prices, making it more competitive.

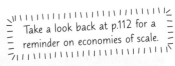

Take a look back at p.112 for a reminder on economies of scale.

2) Firms may enter a merger with a competitor to remove that competitor from the market.

3) Mergers and joint ventures can give firms access to new technologies, expertise, skilled workers and more research and development. This could increase innovation and help in developing new products, which would help the firm increase its competitiveness.

4) Firms might merge with an overseas business to relocate to a country with lower taxes. Tax savings could then be reinvested into more efficient ways of working, such as new machinery, which could lower costs and make the firm more competitive.

5) MNCs can enter mergers or joint ventures with several firms that make similar products to maintain competitiveness through diversification, with different products that each serve a different market. Any loss of sales for one product could be offset by an increase in the sales of one of the firm's other products.

Warm-Up Questions

Q1 What is meant by the terms joint venture and global merger?

Q2 Explain how a global joint venture can help a firm to secure a supply of raw materials.

Q3 Give three ways that a global merger can increase a business's global competitiveness.

Exam Question

Q1 Fultums PLC produces specialist regional UK food dishes and is proud of its use of authentic ingredients. The firm wants to expand both its range and its markets. Assess two benefits to Fultums PLC of pursuing a joint venture with a chain of well-known Chinese restaurants in Chengdu, China, that specialises in Sichuan cuisine. [8 marks]

I'm bringing out a line of stylish knee braces — it's a joint venture...

Some markets can be pretty tricky for a business to enter, so teaming up with a business that's already there can make life a lot easier. Just remember, there are loads of reasons why firms choose global mergers or go into joint ventures.

Global Competition

As the world becomes more connected, customers have more and more products to choose from and firms have to work hard to stand out from the crowd. I think they should use a lot more glitter, that would get my attention...

Businesses Can Aim for Cost Competitiveness or Differentiation

1) Global businesses often try to **maintain** or **improve** their **competitive advantage** through **cost competitiveness** or **differentiation**:

COST COMPETITIVENESS

1) **Cost competitiveness** is when a business has relatively **low costs** compared to its competitors, which allows it to charge **lower prices**.

2) Lower prices **increase competitiveness**, as it can be used to attract **customers** and increase the firm's market share. This can then force **competitors** with **higher prices** out of the market.

There's more on cost leadership on p.105.

3) One way of achieving low prices would be through **cost leadership** — this is when a firm has the **lowest production costs** compared to its **competitors** making similar quality products.

4) **Businesses** that make relatively low quality products are often aiming for **cost competitiveness** — they can **reduce costs** by buying **low quality** raw **materials**. For example, the clothes shop **Primark®** makes relatively **low quality** clothes and is cost competitive, allowing it to charge **lower prices** than its competitors.

Yacob's high protein diet had given him a competitive advantage this time around.

DIFFERENTIATION

1) You met differentiation on p.11 — this is when a product is seen to have unique features that are not possessed by its competitors.

Take a look at p.15 for a reminder on price elasticity of demand.

2) Firms can use differentiation to charge higher prices. This method would be most effective for products with a lower price elasticity of demand.

3) However, differentiation can only be used in the long-term to obtain a competitive advantage if the firm possesses a barrier to entry. Without a barrier to entry, another firm could copy the product's unique features, so it would no longer be differentiated. For example, if a firm owns a trademark or a strong brand name in a country's market, new firms can't copy it, which creates a barrier to entry.

4) Differentiation can be used to attract consumers that place a high value on product characteristics, such as brand or design. For example, Christian Louboutin makes shoes with red soles, which helps to differentiate the product. Differentiation is also common for firms that make high-value products.

2) **Cost competitiveness** could be achieved by lowering production costs. This could be done by **offshoring** production (p.164) or through **selling** to **large global markets** to achieve global **economies of scale**.

3) Businesses that use **differentiation** could **outsource** (p.165) work to **specialist producers** to keep the quality of their products high. For example, Chanel **outsources** the production of **sunglasses** to a specialist company, Luxottica, which helps them to keep **quality high** without having to **find** or **train** their own specialist staff.

Some Industries and Countries Suffer From Skills Shortages

1) Some **industries** in certain **countries** don't have enough **skilled workers** to make their products. This can **reduce** the **relative competitiveness** of a firm by increasing the **costs of production**. For example, firms that lack staff may have to **offer higher wages** to attract people with the right skills and knowledge. This would **increase costs**, and make a firm **less competitive** than one based in a country with **more skilled labour**.

2) Firms could use **less skilled staff**, but this could lead to the **quality** of products going **down** and a **loss of sales**.

3) Businesses can hire unskilled staff and **train them**, but many firms are **reluctant** to do this due to the **high costs** in the short-term. There's also the risk that the firm's investment will be lost if the **staff members leave**.

4) **Whole countries** can have a skills shortage, due to of a lack of **training** or because skilled staff **move** to other countries. For example, the UK has skills shortages in **medicine**, and **Germany** has skills shortages in **science**.

5) A skills shortage in a country can make it less **internationally competitive**. To stop this from happening, some countries and businesses offer **incentives** to **attract skilled workers**.

6) Businesses that rely on product differentiation often need **high levels** of **skills** and **expertise** to make **unique products**. So these firms would be more affected than others by any skills shortage — if they **can't recruit** workers with the right skills they may not be able to **meet customer demand**.

7) A business can use **outsourcing** and **offshoring** as a way to get around this.

Global Competition

Movements in Exchange Rates Affect a Business's Competitiveness

You saw on p.167 that the **exchange rate** between two countries' currencies affects the **price** of **imports** and **exports** between those two countries. This can affect the **competitiveness** of businesses that **import** or **export** products.

Appreciation

1) When one currency **rises in value** relative to another, the currency has **appreciated**.
2) For example, if the UK pound **appreciated** against the euro, the exchange rate might move from £1 = €1.41 to £1 = €1.50 — the pound is **worth more** in euros.
2) When the pound appreciates, UK **exports** will become more **expensive**, which will make them **less competitive** on the global market.
3) **Imports** into the UK will become **cheaper** when the pound appreciates. So UK businesses that buy **raw materials** from overseas will have lower costs and may become more **competitive** in the **UK market**.
4) However, a foreign competitor that **exports completed products** into the UK may also have **lower prices**, reducing UK firms' competitiveness.

Depreciation

1) When a currency **falls in value** relative to another, it has **depreciated**.
2) For example, if the UK pound **depreciated** against the euro, the exchange rate might change from £1 = €1.41 to £1 = €1.19 — the pound is **worth less** in euros.
3) When the pound depreciates, UK **exports** become **cheaper**, which will make them **more competitive** on the global market.
4) Imports into the UK will become **more expensive** when the pound depreciates. So a UK business that **imports raw materials** will have higher costs, making it less competitive in the UK market.
5) A foreign firm that **exports** its products **into the UK** will also have higher prices when the currency depreciates, making it **less competitive** than UK firms.

Example: A UK firm sells watches in Germany.
Each watch is worth £50 000.
In April 2017, £1 = €1.18, so the price in euros was:
£50 000 × 1.18 = €59 000
By August 2017, the pound had depreciated to £1 = €1.09, so the price fell to:
£50 000 × 1.09 = €54 500
So the business was **less competitive** in the German market in April than it was in August.

Little did Beatrice know, the exchange rate had depreciated to one sister to one camel.

Warm-Up Questions

Q1 Describe how a global business could achieve cost competitiveness.
Q2 Why is a business that uses differentiation more affected by skills shortages than one that doesn't?

Exam Question

Q1 Warm & Cosy PLC is a UK based company that imports wool from Australia to produce a range of blankets, which it then sells to several countries within the eurozone. Assess how a depreciation of the pound against the euro and Australian dollar will affect Warm & Cosy PLC. [10 marks]

How do you know a crustacean is happy? They show crab-preciation...

If exchange rates have you in a bit of a pickle, then you might need to read this page several times to get your head around it. You need to know how the price of imports and exports change when exchange rates move, so make sure you really understand it before moving on. Then I think you probably deserve a cup of tea. And some cake.

Global Marketing Strategies

Businesses have a lot to think about when going global, including how to adapt their marketing strategies around the world. It's like changing the accessories that you wear with a dress, depending on the occasion. Sort of...ish... well OK, I guess it's nothing like that really. Just get reading whilst I go and look for some new shoes.

A Business can Use **Different Marketing Strategies** in **Different Countries**

1) You saw on page 18 that a business's marketing strategy is made up of the **4Ps** of the **marketing mix** — **product**, **promotion**, **price** and **place**.

2) A **global marketing strategy** sets out how a business markets its products in **different countries**.

3) Businesses have marketing strategies for **each country** they sell to. These marketing strategies might be exactly the **same** in all countries, or they can be **different** in each country.

4) Businesses might also use the **same marketing strategy** across all countries in one **region** but **change** it for countries in **another region**. For example, a business might have one strategy for **European** countries and another for **South-East Asian** countries.

5) Marketing strategies **don't** have to be **completely different** in different countries. There can be an overall strategy with **adaptations** for each country.

6) Adapting marketing strategies between different countries is called **glocalisation** (global localisation) — this is where firms "**think globally, act locally**". For example, **MTV** operates similar **television channels** around the world, but these are adapted to have local **language**, **music** and **presenters**, e.g. MTV India plays a range of music, including **Hindi pop**.

Martha couldn't decide where to start her world domination plan.

7) **Glocalisation** is often used by international businesses as consumers are more likely to buy a product that's **adapted** to their **needs**, **culture**, or **local tastes**.

8) Another **advantage** of **glocalisation** is that it can lead to **local production**, which can **lower** the **costs** of production for the business, for example if it doesn't have to **transport** its products between countries.

9) The amount that the marketing strategy of a business varies between countries **depends** on the **business** and its **products**. For example, the marketing **strategy** is often **similar** in different countries for **high-end goods**, such as Rolls Royce cars, and **different** in different countries for **mass market** products, such as fast-food or cosmetics.

10) Businesses develop a **marketing approach** to achieve their global marketing strategy. They could use an **ethnocentric**, **polycentric** or **geocentric** approach.

An **Ethnocentric Approach** Keeps a Similar **Marketing Strategy** Everywhere

1) The **ethnocentric** (or **domestic**) approach to global marketing treats all of a firm's markets as being very **similar**, with little or no adaptations to local tastes. This leads to the **marketing strategy** used in global markets being **similar** to the one used in the firm's **domestic market**.

2) For example, Apple® mostly uses an **ethnocentric marketing** approach for its products, based on its **domestic market** in the **USA**. The iPhone® has a **standard design worldwide**, and premium **pricing** is used in all countries.

3) The **ethnocentric approach** has several advantages to businesses:

- Producing the same product for all markets allows a firm to reach economies of scale.

- The firm can use the same marketing and promotional tools worldwide, which helps to reduce its total marketing costs.

- Less time and money needs to be spent on market research for new markets, as it's assumed that all markets will want the same product, and that the promotion and pricing will work as it is.

- The firm also spends less money on maintaining different brand images because it has a smaller range of products that don't have to be adapted to different markets.

- A global brand might make it easier for the firm to deal with suppliers and distributors, as it's more well-known.

- Customers often prefer to buy global brands, especially if they're working or travelling overseas.

4) However, the ethnocentric approach means that the product might **not fit all markets** and might **not sell** well in new markets. It also means that any **negativity** in one country can **impact** the **global brand**.

Global Marketing Strategies

A Firm Using a **Polycentric Approach** Uses **Different Marketing Strategies**

1) A **polycentric** (or **international**) approach means different **products** and **marketing strategies** in each country. **Market research** can be used to create products to suit the different **wants and needs** of international markets.

2) **Mondelēz International** sells different **chocolate products** in different regions — **Lacta** is sold in **Brazil**, **Marabou** is sold in **Scandinavia** and **Côte D'or** is sold in several European countries.

3) Using the polycentric approach to **target products** at particular markets should **ensure sales**.

4) However, it's **expensive** to carry out **market research** and **create** new products and marketing plans. Firms using the polycentric approach also have **fewer chances** to reach **economies of scale**.

The **Geocentric Approach** is a **Mix** Between the Other Approaches

1) The **geocentric** (or **mixed**) approach is an example of **glocalisation**. It's a **combination** of the ethnocentric and polycentric approaches — the **global focus** of the ethnocentric approach is kept, but it also uses some of the **local factors** identified under a polycentric approach. The **global brand** is the **same** in each country, but the **marketing** is **adapted** to suit local consumers.

2) For example, Domino's® pizza has a global brand, but **adjusts** its **menu** to each market.

3) By **adapting** marketing to its **target market** under the geocentric approach, a business should **increase** its **sales**. Another advantage of the geocentric approach is that **money** can be **saved** in other places, for example by **keeping** similar **advertising** for each country. A business can also maintain its **global brand image**, making the brand recognisable around the world.

4) The **disadvantage** of the geocentric approach is that it can be **costly** to **adapt products**. But these costs are still **lower** than in the **polycentric** approach, where different products are developed for **each market**.

The **Marketing Mix** and **Ansoff's Matrix** can be **Applied** to **Global Markets**

1) When determining its **marketing strategy** a global firm needs to consider the 4Ps (p.18):

- **Product** — the firm might need to adapt a product for different markets.
- **Promotion** — different cultures may require different promotional methods.
- **Price** — production and distribution costs, taxes, income and competition will vary between countries, and will affect how much a business can sell its product for.
- **Place** — firms need to know how and where consumers will buy the product. For example, they might buy in a supermarket or online.

An ethnocentric approach generally keeps the 4Ps the same between countries. A polycentric or geocentric approach adapts the 4Ps.

2) For example, when **Starbucks®** expanded into **China** it developed **new food** and **drink** items, and promoted itself as a **premium brand**, with **higher prices** than in other countries and stores in **luxury shopping malls**.

3) A firm aiming to **grow globally** can apply Ansoff's matrix (p.105) to its **global marketing strategy**. For example:
- Risk will increase when a firm **enters** a new market **overseas** because managers **know less** about consumers, competition and the economy. This can make market development **difficult**.
- A **polycentric approach** is often more risky than an ethnocentric one — the firm may develop **new products** for **new markets**, which will have **more uncertainty** than entering a new market with an **existing product**.

Warm-Up Questions
Q1 What does glocalisation mean?
Q2 Give two disadvantages of an ethnocentric marketing approach.
Q3 What is a geocentric marketing approach?

Exam Question
Q1 Jazz PLC makes organic, healthy breakfast cereals that it sells in Spain, and is planning to expand to sell its products in Mexico. It's planning to use a polycentric approach for its global marketing strategy. Assess two changes to its marketing mix that Jazz PLC should consider for expansion. [8 marks]

My ex had an egocentric approach, he was a <the rest of this gag has been censored>...
Some businesses do pretty well if they use the same marketing strategies everywhere, but it won't work for everyone. Just imagine trying to sell American spray cheese in France alongside their Brie and Roquefort. Sacré bleu, non merci.

Global Niche Markets

Skip back to p.2 for a quick recap on niche markets. Then settle down to read about delightful global niche markets.

Products Sold in Global Niche Markets can Meet Specific Customer Needs

1) **Cultural diversity** is the presence of different **cultural groups** in a society. Differences in culture can happen for many reasons, including **religion**, **traditions**, **interests**, **history** and **economic status**.

2) Different **cultural groups** might have different **values and interests**. This can mean that they have **specific wants** and **needs**, which are **not met** by products sold in the **global mass market**.

3) These customers make up **small**, **specialised** parts of global markets, known as **global niche markets**.

4) A global niche market is made up of several **small niche markets** from different countries. A business might sell to a global niche market if a **single niche market** is too small for the business to **survive** or make a profit. For example, the **UK market** for **tandem bicycles** might be **too small** for a business, but all the niche markets for tandem bicycles across **Europe** will have **more customers**, making it a more **profitable market**.

5) Global niche markets have several **advantages** and **disadvantages**:

Advantages

1) Firms serving global niche markets may face **minimal competition**, and often have high **customer loyalty**.

2) Products sold in global niche markets are usually **price inelastic**, so firms can charge **high prices** and therefore **maximise profits**.

3) Risk can be **spread** across many markets if a niche market is made up of several **smaller niche markets**, as it reduces the impact of a downturn in one market.

Disadvantages

1) A firm selling to a global niche market will have a **low sales volume**, so it won't have much chance of getting **economies** of **scale** and can face **high unit costs** of production.

2) A **low sales volume** also means firms **won't** get much **revenue** compared to those in a mass market.

3) If a firm sells to only a **limited number** of niche markets their risk may be high — a **fall in demand** in one country can mean that the firm **struggles to survive**.

4) **High profits** may attract competition, reducing the firm's market share and revenue.

The Marketing Mix can be Adapted for a Global Niche Market

A business should **adapt** the **4Ps** for a global niche market. For example:

- **Product** — products are usually differentiated to meet specific **customer needs**. This is particularly useful if there are **substitute products** available.

- **Promotion** — adverts could highlight the product's **quality**, **uniqueness**, and ability to meet specific **needs**. Firms could use **social media** to **promote** their product to **specific customers**.

- **Price** — a firm could charge **premium prices** to maintain the **exclusivity** of a product.

- **Place** — a firm could sell to a **small number** of exclusive, **high quality** outlets and distributors.

A **global niche market** involves more than one country, so a business might adapt its **marketing mix** to each country using a **geocentric** approach (p.175).

Warm-Up Questions

Q1 What is a global niche market?

Q2 Give two advantages and two disadvantages of a firm selling in a global niche market.

Exam Question

Q1 Sew-sew Ltd makes an embroidery tool for professional crafters, the Stitchatron, which it currently sells in the niche market in the UK. It intends to expand to sell across a global niche market, particularly in North America. Assess the factors that Sew-sew Ltd will need to consider when developing its marketing strategy. [12 marks]

I'm moving into mass marketing — no more Mr. Niche guy...

Global niche markets are great for firms making really specific products, like my jazz-playing robotic vacuum cleaner.

Cultural and Social Differences

Businesses need to take care when marketing abroad. Translating between languages can result in strange, nonsensical or even insulting phrases. Best to hire a real translator, and not just use the internet then...

Marketing Strategies need to Account for Differences in Culture

1) Firms need to think about any differences in **culture** when trading internationally.

2) Businesses could use **market research** to assess how the **local cultural** and **social norms** in a country might **affect** their **marketing strategy**. From this they could consider how to **change the 4Ps** to **adapt** to different cultures and tastes. For example:

> *Remember, an ethnocentric approach has a similar marketing strategy everywhere, so won't take cultural diversity into account.*

- **Product** — A firm making ready-meals might change their ingredients to account for different tastes. For example, some cultures may eat horse meat, whilst others won't.
- **Promotion** — The number four is considered unlucky in China, as it's similar to the word for death. So a firm selling in China might avoid promotions using the number four.
- **Price** — In some cultures, negotiating over price is the norm. So a firm might set a higher price to allow for the lower prices that customers will actually pay after negotiating.
- **Place** — Some states in the USA restrict the sale of wine in supermarkets, so a Chilean wine maker might distribute its product through supermarkets in Europe, but to specialist stores in the USA.

3) The amount that the marketing mix needs to change by can depend on the **cultural differences** between the **domestic** and **overseas markets**. For example, **French** products would require **less adaptation** for the **Spanish** market than for the **Japanese** market.

4) Ignoring cultural differences could lead to inappropriate branding or promotion, which might lead to **poor sales**, and could even **cause offence** to consumers.

5) For example, **Pampers® nappies** were marketed with an **image of a stork** in the USA in the 1970s. The same image was used when Pampers® expanded to sell nappies in **Japan**. However, storks are not associated with delivering babies in Japan, so the image created confusion and the nappies **failed to sell** as well as expected.

Firms should Consider Languages when Marketing Abroad

1) Businesses have to decide which **language** they'll use when going into **overseas markets**.

2) Using a target market's language can **increase costs**, as businesses need to **hire translators**.

3) However, using the **firm's domestic language** overseas could be **offensive** to consumers — it can give the **impression** that the firm doesn't think it's **worth translating**. It also means that messages might not be **understood** by the **target audience**.

4) Sometimes, if a brand name isn't translated into the **target market's language** it can have **unintended meanings**.

Doug wished someone would translate these books for him.

5) If a firm does choose to translate, it has to make sure it **translates** things carefully. An **inaccurate** or **inappropriate translation** from the domestic language could lead to the **wrong message** being given.

6) Firms also need to think about their use of **non-verbal communication** and **body language**, as the **meaning of gestures** can vary. For example, a thumbs-up is a positive gesture in the USA, but is offensive in Greece.

Warm-Up Question

Q1 Give two problems with using a firm's domestic language when marketing abroad.

Exam Question

Q1 Sparkly Skin Ltd produces organic skin care products. Its slogan is "Keep your skin as clean as a whistle.". The business is considering expanding into Spain and North Africa. Assess how cultural and social differences may affect Sparkly Skin Ltd when expanding overseas. **[10 marks]**

The world is like a probiotic yoghurt — full of cultures...
At worst, a firm that makes a cultural blunder could cause real offence to customers that it wants to sell to, and could damage its global brand. At best, it makes for entertaining reading when you're avoiding your revision.

The Effects of MNCs

When businesses choose to operate in new countries, they will affect the economy of their host countries.

Multinational Corporations Operate in Several Countries

1) You saw in **Section 13** (p.116-127) the **reasons** that **firms** might want to **expand abroad**.

2) A **multinational corporation** (**MNC**) is a business that has **branches** or **departments** in more than one country. Its **head office** will be based in **one country** and it will coordinate its **global activities** from there.

3) MNCs can affect the **economies** of the countries they locate in, both at a **local** and a **national** level.

MNCs can Affect Local Economies

POSITIVE EFFECTS

1) MNCs can create jobs, increasing the employment of local labour. For example, an MNC might build a new factory in the host country, creating local jobs for construction workers. More employment reduces the number of people needing benefit payments, reducing local government spending.

2) Increased local employment can improve the local standard of living, especially in LEDCs. This is because employees of MNCs often have better wages and working conditions than staff of local firms.

3) Local firms can benefit from MNCs too. Higher levels of employment and higher wages means more money will be spent in local firms. They might also be able to sell goods or services to the MNC.

4) MNCs might invest in improving infrastructure, which can benefit the local community. This also reduces how much money the local government would need to spend on infrastructure.

NEGATIVE EFFECTS

1) If the MNC brings its **own labour** from other countries this could put a **strain** on the **local community** and its **resources** (such as food supplies). The increased **demand** for resources could increase **prices**.

2) Increased **competition for staff** could force up **local wages**, which **local firms** might **not** be able to **afford**, so local firms could **lose staff** to the MNC. Local people might also start **buying** from MNCs rather than local firms. These could cause local firms to be **forced out** of business. This could reduce the amount of **money** that **stays** in the **local economy** as MNCs might move **profits out** of a region.

3) Although some MNCs improve **working conditions**, others might **employ children** or **exploit workers** by making them work **long hours** in **difficult conditions**. This could cause **increased health problems**, putting a strain on local **healthcare providers**.

4) MNCs might extract large quantities of **unsustainable natural resources**, such as oil, gas or minerals. This might produce large amounts of **pollution** and **waste**, and MNCs might fail to **redevelop** the **landscape** when there are no more resources to extract. So local governments might have to **spend money** to **clean up** after MNCs.

MNCs Pay Tax to Their Host Nations

1) If an MNC has a **branch** or **department** in a country then it will have to **pay taxes** to the **national government**, such as taxes on their **profits**, **exports**, and any **land** they **buy**.

Tax revenue is the money that the government gets through taxes.

2) So an MNC expanding into a country results in increased **government tax revenue** in the country, which might be spent on projects such as **schools** and **hospitals**.

3) MNCs can use **tax avoidance schemes** to **reduce** the amount of tax they pay. Tax avoidance is the use of **legal** accounting methods to **minimise** the tax paid. One tax avoidance method uses **transfer pricing**:

Transfer Pricing

One part of an MNC can sell products to different parts of the same MNC. By doing this, MNCs can move money legally between countries. The MNC can set the prices that it sells products for between the different parts of the MNC — this is transfer pricing. If one part of the MNC is located in a country with a low tax rate, it might sell products to other parts of the MNC for very high prices. This moves its money from a country with a high tax rate to one with a low tax rate. So, at the end of the tax year, more of the MNC's profits are in the country with the low tax rate and it pays less tax overall. If MNCs do this, it can lower the tax paid to governments, which reduces the amount of money in the national economy.

4) **Host governments** with low tax rates might be reliant on the tax revenue from MNCs. So they might be **reluctant** to **enforce** (or introduce) **anti-tax avoidance legislation** against MNCs, because the government fears the MNC will **relocate** to **another country**, reducing their tax revenue.

The Effects of MNCs

MNCs can have Other **Positive Effects** on the **National Economy**

1) MNCs can create large **FDI flows** — this is the **flow** of **money into** and **out of** a country's **economy** from FDI (see p.157). FDI flows contribute towards a country's **balance of payments** — this is the **difference** between the total value of **payments into** and **out** of the country, over a certain period of time.

2) So when an **MNC invests** in a country it causes **FDI inflows**, improving the country's balance of payments. The balance of payments can also improve due to the inflow of **revenue** from an MNC's **exports**.

3) An MNC might need to **train its staff** with new skills or **introduce new technology** to its host nation so it can **make** or **sell** its products.

4) An MNC might also pay for **training** or **technical help** for its **suppliers**, located in the host country. This would be to improve the goods or services **supplied** to the **MNC**.

5) If **staff leave** an **MNC** or the MNC's suppliers to start a **new job**, they will **transfer** their **skills** to different firms, so the skills and technology in the **nation** will **improve**. This can increase the **efficiency** and **productivity** of the nation, helping economic growth.

Anya was determined to share her new skill with anyone who'd listen.

6) The nation's **level of entrepreneurship** might also increase as **individuals** use the **skills** they **learnt** working in MNCs to set up their **own firms**.

7) MNCs often benefit from **economies of scale** and so might be able to offer **cheaper products** than small firms, which is **good** for **consumers**. This can **encourage spending**, which can put **money into** the national economy.

MNCs can have **Negative Effects** on the **National Economy**

1) MNCs can cause **money** to **leave** the national economy, which can have a **negative effect** on a host nation's balance of payments. For example, an MNC might **send profits** back to its home country, or it could **import products** from abroad.

2) MNCs can **force domestic firms out** of business by **undercutting** their prices or offering a **better service** to consumers. In the **short-term** this is **good** news for **consumers**. In the **long-term** it could cause **domestic firms** to **close**, which would lead to **less choice** for consumers and a loss of **tax payments** to the government.

3) A change in **business culture** to reflect that of the MNCs home country could lead to a **loss of national culture**. This could **reduce** the **revenues** of **traditional businesses** if demand for their products falls (e.g. traditional clothes makers). The country could also **lose tourism revenue** if it becomes very **industrial**.

The **Impact** of an MNC will Depend on the **Nature of its Business**

How much an MNC affects its **host nation** depends on the **type** of business. For example:

1) Firms with **highly skilled labour**, such as **technological** firms, will cause more **skills** to be **transferred** than firms with lower skilled labour.

2) An MNC that uses **highly skilled labour**, such as engineers, might **import skilled workers**, so they'll have a **small impact** on the host country's **unemployment rate**. An MNC that needs **lower skilled workers**, such as fruit pickers, won't need to import workers, so it's more likely to **create local jobs**.

3) Some MNCs will have **little choice** over their **location**. For example, **cocoa trees** can only grow under **certain conditions**, so MNCs making chocolate must locate some operations in countries with **suitable climates**.

Warm-Up Question

Q1 Give two positive and two negative effects that an MNC can have on a local economy.

(PRACTICE QUESTIONS)

Exam Question

Q1 Basil PLC is a UK company that carries out highly skilled manufacturing in the UK to produce components for the electronics industry. It owns a copper mine and extraction plant in Uzbekistan, and is considering reducing costs by relocating its manufacturing to Uzbekistan. Compared to the UK, Uzbekistan has lower wages, a lower rate of university education and a lower rate of corporation tax.
Assess how Basil PLC will affect Uzbekistan's economy if it relocates its manufacturing there. [12 marks]

Mango and Nectarine Crumble — my favourite type of MNC...

MNCs can be great for an economy — they create jobs and bring in investments, and may even train staff in new skills. But it's not all roses — MNCs can also force local businesses out, and might avoid paying taxes to the government.

MNCs and Ethics

MNCs have to consider the ethics of their actions, the values of their customers, and the ethics and laws of the countries they operate in. Keeping everyone happy at once sounds about as easy as juggling cats*.

MNCs can have **Conflicts** Between their **Stakeholder Groups**

1) Ethics are **rules** and **principles** that state which **behaviours** are **acceptable** for society, individuals or groups.

2) An MNC needs to act within the **ethical standards** and **legal system** of both its domestic and host countries.

3) Many businesses have an **ethical code** to guide the **decisions** and **behaviours** of its employees according to the firm's values. However, an MNC's **code** can often lead to **conflicts** between its **stakeholders**. For example:

   > Remember, stakeholders are those affected by the firm and its actions (p.133). MNCs have many stakeholders, including shareholders, suppliers, employees, management, governments and communities.

   - An MNCs ethical code might state that it will always **pay a 'fair wage'** to employees. This is **good** for **employees** and local **governments**, but **shareholders** might not be pleased if it reduces the MNC's **profits**.

   - An MNC that mines its resources might have an ethical code that states that it will **clean up** the area around any mining it does to reduce any **negative effects** on local residents living nearby. However, this could **increase** the MNC's **costs**, so it might charge **higher prices** to its customers.

Developing Countries can have **Low Wages** and **Poor Working Conditions**

1) MNCs often set up facilities in **LEDCs**, which usually have **lower rates** of pay than MEDCs. An LEDC's level of **health and safety** could also be lower (e.g. due to less strict legislation, or lack of enforcement).

2) So MNCs that relocate to LEDCs can have **lower labour costs** and might **spend less** on things like **safety equipment** and **proper sanitation**. This **saves money** and **increases profits**. But these money-saving strategies can lead to **poor working conditions**, which some people say is **exploiting labour**.

   > A global supply chain is all the processes and people around the world that are involved in making a product.

3) Labour can be **exploited** in other ways in the **global supply chain** of MNCs. E.g. **suppliers** to an MNC might make staff work for **long hours** — this might be due to a **lack** of **regulation** (or a lack of **enforcement**) over **working hours** in the host country.

4) Some parts of the **global supply chain** might use **child labour**:

   - Child labour generally refers to when children work in jobs that have harmful effects on their well-being. The work may be harmful to their physical, mental or social development, and often means that they don't get a good education. Different countries have different laws about what is classed as child labour.

   - Profits can be increased if children are employed because they can be paid lower wages and are less aware of any rights they may have. For example, if a child employee is not aware of their right to paid breaks, the employer might not pay them for breaks, which will increase the employer's profits.

   - However, it can be difficult for firms to assess whether suppliers use child labour, as company records in LEDCs may not give accurate dates of birth and they might actively hide their use of child labour.

   - In many countries, child labour is acceptable and can be necessary to allow families to have enough income to live on and to pay for school fees. Totally preventing child labour might have negative effects — children might start doing work where they are hidden away, so have even less protection.

5) Host countries have often **encouraged low wages** and ignored poor **working conditions** to attract MNCs and the **revenue** and **FDI** they bring to a country. Governments might be concerned that if **higher wages** or more **health and safety** regulations are applied, the MNC will **relocate** to a different LEDC with lower costs.

6) Consumers have become **increasingly aware** of labour **exploitation** and might think it's unethical for workers in LEDCs to have **lower wages** and more **dangerous working conditions** than they would do in MEDCs.

7) Consumers might **protest** or **refuse to buy** an MNC's products if they are seen to **treat workers unethically**. If an MNC is found to be treating workers unethically, it can lead to a large amount of **public pressure** and **protests**, which could force the MNC to start taking more **control** of the **working conditions** for its employees.

8) Products that are **less** in the **public eye**, such as **business-to-business products** (e.g. industrial machinery), are **less likely** to be subject to **protests** as the general public are **less aware** of them.

9) Some people might argue that there are **lower costs of living** in LEDCs, so wages don't need to be high, and that MNCs aren't **breaking the law** of host countries.

10) Several **initiatives** have been started to try to **improve working conditions** worldwide. For example, **Fairtrade** aims to ensure that suppliers throughout the world have **reasonable working conditions** and a **fair wage**.

* Don't try this at home.

MNCs and Ethics

MNCs can have a **Big Impact** on the **Environment**

MNCs can have large impacts on the **environment** through **greenhouse gas emissions** and **waste disposal**.

1) Most **MEDCs** have **legislation** on a **business's emissions** and how these emissions are **reported**, but LEDCs often have **less strict** legislation. Following **strict legislation** on emissions could be **expensive** for an MNC, or could **restrict** its **operations**, so MNCs might **locate production** in **LEDCs** to avoid this.

2) Most MEDCs have legislation regarding **waste disposal**, because of the potential **environmental** and **health** effects of some waste products. **Disposing** of **waste** safely and legally in MEDCs can be very **costly** for businesses. LEDCs might not have the **legislation** or **infrastructure** to **deal with waste** in an environmentally friendly manner. So MNCs might locate in an LEDC to **reduce** their waste disposal **costs**, but this can mean that they are **disposing** of their waste **unsafely**. Some businesses from MEDCs have also been known to **dump toxic waste** in LEDCs.

3) **Consumers** are becoming more **aware** of the **environmental impacts** of MNCs operating in LEDCs. This puts MNCs **under** increasing **pressure** to act **ethically** and **reduce** their **environmental impacts**.

An **MNC** Might Need to Adapt its **Marketing** to Remain **Ethical**

1) An MNC's **marketing** should be **ethical** in all the **countries** it **operates** in. This might mean that MNCs have to **adapt** their **marketing** for different markets (there's more on adapting to different markets on page 174).

2) MNCs might have to adapt their marketing to avoid **inappropriate promotional** activities. For example, it's the **cultural norm** in Indonesia and Japan to **give gifts** to **business contacts** as a part of promotional activities. But in other countries, like Malaysia, this could be **viewed as a bribe** and so it would be considered **unethical**.

3) Countries can also have different **laws** for how **products are labelled**, and using the same labelling in different countries may be **misleading** to customers, which is unethical.

> Example: The EU requires that food labels include the amount of salt in the food, whereas in the US the label must include the amount of sodium. These are similar, but not exactly the same measure, as it's not just salt in food that can contain sodium. If a business sold an American snack within the EU and advertised that it contained 50% less sodium, this could be misleading for EU customers — it could be interpreted as containing 50% less salt.

Vernon was trying very hard to resist the obvious attempts to bribe him.

Warm-Up Questions

Q1 Why might the government of an LEDC be reluctant to increase the minimum wage in its country if there are MNCs located in the LEDC?

Q2 Why does an MNC need to consider its product labelling in different countries?

Exam Question

Q1 Westlake PLC designs and produces high quality jewellery in the UK. It is considering relocating its production to Ghana, to reduce costs and locate closer to gold mines. If the firm made this move, it would build a factory close to a large city where it would extract gold and carry out the manufacture of jewellery. Low wages and child labour are common in Ghana.

a) Explain one conflict that could occur between Westlake PLC's stakeholders if it moves production to Ghana. [4 marks]

b) Evaluate the ethical considerations of Westlake PLC moving production to Ghana, and recommend whether they should keep production in the UK or move to Ghana. [20 marks]

Good ethics are like head teacher conferences — full of principles...

There are lots of ways that MNCs could make sure that they're acting ethically. Those that don't can end up losing customers. Businesses have to decide if it's worth changing their practices (to keep customers) or not (to keep costs down and profits high). Some are born ethical, some achieve ethical(ness) and some have ethics thrust upon them...

Controlling MNCs

Although they might like to, MNCs can't just do whatever they want. Governments can enforce laws and policies that control their actions, and consumers might use social media to shame some MNCs. Shame...shame...shame...

Governments can try to Influence the Behaviour of MNCs

Governments often try to **control** the **activities** of MNCs, to make sure the MNC doesn't **exploit stakeholders** or have **negative effects** on the **economy**. This can be through **legal control** (changes to the **law**) or **political influences** (changes to **policies**).

Dr. Fluffsome was not impressed by the attempt to control her behaviour.

Governments can Change the Law to Control MNCs

1) **Legislation** and **regulations** can be used to control MNCs:

> - Governments can change **tariffs** and **quotas** — for example, a government might **increase tariffs** on the **import** of **raw materials** to encourage MNCs to **use the resources** from **within** the country, which could help to **reduce FDI outflows**.
> - Some laws prevent MNCs from **exploiting** their stakeholders. This can include **employment laws** that enforce minimum wages, **consumer laws** that ensure product safety standards are met, and **environmental protection laws** that limit greenhouse gas emissions.
> - Governments can introduce laws on **local content provisions**. For example, a government might have regulations that require a **minimum level** of **local labour** that must be **employed** by the MNC, or that the MNC must use **local suppliers** from the host country.
> - Governments might have laws on **competition** to **prevent** an MNC from creating a **monopoly** in the host country and **misusing market powers**.
>   *Take a look at p.97 for a reminder on monopolies.*
> - Governments might introduce laws to **restrict** the use of **transfer pricing** (see p.178 for more on transfer pricing). For example, several countries have laws to make MNCs **sell products** between different **parts** of the business at their **market values**, rather than at **transfer prices**.

2) Using legislation to control MNCs can **reduce tax avoidance** and how much **corporate power** an MNC has. This means that MNCs are less likely to **exploit stakeholders** or have **harmful effects** on **communities** and **economies**.

3) However, **legislation** to control MNCs can be **difficult to enforce** and might even **lead to conflict** between countries with different laws. For example, the **EU** has **imposed fines** on some **US firms** trading within the EU for **breaches** of **European competition law**, which the US government objects to.

Governments can have Political Influences on MNCs

1) Policies are **courses of action** used by a government to **address** an **issue** or **make changes**. For example, a government might have a policy to **reduce** greenhouse gas **emissions**.
   You saw on p.179 the benefits that MNCs can bring to a country's economy.
2) **Governments** can use **policies** to try to **persuade MNCs** to make **particular decisions**. For example, governments might offer **subsidies**, **grants**, or **low** rates of **corporation tax** to try to **attract MNCs** to their country.
3) Countries that offer **low tax rates** could come under **criticism** from **other governments**, as they may be seen to be **stealing** tax revenue from other nations. For example, **Ireland** was criticised in **2018** for its **low rates** of corporation tax.
4) Some MNCs can be **state-owned**, such as the French energy firm **EDF**, which operates in many countries in **Europe** and the rest of the world. State-owned MNCs will be under **more political control**, so it's easier for the government to make sure that the activities of the MNC is in line with government policies. For example, the government may want to **reduce unemployment**, and so they may **create jobs** within **state-owned** businesses to do so.
5) However, state-owned MNCs might be **less efficient** if they don't need to **make a profit** to survive, as the government will **continue to fund** them even if they make a loss.

Controlling MNCs

Pressure Groups Might Want to Change the Behaviour of MNCs

1) **Pressure groups** are groups of people that want to change government policies or the **behaviour** of **businesses**.

2) Pressure groups use several methods to try to change MNCs' behaviour. For example, they **name** and **shame** specific MNCs that they think are **unethical** and may also use **direct action**, like **sit-ins** and **strikes**.

3) They might **target campaigns** at **governments** to cause **legislative change**, which will then **force MNCs** to **change their behaviour** to avoid breaking the law.

4) Pressure groups can raise awareness of issues quickly, particularly by using **social media** (see below).

5) However, pressure groups may not be able to **stop excessive behaviour** by their members (like property damage and intimidating people), which could **harm their campaign** and **weaken their influence** against MNCs.

Social Media is Increasingly Influencing the Behaviour of MNCs

1) Individuals and pressure groups can use **social media** to **influence** an **MNC's** behaviour. Social media allows users to quickly **share information** about an MNC's **unethical practices**, and **organise** large **campaigns**.

2) This can put pressure on a firm to **change** its **practices** to **save** its **brand image**.

> **Example:** Greenpeace led a social media campaign in 2014 against some clothing manufacturers' use of toxic chemicals in children's clothing. Their campaign included a Twitter storm — supporters sent tens of thousands of tweets to several businesses, as well as sharing messages on Facebook® and Instagram. This led to some firms committing to end their use of certain chemicals.

3) Using social media can have problems though. For example, it can lead to the spread of **distorted or incorrect information**. It's also not as effective for **long-term campaigns**, as interests and trends **change** very quickly on social media.

The Amount of Control over MNCs can Vary

1) The level of **control** that a government has on MNCs depends on the **relative power** of a **government** and its **country**. For example, many people in the USA have **high disposable incomes**, so an MNC might do more to make sure it can **operate there** rather than in a country where people have **lower disposable incomes**.

2) The **relative power of the MNC** itself is also a factor. For example, a firm that's **reliant** on a **scarce resource** that's only found in one country is easier to control than one that can **operate anywhere**.

3) Control over an MNC can also be harder if there's a **strong desire** of the government or population to have a **particular MNC** trading there. For example, even if an MNC is known to use **child labour** to make clothes, people might want to **buy the clothes** if they're cheap, or a government might not act against the MNC if it's **paying** large amounts of **tax** (as the government doesn't want to lose tax revenue from the MNC leaving).

4) **Pressure groups** and **social media** campaigns might have less of an effect on MNCs that make **niche products** for a **small number** of consumers — campaigns against them might not get as much **interest**, so are **less likely** to cause them to **lose sales**.

Warm-Up Questions

Q1 Give three ways a government may attempt to control an MNC.

Q2 Give two ways that pressure groups can influence MNCs.

Q3 Give one disadvantage of using social media to attempt to influence an MNC's behaviour.

Exam Question

Q1 Hecate PLC is a large MNC that makes household electrical items, such as clocks and radios. Its head office is in Australia and it sells 40% of its products in Australia, 45% of its products in other nearby MEDCs and 15% of its products in nearby LEDCs. The company uses local staff and suppliers in Australia, and donates to local charities. It's recently been the subject of a social media campaign in Australia over its use of transfer pricing to avoid paying corporation taxes. Assess how likely it is that a social media campaign against Hecate PLC will work.   [10 marks]

My band only plays when stressed — we're an under pressure group...

There are plenty of ways that governments, pressure groups and consumers can try to control MNCs, but they aren't always a success. Make sure you understand why some attempts to control MNCs might work and some might not.

Maths Skills

There are loads of statistics involved in running a business, so you need to be able to understand what they all mean.

Businesses Produce Lots of **Statistics**

1) Businesses have a lot of **figures** — e.g. figures for sales, costs, revenues and profit, and market research data.

2) Businesses need to understand what their figures **mean** so that they know how well the business is **performing**, and can forecast how well it will perform in the **future**. In order to understand the data and be able to use it, they present it in a way that makes it **easy** to understand.

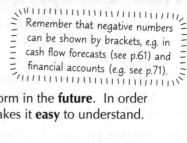
Remember that negative numbers can be shown by brackets, e.g. in cash flow forecasts (see p.61) and financial accounts (e.g. see p.71).

Diagrams Make Data **Easier** to **Understand**

1) **Pie charts** can be used to show **market share**. Each **1% share** is represented by a **3.6°** section of the pie (because there's 360° in a circle and 360 ÷ 100 = 3.6). Pie charts are **simple to use** and **easy** to **understand**. They can be created quickly using **spreadsheets**.

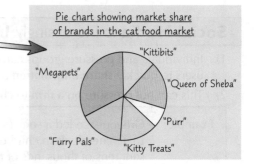
Pie chart showing market share of brands in the cat food market
"Kittibits"
"Megapets"
"Queen of Sheba"
"Purr"
"Furry Pals"
"Kitty Treats"

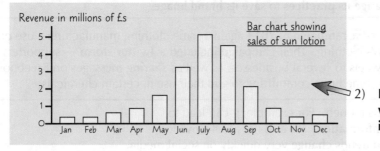
Revenue in millions of £s
Bar chart showing sales of sun lotion

2) **Bar charts** show different values for a **single variable**. They're **easy** to **construct**, easy to **interpret** and they have **high visual impact**.

3) A **histogram** looks quite similar to a bar chart. However, in a histogram the **area** of each block is proportional to the value of the variable measured (not just the height), and there are no gaps between the blocks. So a histogram is different from a bar chart because the bars can vary in both **width** and **height**. Histograms are suitable for comparing variables with **large ranges**.

4) A **pictogram** is a bar chart or histogram where the bars are **pictures** — logos or images. Pictograms are often used in **corporate brochures** — e.g. Cadbury might use pictures of their choccie bars in their sales charts.

5) **Line graphs** plot one variable against another — e.g. sales against time (see p.117). **More than one line** can be shown to make comparisons — they should be in different colours to keep the graph easy to read.

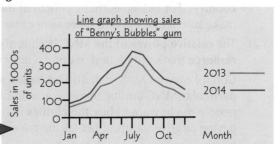
Line graph showing sales of "Benny's Bubbles" gum
Sales in 1000s of units
2013
2014
Jan Apr July Oct   Month

Diagrams can be **Misleading**

1) Graphs and charts can sometimes give a **false impression** of what is actually going on.

2) If the scales on a graph don't start at **zero**, it can be difficult to see what they show and the meaning can be distorted — e.g. the graph on the right seems to show that the profit has **tripled** between 2015 and 2018, but actually it has only gone up by **10%**.

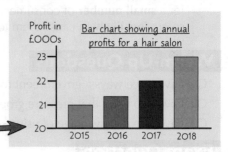
Profit in £000s
Bar chart showing annual profits for a hair salon
2015 2016 2017 2018

You Need to be Able to **Analyse Data** and **Graphs**

- As well as being able to read graphs and charts, you need to be able to **analyse** them.
- This means you need to be able to say what you think is the **important bit** of the chart — e.g. an upward trend in sales, or a big market share.
- You need to be able to say what you think is **causing** it, and what the potential **effects** might be — e.g. a **decrease** in market share might have been caused by the arrival of a new **competitor**, so the **marketing** budget might have to be **increased** to try to get the market share back.

Maths Skills

Data is Clustered Around an **Average** — **Mean, Median** or **Mode**

1) The **mean** is found by **adding together** all numbers in a data set and **dividing** the total by the **number of values** in the data set. Shops could calculate the mean spend per customer:

Example: 5 customers spend £5.90, £27.97, £13.62, £24.95 and £78.81

$$\text{Mean spend} = \frac{5.9 + 27.97 + 13.62 + 24.95 + 78.81}{5} = \frac{151.25}{5} = \pounds30.25$$

2) The **median** is the **middle** value in a data set once all the values are put in **ascending order** — e.g. a business might rank all salespeople by the revenue they've generated over the past month, then identify the **median** and pay everyone above this position a bonus for good performance.

3) The **mode** is the **most common number** in a data set. E.g. Marks & Spencer might check the modal dress size when planning their shop displays so that the mannequins would reflect the most common body size among British women.

4) The **range** is the **difference** between the **largest** and the **smallest** in a group of numbers. It's not an average, but it's often used alongside averages to show how **spread out** the data is.

Index Numbers Show **Changes** in Data Over Time

There's more on index numbers on p.91 and p.93.

1) **Index numbers** are a simple way of showing percentage changes in a set of data over time.

2) Businesses take a set of data showing revenue/profits, etc. over a number of years, and make the earliest year the **base year** — the value for the base year is set as 100, and the figures for the following years are shown as a **percentage** of this figure. E.g. the table below shows the index numbers for revenue for an Italian restaurant:

Year	Total Revenue	Revenue Index (2014 = 100)
2014	£17 000	100
2015	£19 550	115
2016	£21 250	125
2017	£22 440	132
2018	£24 650	145

To work out the revenue index for any year, take the total revenue from that year, divide it by the total revenue in the base year and multiply it by 100, e.g. for 2017:
$$\frac{22\,440}{17\,000} \times 100 = 132$$

3) The main **advantage** of indexing is that it makes it easy to see **trends** within the business.

Rearrange Formulas to Get Them Into the Form You Want

Sometimes you'll have to **rearrange** a formula before you put the numbers in. Rearrange so that the value you're trying to find is on one side of the formula, and everything else is on the other side.

Example: A business selling novelty doorbells has fixed costs of £6000 and the variable cost per unit is £15. They have to sell 1500 units to break even. What is the selling price per unit?

Use the formula: **Contribution per unit = selling price – variable cost per unit**

See p.64 for a reminder of the break-even formulas.

Rearrange to get the value you're looking for on its own:

Selling price = contribution per unit + variable cost per unit

But you don't know the contribution per unit, so you'll need another formula to work this out:

$$\text{Break-even point} = \frac{\text{total fixed costs}}{\text{contribution per unit}}$$

Rearrange to get contribution per unit on its own: $\text{Contribution per unit} = \frac{\text{total fixed costs}}{\text{break-even point}}$

Replace 'contribution per unit' in the selling price formula:

$$\text{Selling price} = \frac{\text{total fixed costs}}{\text{break-even point}} + \text{variable cost per unit}$$

$$= \frac{6000}{1500} + 15 = 4 + 15 = \mathbf{19}. \quad \text{So each novelty doorbell must sell for } \mathbf{£19}.$$

Maths Skills

Maths Skills

Businesses use **Percentage Changes** to **Analyse** Figures

1) Businesses work out **percentage** increases or decreases in figures like sales volume, revenue, profit and market share in order to see how performance is **progressing** over time. By looking at percentage changes over a number of months or years, they can see **trends** in the business's performance.

2) This is the **formula** for working out percentage change:

$$\text{Percentage change} = \frac{\text{new figure} - \text{previous figure}}{\text{previous figure}} \times 100$$

E.g. if sales of hats have gone up from 9000 to 11 000,

the percentage increase in sales is: $\frac{11\,000 - 9000}{9000} \times 100 = 22.2\%$.

3) By rearranging the formula, you can **increase a figure** by a **percentage**:

$$\text{New figure} = \text{previous figure} + \left(\frac{\text{previous figure}}{100} \times \text{percentage change}\right)$$

E.g. if a business's profit was £40 000 in 2013 and it increased by 20% in 2014, then the 2014 profit was: $40\,000 + \left(\frac{40\,000}{100} \times 20\right) = 40\,000 + 8000 = £48\,000$.

Percentages, Fractions and Ratios are all Related

Related: 100 percentages that will restore your faith in humanity. (#148 BLEW MY MIND)

1) You could be given **data** about a business or a product in a **few different ways**, and you should be able to **convert** between them.

2) To get from **fractions to percentages**, times by 100. And to get from **percentages to fractions**, divide by 100 and simplify.
For example, if $\frac{1}{4}$ of a business's total revenue is profit, then $\frac{1}{4} \times 100 = $ **25%** of its total revenue is profit.

3) You can also convert from **fractions to ratios** — a ratio is a way of comparing one amount to another. Here, there is 1 part profit to 4 parts revenue, so the ratio of **total revenue to profit** is 4:1. This means that for every £4 of revenue, the business makes £1 of profit.

4) You might also have to find the **percentage of a number**. To do this, you turn the percentage you're finding into a **decimal** by dividing by 100 (e.g. $77\% = \frac{77}{100} = 0.77$), and **multiply** this by your number.

Example: During one year, a business's labour turnover was 20%. The average number of employees that year was 2680. Calculate: a) the labour turnover as a fraction, b) the labour turnover as a ratio of the number of employees leaving to the average number of employees, c) the number of employees that left the business.

See p.34 for more on labour turnover (and p.143 if you're doing the full A-level course).

a) Labour turnover is 20%, which as a **fraction** is simply $\frac{20}{100} = \frac{1}{5}$.

b) The **ratio** of the number of employees leaving to the average number of employees is 20:100 or **1:5**.

c) The **number of employees** that left the business is 20% of 2680 = $0.2 \times 2680 = $ **536**.

Warm-Up Questions

Q1 Why can graphs and charts sometimes be misleading?

Q2 Explain the difference between the "mean", "median" and "mode" of a set of data.

Q3 What do index numbers show?

Exam Question

Q1 A business's total costs to profit ratio is 1:2.5. In 2018, it made a profit of £500 000. Calculate the business's total revenue in 2018. You are advised to show your working. [4 marks]

Ladies and gentlemen, you have been warned — maths kills...

All this maths stuff can be very helpful, but it can also be biased. If you're given a table or graph as part of an exam question, watch out for things like how the axes are labelled, whether the axes start at zero, and whether important info is left out. Businesses often use graphs and charts to put their facts and figures in as good a light as possible.

Exam Structure

This page will get you familiar with how the Business exams are set out, so there'll be no nasty surprises on the day. There are differences between the way AS and A-Level Business are examined, so make sure you're paying attention to the relevant bits here, depending on what course you're doing.

AS Business has Two Papers

This table shows you how **AS Business** is examined:

Paper	Total Marks	Time	% of Total Qualification	Section	Themes Tested
Paper 1: Marketing and People	80	1 hour and 30 minutes	50	A	1
				B	
				C	1 and 2
Paper 2: Managing Business Activities	80	1 hour and 30 minutes	50	A	2
				B	
				C	1 and 2

In section C (for both AS papers) there'll just be one longer-answer question — this is likely to be a 20 mark 'evaluate' question (see page 189).

A-Level Business has Three Papers

This table shows you how **A-Level Business** is examined:

Paper	Total Marks	Time	% of Total Qualification	Section	Themes Tested
Paper 1: Marketing, People and Global Businesses	100	2 hours	35	A	1 and 4
				B	
Paper 2: Business Activities, Decisions and Strategy	100	2 hours	35	A	2 and 3
				B	
Paper 3: Investigating Business in a Competitive Environment	100	2 hours	30	A	1, 2, 3 and 4
				B	

For **Paper 3**, you'll be given some material **before the exam** about a **broad context** that you have to **research**, e.g. it could be about a particular **market** or **industry**. The **questions** in Paper 3 will be **based around this context** — the **more research** you've done on the context, the **better prepared** you'll be to answer the questions (but you're **not allowed** to take any of your research notes **into the exam** with you).

The material is available to your teacher several months before your exams, so you should get plenty of time to do your research.

All Questions are Based on Extracts About Businesses

1) No matter what paper you're doing, for **each section** you'll be given an **extract** (or **extracts**) about a **business** (or **businesses**) to read. You'll then have to **answer questions related** to the information you've just read. (For the **A-Level Paper 3**, you might also have to draw on your knowledge from the **research** you've done — see above.)

2) The **extracts** could be made up of **written information** (which could be a combination of both **qualitative** and **quantitative** information) or **data** given in **graphs**, **diagrams** or **tables** (e.g. you might get a table showing a firm's financial data, or a graph showing information about market share).

3) **All questions** could test your knowledge about businesses in a **local**, **national** or **global context**.

4) You **don't** get a **choice** of which questions to answer — you're expected to **answer all of them**.

5) **At least 10% of the marks** for **each qualification** will be for **maths**, so make sure you've brushed up on your **maths skills** (see pages 184-186) and take your **calculator** to **each exam**.

Ava was confident she'd get plenty of marks on this paper.

Get Marks In Your Exams

These pages explain what type of questions you're likely to meet in your exams, as well as how they're marked. Basically, the marks are split up into four different skills, and to get all the marks, you need to demonstrate all the skills.

Exam Questions Have **Different Assessment Objectives**

1) **Different questions** in the Business exams will require the use of **different skills**.

2) The skills you need can be divided into **four broad categories** — these are called **assessment objectives** (**AOs**).

3) Here's a **brief description** of what each **assessment objective** covers:

- **AO1** — **knowledge** and **understanding**, e.g. of terms, methods and theories. This means things like knowing the **proper definitions** for **business terms**.
- **AO2** — **application**. This means thinking about the **type of business** in the **question**, the **product** it's selling and the **type of market** it's in, and **applying your knowledge** to that situation.
- **AO3** — **analysis**. This means explaining likely **benefits**, **drawbacks**, **influences**, **effects** and **limitations**.
- **AO4** — **evaluation**. This means using your **judgement** to come up with **solutions** (backed up by clear reasoning or evidence). It also means providing a **balanced argument** — e.g. discussing both the pros and cons of something.

You Should be **Familiar** With the **Types of Questions** You Could be Asked

Here are **descriptions** of the **types of questions** that are likely to come up in your exams and information about how the **marks** are **usually allocated**.

Short-Answer, Calculate or Construct Questions

WHAT IS MEANT BY...? (2 MARKS)

These questions are worth **2 AO1 marks** and you need to write a **clear definition** of a term to get the marks. A **simple example** can help to strengthen your answer.

'What is meant by' questions only come up in the AS papers.

EXPLAIN HOW... (4 MARKS)

1) These questions are worth **1 AO1 mark**, **2 AO2 marks** and **1 AO3 mark**.

2) To get the **AO1 mark**, you need to show that you really know what the term you're explaining **means**, so it's usually a good idea to **start** your answer with a **definition**.

3) To get the **2 AO2 marks** you should give **two examples** of what the question's asking about that **relate** to the **business** or **scenario** in the question.

4) To get the **AO3 mark**, you need to explain **how** or **why** the examples you've given could **affect the business** in the context.

Lucinda, Tarquin, Jemima and Angelica were experts at demonstrating AOs 1-4.

CALCULATE... (4 MARKS)

1) There's **1 AO1 mark**, which is usually given for using the **correct formula**.

2) There are **3 AO2 marks**, which are usually given for evidence of the **correct working**.

3) You can get the **full 4 marks** if you just write down the **correct answer**, but it's always a good idea to show your working — that way you might still **pick up marks** even if your final answer's **wrong**.

CONSTRUCT / DRAW... (4 MARKS)

1) You have to **draw** a 'business diagram' (e.g. a supply and demand diagram, see p.12) **using information** you're given in the question.

2) You'll get **at least 1 AO1 mark** for correctly drawing the thing you've been asked to construct — make sure you remember any **relevant labels** (e.g. axes labels).

3) The other marks are **AO2** and **AO3**, as you'll need to relate your drawing to the **context** of the question and may need to **analyse the information** you've been given.

Get Marks In Your Exams

Longer-Answer Questions

You might have to do some maths as part of a longer-answer question.

ASSESS TWO... e.g. benefits, ways. (8 MARKS)

1) There are **2 AO1 marks**, 2 AO2 marks, **2 AO3 marks** and **2 AO4 marks** in these questions.

2) In order to **make an assessment**, you need to **present a balanced argument** for whatever it is you're being asked to assess, e.g. if you're **assessing a benefit** of something, you should explain why you think it's a **benefit** but then **counter this** by explaining why it could be a **drawback** as well. In these **8 mark** assess questions you're asked to assess **two** factors, so you need to provide **two balanced arguments** — one for each **factor**.

3) To get the **2 AO1** and 2 AO2 marks, it's really important to show that you **understand** any **business terms** in the question (e.g. by stating the **definitions**), and are clearly **linking** your definitions and arguments to the **business context** in the question (using **examples** from the extracts where you can).

4) To get **AO3 marks**, you need to give **reasons** that **clearly explain** your points. If there's numerical **data**, you could say what the figures **mean** and talk about what might have **caused** them or what **effect** they could have on the business. Make sure you **link** your **ideas together** in a **logical way** and explain how one thing **causes**, **influences** or **affects** another.

5) Your **AO4 skills** will be demonstrated by making **judgements** supported with a **balanced argument**. You **don't** need to write a **conclusion** for these **8 mark** assess questions.

ASSESS... e.g. the possible benefits, the likely consequences. (10 or 12 MARKS)

1) For the **10 mark** questions, there are **2 AO1**, 2 AO2, **3 AO3** and **3 AO4 marks**. For the **12 mark** questions, there are **2 AO1**, 2 AO2, **4 AO3** and **4 AO4 marks**.

2) As with the 8 mark questions (see above), you need to **make it clear** you **understand** the **business terms** you write about, **clearly link** your answer to the **context**, give clear **reasoning** and **explanations** of how things are linked, and provide a **balanced argument**.

3) For these 10 and 12 mark assess questions, it's **crucial** that you **sum up your answer** with a **justified conclusion**, in which you make a **clear judgement** based on the arguments you've made (e.g. if you've been asked to assess the **likely effects** of something, your judgement could be whether the effects would be **positive or negative overall**).

There isn't a set number of factors you have to write about for the 10 and 12 mark assess questions or the evaluate questions. However, the more marks the question is worth, the more wide-ranging, fully-developed and justified the examiner will expect your answer to be.

EVALUATE... (20 MARKS)

1) These questions are worth **4 AO1**, 4 AO2, **6 AO3** and **6 AO4 marks**.

2) You have to evaluate **two options** and then make a **recommendation** as to which option you think is best, depending on **what factor** you're being asked about (e.g. you might have to say which option would make a firm more profitable or more competitive).

3) You need to **thoroughly assess** each option (see the advice from how to answer the 8 mark assess questions above). You also need to show that you've considered the **validity** and **significance** of the points you're making in your arguments. Your recommendation needs to be **supported** by your **arguments** for and against each option.

Make Sure You Write **Clearly** and **Structure** Your Answers Well

1) You have to use the **right style** of writing and **arrange relevant information clearly** — write in **full sentences** and **link** your points together. Writing a **quick plan** could help you structure longer-answer questions. You need to use **specialist vocabulary** when it's appropriate, so it's well worth **learning** the **fancy terms** used in this book.

2) Generally, the **more marks** a question is worth, the **more you need to write**. The number of marks the questions are worth **increase** throughout each section, so the ones worth the **most marks** are always at the **end**. Bear this in mind and make sure you leave yourself **enough time** to really get stuck into the **longer-answer questions**.

It's exam time — let's get down to business...

These pages should take some of the surprise out of your exams. You should realise that examiners aren't just checking that you know the facts, but also that you understand what you've learnt and can apply it to unfamiliar contexts.

Worked Exam Questions

Here's an example of the kind of extracts and questions you might get in the exams.

Extract A

Crinkle Cakes Ltd

Crinkle Cakes Ltd is a business that makes cakes, set up by Janet Jones, who made cakes in her own kitchen to sell to family and friends. Over eight years, it has grown from a sole trader business to a medium-sized private limited company. The business now operates out of premises equipped with machinery which allows it to produce 50 cakes per hour. Crinkle Cakes employs 40 staff, some on full-time contracts and some on part-time contracts.

Crinkle Cakes aims to sell its products in the big supermarkets, but so far has been unable to secure a deal to supply any of the major chains. The main reasons the supermarkets gave for not stocking Crinkle Cakes's products were that it had a very narrow product range (selling only whole cakes rather than multi-pack slices or individual portions), and that its cakes were priced higher than competing bakeries.

The marketing manager has been looking at secondary market research data about the cake market. For example, he has looked at the types of cakes consumers buy and the prices of cakes in the market. Crinkle Cakes had originally aimed to charge prices that could compete with its main local competitor, but the reality is that Crinkle Cakes's prices are on average 10% higher than the local competitor's and approximately 30% higher than the national competitors'.

The operations manager has been looking at ways to cut costs. She has discovered that one problem is the rising cost of ingredients from suppliers.

Extract B

Results from secondary market research into the types of cakes consumers buy (percentage of people asked)

Product	Purchased weekly	Purchased monthly	Purchased rarely	Never purchased
Whole cakes	2	8	62	28
Multi-pack, e.g. slices	55	23	14	8
Individual portions	67	17	10	6

Extract C

Crinkle Cakes Ltd expenditure budget and actual expenditure for a typical month

	Budget	Actual	Variance
Raw materials	£20k	£30k	£10k (A)
Staff costs	£50k	£48k	£2k (F)
Marketing	£5k	£8k	£3k (A)
Insurance & utility bills	£10k	£8k	£2k (F)
Other	£5k	£4k	£1k (F)

An **Example Short Question and Answer** to Give You Some Tips:

Q1 Explain how changing from a sole trader to a private limited company is likely to have benefited Crinkle Cakes Ltd. **[4 marks]**

Being a private limited company means that Crinkle Cakes is owned by private shareholders, who all have limited liability.

Crinkle Cakes is now a much bigger business than it was when it was set up. For example, it now operates from a premises equipped with machinery rather than operating out of the owner's kitchen. Also, the business is now able to produce up to 50 cakes an hour rather than just producing enough to sell to family and friends.

Allowing people to buy shares in Crinkle Cakes would have raised finance for the business, which it's likely to have used to fund the expansion into a medium-sized firm.

AO1: Shows knowledge of what a private limited company is.

AO2: Uses two examples of growth from the extract.

AO3: Gives a reason as to why becoming a Ltd company is beneficial.

This answer would probably get the full **4 marks**. You could have also talked about the fact that having **limited liability** might have encouraged the owners to take more **financial risks**, allowing it to grow quickly.

Worked Exam Questions

Q2 Assess the importance of secondary market research to a business, such as Crinkle Cakes Ltd, as a way to stay competitive.

[10 marks]

AO1: Shows understanding of what secondary market research is.

Secondary market research involves using data that's already available. For example, it could be data that's available in a trade magazine, or via reliable internet sources.

AO2: Applies knowledge about secondary market research to the business in question.

AO3: Explains how secondary market research can affect competitiveness.

Secondary market research could allow a business to find out information about what consumers in the market want. For example, Crinkle Cakes found out information about whether consumers in its market were more likely to buy whole cakes, multi-packs of cakes or individual cake portions. Knowing what consumers want means that a business can tailor its products to meet consumer needs. If it does this better than its competitors, then consumers may be more likely to buy the firm's products rather than those of competitors, meaning it remains competitive.

AO3: Identifies another way in which secondary market research can be used to gain information on factors that affect competitiveness.

This could have been related to the information that Crinkle Cakes found out about its prices.

Secondary market research may allow a business to gain more information about competitors' products, such as their product ranges, their promotional methods and their prices. Knowing this information could allow a business to make sure its products are in-line with those of its competitors. For example, it could ensure that its prices were similar to those of competitors.

This analysis could be improved by explaining how the price of products is linked to sales and how this affects how competitive a firm is.

AO4: Provides a balanced argument about why secondary market research might not be important for improving competitiveness.

However, although secondary market research may be useful to a firm, its use may be limited depending on the data that's available. If the data is very generic, it might not provide specific enough information to give a firm an insight into how it could adapt its business to make it more competitive. For example, the secondary market research data in Extract B provided information to Crinkle Cakes about how consumers like to buy their cakes (i.e. what they get in each packet). But there might have been little or no data available about other factors that would affect consumers' decisions when buying cakes, such as flavour or appearance.

AO2: Links directly to evidence from the extract as well as the general business context (i.e. the cake market).

AO1: Shows knowledge of other types of market research.

Information gathered from primary research is likely to be more important to a business than secondary market research data. The business may have already identified factors that it needs to work on to remain competitive, and primary market research would allow it to gain information about these factors specifically.

The conclusion could be improved by talking about Crinkle Cakes or the cake market specifically.

Overall, although secondary market research might not provide information about specific factors that affect a business's competitiveness, it's still a very important way for a firm to make sure it stays competitive. It can give a business insight into the overall patterns and trends in a market, which might trigger it to take steps to improve a certain area of its business in order to remain competitive.

The conclusion directly answers the question.

AO4: Provides a justified conclusion.

This answer would probably get about **8 marks**. It analyses **reasons** why secondary market research would be **important** to stay **competitive**, as well as reasons why it might **not** be so important. There is a clear understanding of both **secondary** and **primary market research**. The **conclusion is justified, answers** the **question** directly and gives a **judgement** as to how important secondary market research is likely to be.

However, **more marks** could have been gained if the answer **related more to the context** in the extract, especially about the market research on prices. Also, there are places where the **chain of reasoning** could be **clearer**, such as explaining how a firm's competitiveness is linked to its prices.

Worked Exam Questions

An **Example Evaluate Question and Answer** to Give You Some Tips:

> Q3 Crinkle Cakes Ltd is considering changing its marketing mix in order to increase its market share. In particular, it is considering changing either its product or its price. Evaluate these two options and recommend which option would be the most effective at increasing Crinkle Cakes Ltd's market share. [20 marks]

The definitions are clear and accurate.

AO2: Links knowledge about the marketing mix to the business in question.

The suggestions have been applied specifically to the business in the context, i.e. a cake manufacturer.

AO3: Logical line of reasoning linking wider effects of changing product on the business.

AO3: Explains how high costs are linked to high prices.

Draw on your own knowledge of a market if you can (i.e. you probably know the cake market is competitive).

AO1: Defines both market share and marketing mix.

A specific figure from Extract B has been used.

AO3: Links together a cause and effect.

AO4: Evaluates the impact of changes to the product.

AO2: Links issue of price to the business in question.

The knock-on effects could have been discussed here (e.g. changing suppliers could affect the quality of the products).

AO4: Evaluates the impact of changes to the price.

AO1: Understanding of a business term (price elasticity of demand).

The market share of a business is the proportion of the total market sales that the business holds. A business is usually able to increase its market share by increasing the volume of products it sells.

The marketing mix is all the factors a business has to take into account when marketing a product. This is commonly referred to as "the four Ps" of product, promotion, pricing and place. In order to adapt a marketing mix it is necessary to consider these factors.

There are a number of ways in which Crinkle Cakes could make changes to the product. At present it produces mainly whole cakes, which 28% of customers never buy according to the research findings in Extract B. This has meant that few supermarkets have shown a willingness to sell Crinkle Cakes' products. Based on this, one change could be to make a wider range of cake sizes. So, in addition to the whole cakes, it could introduce a multi-pack containing cake slices, aimed at families, and single-slice packs, perhaps aimed at single people or impulse buyers. This would increase the market segments it appeals to and increase the likelihood of sales to the big supermarkets. Another alteration that Crinkle Cakes could make to its products is to start targeting niche markets rather than mass markets (e.g. by making gluten-free products). This would reduce its competition and would mean that it could charge higher prices and still be competitive. However, this may require further market research. Also, the costs of developing and then manufacturing new products would have to be considered. For example, the business may need to invest in new machinery and training staff in order to produce different types of cakes. The business may need to raise extra money to finance these changes, which could be costly, e.g. if it needs to take out a loan. The increased costs may also mean that the business's profits fall in the short-term, which shareholders might be opposed to as it will mean they get fewer dividends.

The other element of the marketing mix that Crinkle Cakes is considering changing is price. Extract A states that Crinkle Cakes charges higher prices than its competitors and that the cost of ingredients is rising. Extract C shows that the business is paying £10K per month more for its raw materials than budgeted. These high costs may explain why Crinkle Cakes has to charge higher prices in order to make a reasonable amount of profit. To be able to charge more competitive prices and therefore increase sales volume, Crinkle Cakes could cut costs, e.g. by negotiating a better deal with its supplier, or by changing suppliers. Lower prices would make the cakes more appealing to consumers and the big supermarkets. Or, instead of trying to reduce prices, the company could keep its high prices (or even make them higher) and promote the cakes as a luxury item to justify the prices and increase sales. However, this may be difficult to do as the cake market is highly competitive, as there are a lot of firms that sell very similar products. Cakes are likely to be price elastic, so if Crinkle Cakes increases its prices too much, it's likely that sales will fall as consumers will just buy competitors' cakes.

In conclusion, adapting the product is very important to the success of Crinkle Cakes, but changing its prices would help it increase its market share more.

This answer would get about **14 marks**. It gives a good **balanced argument** about how a business could change its **product** or **price** to **increase sales** and frequently **relates** to the **business context** directly. However, it **fails** to **fully develop the arguments** and produce a **clear conclusion** and overall **recommendation**.

Answers to Numerical Questions

Theme 1: Section 2

Page 17 — Warm-Up Questions

Q4 Income elasticity of demand

$$= \frac{\% \text{ change in quantity demanded}}{\% \text{ change in income}}$$

So, % change in quantity demanded
= income elasticity of demand × % change in income
= 2.8 × –1.2% = –3.36%

Page 17 — Exam Questions

Q1 Price elasticity of demand

$$= \frac{\% \text{ change in quantity demanded}}{\% \text{ change in price}}$$

So, % change in quantity demanded
= price elasticity of demand × % change in price
= –0.7 × 15% = –10.5%
100 – 10.5 = 89.5%
The company will sell: 200 × 89.5% = 179 horses
The new price of a horse will be:
£1500 + (£1500 × 15%) = £1725
The company's new sales revenue will be:
sales revenue = selling price × sales volume
= £1725 × 179 = £308 775
[4 marks for the correct answer, otherwise 1 mark for giving the correct equation for the price elasticity of demand, 1 mark for correctly calculating the change in quantity demanded and 1 mark for correctly calculating the new number of horses sold (the new sales volume)]

Theme 2: Section 6

Page 61 — Exam Question

Q1 Total cash inflows = £4500 + £0 = £4500
Total cash outflows = £2500 + £500 = £3000
Net cash flow = £4500 – £3000 = £1500
Opening balance for March equals the closing balance for February = £3250
Closing balance = net cash flow + opening balance
= £1500 + £3250 = £4750
The closing balance for March is £4750
[4 marks for the correct answer, otherwise 1 mark for the correct formula for calculating a closing balance (net cash flow + opening balance), 1 mark for correctly calculating the total cash inflows and outflows and 1 mark for correctly calculating the net cash flow]

Theme 2: Section 7

Page 63 — Warm-Up Questions

Q2 Sales volume = sales revenue ÷ selling price
= £50 299 ÷ £89.50 = 562 coats

Page 63 — Exam Question

Q1 Sales revenue = selling price × sales volume
= £3.95 × 7800 = £30 810
Total variable costs = AVC × quantity produced
= £1.47 × 8200 = £12 054
Total costs = fixed costs + total variable costs
= £7400 + £12 054 = £19 454
Profit = total revenue – total costs
= £30 810 – £19 454 = £11 356
[4 marks for the correct answer, otherwise 1 mark for correctly calculating sales revenue, 1 mark for correctly calculating total variable costs and 1 mark for correctly recognising that profit = total revenue – total costs]

Page 65 — Exam Questions

Q1 Contribution = selling price – variable costs per unit
= £13 – £5 = £8
Fixed costs per month = £15 000 ÷ 12
= £1250

$$\text{Break-even point} = \frac{\text{total fixed costs}}{\text{contribution per unit}}$$

$$= \frac{£1250}{£8} = 156.25 = 157 \text{ customers}$$

[4 marks for the correct answer, otherwise 1 mark for calculating the contribution, 1 mark for calculating the fixed costs per month and 1 mark for the correct equation for break-even point]

Page 69 — Warm-Up Questions

Q2 Variance = £18 000 – £15 000 = £3000
so there is a £3000 adverse (or negative) variance.

Theme 2: Section 8

Page 71 — Exam Question

Q1 Profit for the year = operating profit – interest,
so operating profit = profit for the year + interest
= £650 000 + £100 000 = £750 000
Operating profit = gross profit – operating expenses,
so gross profit = operating profit + operating expenses
= £750 000 + £250 000 = £1 000 000
[4 marks for correct answer, otherwise 1 mark for showing the correct formula for either operating profit or gross profit, 1 mark for correctly rearranging either formula and 1 mark for correctly calculating operating profit]

Page 73 — Exam Question

Q1 GPM in 2017 = $\frac{43}{85}$ × 100 = 50.6% (to 1 d.p.)

OPM in 2017 = $\frac{12}{85}$ × 100 = 14.1% (to 1 d.p.)

Profit for the year margin in 2017 = $\frac{7}{85}$ × 100

= 8.2% (to 1 d.p.)
[Up to 3 marks are available for the calculations of profit margins — 1 mark for each correct profit margin]

Theme 2: Section 9

Page 87 — Exam Question

Q1 a) Previous re-order amount = 500 – 200 = 300 units
(300 ÷ 100) × 10 = 30
Quantity re-ordered at point A = 300 + 30 = 330 units
Maximum stock = buffer stock + re-order quantity
= 200 + 330 = 530 units
[4 marks for the correct answer, otherwise 1 mark for correctly calculating the previous re-order amount, 1 mark for correctly calculating the number of units re-ordered at point A and 1 mark for recognising that maximum stock = buffer stock + re-order amount]

Answers to Numerical Questions

Theme 2: Section 10

Page 91 — Warm-Up Questions

Q2 average value of the 'basket'
$$= \frac{\text{index number}}{100} \times \text{base value of the 'basket'}$$
$$= \frac{101.2}{100} \times 863.42 = \$873.78 \text{ (to 2 d.p.)}$$

Page 93 — Warm-Up Questions

Q1 $1 = £0.55
$80 \div 0.55 = 145.4545...$, so $80 = \$145.45$

Q2 currency index number $= \dfrac{\text{exchange rate}}{\text{base exchange rate}} \times 100$

base exchange rate = 1480

currency index number $= \dfrac{1441}{1480} \times 100 = 97.36$ (to 2 d.p.)

Q3 exchange rate
$$= \frac{\text{currency index number}}{100} \times \text{base exchange rate}$$
$$= \frac{95}{100} \times 1.36 = 1.29 \text{ (to 2 d.p.)}$$

Theme 3: Section 13

Page 118 — Exam Question

Q1 a) E.g.

In 2015 the estimated sales are £150 000.

Percentage change $= \dfrac{2015 \text{ sales} - 2010 \text{ sales}}{2010 \text{ sales}} \times 100$

$= \dfrac{£150\,000 - £100\,000}{£100\,000} \times 100$

$= 50\%$

[4 marks for an answer between 50% and 55%, otherwise 1 mark for the correct formula for calculating a percentage change, 1 mark for drawing an extrapolated line of best fit and correctly reading a 2015 sales value from that line, and 1 mark for calculating the difference in sales between 2010 and 2015]

Page 123 — Exam Question

Q1

EMV of each outcome
= probability of outcome occurring × profit.
EMV of increase in capacity
= EMV of success + EMV of failure
= (0.6 × £500m) + (0.4 × –£100m)
= £300m – £40m = £260m

[1 mark for drawing a square decision node with 2 correctly labelled courses of action, 1 mark for drawing a circular chance node with 2 correctly labelled outcomes, 1 mark for using the correct formula to calculate the EMV of each outcome, 1 mark for the correct EMV of £260m (if £260m is given but no working is shown, award 2 marks)]

Theme 3: Section 15

Page 142 — Warm-Up Questions

Q4 Capital employed = non-current liabilities + total equity
= £40 000 + £85 000
= £125 000
ROCE = (operating profit ÷ capital employed) × 100
= (£50 000 ÷ £125 000) × 100
= 40%

Page 142 — Exam Question

Q1 Capital employed = non-current liabilities + total equity
= £300 000 + £1 300 000
= £1 600 000
Gearing ratio = (non-current liabilities ÷
capital employed) × 100
= (£300 000 ÷ £1 600 000) × 100
= 18.75%
ROCE = (operating profit ÷ capital employed) × 100
= (£850 000 ÷ £1 600 000) × 100
= 53.125%

[Up to 6 marks are available for the calculations of gearing and ROCE — 1 mark for the correct formula for capital employed, 1 mark for the correct calculation of capital employed, 1 mark for the correct formula for gearing, 1 mark for the correct calculation of gearing, 1 mark for the correct formula for ROCE and 1 mark for the correct calculation of ROCE]

Page 145 — Warm-Up Questions

Q1 Labour productivity = output per period ÷
number of employees
= 24 000 ÷ 25
= 960 bath bombs per employee
per week

Page 145 — Exam Question

Q1 Absenteeism = (number of days of staff absence ÷
(number of staff × time period)) × 100
Absenteeism in 2016 = (120 ÷ (24 × 225)) × 100
= (120 ÷ 5400) × 100
= 2.22% (to 2 d.p.)
Absenteeism in 2017 = (360 ÷ (24 × 225)) × 100
= (360 ÷ 5400) × 100
= 6.67% (to 2 d.p.)

[Up to 3 marks are available for the calculations of absenteeism — 1 mark for giving the correct formula for absenteeism, 1 mark for correctly calculating the absenteeism in 2016 and 1 mark for correctly calculating the absenteeism in 2017]

Maths Skills

Page 186 — Exam Question

Q1 Total costs to profit ratio is 1 : 2.5.
So profit of £500 000 means total costs in 2018 were
$$\frac{£500\,000}{2.5} = £200\,000$$
Profit = total revenue – total costs,
so total revenue = profit + total costs
Total revenue in 2018 = £500 000 + £200 000
= £700 000

[4 marks for correct answer, otherwise 1 mark for using total costs to profit ratio to correctly calculate total costs, 1 mark for showing the correct formula for profit and 1 mark for correctly rearranging the formula for profit]

Glossary

absenteeism The percentage of the labour force that is absent during a certain time period.

accounting ratio A ratio that's calculated from a firm's financial statements and used to evaluate its financial performance, e.g. a profitability ratio, a liquidity ratio, a gearing ratio.

acid test ratio A liquidity ratio that compares current assets minus inventories to current liabilities.

added value The difference between the cost of making a product and the price that a customer pays for it.

Ansoff's matrix Shows the strategies that a business can use to expand, according to how risky they are.

appreciation When the value of a currency increases relative to that of another.

appropriable (capability) A distinct capability that one business isn't able to copy from another business.

architecture (Kay's model) Describes the relationships a business has with its stakeholders.

asset Anything a business has which is valuable.

autocratic leadership style A leadership style where the leader makes all the decisions on their own.

average rate of return (ARR) A figure that compares the average net return with the initial investment. Used in investment appraisal.

B2B marketing The marketing of one business's product to another business or organisation.

B2C marketing The marketing of a business's product to a consumer.

balance of payments A country's record of its international transactions — the difference between the total value of payments into the country and the total value of payments out of the country, over a certain period of time.

batch production A production method in which products are made in small batches (or sets) of different products, with the products in each batch being identical to each other.

Boston Matrix A matrix that compares a business's products based on their market growth and market share.

brand A clear and obvious logo, name or statement that customers can instantly recognise as being related to a certain product or business.

brandnomer When a product becomes known by the name of a brand rather than its general name.

break-even analysis A process that identifies the point where a business's total revenue equals its total costs.

budget A forecast of future earnings and/or future spending.

buffer stock The minimum level of stock a business needs to hold to make sure that it won't run out of raw materials or finished goods.

business angel A wealthy individual that invests money into new or innovative businesses that they think have the potential to be successful.

business cycle diagram A graph that shows how the gross domestic product (GDP) of an area changes over time — it shows booms, recessions, slumps and recoveries.

business failure When a business is no longer making enough money to cover its costs and so shuts down still owing people money.

business objective A specific short- to medium-term goal of a business to help it achieve an aim.

business plan A document that outlines what a business plans to achieve and how it plans to achieve it.

capacity utilisation How much of its maximum capacity a business is using.

capital A business's (or person's) wealth in the form of money or other assets.

capital employed The total amount of finance in a business, from non-current liabilities, share capital and reserves.

capital-intensive production When a firm uses lots of machinery and relatively few workers to make its product.

cash cow (Boston Matrix) A product that has high market share but low market growth.

cash flow Money that moves in and out of a business over a set period of time.

cell production A production method in which an assembly line is divided into sets of tasks, each of which is completed by a work group.

centralisation A way to structure a business where all decisions come from a few key people.

chain of command The path of communication and authority up and down the hierarchy of a business.

change management The processes and procedures performed by managers to plan and prepare for changes, carry out the changes and assess the possible effect of the changes on the business and its stakeholders.

collective bargaining When a group of employees is represented by workforce representatives who negotiate work-related issues.

competitive advantage A condition which allows a business to generate more sales or be more profitable than its rivals.

complementary products Products that are used together.

Consumer Prices Index An index that tracks the changes in the average cost of a 'basket' of goods and services that an average household regularly buys.

continuity planning Making a recovery plan for an unspecified incident — this is done by identifying a minimum acceptable level of operations to allow a firm to resume normal business, and planning how to achieve this minimum acceptable level.

contribution The difference between the selling price and the variable costs of a product.

corporate culture The way things are done within a business, in relation to expectations, attitudes and how staff make decisions.

corporate objective A goal of a business as a whole.

corporate social responsibility (CSR) A business's policy regarding its contribution to society.

corporation tax The tax paid by limited companies based on their profits.

cost leadership (Porter's generic strategies) Producing a product for the lowest cost possible, for a given quality.

creditor Someone who a business owes money to.

critical path In critical path analysis, the series of activities that are critical in the timing of the overall project.

critical path analysis A method of calculating the most efficient order in which to carry out a series of activities.

crowd funding A source of finance in which a large number of people typically each give a small sum of money, usually via the internet.

current asset An asset that the business is likely to exchange for cash within the accounting year.

current liability A debt which needs to be paid off within a year.

current ratio A liquidity ratio that compares current assets to current liabilities.

debtor Someone who owes money to a business.

decentralisation A way to structure a business where decisions are shared across the firm.

decision tree A method of analysing the expected pay-offs of different business decisions.

deflation An overall decrease in the price of products within an economy.

delayering Reducing the number of levels in the hierarchy of an organisation.

demand A measure of the quantity of a product that consumers want and are able to buy at a given price, at a particular time.

democratic leadership style A leadership style where the leader encourages the workforce to participate in the decision-making process.

depreciation When the value of a currency decreases relative to that of another.

design mix The factors that are considered when designing a product — function, aesthetics and costs.

differentiation (Porter's generic strategies) Selling a product with unique attributes or features.

direct competition When two or more businesses sell a similar product and are competing for the same group of customers.

discounted cash flow (DCF) An investment appraisal method that estimates the return on an investment by discounting the value of future cash flows to their present value.

diseconomies of scale When the cost of producing each item increases as the scale of production increases.

dismissal When an employer ends an employee's contract of employment because the worker has breached the contract.

distinctive capability Something that a business is good at that other businesses don't do, therefore setting it apart from its competitors.

distribution channel The route used to transport a product from the producer to the consumer.

diversification Selling new products to new markets.

dog (Boston Matrix) A product that has a low market share and low market growth.

economies of scale When the cost of producing each item decreases as the scale of production increases.

efficiency When something is produced at an overall minimum average cost. It can also mean a measure of the extent to which this is achieved.

embargo A ban on trade with a particular country.

empowerment When workers are given more control over their work and a greater role in decision-making.

entrepreneur A person who takes on the risks of a new business activity with the aim of gaining a reward (usually profit).

equilibrium price The price on a supply and demand diagram at which the demand and supply curves meet.

ethics The rules and principles that state which behaviours are morally acceptable for society, individuals, groups or organisations.

ethnocentric A global marketing approach that keeps the marketing strategy similar to the one used in the firm's domestic market across all countries.

exchange rate The value of one currency in terms of another currency — for example, £1 might be worth €1.20.

extension strategies Used to increase the sales of a product, and so extend its life cycle.

external shock An unexpected change which takes place outside of a business and affects the economy.

FDI flows The flow of money into and out of a country's economy from foreign direct investment.

fixed cost A cost that stays the same no matter how much or how little a firm produces.

flat structure An organisational structure that has few layers of management.

flexible workforce A group of employees with a range of skills or who work a range of employment patterns.

flow production A production method in which lots of identical products are made using an assembly line.

focus (Porter's generic strategies) Focusing on a niche market to achieve either cost advantage or differentiation.

foreign direct investment (FDI) When a firm in one country invests in a business in another country. The firm must have some (or total) managerial control of the business in the foreign country.

franchising An agreement which allows one business to use the business idea, name, model and reputation of an established business, in return for a fee.

free trade agreement An agreement between two or more countries to reduce (or remove) trade barriers.

gearing ratio The proportion of a business financed through long-term debt rather than share capital or reserves.

geocentric A global marketing approach that combines the ethnocentric and polycentric approaches. A global brand is maintained, but the marketing strategy is adapted to different regions or countries.

global niche market A smaller part of the global market, with specific product requirements. It's made up of niche markets across several countries.

globalisation The increase in how interconnected the world is.

glocalisation Where businesses "think global, act local" and adapt their marketing strategies between different countries.

gross domestic product (GDP) The total market value of goods and services produced within a nation over a period of time (usually a year).

gross profit The difference between total revenue and cost of sales.

hierarchy (organisational structure) The series of levels in a business, organised by the amount of authority and responsibility that workers have.

historical budget A budget based on previous budgets.

horizontal communication Getting messages throughout one level of an organisation's hierarchy.

horizontal integration When a business combines with another business in the same industry at the same stage of the production process.

income elasticity of demand Shows the relationship between a change in income and the change in demand for a product.

income tax The tax paid by individuals on their income or by sole traders and partnerships on their profits.

indirect competition When two or more businesses sell different products but are competing for the same group of customers.

individual bargaining When a single employee negotiates work-related issues with their employer.

induction training Training provided to new employees to introduce them to the business and their job role.

inferior product A product that has a negative income elasticity of demand.

inflation An overall increase in the price of goods and services within an economy.

infrastructure The basic facilities such as roads, railways, power lines, water pipes and communication networks that allow society to function.

innovation (Kay's model) Describes the extent to which a business produces new and unique products.

inorganic growth When a business grows by combining two or more businesses, e.g. through mergers or takeovers.

interest rate The money charged for borrowing money — usually quoted as a percentage of the amount borrowed.

intrapreneurship When an employee of a business shows entrepreneurial skills within the business.

investment appraisal Assessing how favourable investment opportunities are, based on their cash flow forecasts.

job description A summary of a job role, including working hours, salary and duties.

job enlargement When workers are given a greater range of work at the same level.

job enrichment When workers are given more challenging work and the training they need to do it.

job production A production method in which one-off items are made.

job rotation When workers are moved between different tasks.

job specification A summary of the qualities and qualifications required for a job.

joint venture A legal agreement between two or more businesses to undertake a joint project, which then exists as a separate entity to the parent businesses.

just-in-time (JIT) management A method of lean production where the aim of reducing waste is met by having as little stock as possible.

kaizen A method of lean production that involves encouraging everyone to constantly improve quality (continuous improvement).

Kay's model Three distinctive capabilities (architecture, reputation and innovation) that would give a business a competitive advantage if successfully exploited.

labour productivity The production output per employee during a given period.

labour retention The proportion of staff that stay at a business during a given period.

labour turnover The proportion of staff that leave a business during a given period.

labour-intensive production When a firm uses lots of workers and relatively little machinery to make its product.

laissez-faire leadership style A leadership style where the leader may offer coaching and support to employees, but will rarely interfere in the running of the business.

leader A person who has a vision which they share with others, while pushing them in the right direction.

lean production An efficient form of production that focuses on waste minimisation.

leasing Where monthly sums of money are paid over a set period of time, in return for the use of an asset. After the lease period, the asset is often returned to the leasing firm.

legislation A law or a set of laws.

liability A financial debt a business owes.

lifestyle business A type of business that focuses on profit satisficing to obtain and maintain a desired lifestyle.

limited liability A state where the owners of a business are not legally responsible for all of the business's debts, so each owner only risks losing the money they invested if the firm goes bust.

liquidity The ability of a business to turn assets into cash.

liquidity ratio A ratio that shows whether a business has enough liquid assets (e.g. money) to pay its short-term debts.

long-termism Where a business focuses more on strategies that will benefit the business in the long term, rather than maximising financial rewards in the short term.

macroeconomy The economy as a whole (including all businesses and consumers).

margin of safety The difference between break-even output and actual output.

market development Selling existing products to new markets.

Glossary

market map A graph that compares two aspects (e.g. quality and price) of different products or brands in a market.

market orientation When a business focuses most heavily on selling products that match consumer preferences.

market penetration When a business tries to increase market share in its existing market.

market share The proportion of sales in a market made by one firm or brand, usually expressed as a percentage.

market size The total value of sales or total number of consumers in a market.

marketing mix The 4Ps businesses use to market their products — product, promotion, price and place.

mass market A market with a large number of customers, which is not segmented into groups based on customer needs or interests.

matrix structure A way of organising staff by two different criteria, e.g. into a combination of projects and functions.

merger Where two businesses agree to join together into one business.

microeconomy A part of the economy that consists of only the individual consumers and firms that make up a specific market.

minimum wage The lowest amount that someone can legally be paid in a given time period (e.g. per hour). In the UK, it depends on a person's age and whether or not they are an apprentice.

mission statement A written description of a business's corporate aims.

monopoly Where one business has complete control over its market.

moving average A series of averages taken from time-series data, using overlapping periods of time.

multinational corporation (MNC) A business with its head office in one country, and branches or departments in one or more other countries.

net present value (NPV) The value of all cash flows from a project after the future cash flows have been discounted to their present values.

niche market A market that has customers with specific needs or requirements.

non-current asset An asset that the business is likely to keep for more than a year.

non-current liability A debt that the business will pay off over several years.

normal product A product that has a positive income elasticity of demand.

off-the-job training When an employee is trained outside of their work environment.

offshoring When a business locates one or more of its departments overseas.

oligopoly Where a small number of firms dominate a single market.

on-the-job training When an employee is trained at work whilst they are doing the actual job.

operating profit The difference between gross profit and operating expenses that aren't directly related to making the product.

opportunity cost The value of the next best alternative that's given up in order to do something else.

organic growth When a business grows from within and doesn't involve any other businesses.

organisational culture See corporate culture.

outsourcing When a business has one or more of its activities carried out by another business.

overdraft Where a bank account has a negative amount of money in it.

overtrading When an increase in demand leads a business to buy more raw materials and employ more staff, resulting in high costs before it's been paid by customers.

partnership A form of legal ownership of a business that usually has between two and twenty owners. It has unlimited liability.

patent The exclusive right to make, use or sell a product or feature for a certain amount of time, in a certain place (e.g. a country).

paternalistic leadership style A leadership style similar to the autocratic style, but where the leader focuses on employee wellbeing and motivation.

payable Money that a business owes.

payback period The time that it takes for a project to make enough money to pay back the initial investment. Used in investment appraisal.

peer-to-peer lending Where individuals lend money to other individuals or businesses via an online lending company.

penetration pricing A pricing strategy where a product is sold at a low price when it first reaches the market, to attract customers.

perfect competition A theoretical type of competition where all firms compete on an equal basis.

PESTLE analysis A method of assessing the external influences on a business by considering the political, economic, social, technological, legal and environmental influences on a business.

piecework When workers are paid per unit produced.

polycentric A global marketing approach that has different products and marketing strategies in different countries to suit differences in customer wants and needs.

Porter's Five Forces model A framework for analysing competition within an industry and judging how attractive the market is.

Porter's strategic matrix Identifies a competitive strategy, based on competitive advantage and market scope.

pressure group A group of people who want to change the behaviour of businesses or cause a change in a government's policies.

price elasticity of demand Shows the relationship between a change in the price of a product and the change in demand for the product.

price skimming A pricing strategy where a new or innovative product is sold at a high price when it first reaches the market — consumers will pay more because it has scarcity value.

Glossary

primary market research When a business does market research by gathering new data.

private limited company A form of legal ownership of a business in which shares are sold privately. It has limited liability.

product A good or service provided by a business.

product development When a business sells new products in its existing market.

product differentiation A way in which businesses distinguish their products against competitor products, usually by emphasising unique features of their products that competitor products do not have.

product life cycle Shows how the sales of a product change over time.

product orientation When a business focuses most heavily on design, quality and performance when creating and selling products.

product portfolio The combination of all of the product lines that a business produces.

productivity The output per unit of input (worker or machine) in a given time period.

profit The difference between total revenue and total costs.

profit for the year (net profit) The difference between operating profit and interest payments (money made or lost from one-off events is also deducted from operating profit here).

profit satisficing Where a business focuses on making enough profit so that the owner has a desirable quality of life, or that shareholders are paid satisfactory dividends, and not on maximising profit levels.

profitability The amount of profit that has been (or can be) generated by a business, relative to revenue or investment.

promotion The methods used by a business to inform consumers about a product, or to persuade them to buy it.

protectionism Measures taken by a government to protect domestic businesses from foreign competition (e.g. by using tariffs or quotas).

public limited company A form of legal ownership of a business in which shares are sold publicly on the stock market. It has limited liability.

quality assurance Measures that are introduced to the production process to ensure quality products, with products being checked at each stage of the production process.

quality circle A meeting of a group of employees to discuss quality.

quality control Checking goods as they are made or when they arrive from suppliers to see if anything is wrong with them.

question mark (Boston Matrix) A product that has small market share but high market growth.

quota (import) A type of trade restriction that put limits on the volume of particular products that can be imported into a country in a certain time period.

rate of inflation The percentage change in the price of goods and services within an economy, in one year compared to the previous year.

receivable Money owed to a business.

recession A temporary decline in a country's economic activity.

recruitment The process of finding and hiring a person for a specific job role that needs filling within a business.

redundancy When an employee loses their job because their job role is no longer required.

reputation (Kay's model) Describes the reputation, customer satisfaction and brand loyalty towards a business.

retained profit Profit that is saved by the business and can be used to fund later investment.

return on capital employed (ROCE) Shows how much money is made by the business compared to how much money's been put into the business.

revenue The amount of money a firm has earned in a given time period, usually from sales. Also called sales, sales revenue or turnover.

risk acceptance When the business decides to accept a risk, without creating a plan for it.

risk assessment The identification of potential risks to a business, and the calculation of the probabilities that they will happen and the possible detrimental effects they could cause to the business if they do.

risk avoidance When a risk is avoided altogether by ensuring that the business doesn't put itself in a position where the risk is possible.

risk limitation When a business takes action so that the impact of a risk is reduced.

risk mitigation When a plan is created to reduce the probability of a risk occurring to a business, or to reduce the negative effects on the business if the risk does occur.

risk transference When a business transfers a risk to a third party.

sales forecasts A prediction of future sales volume and revenue based on past sales data and market research.

sales revenue See revenue.

sanction A restriction on trade with a particular country.

saturated market A market in which all consumer demand has been (or is being) met.

scenario planning Where a business considers specific events that may happen in the future, plans how it would operate should one of the events occur, and plans how it would mitigate the effects of any negative changes the event might cause.

secondary market research When a business does market research using data that is already available.

segmentation Dividing a market into identifiable segments in which consumers share one or more characteristic.

share capital Money raised by selling shares in a business.

shareholder An individual that owns shares in a business.

short-termism Where a business frequently makes decisions to increase short-term financial rewards, rather than focusing on long-term performance.

single market A market in which there are very few barriers to trade between the countries that operate in it. Goods and labour can move freely within the single market.

Glossary

SMART objectives SMART objectives are specific, measurable, agreed, realistic and timely.

social enterprise A business that's set up with a core aim to use its profits to benefit society in some way.

social entrepreneur A person that sets up a social enterprise.

sole trader A form of legal ownership of a business where there is just one owner. It has unlimited liability.

solvency A business's ability to pay its debts.

span of control The number of people who report directly to a manager.

specialisation When a business or country focuses on producing just one product (or a very narrow range of products).

stakeholder Anyone who is affected by a business, including workers, shareholders and customers.

star (Boston Matrix) A product that has high market share and high market growth.

statement of comprehensive income A financial statement showing how much money's gone into and out of a business over a period of time.

statement of financial position A snapshot of a firm's finances at a particular time.

stock-in costs The costs associated with holding too much stock.

stock-out costs The costs associated with running out of stock.

strategy A medium- to long-term plan for achieving a business's objectives.

subsidy (domestic) An amount of money paid by a government to domestic firms to lower their costs of production.

substitute A product that can be used to replace another because customers see them as being very similar products.

succession planning Making plans to identify and prepare staff members to fill key roles, in the event that key members of staff leave the business.

supply The quantity of a product that suppliers are willing and able to supply to a market at a given price, at a particular time.

sustainable (capability) A distinct capability that can be maintained over time.

SWOT analysis A method of assessing a business's current situation — it looks at the strengths, weaknesses, opportunities and threats facing the business.

tactic A short-term plan in order to achieve a strategy.

takeover Where one business buys over 50% of the shares of another business, giving them a controlling interest.

tall structure An organisational structure that has many layers of management.

tariff A form of tax placed on certain imports to make them more expensive.

tax avoidance Using legal accounting methods to reduce the amount of tax a business pays.

time-series analysis Analysis of data that has been recorded over a period of time, to help identify trends.

total float In critical path analysis, the length of time a non-critical activity can be delayed without causing a delay to the entire project.

total quality management (TQM) A system that involves the whole workforce having input into quality improvements.

trade credit When a business buys a good or service and can delay payment for a period of time (the agreed period is usually between 30 and 90 days).

trade liberalisation The reduction or total removal of barriers to trade between countries, which encourages increased international trade.

trade union A group that acts on behalf of a group of employees in negotiations with employers.

trade-off When one thing has to be reduced or given up in order to increase or gain another.

trading bloc A group of countries with few trade barriers between them.

transfer pricing The action of setting prices for goods and services transferred between different parts of a business based in different countries.

transformational leadership A leadership style where the leader has highly innovative ideas to improve a business and can inspire the employees to make these changes.

turnover See revenue.

unique selling point (USP) An aspect of a product that makes it different from any other on the market.

unlimited liability A state where the owners of a business are legally responsible for all of the business's debts.

variable cost A cost that varies, depending on how much a business outputs.

variance The difference between a budgeted figure and an actual figure.

venture capital Money invested in a business with high growth potential. Investors get a share of the business in return for their investment.

vertical communication Getting messages between the different levels of an organisation's hierarchy.

vertical integration When a business combines with another business in the same industry at a different stage of the production process.

viral marketing The use of social networks to rapidly raise awareness of a new product or service.

wholesaler A business that buys goods from manufacturers in bulk and sells them in smaller quantities to retailers.

working capital Money available for day-to-day spending.

World Trade Organisation (WTO) An international organisation that encourages trade between member countries. It deals with trade rules and negotiations.

zero-based budget A budget that is based on the specific spending plans for the year ahead.

Index

4Ps 18

A

absenteeism 144
accounting ratios
  analysing 142
  gearing ratios 140
  liquidity ratios 76
  profit margins 72, 73
  ROCE 141
acid test ratios 76
added value 11
advertising 19
aims 48, 102
analysing data 184
Ansoff's matrix 104, 105
  global markets 175
appreciation 173
ASEAN (Association of Southeast Asian Nations) 160
assessment days 33
assets 74, 75, 77
  selling 54
autocratic leadership 42
average (accounting) rate of return (ARR) 120
averages 185
  moving 116-118

B

B2B marketing 28
B2C marketing 28
balance of payments 178, 179
balance sheets 74, 75, 139
banks 55
bar charts 184
barriers to entry 110
batch production 80
bias (in market research) 7
bonus schemes 41
Boston Matrix 27, 107
branding 2, 20, 21
break-even analysis 64, 65
BRICS economies 155
budgets 66-68
  historical budgeting 67
  variance 68, 69
  zero-based budgeting 67
buffer stocks 86
business
  aims 48, 102
  objectives 48, 49, 103
  plans 59
business angels 55, 57
business cycle 94, 95
buyer power 110

C

capabilities 106, 107
capacity utilisation 84, 85
capital
  owner's capital 54
  share capital 51, 57
  venture capital 57
  working capital 77
capital employed 140
capital-intensive production 83
cash 73, 77
cash cows 27
cash flow forecasts 60, 61
cell production 80
centralised organisational structures 37
chains of command 36
change
  external factors 149
  in culture 150
  in organisational size 146, 150
  internal factors 146-148
  management 150
  resistance to 151
child labour 180
collective bargaining 32
commission 40
competition 4, 5, 97, 100, 101, 111, 162
  global 171-173
competitive advantage 11
  global 172
competitive pricing 23
consultation (non-financial motivation) 40
  strategies 145
Consumer Prices Index 91
continuity planning 153
continuous improvement (quality management) 89
contribution 64
corporate
  aims 48, 102
  branding 20
  culture 130-132, 150
  objectives 48, 49, 103
  timescales 128
corporate social responsibility (CSR) 137
corporation tax 94
cost competitiveness 172
cost leadership 105, 106, 172
cost-plus pricing 23
critical path analysis 124-127
crowd funding 55
cultural diversity 176, 177

D

databases 8
debts 75
decentralised organisational structures 37
decision trees 122, 123
deflation 90
delayering 36
delegation (non-financial motivation) 40
demand 12-17
democratic leadership 42
demographics 9
depreciation 173
design mix 18
differentiation 11, 105, 106, 172
discounted cash flow (DCF) 121
discrimination 98
diseconomies of scale 114
dismissal 30
distinctive capabilities 106, 107
distribution channels 24, 25
diversification 104, 105
dogs 27
domestic approach 174
domestic subsidies 160
dynamic markets 2

E

earliest finishing times (EFTs) 125
earliest start times (ESTs) 125
economic growth 154, 155
economies of scale 49, 112, 114
effective demand 12
efficiency 82, 83
elasticity of demand 15-17
embargoes 160
emerging economies 155
employee share ownership 145
employees 30-32
  productivity 81
employer-employee relationships 32
empowerment 40
  strategies 145

culture (of a business) 130-132, 150

culture (of a business) 130-132, 150
  corporate 130-132
currency indices 93
current assets 75
current liabilities 75
current ratios 76
customer loyalty 29
cyclical variations 118

Index

Index

Index

M

machinery
  productivity 81
management buyouts 147
managers 42
margin of safety 65
market
  development 104, 105
  maps 10
  orientation 6
  penetration 104, 105
  positioning 10, 11
  research 6-9
  saturation 162
  share 2
  size 2
marketing
  approaches 174, 175
  ethics 181
marketing mix 4, 18
  global markets 174-177
marketing strategies 18, 26-29
  global 174-177
  mass markets 28
  niche markets 28
Maslow (motivational theorist) 38
mass markets 2
  marketing strategies 28
matrix organisational structures 37
Mayo (motivational theorist) 39
mean 185
median 185
mergers 112-114
  global 170, 171
MINT economies 155
mission statements 102
mixed approach 175
mode 185
monopolies 100
More Economically Developed
    Countries (MEDCs) 154
motivation (of employees) 38-41
motivational theories 38, 39
moving averages 116-118
multinational corporations (MNCs)
    178-183
  controlling 182, 183
  environmental impacts 181
multi-skilled workforce 31

N

NAFTA (North American Free Trade
    Agreement) 160
National Living Wage 30, 99
National Minimum Wage 30, 99
net present value (NPV) 121
net profit 70
  margins 72, 73
networks (critical path analysis)
    124-127
niche markets 2
  global 176
  marketing strategies 28
non-current assets 75
non-current liabilities 75
non-financial motivation 40
non-financial motives (of entrepreneurs)
    46

O

objectives 48, 49, 103
off-shoring 164, 165
off-the-job training 35
oligopolies 100
online
  businesses 52
  distribution 25
  retailing 3, 23
on-the-job training 35
operating profit 70
  margins 72, 73
opportunity costs 53
organic growth 113
organisational size 146, 150
organisational structures 36, 37
outsourcing 31, 165
overdrafts 56
own branding 20
owner's capital 54
ownership 50, 51, 147

P

partnerships 50
patents 171
paternalistic leadership 42
payback period 119, 120
peer-to-peer lenders 55
penetration pricing 22
percentages 186
perfect competition 100
performance-related pay 41
PESTLE analysis 109, 149
pictograms 184
pie charts 184
piecework 40
polycentric approach 175
Porter's Five Forces model 110, 111
Porter's generic strategies 105
Porter's strategic matrix 106
predatory pricing 23
pressure groups 183
price elasticity of demand 15-17
price skimming 22
pricing strategies 22, 23
primary market research 7
private limited companies (Ltds) 51
product
  branding 20
  development 104, 105
  differentiation 11, 105, 106, 172
  life cycle 26
  lines 27
  orientation 6
  portfolios 27, 107
production location 168, 169
production methods 80
productivity 81
  labour 143
profit 63, 70-73
  gross profit 70
  margins 72, 73
  maximisation 46, 48, 49
  operating profit 70
  profit for the year (net profit) 70
  satisficing 46
profit and loss accounts 71, 138
profit for the year (net profit) 70
  margins 72, 73
profit sharing schemes 41
profitability 72, 73
profitability ratios
  profit margins 72, 73
  ROCE 141
promotion 19-21
protectionism 160
psychological pricing 23
public limited companies (PLCs) 51
pull factors 163
push factors 162

Index